WITHDRA[WN]

‖‖‖‖‖‖‖‖‖‖‖‖‖‖‖‖‖‖‖‖‖‖

W9-CQK-806

COLLEGE OF ALAMEDA LIBRARY

PS
668   Brandt, Carl G.
B6   Selected American
         speeches on basic issues
         1850–1950

FEB 19 '92

LENDING POLICY
IF YOU DAMAGE OR LOSE LIBRARY
MATERIALS, THEN YOU WILL BE
CHARGED FOR REPLACEMENT. FAIL
URE TO PAY AFFECTS LIBRARY
PRIVILEGES, GRADES, TRANSCRIPTS,
DIPLOMAS, AND REGISTRATION
PRIVILEGES OR ANY COMBINATION
THEREOF.

WITHDRAWN

SELECTED
AMERICAN SPEECHES
ON BASIC ISSUES
(1850-1950)

SELECTED

AMERICAN SPEECHES

ON BASIC ISSUES

(1850-1950)

EDITED BY

CARL G. BRANDT AND EDWARD M. SHAFTER, JR.

The University of Michigan

HOUGHTON MIFFLIN COMPANY • BOSTON

The Riverside Press Cambridge

COPYRIGHT ©, 1960, by Carl G. Brandt and Edward
M. Shafter, Jr. All rights reserved.

The Riverside Press Cambridge

PRINTED IN THE U.S.A.

CONTENTS

Part One

Time of Civil Strife: Slavery and States' Rights

Part Two

The Dawn of the Twentieth Century: American Nationalism and Expansion

Part Three

World Wars I and II: Crises and Controversies

INTRODUCTION

A speech which has survived the passage of time and has become part of our American heritage is one which either had an unusual impact on the thinking of the time at which it was delivered or which made a vital contribution to the later understanding of the history of the period. It is the product of some event which gives rise to a speech situation of unusual importance, but it does not happen without an accomplished speaker who rises to the occasion. Undoubtedly many excellent speakers would have made noteworthy speeches if the occasion had presented itself. But the speech situation and the speaker must both appear together. "True eloquence," said Webster, "must exist in the man, in the subject, and in the occasion." This collection of speeches will concern itself with those exciting instances when the speech situation and the speaker were both on the stage of history at the same time.

This book is designed not only for the student of public speaking but also for the reader who enjoys history and biography. It will give him nineteen examples of modern eloquence from the minds and mouths of seventeen famous Americans. Many of these examples are not easily obtainable and rarely can be found in any anthology. The speeches are especially significant because they are drawn from certain selected moments of American history and show the speaker as a human force in a time of stress. He is not a mere worker with words and phrases but rather a brilliant molder of public opinion and a shaper of man's destiny. While there is much to be said for the value of edited and abridged versions of speeches, this book provides, as far as it is practicable to do so, the complete texts of a selected collection of outstanding American speeches. Such a volume should thereby furnish a greater opportunity for careful study and analysis.

Perhaps a whole new expanse of interest in history and government may be found in these speeches. How better can critical issues be understood than from the lips of those distinguished men who actually debated those issues and who, in many instances, were willing to sacrifice not only political advantage (as did Webster) but even their own physical well-being (as did Clay, Calhoun, and Grady)? Even the reader with no specialized interests should find these speeches both challenging and enlightening.

For the purposes of this collection the editors narrowed the period from which the speeches were selected to about one hundred years—roughly from 1850 to 1950. They then selected three important historical periods which occurred during this space of time. These periods are: (1) Time of Civil Strife: Slavery and States' Rights, (2) Dawn of the Twentieth Century: American Nationalism and Expansion, and (3) World Wars I and II: Crises and Controversies. The next step for limitation was to select those issues in each period which seemed particularly stirring and eventful. The last step was to select the speakers who would best express those issues.

As a result of these processes, the speeches in the period of "Civil Strife" present the unforgettable words of such great men as Henry Clay, John C. Calhoun, Daniel Webster, Abraham Lincoln, and Stephen A. Douglas on states' rights and slavery; and of Henry W. Grady on the problems of Civil War reconstruction. "The Dawn of the Twentieth Century" contains the brilliant eloquence of William Jennings Bryan and of Robert J. Ingersoll on the gold standard, of Albert J. Beveridge and Carl Schurz on American imperialism, and of Theodore Roosevelt on social reform. The World War I period, a time of vigorous and vital speaking, includes Woodrow Wilson's speeches for neutrality and for war; Robert M. LaFollette's speech against the declaration of war; William Howard Taft's, Henry Cabot Lodge's, and William E. Borah's on the League of Nations. The period ends with the beginning of World War II and offers President Franklin D. Roosevelt's speeches for neutrality and for war in strange coincidence with the speeches of Woodrow Wilson some twenty-five years before. The anthology ends at this point in history.

A last point should be made regarding the selection and arrangement of the speeches. They have been so chosen that the reader may know the qualities of individual speakers and speeches and that he may appreciate their strategy and materials of debate. In order to accomplish the latter purpose, the editors have, in the main, selected speeches with opposing views on most of the principal issues covered in the collection.

Although the book exists primarily for the authentic reproduction of the speeches, at the same time the editors have offered what they consider necessary editorial comment. Each of the three historical periods in the book is preceded by a statement describing the period, and each speech is preceded by a discussion of the speaker and of the significance of the speech. These comments are necessarily brief because of the demands of space but they are a condensation of a wealth of materials. The reader should, in the estimation of the editors, read the editorial matter with some care for a proper appreciation of the speeches and the speakers. The editors have included a selected bibliography which they found of value in the preparation of this collection. The list of references is in no sense complete. Except for these intrusions, the book consists of speeches which have strongly influenced American history.

The editors express their appreciation to their colleagues who have contributed in many ways to the preparation of this volume. The cooperation of Donald R. Browne has been particularly helpful.

Without further explanation or apology, the editors dedicate to their readers this volume.

CARL G. BRANDT
EDWARD M. SHAFTER, JR.

Ann Arbor, Michigan

SELECTED
AMERICAN SPEECHES
ON BASIC ISSUES
(1850-1950)

PART ONE

Time of Civil Strife: Slavery and States' Rights

The thirty-year period preceding the Civil War is perhaps the Golden Age of American oratory. Such noted orators as John Quincy Adams, Thomas H. Benton, John C. Calhoun, Salmon P. Chase, Rufus Choate, Henry Clay, Thomas Corwin, Stephen Douglas, Robert Y. Hayne, Abraham Lincoln, Theodore Parker, Seargent S. Prentiss, William H. Seward, Charles Sumner, Daniel Webster, and William L. Yancey dominated the American political scene, and their eloquence helped to shape the events of their time and drew a blueprint for the years which were to follow. The significant pre-Civil War events began with the Missouri Compromise of 1820, representing the first great clash between the North and the South over the issue of slavery in the states and territories, and led through many subsequent crises to the Civil War itself. The North, on the one hand, consistently condemned the reprehensible institution of slavery. In his "Springfield Speech" (June 17, 1858), Lincoln earnestly pleaded that " 'a house divided against itself cannot stand.' . . . this government cannot endure permanently half slave and half free." The South, on the other hand, militantly defended the economically profitable institution of slavery, often on the grounds that it was clearly God's will that

2

some men were masters, some slaves. But the South was not fighting for the retention of slavery alone; it was fighting to maintain and promote a way of life, of which slavery was an indispensable part. It was the misfortune of the South that a defense of its culture necessitated a defense of slavery. The wife of Stonewall Jackson wrote of her husband

> . . . that he would never have fought for the sole object of perpetuating slavery. . . . He found the institution a troublesome and responsible one, and I have heard him say that he would prefer to see the negroes free, but he believed that the Bible taught that slavery was sanctioned by the Creator Himself, who maketh all men to differ, and instituted laws for the bond and the free. He therefore accepted slavery, as it existed in the South, not as anything desirable in itself, but as allowed by Providence for ends which it was not his business to determine.[1]

While slavery was the great rallying issue between the North and the South, the real issue was state sovereignty — the South did not believe that the Federal government could control its right to own slaves or any other rights which it felt belonged to free, independent states. In his Confederate Congress Speech (April 29, 1860), Jefferson Davis succinctly stated the Southern case when he remarked that the Constitution of 1787 was "a compact *between* the States" and not, as so many in the North seemed to think, "a national government set up *above* and *over* the States." The states were to retain all powers not expressly delegated to the national government by the Constitution. And "in no clause," asserted Davis, "can there be found any delegation of power to the Congress authorizing it in any manner to legislate to the prejudice, detriment,

[1] Robert Birley, ed., *Speeches and Documents in American History*, I, xiii.

or discouragement of the owners of that species of property [slaves], or excluding it from the protection of the government."

In the estimation of the editors, the speeches of this pre-Civil War period in American oratory may best be represented by those of Clay, Calhoun, and Webster in the matter of the Crisis of 1850 when Henry Clay sought a compromise between the North and the South over the question of slavery in territory recently acquired from Mexico, by the renowned effort of Stephen Douglas in support of the Kansas-Nebraska Bill in 1854, and by the superlative address of Abraham Lincoln at Cooper Institute in 1858.

The years 1860-1865, of course, produced such sublime public utterances as Lincoln's First and Second Inaugural Addresses and Gettysburg Address. But since space is at a premium and since these are so frequently anthologized, they have been omitted here.

The several decades following the Civil War were confusing and chaotic in many respects. Of the manifold problems of the Reconstruction, one overshadowed all others — the Negro problem. To be sure, the war had emancipated the Negro, but the North and South differed sharply on what political, economic, and social status he was to assume. The question of what to do with the Negro now that he was free absorbed the attention of both Northern and Southern spokesmen, speakers like Henry Ward Beecher, Wendell Phillips, Andrew Johnson, Benjamin H. Hill, Lucius Q. C. Lamar, and Alexander H. Stephens. By the time Henry W. Grady of Atlanta appeared on the public platform, some progress toward sectional harmony had been achieved, but much remained to be done. Of paramount importance was the need for a Southern leader who could help dispel Northern suspicions and doubts concerning the South's intentions toward the Negro. Grady fulfilled that need; he quickly became the symbol of the "New South" and the recognized ambassador of good will between North and South. Grady's genius as an arbiter is clearly revealed in what the editors consider his finest speech, his Boston address of 1889 on "The Race Problem in the South."

HENRY CLAY

(1777-1852)

Often referred to as "the Great Compromiser," Henry Clay probably is best known as a member of that famous Senate Triumvirate of Clay, Calhoun, and Webster. But he merits recognition also as perhaps America's finest "natural" orator and the most sparkling and celebrated political speaker of the first half of the nineteenth century. His ability to captivate and thrill a popular audience seldom has been equaled. The secret of such rapport with an audience lay in a voice and manner that were compelling and magnetic. No better description exists of Clay the speaker than that of William Mathews who, in January of 1840, heard him speak in the Senate chamber:

. . . our attention was at once arrested by a voice that seemed like the music of the spheres. It came from the lips of a tall, well-formed man, with a wide mouth, a flashing eye, and a countenance that revealed every change of thought within. It had a wonderful flexibility and compass, at one moment crashing upon the ear in thunderpeals, and the next falling in music as soft as that of "summer winds a-wooing flowers." It rarely startled the hearer, however, with violent contrasts of pitch, and was equally distinct and clear when it rang out in trumpet tones, and when it sank to the lowest whisper. Every syllable, we had almost said, every letter, was perfectly audible, and as "musical as is Apollo's lute." There was not a word of rant, not one tone of vociferation; in the very climax of his passion he spoke deliberately, and his outpouring of denunciation was as slow and steady as the tread of Nemesis. He gesticulated all over. As he spoke, he stepped forward and backward with effect; and the nodding of his head, hung on a long neck, — his arms, hands, fingers, feet,

5

and even his spectacles and blue handkerchief, aided him in debate. Who could it be? It took but a minute to answer the question. It was — it could be no other than — Henry Clay.[1]

In 1849, the people of Kentucky seemed to feel that if any man could ease the critically strained relations between North and South over the matter of slavery, that man was Henry Clay. Clay, consequently, was unanimously elected to fill the Senate seat that he had left voluntarily in 1842. At the age of seventy-three, and with considerable apprehension, Clay emerged from retirement to accept the duty thrust upon him. On January 29, 1850, in his role as peacemaker, he submitted to the Senate eight proposals which he felt embodied the most insistent demands of both North and South over the disposition of slavery in territories recently acquired from Mexico. One of the most stirring and memorable debates in American political history was thus initiated, a debate fraught with the gravest consequences.

On February 5 and 6, Clay delivered his remarkable and crucial "Compromise Speech" in support of his previously offered resolutions which, ultimately, evolved from a lengthy legislative process as the Compromise of 1850. He took almost three hours the first day to cover but half his speech; he talked nearly as long the next day. Convincingly and from the heart he pleaded fervently for concession from the North and peace from the South. With all his remaining strength and with full sense of the decisive hour at hand he fought to preserve the Union which he loved. He harbored no inclination to further personal ambition, for physically he was exhausted and had not long to live. Clay — weak, ill — actually had to be assisted up the Capitol steps that February day, and a friend even sought to dissuade him from exerting himself. "I consider our country in danger," Clay replied, "and if I can be the means in any measure of averting that danger, my health and life is of little consequence." That he did help is generally acknowledged, for his strenuous efforts to hold the Union together were, in large measure, responsible for postponing the horrors of war eleven years to a time when the North, at last the stronger, was barely able to defeat the South. But the Crisis of 1850 was Clay's last great fight; little more than two years later he was dead.

[1] Oratory and Orators, pp. 311-312.

COMPROMISE SPEECH OF 1850

by

Henry Clay

Delivered in the United States Senate on February 5 and 6, 1850.

MR. PRESIDENT, NEVER on any former occasion have I risen under feelings of such painful solicitude. I have seen many periods of great anxiety, of peril, and of danger in this country, and I have never before risen to address any assemblage so oppressed, so appalled, and so anxious; and sir, I hope it will not be out of place to do here, what again and again I have done in my private chamber, to implore of Him who holds the destinies of nations and individuals in His hands, to bestow upon our country His blessing, to calm the violence and rage of party, to still passion, to allow reason once more to resume its empire. And may I not ask of Him too, sir, to bestow on his humble servant, now before him, the blessing of his smiles, and of strength and ability to perform the work which now lies before him? Sir, I have said that I have seen other anxious periods in the history of our country, and if I were to venture, Mr. President, to trace to their original source the cause of all our present dangers, difficulties, and distraction, I should ascribe it to the violence and intemperance of party spirit. To party spirit! Sir, in the progress of this session we have had the testimony of two senators here, who, however they may differ on other matters, concur in the existence of that cause in originating the unhappy differences which prevail throughout the country, on the subject of the institution of slavery.

Parties, in their endeavors to obtain, the one ascendancy over the other, catch at every passing or floating plank in order to add strength and power to each. We have been told by the two senators to whom I have referred, that each of the parties at the North, in its turn, has moved and endeavored to obtain the assistance of a small party called Abolitionists, in order that the scale in its favor might preponderate against that of its adversary. And all around us, every where, we see too many evidences of the existence of the spirit and intemperance of party. I might go to other legislative bodies than that which is assembled in Congress, and I might draw from them illustrations of the melancholy truth upon which I am dwelling, but I need not pass out of this Capitol itself. I say it, sir, with all deference and respect to that other portion of Congress assembled in the other wing of this Capitol; but what have we seen there? During this very session one whole week has been exhausted — I think about a week — in the vain endeavor to elect a door-keeper of the House.

And, Mr. President, what was the question in this struggle to elect a doorkeeper? It was not as to the man or the qualities of the man, or who is best adapted to the situation. It was whether the doorkeeper entertained opinions upon certain national mea-sures coincident with this or that side of the House. That was the sole question which prevented the election of a doorkeeper for about the period of a week. Sir, I make no reproaches — none, to either portion of that House; I state the fact; and I state the fact to draw from it the conclusion and to express the hope that there will be an endeavor to check this violence of party.

Sir, what vicissitudes do we not pass through in this short mortal career of ours? Eight years, or nearly eight years ago, I took my leave finally, and, as I supposed, forever, from this body. At that time I did not conceive of the possibility of ever again returning to it. And if my private wishes and particular inclinations, and the desire during the short remnant of my days to remain in repose and quiet, could have prevailed, you would never have seen me occupying the seat which I now occupy upon this floor. The Legislature of the State to which I belong, unsolicited by me, chose to designate me for this station, and I have come here, sir, in obedience to a sense of stern duty, with no personal objects, no private views, now or hereafter, to gratify. I know, sir, the jealousies, the fears, the apprehensions which are engendered by the existence of that party spirit to which I have referred; but if there be in my hearing now, in or out of this Capitol, any one who hopes, in his race for honors and elevation, for higher honors and higher eleva-tion than that which he now occupies, I beg him to believe that I, at least, will never jostle him in the pursuit of those honors or that elevation. I beg him to be perfectly persuaded that, if my wishes prevail, my name shall never be used in competition with his. I beg to assure him that when my service is terminated in this body, my mission, so far as respects the public affairs of this world and upon this earth, is closed, and closed, if my wishes prevail, forever.

But, sir, it is impossible for us to be blind to the facts which are daily transpiring before us. It is impossible for us not to perceive that party spirit and future elevation mix more or less in all our affairs, in all our deliberations. At a moment when the White House itself is in danger of conflagration, instead of all hands uniting to extinguish the flames, we are contending about who shall be its next occupant. When a dreadful crevasse has occurred, which threatens inundation and destruction to all around it, we are contending and disputing about the profits of an estate which is threatened with total submersion.

Mr. President, it is passion, passion — party, party, and intemperance — that is all I dread in the adjustment of the great questions which unhappily at this time divide our distracted country. Sir, at this moment we have in the legislative bodies of this Capitol and in the States, twenty old furnaces in full blast, emitting heat, and passion, and intemperance, and diffusing them throughout the whole extent of this broad land. Two months ago all was calm in comparison to the present moment. All now is uproar, confusion, and menace to the existence of the Union, and to the happiness and safety of this people. Sir, I implore senators, I entreat them, by all that they expect hereafter, and by all that is dear to them here below, to repress the ardor of these passions, to look to their country, to its interests, to listen to the voice of reason — not as it shall be attempted to be uttered by me, for I am not so presumptuous as to indulge the hope that anything I may say will avert the effects which I have described, but to listen to their own reason, their own judgment, their own good sense, in determining upon what is best to be done for our country in the actual posture in which we find her. Sir, to this great object have my efforts been directed during the whole session.

I have cut myself off from all the usual enjoyments of social life, I have confined myself almost entirely, with very few exceptions, to my own chamber, and from the beginning of the session to the present time my thoughts have been anxiously directed to the

object of finding some plan, of proposing some mode of accommodation, which would once more restore the blessings of concord,
harmony and peace to this great country. I am not vain enough to
suppose that I have been successful in the accomplishment of this
object, but I have presented a scheme, and allow me to say to
honorable senators that, if they find in that plan any thing that is
defective, if they find in it any thing that is worthy of acceptance,
but is susceptible of improvement by amendment, it seems to me
that the true and patriotic course is not to denounce it, but to
improve it — not to reject without examination any project of
accommodation having for its object the restoration of harmony
in this country, but to look at it to see if it be susceptible of elab-
oration or improvement, so as to accomplish the object which I
indulge the hope is common to all and every one of us, to restore
peace and quiet, and harmony and happiness to this country.

Sir, when I came to consider this subject, there were two or three
general purposes which it seemed to me to be most desirable, if
possible, to accomplish. The one was, to settle all the controverted
questions arising out of the subject of slavery. It seemed to me to
be doing very little, if we settled one question and left other dis-
tracting questions unadjusted, it seemed to me to be doing but
little, if we stopped one leak only in the ship of State, and left
other leaks capable of producing danger, if not destruction, to the
vessel. I therefore turned my attention to every subject connected
with the institution of slavery, and out of which controverted
questions had sprung, to see if it were possible or practicable to
accommodate and adjust the whole of them. Another principal
object which attracted my attention was, to endeavor to form such
a scheme of accommodation that neither of the two classes of
States into which our country is so unhappily divided should make
any sacrifice of any great principle. I believe, sir, the series of
resolutions which I have had the honor to present to the Senate
accomplishes that object.

Sir, another purpose which I had in view was this: I was aware
of the difference of opinion prevailing between these two classes
of States. I was aware that, while one portion of the Union was
pushing matters, as it seemed to me, to the greatest extremity,
another portion of the Union was pushing them to an opposite,
perhaps not less dangerous extremity. It appeared to me, then,
that if any arrangement, any satisfactory adjustment could be made

of the controverted questions between the two classes of States, that adjustment, that arrangement, could only be successful and effectual by extracting from both parties some concessions — not of principle, not of principle at all, but of feeling, of opinion, in relation to matters in controversy between them. Sir, I believe the resolutions which I have prepared fulfill that object. I believe, sir, that you will find, upon that careful, rational, and attentive examination of them, which I think they deserve, that neither party in some of them make any concession at all; in others the concessions of forbearance are mutual; and in the third place, in reference to the slaveholding States, there are resolutions making concessions to them by the opposite class of States, without any compensation whatever being rendered by them to the non-slaveholding States. I think every one of these characteristics which I have assigned, and the measures which I proposed, is susceptible of clear and satisfactory demonstration by an attentive perusal and critical examination of the resolutions themselves. Let us take up the first resolution.

The first resolution, Mr. President, as you are aware, relates to California, and it declares that California, with suitable limits, ought to be admitted as a member of this Union, without the imposition of any restriction either to interdict or to introduce slavery within her limits. Well now, is there any concession in this resolution by either party to the other? I know that gentlemen who come from slaveholding States say the North gets all that it desires; but by whom does it get it? Does it get it by any action of Congress? If slavery be interdicted within the limits of California, has it been done by Congress — by this Government? No, sir. That interdiction is imposed by California herself. And has it not been the doctrine of all parties that when a State is about to be admitted into the Union, the State has a right to decide for itself whether it will or will not have slavery within its limits?

The great principle, sir, which was in contest upon the memorable occasion of the introduction of Missouri into the Union, was, whether it was competent or not competent for Congress to impose any restrictions which should exist after she became a member of the Union. We who were in favor of the admission of Missouri, contended that no such restriction should be imposed. We contended that, whenever she was once admitted into the Union, she had all the rights and privileges of any pre-existing State in the

Union, and that among these rights and privileges was one to decide for herself whether slavery should or should not exist within her limits; that she had as much a right to decide upon the introduction of slavery or its abolition as New York had a right to decide upon the introduction or abolition of slavery; and that, although subsequently admitted, she stood among her peers, equally invested with all the privileges that any one of the original thirteen States had a right to enjoy.

Sir, I think that those who have been contending with so much earnestness and perseverance for the Wilmot proviso, ought to reflect that, even if they could carry their object and adopt the proviso, it ceases the moment any State or Territory to which it was applicable came to be admitted as a member of the Union. Why, sir, no one contends now, no one believes, that with regard to those North-western States to which the ordinance of 1787 applied — Ohio, Indiana, Illinois, and Michigan — no one can now believe but that any one of those States, if they thought proper to do it, have just as much right to introduce slavery within their borders, as Virginia has to maintain the existence of slavery within hers. Then, sir, if in the struggle for power and empire between the two classes of States a decision in California has taken place adverse to the wishes of the Southern States, it is a decision not made by the General Government.

It is a decision respecting which they can utter no complaint toward the General Government. It is a decision made by California herself; which California had unquestionably the right to make under the Constitution of the United States. There is, then, in the first resolution, according to the observation which I made some time ago, a case where neither party concedes; where the question of slavery, neither its introduction nor interdiction, is decided in reference to the action of this Government; and if it has been decided, it has been by a different body — by a different power — by California itself, which had a right to make the decision.

Mr. President, the next resolution in the series which I have offered I beg gentlemen candidly now to look at. I was aware, perfectly aware, of the perseverance with which the Wilmot proviso was insisted upon. I knew that every one of the free States in this Union, without exception, had by its Legislative body passed resolutions instructing their Senators and requesting their Representatives to get that restriction incorporated in any Territorial Government which might be established under the auspices of Congress. I knew how much, and I regretted how much, the free States had put their hearts upon the adoption of this measure. In the second resolution I call upon them to waive persisting in it. I ask them, for the sake of peace and in the spirit of mutual forbearance to other members of the Union, to give it up — to no longer insist upon it — to see, as they must see, if their eyes are open, the dangers which lie ahead, if they persevere in insisting upon it.

When I called upon them in this resolution to do this, was I not bound to offer, for a surrender of that favorite principle or measure of theirs, some compensation, not as an equivalent by any means, but some compensation in the spirit of mutual forbearance, which, animating one side, ought at the same time to actuate the other side? Well, sir, what is it that is offered them? It is a declaration of what I characterized, and must still characterize, with great deference to all those who entertain opposite opinions, as two truths, I will not say incontestible, but to me clear, and I think they ought to be regarded as indisputable truths. What are they? The first is, that by law slavery no longer exists in any part of the acquisitions made by us from the Republic of Mexico; and the other is, that in our opinion, according to the probabilities of the case, slavery never will be introduced into any portion of the territories so acquired from Mexico. Now, I have heard it said that this declaration of what I call these two truths is equivalent to the enactment of the Wilmot proviso.

I have heard this asserted, but is that the case? If the Wilmot proviso be adopted in Territorial Governments established over these countries acquired from Mexico, it would be a positive enactment, a prohibition, an interdiction as to the introduction of slavery within them; but with regard to these opinions I had hoped, and I shall still indulge the hope, that those who represent the free States will be inclined not to insist — indeed it would be extremely difficult to give to these declarations the form of positive enactment. I had hoped that they would be satisfied with the simple expression of the opinion of Congress, leaving it upon the basis of that opinion, without asking for what seems to me almost impracticable, if not impossible — for any subsequent enactment to be introduced into the bill by which Territorial Governments should be established.

And I can only say that the second resolution, even without the declaration of these two truths expressed, would be much more acceptable to me than with them — but I could not forget that I was proposing a scheme of arrangement and compromise, and I could not, therefore, depart from the duty which the preparation of such a scheme seems to me to impose, of offering, while we ask the surrender on one side of a favorite measure, of offering to the other side some compensation for that surrender or sacrifice. What are the truths, Mr. President? The first is, that by law slavery does not exist within the Territories ceded to us by the Republic of Mexico. It is a misfortune, sir, in the various weighty and important topics which are connected with the subject that I am now addressing you upon, that any one of the five or six furnishes a theme for a lengthened speech; and I am therefore reduced to the necessity, I think — at least in this stage of the discussion — of limiting myself rather to the expression of opinions, than going at any great length into the discussion of all these various topics.

With respect to the opinion that slavery does not exist in the Territories ceded to the United States by Mexico, I can only refer to the fact of the passage of the law by the Supreme Government of Mexico abolishing it, I think, in 1824; and to the subsequent passage of a law by the Legislative body of Mexico, I forget in what year, by which they proposed — what it is true they have never yet carried into full effect — compensation to the owners of slaves for the property of which they were stripped by the act of abolition. I can only refer to the acquiescence of Mexico in the abolition of slavery from the time of its extinction down to the time of the treaty by which we acquired these countries. But all Mexico, so far as I know, acquiesced in the non-existence of slavery. Gentlemen, I know, talk about the irregularity of the law by which that act was accomplished; but does it become us, a foreign power, to look into the mode by which an object has been accomplished by another foreign power, when she herself is satisfied with what she has done; and when, too, she is the exclusive judge whether an object which is local and municipal to herself, has been or has not been accomplished in conformity with her fundamental laws? Why, Mexico upon this subject showed to the last moment, her anxiety in the documents which were laid before the country upon the subject of the negotiation of this treaty, by Mr. Trist.

In the very act, in the very negotiation by which the treaty was concluded, ceding to us the countries in question, the diplomatic representatives of the Mexican Republic urged the abhorrence with which Mexico would view the introduction of slavery into any portion of the Territory which she was about to cede to the United States. The clause of prohibition was not inserted in consequence of the firm ground taken by Mr. Trist, and his declaration that it was an utter impossibility to mention the subject.

I take it then, sir — and availing myself of the benefit of the discussions which took place on a former occasion on this question, and which I think have left the whole country under the impression of the non-existence of slavery within the whole of the Territory in the ceded Territories — I take it for granted that what I have said, aided by the reflection of gentlemen, will satisfy them of that first truth, that slavery does not exist there by law, unless slavery was carried there the moment the treaty was ratified by the two parties, and under the operation of the Constitution of the United States. Now, really, I must say that upon the idea that *eo instanti* upon the consummation of the treaty, the Constitution of the United States spread itself over the acquired Territory, and carried along with it the institution of slavery, the proposition is so irreconcilable with any comprehension or reason that I possess, that I hardly know how to meet it.

Why, these United States consist of thirty States. In fifteen of them there was slavery, in fifteen of them slavery did not exist. Well, how can it be argued that the fifteen slave States, by the operation of the Constitution of the United States, carried into the ceded Territory their institution of slavery, any more than it can be argued on the other side that, by the operation of the same Constitution, the fifteen free States carried into the ceded territory the principle of freedom which they from policy have chosen to adopt within their limits? Why, sir, let me suppose a case. Let me imagine that Mexico had never abolished slavery there at all — let me suppose that it was existing in point of fact and in virtue of law, from the shores of the Pacific to those of the Gulf of Mexico, at the moment of the cession of these countries to us by the treaty in question.

With what patience would gentlemen coming from slaveholding

States listen to any argument which should be urged by the free States, that notwithstanding the existence of slavery within those territories, the Constitution of the United States abolished it the moment it operated and took effect in the ceded territory? Well, is there not just as much ground to contend that, where a moiety of the States is free, and the other moiety is slaveholding, the principle of freedom which prevails in the one class shall operate as much as the principle of slavery which prevails in the other? Can you come, amid this conflict of interests, principles, and legislation which prevails in the two parts of the Union, to any other conclusion than that which I understand to be the conclusion of the public law of the world, of reason, and justice — that the *status of law*, as it existed at the moment of the conquest or the acquisition, remains until it is altered by the sovereign authority of the conquering or acquiring power? That is the great principle which you can scarcely turn over a page of the public law of the world without finding recognized, and every where established. The laws of Mexico, as they existed at the moment of the cession of the ceded Territories to this country, remained the laws until, and unless, they were altered by that new sovereign power which this people and these Territories come under, in consequence of the treaty of cession to the United States.

I think, then, Mr. President, that without trespassing further, or exhausting the little stock of strength which I have, and for which I shall have abundant use in the progress of the argument, I may leave that part of the subject with two or three observations only upon the general power which I think appertains to this Government on the subject of slavery.

Sir, before I approach that subject, allow me to say that, in my humble judgment, the institution of slavery presents two questions totally distinct, and resting on entirely different grounds — slavery within the States, and slavery without the States. Congress, the General Government, has no power, under the Constitution of the United States, to touch slavery within the States, except in three specified particulars in that instrument; to adjust the subject of representation; to impose taxes when a system of direct taxation is made; and to perform the duty of surrendering, or causing to be delivered up, fugitive slaves that may escape from service which they owe in slave States, and take refuge in free States. And, sir, I am ready to say that if Congress were to attack, within the

States, the institution of slavery, for the purpose of the overthrow or extinction of slavery, then, Mr. President, my voice would be for war; then would be made a case which would justify in the sight of God, and in the presence of the nations of the earth, resistance on the part of the slave States to such an unconstitutional and usurped attempt as would be made on the supposition which I have stated.

Then we should be acting in defense of our rights, our domicils, our property, our safety, our lives; and then, I think, would be furnished a case in which the slaveholding States would be justified by all considerations which pertain to the happiness and security of man, to employ every instrument which God or nature had placed in their hands, to resist such an attempt on the part of the free States. And then, if unfortunately civil war should break out, and we should present to the nations of the earth the spectacle of one portion of this Union endeavoring to subvert an institution in violation of the Constitution and the most sacred obligations which can bind men; we should present the spectacle in which we should have the sympathies, the good wishes, and the desire for our success of all men who love justice and truth. Far different, I fear, would be our case — if unhappily we should be plunged into civil war — if the two parts of this country should be placed in a position hostile toward each other, in order to carry slavery into the new Territories acquired from Mexico.

Mr. President, we have heard, all of us have read of the efforts of France to propagate — what, on the continent of Europe? Not slavery, sir; not slavery, but the rights of man; and we know the fate of her efforts in a work of that kind. But if the two portions of this Confederacy should unhappily be involved in civil war, in which the effort on the one side would be to restrain the introduction of slavery into new Territories, and on the other side to force its introduction there, what a spectacle should we present to the contemplation of astonished mankind! An effort not to propagate right, but I must say — though I trust it will be understood to be said with no desire to excite feeling — an effort to propagate wrong in the territories thus acquired from Mexico. It would be a war in which we should have no sympathy, no good wishes, and in which all mankind would be against us, and in which our own history itself would be against us; for, from the commencement of the Revolution down to the present time, we have constantly reproached our British ancestors for the introduction of slavery into this country; and allow me to say that, in my opinion, it is one of the best defenses which can be made to preserve the institution in this country, that it was forced upon us against the wishes of our ancestors, our own colonial ancestors, and by the cupidity of our British commercial ancestors.

The power then, Mr. President, in my opinion — and I will extend it to the introduction as well as the prohibition of slavery in the new territories — I think the power does exist in Congress, and I think there is that important distinction between slavery outside of the States and slavery inside of the States, that all outside is debatable, all inside of the States is undebatable. The Government has no right to touch the institution within the States; but whether she has, and to what extent she has the right or not to touch it outside of the States, is a question which is debatable, and upon which men may honestly and fairly differ, but which, decided however it may be decided, furnishes, in my judgment, no just occasion for breaking up this happy and glorious Union of ours.

Now, I am not going to take up that part of the subject which relates to the power of Congress to legislate either within this District — (I shall have occasion to make some observations upon that when I approach the resolution relating to the District) — either within this District or the Territories. But I must say, in a few words, that I think there are two sources of power, either of which is, in my judgment, sufficient to warrant the exercise of the power, if it was deemed proper to exercise it, either to introduce or to keep out slavery outside the States, within the territories.

Mr. President, I shall not take up time, of which already so much has been consumed, to show that, according to my sense of the Constitution of the United States, or rather according to the sense in which the clause has been interpreted for the last fifty years, the clause which confers on Congress the power to regulate the Territories and other property of the United States conveys the authority.

Mr. President, with my worthy friend from Michigan — and I use the term in the best and most emphatic sense, for I believe he and I have known each other longer than he and I have known any other senator in this hall — I can not concur, although I entertain the most profound respect for the opinions he has advanced upon the subject, adverse to my own; but I must say, when a point is settled bv all the elementary writers of our country, by all the departments of our Government, legislative, executive, and judicial — when it has been so settled for a period of fifty years, and never was seriously disturbed until recently, that I think, if we are to regard any thing as fixed and settled under the administration of this Constitution of ours, it is a question which has thus been invariably and uniformly settled in a particular way. Or are we to come to this conclusion that nothing, nothing on earth is settled under this Constitution, but that every thing is unsettled?

Mr. President, we have to recollect it is very possible — sir, it is quite likely — that when that Constitution was framed, the application of it to such Territories as Louisiana, Florida, California, and New Mexico was never within the contemplation of its framers. It will be recollected that when that Constitution was framed the whole country northwest of the river Ohio was unpeopled; and it will be recollected also, that the exercise and the assertion of the power to make governments for Territories in their infant state, are, in the nature of the power, temporary, and to terminate whenever they have acquired a population competent for self-government. Sixty thousand is the number fixed by the ordinance of 1787. Now, sir, recollect that when this Constitution was adopted, and that Territory was unpeopled, is it possible that Congress, to whom it had been ceded by the States for the common benefit of the ceding State and all other members of the Union — is it possible that Congress had no right whatever to declare what description of settlers should occupy the public lands?

Suppose they took up the opinion that the introduction of slavery would enhance the value of the land, and enable them to command for the public treasury a greater amount from that source of revenue than by the exclusion of slaves, would they not have had the right to say, in fixing the rules, regulations, or whatever you choose to call them, for the government of that Territory, that any one that chooses to bring slaves may bring them, if it will enhance the value of the property, in the clearing and cultivation of the soil, and add to the importance of the country? Or take the reverse: — Suppose Congress had thought that a greater amount of revenue would be derived from the waste lands beyond the Ohio river by the interdiction of slavery, would they not have had a right to interdict it? Why, sir, remember how these settlements were made, and what was their progress. They began with a few. I believe that about Marietta the first settlement was made.

It was a settlement of some two or three hundred persons from New England. Cincinnati, I believe, was the next point where a settlement was made. It was settled perhaps by a few persons from New Jersey, or some other state. Did those few settlers, the moment they arrived there, acquire sovereign rights? Had those few persons power to dispose of these territories? Had they even power to govern themselves — the handful of men who established themselves at Marietta or Cincinnati? No, sir, the contemplation of the Constitution no doubt was, that, inasmuch as this power was temporary, as it is applicable to unpeopled territory, and as that territory will become peopled gradually, insensibly, until it reaches a population which may entitle it to the benefit of self-government, in the mean time it is right and proper that Congress, who owns the soil, should regulate the settlement of the soil, and govern the settlers on the soil, until those settlers acquire number and capacity to govern themselves.

Sir, I will not further dwell upon this part of the subject; but I said there is another source of power equally satisfactory, equally conclusive in my mind, as that which relates to the territories, and that is the treaty-making power — the acquiring power. Now, I put it to gentlemen, is there not at this moment a power somewhere existing either to admit or exclude slavery from the ceded territory? Is it not an annihilated power. This is impossible. It is a subsisting, actual, existing power; and where does it exist? It existed, I presume no one will controvert, in Mexico prior to the cession of these territories. Mexico could have abolished slavery or introduced slavery either in California or New Mexico. That must be conceded. Who will controvert this position? Well, Mexico has parted from the territory and from the sovereignty over the territory; and to whom did she transfer it? She transferred the territory and the sovereignty of the territory to the Government of the United States.

The Government of the United States acquires in sovereignty and in territory over California and New Mexico, all, either in sovereignty or territory, that Mexico held in California or New Mexico, by the cession of those territories. Sir, dispute that who can. The power exists or it does not; no one will contend for its annihilation. It existed in Mexico. No one, I think, can deny that. Mexico alienates the sovereignty over the territory, and her alience is the Government of the United States. The Government of the

United States, then, possesses all power which Mexico possessed over the ceded territories, and the Government of the United States can do in reference to them — within, I admit, certain limits of the Constitution — whatever Mexico could have done. There are prohibitions upon the power of Congress within the Constitution, which prohibitions, I admit, must apply to Congress whenever she legislates, whether for the old States or for new territories; but, within those prohibitions, the powers of the United States over the ceded territories are co-extensive and equal to the powers of Mexico in the ceded territories, prior to the cession.

Sir, in regard to this treaty-making power, all who have any occasion to examine into its character and to the possible extent to which it may be carried, know that it is a power unlimited in its nature, except in so far as any limitation may be found in the Constitution of the United States; and upon this subject there is no limitation which prescribes the extent to which the powers should be exercised. I know, sir, it is argued that there is no grant of power in the Constitution, in specific terms, over the subject of slavery any where; and there is no grant in the Constitution to Congress specifically over the subject of a vast variety of matters upon which the powers of Congress may unquestionably operate. The major includes the minor. The general grant of power comprehends all the particulars and elements of which that power consists. The power of acquisition by treaty draws after it the power of government of the country acquired.

If there be a power to acquire, there must be, to use the language of the tribunal that sits below, a power to govern. I think, therefore, sir, without, at least for the present, dwelling further on this part of the subject, that to the two sources of authority in Congress to which I have referred, and especially to the last, may be traced the power of Congress to act in the territories in question; and, sir, I go to the extent, and I think it is a power in Congress equal to the introduction or exclusion of slavery. I admit the argument in both its forms; I admit if the argument be maintained that the power exists to exclude slavery, it necessarily follows that the power must exist, if Congress choose to exercise it, to tolerate or introduce slavery within the territories.

But, sir, I have been drawn off so far from the second resolution — not from the object of it, but from a particular view of it — that it has almost gone out of my recollection. The resolution asserts —

That as slavery does not exist by law, and is not likely to be introduced into any of the territory acquired by the United States from the Republic of Mexico, it is inexpedient for Congress to provide by law either for its introduction into or exclusion from any part of the said territory; and that appropriate territorial governments ought to be established by Congress in all of the said territory, not assigned as the boundaries of the proposed State of California, without the adoption of any restriction or condition on the subject of slavery.

The other truth which I respectfully and with great deference conceive to exist, and which is announced in this resolution, is, that slavery is not likely to be introduced into any of these territories. Well, sir, is not that a fact? Is there a member who hears me that will not confirm the fact? What has occurred within the last three months? In California, more than in any other portion of the ceded territory, was it most probable, if slavery was adapted to the interests of the industrial pursuits of the inhabitants, that slavery would have been introduced. Yet, within the space of three or four months, California herself has declared, by a unanimous vote of her convention, against the introduction of slavery within her limits. And, as I remarked on a former occasion, this declaration was not confined to non-slaveholders.

There were persons from the slaveholding States who concurred in that declaration. Thus this fact which is asserted in the resolution is responded to by the act of California. Then, sir, if we come down to those mountain regions which are to be found in New Mexico, the nature of its soil and country, its barrenness, its unproductive character, every thing which relates to it, and every thing which we hear of it and about it, must necessarily lead to the conclusion which I have mentioned, that slavery is not likely to be introduced into them. — Well, sir, if it be true that by law slavery does not now exist in the ceded territories, and that it is not likely to be introduced into the ceded territories — if you, senators, agree to these truths, or a majority of you, as I am persuaded a large majority of you must agree to them — where is the objection or the difficulty to your announcing them to the whole world? Why should you hesitate or falter in the promulgation of incontestable truths? On the other hand, with regard to senators coming from the free States, allow me here to make, with reference to California, one or two observations.

When this feeling within the limits of your States was gotten up;

when the Wilmot proviso was disseminated through them, and your people and yourselves attached themselves to that proviso, what was the state of facts? The state of facts at the time was, that you apprehended the introduction of slavery there. You did not know much — very few of us now know much — about those very territories. They were far distant from you. You were apprehensive that slavery might be introduced there. You wanted as a protection to introduce the interdiction called the Wilmot proviso. It was in this state of want of information that the whole North blazed up in behalf of this Wilmot proviso. It was under the apprehension that slavery might be introduced there that you left your constituents. For when you came from home, at the time you left your respective residences, you did not know the fact, which has only reached us since the commencement of the session of Congress, that a constitution has been unanimously adopted by the people of California, excluding slavery from their Territory.

Well, now, let me suppose that two years ago it had been known in the free states that such a constitution would be adopted; let me suppose that it had been believed that in no other portion of these ceded territories would slavery be introduced; let me suppose that upon this great subject of solicitude, negro slavery, the people of the North had been perfectly satisfied that there was no danger; let me also suppose that they had foreseen the excitement, the danger, the irritation, the resolutions which have been adopted by Southern Legislatures, and the manifestations of opinion by the people of the slaveholding States — let me suppose that all this had been known at the North at the time when the agitation was first got up upon the subject of this Wilmot proviso — do you believe that it would have ever reached the height to which it has attained? Do any of you believe it? And if, prior to your departure from your respective homes, you had had an opportunity of conferring with your constituents upon this most leading and important fact — of the adoption of a constitution excluding slavery in California — do you not believe, senators and representatives coming from the free States, that if you had the advantage of that fact told in serious, calm, fire-side conversation with your constituents, they would not have told you to come here and to settle all these agitating questions without danger to this Union?

What do you want? What do you want who reside in the free States? You want that there shall be no slavery introduced into the territories acquired from Mexico. Well, have not you got it in California already, if admitted as a State? Have you not got it in New Mexico, in all human probability, also? What more do you want? You have got what is worth a thousand Wilmot provisos. You have got nature itself on your side. You have the fact itself on your side. You have the truth staring you in the face that no slavery is existing there. Well, if you are men; if you can rise from the mud and slough of party struggles and elevate yourselves to the height of patriots, what will you do? You will look at the fact as it exists. You will say, this fact was unknown to my people. You will say, they acted on one set of facts, we have got another set of facts here influencing us, and we will act as patriots, as responsible men, as lovers of unity and above all of this Union. We will act on the altered set of facts unknown to our constituents, and we will appeal to their justice, their honor, their magnanimity, to concur with us on this occasion, for establishing concord and harmony, and maintaining the existence of this glorious Union.

Well, Mr. President, I think, entertaining these views, that there was nothing extravagant in the hope in which I indulged when these resolutions were prepared and offered — nothing extravagant in the hope that the North might content itself even with striking out as unnecessary these two declarations. They are unnecessary for any purpose the free States have in view. At all events, if they should insist upon Congress expressing the opinions which are here asserted, they should limit their wishes to the simple assertion of them, without insisting on their being incorporated in any territorial Government which Congress may establish in the territories.

I pass on from the second resolution to the third and fourth, which relate to Texas; and allow me to say, Mr. President, that I approach the subject with a full knowledge of all its difficulties; and of all the questions connected with or growing out of this institution of slavery, which Congress is called upon to pass upon and decide, there are none so difficult and troublesome as those which relate to Texas, because, sir, Texas has a question of boundary to settle, and the question of slavery, or the feelings connected with it, run into the question of boundary. The North, perhaps, will be anxious to contract Texas within the narrowest possible limits, in order to exclude all beyond her to make it a free territory; the South, on the contrary, may be anxious to extend their limits to the source of the Rio Grande, for the purpose of creating an additional theater for slavery; and thus, to the question of the limits of Texas, and the settlement of her boundary, the slavery question, with all its troubles and difficulties, is added, meeting us at every step we take.

There is, sir, a third question, also, adding to the difficulty. By the resolution of annexation, slavery was interdicted in all north of 36° 30'; but of New Mexico, that portion of it which lies north or 36° 30' embraces, I think, about one third of the whole of New Mexico east of the Rio Grande; so that you have free and slave territory mixed, boundary and slavery mixed together, and all these difficulties are to be encountered. And allow me to say, sir, that among the considerations which induced me to think it was necessary to settle all these questions, was the state of things that now exists in New Mexico, and the state of things to be apprehended both there and in other portions of the territories. Why, sir, at this moment — and I think I shall have the concurrence of the two senators from that State when I announce the fact — at this moment there is a feeling approximating to abhorrence on the part of the people of New Mexico at the idea of any union with Texas.

(MR. RUSK. Only, sir, on the part of the office-seekers and army followers, who have settled there, and attempted to mislead the people.

MR. CLAY. Ah! sir, that may be, and I am afraid that New Mexico is not the only place where this class composes a majority of the whole population of the country. [Laughter.])

Now, sir, if the questions are not settled which relate to Texas, her boundaries, and so forth, and to the territory now claimed by Texas and disputed by New Mexico — the territories beyond New Mexico which are excluded from California — if these questions are not all settled, I think they will give rise to future confusion, disorder and anarchy there, and to agitation here. There will be, I have no doubt, a party still at the North crying out, if these questions are not settled this session, for the Wilmot proviso, or some other restriction upon them, and we shall absolutely do nothing, in my opinion, if we do not accommodate all these difficulties and provide against the recurrence of all these dangers.

Sir, with respect to the state of things in New Mexico, allow me to call the attention of the Senate to what I consider as the highest authority I could offer to them as to the state of things there existing. I mean the acts of their Convention, unless that Convention happens to have been composed altogether of office-seekers, office-holders, and so forth. Now, sir, I call your attention to what they say in depicting their own situation.

(MR. UNDERWOOD, at Mr. Clay's request, read the following extract from instructions adopted by the Convention, appended to the journal of the Convention of the Territory of New Mexico, held at the city of Santa Fé, in September, 1849.

We, the people of New Mexico, in Convention assembled, having elected a delegate to represent this Territory in the Congress of the United States, and to urge upon the Supreme Government a redress of our grievances, and the protection due to us as citizens of our common country, under the Constitution, instruct him as follows: That whereas, for the last three years we have suffered under the paralyzing effects of a government undefined and doubtful in its character, inefficient to protect the rights of the people, or to discharge the high and absolute duty of every Government, the enforcement and regular administration of its own laws, in consequence of which, industry and enterprise are paralyzed and discontent and confusion prevail throughout the land. The want of proper protection against the various barbarous tribes of Indians that surround us on every side has prevented the extension of settlements upon our valuable public domain, and rendered utterly futile every attempt to explore or develop the great resources of the territory.

Surrounded by the Utahs, Camanches, and Apaches, on the North, East and South, by the Navajos on the West, with Jicarillas within our limits, and without any adequate protection against their hostile inroads, our flocks and herds are driven off by thousands, our fellow-citizens, men, women, and children, are murdered or carried into captivity. Many of our citizens, of all ages and sexes, are at this moment suffering all the horrors of barbarian bondage, and it is utterly out of our power to obtain their release from a condition to which death would be preferable. The wealth of our territory is being diminished. We have neither the means nor any adopted plan of Government for the education of the rising generation. In fine, with a government temporary, doubtful, uncertain, and inefficient in character and in operation, surrounded and despoiled by barbarous foes, ruin appears inevitably before us, unless speedy and effectual protection be extended to us by the Congress of the United States.)

There is a series of resolutions, Mr. President, which any gentleman may look at, if he chooses; but I think it is not worth while to take up the time of the Senate in reading them.

That is the condition, sir, of New Mexico. Well, I suspect that to go beyond it, to go beyond the Rio Grande to the territory which is not claimed by Texas, you will not find a much better state of things. In fact, sir, I can not for a moment reconcile it to my sense of duty to suffer Congress to adjourn without an effort, at least, being made to extend the benefits, the blessings of government to those people who have recently been acquired by us.

Sir, with regard to that portion of New Mexico which lies east of the Rio Grande, undoubtedly, if it is conceded to Texas, while she has two parties, disliking each other as much as those office-holders and office-seekers alluded to by the senator from Texas, if they could possibly be drawn together and governed quietly, peaceably, and comfortably, there might be a remedy, so far as relates to the country east of the Rio Grande; but all beyond it — Deseret and the North of California — would be still open and liable to all the consequences of disunion, confusion and anarchy, without some stable government emanating from the authority of the nation of which they now compose a part, and with which they are but little acquainted. I think, therefore, that all these questions, difficult and troublesome as they may be, ought to be met — met in a spirit of candor and calmness, and decided upon as a matter of duty.

Now, these two resolutions which we have immediately under consideration propose a decision of these questions. I have said, sir, that there is scarcely a resolution in the series which I have offered that does not contain some mutual concession or evidence of mutual forbearance, where the concession was not altogether from the non-slaveholding to the slaveholding States.

Now, with respect to this resolution proposing a boundary for Texas, what is it? We know the difference of opinion which has existed in this country with respect to that boundary. We know that a very large portion of the people of the United States have supposed that the western limit of Texas was the Nueces, and that it did not extend to the Rio Grande. We know, by the resolution of annexation, that the question of what is the western limit and the northern limit of Texas was an open question — that it has been all along an open question. It was an open question when the boundary was run, in virtue of the Act of 1838, marking the boundary between the United States and Texas. Sir, at that time the boundary authorized by the Act of 1838 was a boundary commencing at the mouth of the Sabine and running up to its head, thence to Red River, thence westwardly with Red River to, I think, the hundredth degree of west longitude. Well, sir, that did not go so far as Texas now claims, and why? Because it was an open question. War was yet raging between Texas and Mexico; it was not foreseen exactly what might be her ultimate limits. But, sir, we will come to the question of what was done at the time of her annexation.

The whole resolution which relates to the question of boundary, from beginning to end, assumes an open boundary, an unascertained, unfixed boundary to Texas on the West. Sir, what is the first part of the resolution? It is that "Congress doth consent that the Territory properly included within and rightfully belonging to the Republic of Texas may be erected into a new State." Properly including — rightfully belonging to. The resolution specifies no boundary. It could specify none. It has specified no western or northern boundary for Texas. It has assumed in this state of uncertainty what we know in point of fact existed. But then the latter part of it: "Said State to be formed subject to the adjustment of all questions of boundary that may arise with other Governments, and the constitution thereof," &c. That is to say, she is annexed with her rightful and proper boundaries, without a specification of them; but inasmuch as it was known that these boundaries at the west and the north were unsettled, the Government of the United States retained to itself the power of settling with any foreign nation what the boundary should be.

Now, sir, it is impossible for me to go into the whole question and to argue it fully. I mean to express opinions or impressions, rather than to go into the entire argument. The western and northern limit of Texas being unsettled, and the Government of the United States having retained the power of settling it, I ask, suppose the power had been exercised, and that there had been no cession of territory by Mexico to the United States, but that the negotiations between the countries had been limited simply to the fixation of the western and northern limits of Texas, could it not have been done by the United States and Mexico conjointly? Will any one dispute it? Suppose there had been a treaty of limits of Texas concluded between Mexico and the United States, fixing the Nueces as the western limit of Texas, would not Texas have been bound by it? Why, by the express terms of the resolution she would have been bound by it; or if it had been the Colorado or the Rio Grande, or any other boundary, whatever western limit had been fixed by the joint action of the two powers, would have been binding and obligatory upon Texas by the express terms of the resolution by which she was admitted into the Union. Now, sir, Mexico and the United States conjointly, by treaty, might have fixed upon the western and northern limits of Texas, and if the United States have acquired by treaty all the subjects upon which the limits of Texas might have operated, have not the United States now the power solely and exclusively which Mexico and the United States conjointly possessed prior to the late treaty between the two countries? It seems to me, sir, that this conclusion and reasoning are perfectly irresistible. If Mexico and the United States could have fixed upon any western limit for Texas, and did not do it, and if the United States have acquired to themselves, or acquired by the treaty in question, all the territory upon which the western limit must have been fixed, when it was fixed, it seems to me that no one can resist the logical conclusion, that the United States now have themselves a power to do what the United States and Mexico conjointly could have done.

Sir, I admit it is a delicate power — an extremely delicate power. I admit that it ought to be exercised in a spirit of justice, liberality, and generosity toward this the youngest member of the great American family. But here the power is. Possibly, sir, upon that question — however I offer no positive opinion — possibly, if the United States were to fix it in a way unjust in the opinion of Texas, and contrary to her rights, she might bring the question before the Supreme Court of the United States, and have it there again investigated and decided. I say possibly, sir, because I am not one of that class of politicians who believe that every question is a competent and proper question for the Supreme Court of the United States. There are questions too large for any tribunal of that kind to try; great political questions, national territorial questions, which transcend their limits; for such questions their powers are utterly incompetent. Whether this be one of those questions or not, I shall not decide; but I will maintain that the United States are now invested solely and exclusively with that power which was common to both nations — to fix, ascertain, and settle the western and northern limits of Texas.

Sir, the other day my honorable friend who represents so well the State of Texas said that we had no more right to touch the limits of Texas than we had to touch the limits of Kentucky. I think that was the illustration he gave us — that a State is one and indivisible, and that the General Government has no right to sever it. I agree with him, sir, in that; where the limits are ascertained and certain, where they are undisputed and indisputable. The General Government has no right, nor has any other earthly power the right, to interfere with the limits of a State whose boundaries are thus fixed, thus ascertained, known, and recognized. The whole power, at least, to interfere with it is voluntary. The extreme case may be put — one which I trust in God may never happen in this nation — of a conquered nation, and of a constitution adapting itself to the state of subjugation or conquest to which it has been reduced; and giving up whole States, as well as parts of States, in order to save from the conquering arms of the invader what remains. I say such a power in case of extremity may exist. But I admit that, short of such extremity, voluntarily, the General Government has no right to separate a State — to take a portion of its territory from it, or to regard it otherwise than as integral, one and indivisible, and not to be affected by any legislation of ours. But, then, I assume what does not exist in the case of Texas, and these boundaries must be known, ascertained, and indisputable. With regard to Texas, all was open, all was unfixed; all is unfixed at this moment, with respect to her limits west and north of the Nueces.

But, sir, we gave fifteen millions of dollars for this territory that we bought, and God knows what a costly bargain to this now distracted country it has been! We gave fifteen millions of dollars for the territory ceded to us by Mexico. Can Texas justly, fairly, and honorably come into the Union and claim all that she asserted a right to, without paying any portion of the fifteen millions of dollars which constituted the consideration of the grant by the ceding nation to the United States? She proposes no such thing. She talks, indeed, about the United States having been her agent, her trustee. Why, sir, the United States was no more her agent or her trustee than she was the agent or trustee of the whole people of the United States. Texas involved herself in war — (I mean to make this no reproach — none — none — upon the past) — Texas brought herself into a state of war, and when she got into that war, it was not the war of Texas and Mexico, but it was the war of the whole thirty United States and Mexico; it was a war in which the Government of the United States, which created the hostilities, was as much the trustee and agent of the twenty-nine other States composing the Union as she was the trustee and agent of Texas. And, sir, with respect to all these circumstances — such, for example, as a treaty with a map annexed, as in the case of the recent treaty with Mexico; such as the opinion of individuals highly respected and eminent, like the lamented Mr. Polk, late President of the United States, whose opinion was that he had no right, as President of the United States, or in any character otherwise than as negotiating with Mexico — and in that the Senate would have to act in concurrence with him — that he had no right to fix the boundary; and as to the map attached to the treaty, it is sufficient to say that the treaty itself is silent from beginning to end on the subject of the fixation of the boundary of Texas. The annexation of the map to the treaty was a matter of no utility, for the treaty is not strengthened by it; it no more affirms the truth of any thing delineated upon the map in relation to Texas than it does any thing in relation to any other geographical subject that composed the map.

Mr. President, I have said that I think the power has been concentrated in the Government of the United States to fix upon the limits of the State of Texas. I have said also that this power ought to be exercised in a spirit of great liberality and justice; and I put it to you, sir, to say, in reference to this second resolution of mine, whether that liberality and justice have not been displayed in the resolution which I have proposed. In the resolution, what is proposed? To confine her to the Nueces? No, sir. To extend her boundary to the mouth of the Rio Grande, and thence up that river to the southern limit of New Mexico; and thence along that limit to the boundary between the United States and Spain, as marked under the treaty of 1819.

Why, sir, here is a vast country. I believe — although I have made no estimate about it — that it is not inferior in extent of land, of acres, of square miles, to what Texas east of the river

Nueces, extending to the Sabine, had before. And who is there can say with truth and justice that there is no reciprocity, nor mutuality, no concession in this resolution, made to Texas, even in reference to the question of boundary alone? You give her a vast country, equal, I repeat, in extent nearly to what she indisputably possessed before; a country sufficiently large, with her consent, hereafter to carve out of it some two or three additional States when the condition of the population may render it expedient to make new States. Sir, is there not in this resolution concession, liberality, justice? But this is not all that we propose to do. The second resolution proposes to pay off a certain amount of the debt of Texas. A blank is left in the resolution, because I have not heretofore been able to ascertain the amount.

(Mr. Foote — *Will the honorable Senator allow me to suggest that it may be agreeable to him to finish his remarks to-morrow? If such be the case, I will move that the Senate now go into Executive session.*

Mr. Clay — *I am obliged to the worthy Senator from Mississippi; I do not think it possible for me to conclude to-day, and I will yield with great pleasure if* —

Mr. Foote — *I now move* —

Mr. Clay — *If the Senator will permit to conclude what I have to say in relation to Texas, I will then cheerfully yield the floor for his motion.*)

I was about to remark that, independently of this most liberal and generous boundary which is tendered to Texas, we propose to offer her in this second resolution a sum which the worthy Senator from Texas thinks will not be less than three millions of dollars — the exact amount neither he nor I can furnish, not having the materials at hand upon which to make a statement. Well, sir, you get this large boundary and three millions of your debt paid. I shall not repeat the argument which I urged upon a former occasion, as to the obligation of the United States to pay a portion of this debt, but was struck the other day, upon reading the treaty of limits, first between the United States and Mexico, and next the treaty of limits between the United States and Texas, to find, in the preamble of both those treaties, a direct recognition of the principle from which I think springs our obligation to pay a portion of this debt, for the payment of which the revenue of Texas was pledged before her annexation. The principle asserted in the treaty of limits with Mexico is, that whereas by the treaty of 1819, between Spain and the United States, a limit was fixed between Mexico and the United States, Mexico comprising then a portion of the possessions of the Spanish Government, although Mexico was at the date of the treaty severed from the crown of Spain, yet she, as having been a part of the possessions of the crown of Spain when the treaty of 1819 was made, was bound by that treaty as much as if it had been made by herself instead of Spain — in other words, that the severance of no part of a common empire can exonerate either portion of that empire from the obligations contracted when the empire was entire and unsevered. And, sir, the same principle is asserted in the treaty of 1838, between Texas and the United States. The principle asserted is, that the treaty of 1828 between Mexico and the United States having been made when Texas was a part of Mexico, and that now Texas being dissevered from Mexico, she nevertheless remains bound by that treaty as much as if no such severance had taken place. In other words, the principle is this — that when an independent power creates an obligation or debt, no subsequent political misfortune, no subsequent severance of the territories of that power, can exonerate it from the obligation that was created while an integral and independent power; in other words, to bring it down and apply it to this specific case — that, Texas being an independent power, and having a right to make loans and to make pledges, having raised a loan and pledged specifically the revenues arising from the customs to the public creditor, the public creditor became invested with a right to that fund; and it is a right of which he could not be divested by any other act than one to which his own consent was given — it could be divested by no political change which Texas might think proper to make. In consequence of the absorption or merging of Texas into the United States, the creditor, being no party to the treaty which was formed, does not lose his right — he retains his right to demand the fulfillment of the pledge that was made upon this specific fund, just as if there had not been any annexation of Texas to the United States.

That was the foundation upon which I arrived at the conclusion expressed in the resolution — that the United States having appropriated to themselves the revenue arising from the imports, which revenue had been pledged to the creditor of Texas, the United States as an honorable and just power ought now to pay the debt for which those duties were solemnly pledged by a power independent in itself, and competent to make the pledge. Well, sir, I think that when you consider the large boundary which is assigned to Texas — and when you take into view the abhorrence, for I think I am warranted in using this expression — with which the people of New Mexico east of the Rio Grande will look upon any political connection with Texas — and when, in addition to this, you take into view the large grant of money that we propose to make, and our liberality in exonerating her from a portion of her public debt, equal to that grant — when we take all these circumstances into consideration, I think I have presented a case in regard to which I confess I shall be greatly surprised if the people of Texas themselves, when they come to deliberate upon these liberal offers, hesitate a moment to accede to them.

I have now got through with what I had to say in reference to this resolution, and if the Senator from Mississippi wishes it, I will give way for a motion for adjournment.

(On motion of MR. FOOTE the further consideration of the resolution was postponed, and on motion.

*The Senate adjourned.)**

WEDNESDAY, Feb. 6.

MR. PRESIDENT, IF there be in this vast assembly of beauty, grace, elegance, and intelligence, any who have come here under an expectation that the humble individual who now addresses you means to attempt any display, any use of ambitious language, any extraordinary ornament or decoration of speech, they will be utterly disappointed. The season of the year, and my own season of life, both admonish me to abstain from the use of any such ornaments;

---

*Editors' Note: Clay's speech was delivered over a period of two days. The remarks of the first day have been presented in full. The part which is to follow was delivered on the second day and has been abridged because of its length. The editors are including the introductory statement which Clay made upon resuming his speech and then skipping to his powerful conclusion which actually is a summary of the speech of both days.

but, above all, Mr. President, the awful subject upon which it is my duty to address the Senate and the country forbids my saying any thing but what pertains strictly to that subject, and my sole desire is to make myself, in seriousness, soberness, and plainness, understood by you and by those who think proper to listen to me. . . .

Sir, our prosperity is unbounded — nay, Mr. President, I sometimes fear that it is in the wantonness of that prosperity that many of the threatening ills of the moment have arisen. Wild and erratic schemes have sprung up throughout the whole country, some of which have even found their way into legislative halls; and there is a restlessness existing among us which I fear will require the chastisement of Heaven to bring us back to a sense of the immeasurable benefits and blessings which have been bestowed upon us by Providence. At this moment — with the exception of here and there a particular department in the manufacturing business of the country — all is prosperity and peace, and the nation is rich and powerful. Our country has grown to a magnitude, to a power and greatness, such as to command the respect, if it does not awe the apprehensions, of the powers of the earth, with whom we come in contact.

Sir, do I depict with colors too lively the prosperity which has resulted to us from the operations of this Union? Have I exaggerated in any particular her power, her prosperity, or her greatness? And now, sir, let me go a little into detail with respect to sway in the councils of the nation, whether from the North or the South, during the sixty years of unparalleled prosperity that we have enjoyed. During the first twelve years of the administration of the Government Northern counsels rather prevailed; and out of them sprang the Bank of the United States, the assumption of the State debts, bounties to the fisheries, protection to our domestic manufactures — I allude to the act of 1789 — neutrality in the wars of Europe, Jay's treaty, the alien and sedition laws, and war with France. I do not say, sir, that these, the leading and prominent measures which were adopted during the administrations of Washington and the elder Adams, were carried exclusively by Northern counsels — they could not have been — but mainly by the ascendency which Northern counsels had obtained in the affairs of the nation. So, sir, of the later period — for the last fifty years.

I do not mean to say that Southern counsels alone have carried the measures which I am about to enumerate. I know they could not exclusively have carried them, but I say that they have been carried by their prepondering influence, with the co-operation, it is true — the large co-operation in some instances — of the Northern section of the Union. And what are those measures? During that fifty years, or nearly that period, in which Southern counsels have preponderated, the embargo and other commercial restrictions of non-intercourse and non-importation were imposed; war with Great Britain, the Bank of the United States overthrown, protection enlarged and extended to domestic manufactures — I allude to the passage of the act of 1815 or 1816 — the Bank of the United States re-established, the same bank put down, re-established by Southern counsels and put down by Southern counsels, Louisiana acquired, Florida bought, Texas annexed, war with Mexico, California and other territories acquired from Mexico by conquest and purchase, protection superseded, and free trade established, Indians removed west of the Mississippi, and fifteen new States admitted into the Union. It is very possible, sir, that in this enumeration I may have omitted some of the important measures which have been adopted during this later period of time — the last fifty years — but these I believe to be the most prominent ones.

Now, sir, I do not deduce from the enumeration of the measures adopted by the one side or the other any just cause of reproach either upon one side or the other; though one side or the other has predominated in the two periods to which I have referred. These measures were, to say the least, the joint work of both parties, and neither of them have any just cause to reproach the other. But, sir, I must say, in all kindness and sincerity, that least of all ought the South to reproach the North, when we look at the long list of measures which, under her sway in the counsels of the nation, have been adopted; when we reflect that even opposite doctrines have been from time to time advanced by her; that the establishment of the Bank of the United States, which was done under the administration of Mr. Madison, met with the co-operation of the South — I do not say the whole South — I do not, when I speak of the South or the North, speak of the entire South or the entire North; I speak of the prominent and larger proportion of Southern and Northern men. It was during Mr. Madison's administration that the Bank of the United States was established. My friend, whose sickness — which I very much deplore — prevents us from having his attendance upon this occasion (Mr. Calhoun), was the chairman of the committee, and carried the measure through Congress. I voted for it with all my heart. Although I had been instrumental with other Southern votes in putting down the Bank of the United States, I changed my opinion and co-operated in the establishment of the Bank of 1816. The same bank was again put down by Southern counsels, with General Jackson at their head, at a later period. Again, with respect to the policy of protection. The South in 1815 — I mean the prominent Southern men, the lamented Lowndes, Mr. Calhoun, and others — united in extending a certain measure of protection to domestic manufactures as well as the North.

We find a few years afterward the South interposing most serious objections to this policy, and one member of the South, threatening on that occasion, a dissolution of the Union or separation. Now, sir, let us take another view of the question — and I would remark that all these views are brought forward not in a spirit of reproach, but of conciliation — not to provoke or exasperate, but to quiet, to produce harmony and repose, if possible. What have been the territorial acquisitions made by this country, and to what interests have they conduced? Florida, where slavery exists, has been introduced; Louisiana, or all the most valuable part of that State — for although there is a large extent of territory north of the line 36° 30′, in point of intrinsic value and importance, I would not give the single State of Louisiana for the whole of it — all Louisiana, I say, with the exception of that which lies north of 36° 30′, including Oregon, to which we obtained title mainly on the ground of its being a part of the acquisition of Louisiana; all Texas; all the territories which have been acquired by the Government of the United States during its sixty years' operation have been slave territories, the theater of slavery, with the exception that I have mentioned of that lying north of the line 36° 30′.

And here, in the case of a war made essentially by the South — growing out of the annexation of Texas, which was a measure proposed by the South in the councils of the country, and which led to the war with Mexico — I do not say all of the South, but the major portion of the South pressed the annexation of Texas upon the country — that measure, as I have said, led to the war with Mexico, and the war with Mexico led to the acquisition of those territories which now constitute the bone of contention between the different members of the Confederacy. And now, sir, for the first time after the three great acquisitions of Texas, Florida, and Louisiana have been made and have redounded to the benefit of the South — now, for the first time, when three territories are attempted to be introduced without the institution of slavery, I put it to the hearts of my countrymen of the South, if it is right to press matters to the disastrous consequences which have been indicated no longer ago than this very morning, on the occasion of the presentation of certain resolutions — even extending to a dissolution of the Union. Mr. President, I can not believe it.

(Mr. UNDERWOOD — *Will the Senator give way for an adjournment?*)

Oh, no; if I do not weary the patience of the Senate, I prefer to go on. I think I can begin to see land. I shall soon come to the conclusion of what I have to say. Such is the Union, and such are the glorious fruits which are now threatened with subversion and destruction. Well, sir, the first question which naturally arises is, supposing the Union to be dissolved for any of the causes or grievances which are complained of, how far will dissolution furnish a remedy for those grievances? If the Union is to be dissolved for any existing cause, it will be because slavery is interdicted or not allowed to be introduced into the ceded territories; or because slavery is threatened to be abolished in the District of Columbia; or because fugitive slaves are not restored, as in my opinion they ought to be, to their masters. These, I believe, would be the causes, if there be any causes which can lead to the dreadful event to which I have referred. Let us suppose the Union dissolved; what remedy does it, in a severed state, furnish for the grievances complained of in its united condition? Will you be able at the South to push slavery into the ceded territory? How are you to do it, supposing the North, or all the States north of the Potomac, in possession of the navy and army of the United States? Can you expect, I say, under these circumstances, that if there is a dissolution of the Union you can carry slavery into California and New Mexico? Sir, you can not dream of such an occurrence.

If it were abolished in the District of Columbia and the Union were dissolved, would the dissolution of the Union restore slavery in the District of Columbia? Is your chance for the recovery of your fugitive slaves safer in a state of dissolution or of severance of the Union than when in the Union itself? Why, sir, what is the state of the fact? In the Union you lose some slaves and recover others; but here let me revert to a fact which I ought to have noticed before, because it is highly creditable to the courts and juries of the free States. In every instance, as far as my information extends, in which an appeal has been made to the courts of justice to recover penalties from those who have assisted in decoying slaves from their masters — in every instance, as far as I have heard, the court has asserted the rights of the owner, and the jury has promptly returned an adequate verdict on his behalf. Well, sir, there is then some remedy while you are a part of the Union for the recovery of your slaves, and some indemnification for their loss. What would you have, if the Union was severed? Why, then the several parts would be independent of each other — foreign countries — and slaves escaping from one to the other would be like slaves escaping from the United States to Canada. There would be no right of extradition, no right to demand your slaves; no right to appeal to the courts of justice to indemnify you for the loss of your slaves. Where one slave escapes now by running away from his master, hundreds and thousands would escape if the Union were dissevered — I care not how or where you run the line, or whether independent sovereignties be established. Well, sir, finally, will you, in case of a dissolution of the Union, be safer with your slaves within the separated portions of the States than you are now? Mr. President, that they will escape much more frequently from the border States no one will deny.

And, sir, I must take occasion here to say that in my opinion there is no right on the part of any one or more of the States to secede from the Union. War and dissolution of the Union are identical and inevitable, in my opinion. There can be a dissolution of the Union only by consent or by war. Consent no one can anticipate, from any existing state of things, is likely to be given, and war is the only alternative by which a dissolution could be accomplished. If consent were given — if it were possible that we were to be separated by one great line — in less than sixty days after such consent was given war would break out between the slaveholding and non-slaveholding portions of this Union — between the two independent parts into which it would be erected in virtue of the act of separation. In less than sixty days, I believe, our slaves from Kentucky, flocking over in numbers to the other side of the river, would be pursued by their owners. Our hot and ardent spirits would be restrained by no sense of the right which appertains to the independence of the other side of the river, should that be the line of separation. They would pursue their slaves into the adjacent free States; they would be repelled, and the consequence would be that, in less than sixty days, war would be blazing in every part of this now happy and peaceful land.

And, sir, how are you going to separate the States of this Confederacy? In my humble opinion, Mr. President, we should begin with at least three separate Confederacies. There would be a Confederacy of the North, a Confederacy of the Southern Atlantic slaveholding States, and a Confederacy of the valley of the Mississippi. My life upon it, that the vast population which has already concentrated and will concentrate on the head-waters and the tributaries of the Mississippi will never give their consent that the mouth of that river shall be held subject to the power of any foreign State or community whatever. Such, I believe, would be the consequences of a dissolution of the Union, immediately ensuing; but other Confederacies would spring up from time to time, as dissatisfaction and discontent were disseminated throughout the country — the Confederacy of the lakes, perhaps the Confederacy of New England, or of the middle States. Ah, sir, the veil which covers these sad and disastrous events that lie beyond it, is too thick to be penetrated or lifted by any mortal eye or hand.

Mr. President, I am directly opposed to any purpose of secession or separation. I am for staying within the Union, and defying any portion of this Confederacy to expel me or drive me out of the Union. I am for staying within the Union and fighting for my rights, if necessary, with the sword, within the bounds and under the safeguard of the Union. I am for vindicating those rights, not by being driven out of the Union harshly and unceremoniously by any portion of this Confederacy. Here I am within it, and here I mean to stand and die, as far as my individual wishes or purposes can go — within it to protect my property and defend myself, defying all the power on earth to expel me or drive me from the situation in which I am placed. And would there not be more safety in fighting within the Union than out of it? Suppose your rights to be violated, suppose wrong to be done you, aggressions to be perpetrated upon you, can you not better vindicate them — if you have occasion to resort to the last necessity, the sword, for a restoration of those rights — within, and with the sympathies of a large portion of the population of the Union, than by being without the Union, when a large portion of the population have sympathies adverse to your own? You can vindicate your rights within the Union better than if expelled from the Union, and driven from it without ceremony and without authority.

Sir, I have said that I thought there was no right on the part of one or more States to secede from the Union. I think so. The Constitution of the United States was made not merely for the generation that then existed, but for posterity — unlimited, undefined, endless, perpetual posterity. And every State that then came into the Union, and every State that has since come into the Union, came into it binding itself, by indissoluble bands, to remain within the Union itself, and to remain within it by its posterity forever. Like another of the sacred connections, in private life, it is a marriage which no human authority can dissolve or divorce the parties from. And if I may be allowed to refer to some examples in private life, let me say to the North and to the South, what husband and wife say to each other. We have mutual faults; neither of us is perfect; nothing in the form of humanity is perfect; let us, then, be kind to each other — forbearing, forgiving each other's faults — and above all, let us live in happiness and peace together.

Mr. President, I have said, what I solemnly believe, that dissolution of the Union and war are identical and inevitable; and they are convertible terms; and such a war as it would be, following a dissolution of the Union! Sir, we may search the pages of history, and none so ferocious, so bloody, so implacable, so exterminating — not even the wars of Greece, including those of the Commoners of England and the revolutions of France — none, none of them all would rage with such violence, or be characterized with such bloodshed and enormities as would the war which must succeed, if that ever happens, the dissolution of the Union. And what would be its termination? Standing armies, and navies, to an extent stretching the revenues of each portion of the dissevered members, would take place. An exterminating war would follow — not, sir, a war of two or three years' duration, but a war of interminable duration — and exterminating wars would ensue, until, after the struggles and exhaustion of both parties, some Philip or Alexander, some Cæsar or Napoleon, would arise and cut the Gordian knot, and solve the problem of the capacity of man for self-government, and crush the liberties of both the severed portions of this common empire. Can you doubt it?

Look at all history — consult her pages, ancient or modern — look at human nature; look at the contest in which you would be engaged in the supposition of war following upon the dissolution of the Union, such as I have suggested; and I ask you if it is possible for you to doubt that the final disposition of the whole would be some despot treading down the liberties of the people — the final result would be the extinction of this last and glorious light which is leading all mankind, who are gazing upon it, in the hope and anxious expectation that the liberty which prevails here will sooner or later be diffused throughout the whole of the civilized world. Sir, can you lightly contemplate these consequences? Can you yield yourself to the tyranny of passion, amid dangers which I have depicted in colors far too tame of what the result would be if that direful event to which I have referred should ever occur? Sir, I implore gentlemen, I adjure them, whether from the South or the North, by all that they hold dear in this world — by all their love of liberty — by all their veneration for their ancestors — by all their regard for posterity — by all their gratitude to Him who has bestowed on them such unnumbered and countless blessings — by all the duties which they owe to mankind — and by all the duties which they owe to themselves, to pause, solemnly to pause at the edge of the precipice, before the fearful and dangerous leap be taken into the yawning abyss below, from which none who ever take it shall return in safety.

Finally, Mr. President, and in conclusion, I implore, as the best blessing which Heaven can bestow upon me, upon earth, that if the direful event of the dissolution of this Union is to happen, I shall not survive to behold the sad and heart-rending spectacle.

JOHN C. CALHOUN

(1782-1850)

Unlike his colleague and frequent opponent in the Senate, Henry Clay, John C. Calhoun was no advocate of compromise. To the contrary, he doggedly maintained a rigid, unflinching position in defense of state sovereignty. Until his death in 1850, he was the champion spokesman of the Southern cause, a staunch defender of the right of the individual state to nullify any Federal law which it believed unconstitutional. For his adherence to such a doctrine he was frequently called the "Great Nullifier." Although Calhoun, as a member of the famed Triumvirate, could not match the magnificent voices of Clay and Webster, he is numbered nevertheless among the great orators of the time. He had the supreme gift of a keen logical faculty which enabled him to reduce a complex issue to its few basic essentials. This analytical power was coupled with an obvious and deep sense of conviction in the rightness of his cause. His style was direct, blunt, factual, with little of the imaginative and rhetorical touches of a Clay or a Webster. Oliver Dyer, a newspaper reporter who saw and heard Calhoun speak on many occasions, observed that he "talked on the most abstruse subjects with the guileless simplicity of a prattling child. His ideas were so clear and his language so plain that he made a path of light through any subject he discussed." In his tribute to Mr. Calhoun in the Senate on April 1, 1850, Daniel Webster remarked:

. . . the eloquence of Mr. Calhoun, or the manner in which he exhibited his sentiments in public bodies, was part of his intellectual character. It grew out of the qualities of his mind. It was plain, strong, terse, condensed, concise; sometimes impassioned, still always severe. Rejecting ornament, not often seeking far for illustration, his power consisted in the plainness of his propositions, in the closeness of his logic, and in the earnestness and energy of his manner. These are the qualities, as I think, which have enabled him through such a long course of years to speak often, and yet always command attention. His demeanor as a Senator is known to us all, is appreciated, venerated, by us all. No man was more respectful to others; no man carried himself with greater decorum, no man with superior dignity. I think there is not one of us, when he last addressed us from his seat in the Senate, his form still erect, with a voice by no means indicating such a degree of physical weakness as did in fact possess him, with clear tones, and an impressive, and, I may say, an imposing manner, who did not feel that he might imagine that we saw before us a Senator of Rome, while Rome survived.

Calhoun's brilliant address to the Senate on March 4, 1850, in opposition to Clay's compromise proposals was his last major speech and one of the most extraordinary ever heard in that chamber. The speech was a masterpiece of logical analysis. With dignity and precision it set forth the cause and nature of the present danger to the Union, how the Union could not be saved, and finally how it could be saved. The only hope for preservation of the Union was that the North must make concessions; otherwise the South would secede. Too ill to deliver the speech himself, he had it read by his friend, Senator James Mason of Virginia. The setting, certainly, was one of the most dramatic and impressive in Senate history — a dying man who sat and listened to his own fateful words spoken by another. Twenty-seven days later, in the early morning of March 31, John C. Calhoun died, troubled to the last by what would happen to his beloved South.

COMPROMISE SPEECH OF 1850

by

John C. Calhoun

Delivered in the United States Senate on March 4, 1850.

I HAVE, SENATORS, believed from the first that the agitation of the subject of slavery would, if not prevented by some timely and effective measure, end in disunion. Entertaining this opinion, I have, on all proper occasions, endeavored to call the attention of both the two great parties which divide the country to adopt some measure to prevent so great a disaster, but without success. The agitation has been permitted to proceed, with almost no attempt to resist it, until it has reached a point when it can no longer be disguised or denied that the Union is in danger. You have thus had forced upon you the greatest and gravest question that can ever come under your consideration — How can the Union be preserved?

To give a satisfactory answer to this mighty question, it is indispensable to have an accurate and thorough knowledge of the nature and the character of the cause by which the Union is endangered. Without such knowledge it is impossible to pronounce, with any certainty, by what measure it can be saved; just as it would be impossible for a physician to pronounce, in the case of some dangerous disease, with any certainty, by what remedy the patient could be saved, without similar knowledge of the nature and character of the cause which produced it. The first question, then, presented for consideration, in the investigation I propose to make, in order to obtain such knowledge, is — What is it that has endangered the Union?

To this question there can be but one answer, — that the immediate cause is the almost universal discontent which pervades all the States composing the Southern section of the Union. This widely-extended discontent is not of recent origin. It commenced with the agitation of the slavery question, and has been increasing ever since. The next question, going one step further back, is — What has caused this widely diffused and almost universal discontent?

It is a great mistake to suppose, as is by some, that it originated with demagogues, who excited the discontent with the intention of aiding their personal advancement, or with the disappointed ambition of certain politicians, who resorted to it as the means of retrieving their fortunes. On the contrary, all the great political influences of the section were arrayed against excitement, and exerted to the utmost to keep the people quiet. The great mass of the people of the South were divided, as in the other section, into Whigs and Democrats. The leaders and the presses of both parties in the South were very solicitous to prevent excitement and to preserve quiet; because it was seen that the effects of the former would necessarily tend to weaken, if not destroy, the political ties which united them with their respective parties in the other section. Those who know the strength of party ties will readily appreciate the immense force which this cause exerted against agitation, and in favor of preserving quiet. But, great as it was, it was not sufficient to prevent the wide-spread discontent which now pervades the section. No; some cause, far deeper and more powerful than the one supposed, must exist, to account for discontent so wide and deep. The question then recurs — What is the cause of this discontent? It will be found in the belief of the people of the Southern States, as prevalent as the discontent itself, that they cannot remain, as things now are, consistently with honor and safety, in the Union. The next question to be considered is — What has caused this belief?

One of the causes is, undoubtedly, to be traced to the long-continued agitation of the slave question on the part of the North, and the many aggressions which they have made on the rights of the South during the time. I will not enumerate them at present, as it will be done hereafter in its proper place.

There is another lying back of it — with which this is intimately connected — that may be regarded as the great and primary cause. This is to be found in the fact that the equilibrium between the two sections, in the Government as it stood when the constitution was ratified and the Government put in action, has been destroyed. At that time there was nearly a perfect equilibrium between the two, which afforded ample means to each to protect itself against the aggression of the other; but, as it now stands, one section has the exclusive power of controlling the Government, which leaves the other without any adequate means of protecting itself against its encroachment and oppression. To place this subject distinctly before you, I have, Senators, prepared a brief statistical statement, showing the relative weight of the two sections in the Government under the first census of 1790 and the last census of 1840.

According to the former, the population of the United States, including Vermont, Kentucky, and Tennessee, which then were in their incipient condition of becoming States, but were not actually admitted, amounted to 3,929,827. Of this number the Northern States had 1,997,899, and the Southern 1,952,072, making a difference of only 45,827 in favor of the former States. The number of States, including Vermont, Kentucky, and Tennessee, were sixteen; of which eight, including Vermont, belonged to the Northern section, and eight, including Kentucky and Tennessee, to the Southern — making an equal division of the States between the two sections under the first census. There was a small preponderance in the House of Representatives, and in the electoral college, in favor of the Northern, owing to the fact that, according to the provisions of the constitution, in estimating federal numbers five slaves count but three; but it was too small to affect sensibly the perfect equilibrium which, with that exception, existed at the time. Such was the equality of the two sections when the States composing them agreed to enter into a Federal Union. Since then the equilibrium between them has been greatly disturbed.

According to the last census the aggregate population of the United States amounted to 17,063,357, of which the Northern section contained 9,728,920, and the Southern 7,334,437, making a difference, in round numbers, of 2,400,000. The number of States had increased from sixteen to twenty-six, making an addition of ten States. In the mean time the position of Delaware had become doubtful as to which section she properly belonged. Considering her as neutral, the Northern States will have thirteen and the Southern States twelve, making a difference in the Senate of two Senators in favor of the former. According to the apportionment under the census of 1840, there were two hundred and twenty-three members of the House of Representatives, of which the Northern States had one hundred and thirty-five, and the Southern States (considering Delaware as neutral) eighty-seven, making a difference in favor of the former in the House of Representatives of forty-eight. The difference in the Senate of two members, added to this, gives to the North, in the electoral college, a majority of fifty. Since the census of 1840, four States have been added to the Union — Iowa, Wisconsin, Florida, and Texas. They leave the difference in the Senate as it stood when the census was taken; but add two to the side of the North in the House, making the present majority in the House in its favor fifty, and in the electoral college fifty-two.

The result of the whole is to give the Northern section a predominance in every department of the Government, and thereby concentrate in it the two elements which constitute the Federal Government, — majority of States, and a majority of their population, estimated in federal numbers. Whatever section concentrates the two in itself possesses the control of the entire Government.

But we are just at the close of the sixth decade, and the commencement of the seventh. The census is to be taken this year, which must add greatly to the decided preponderance of the North in the House of Representatives and in the electoral college. The prospect is, also, that a great increase will be added to its present preponderance in the Senate, during the period of the decade, by the addition of new States. Two territories, Oregon and Minnesota, are already in progress, and strenuous efforts are making to bring in three additional States from the territory recently conquered from Mexico; which, if successful, will add three other States in a short time to the Northern section, making five States; and increasing the present number of its States from fifteen to twenty, and of its Senators from thirty to forty. On the contrary, there is not a single territory in progress in the Southern section, and no certainty that any additional State will be added to it during the decade. The prospect then is, that the two sections in the Senate, should the efforts now made to exclude the South from the newly acquired territories succeed, will stand, before the end of the decade, twenty Northern States to fourteen Southern (considering Delaware as neutral), and forty Northern Senators to twenty-eight Southern. This great increase of Senators, added to the great increase of members of the House of Representatives and the electoral college on the part of the North, which must take place under the next decade, will effectually and irretrievably destroy the equilibrium which existed when the Government commenced.

Had this destruction been the operation of time, without the interference of Government, the South would have had no reason to complain; but such was not the fact. It was caused by the legislation of this Government, which was appointed, as the common agent of all, and charged with the protection of the interests and security of all. The legislation by which it has been effected, may be classed under three heads. The first is, that series of acts by which the South has been excluded from the common territory belonging to all the States as members of the Federal Union —

which have had the effect of extending vastly the portion allotted to the Northern section, and restricting within narrow limits the portion left the South. The next consists in adopting a system of revenue and disbursements, by which an undue proportion of the burden of taxation has been imposed upon the South, and an undue proportion of its proceeds appropriated to the North; and the last is a system of political measures, by which the original character of the Government has been radically changed. I propose to bestow upon each of these, in the order they stand, a few remarks, with the view of showing that it is owing to the action of this Government, that the equilibrium between the two sections has been destroyed, and the whole powers of the system centered in a sectional majority.

The first of the series of acts by which the South was deprived of its due share of the territories, originated with the confederacy which preceded the existence of this Government. It is to be found in the provision of the ordinance of 1787. Its effect was to exclude the South entirely from that vast and fertile region which lies between the Ohio and the Mississippi rivers, now embracing five States and one territory. The next of the series is the Missouri compromise, which excluded the South from that large portion of Louisiana which lies north of 36° 30', excepting what is included in the State of Missouri. The last of the series excluded the South from the whole of the Oregon Territory. All these, in the slang of the day, were what are called slave territories, and not free soil; that is, territories belonging to slaveholding powers and open to the emigration of masters with their slaves. By these several acts, the South was excluded from 1,238,025 square miles — an extent of country considerably exceeding the entire valley of the Mississippi. To the South was left the portion of the Territory of Louisiana lying south of 36° 30', and the portion north of it included in the State of Missouri, with the portion lying south of 36° 30', including the States of Louisiana and Arkansas, and the territory lying west of the latter, and south of 36° 30', called the Indian country. These, with the Territory of Florida, now the State, make, in the whole, 283,503 square miles. To this must be added the territory acquired with Texas. If the whole should be added to the Southern section, it would make an increase of 325,520, which would make the whole left to the South, 609,023. But a large part of Texas is still in contest between the two sections, which leaves it uncertain what will be the real extent of the portion of territory that may be left to the South.

I have not included the territory recently acquired by the treaty with Mexico. The North is making the most strenuous efforts to appropriate the whole to herself, by excluding the South from every foot of it. If she should succeed, it will add to that from which the South has already been excluded, 526,078 square miles, and would increase the whole which the North has appropriated to herself, to 1,764,023, not including the portion that she may succeed in excluding us from in Texas. To sum up the whole, the United States, since they declared their independence, have acquired 2,373,046 square miles of territory, from which the North will have excluded the South, if she should succeed in monopolizing the newly acquired territories, about three-fourths of the whole, leaving to the South but about one-fourth.

Such is the first and great cause that has destroyed the equilibrium between the two sections in the Government.

The next is the system of revenue and disbursements which has been adopted by the Government. It is well known that the Government has derived its revenue mainly from duties on imports. I shall not undertake to show that such duties must necessarily fall mainly on the exporting States, and that the South, as the great exporting portion of the Union, has in reality paid vastly more than her due proportion of the revenue; because I deem it unnecessary, as the subject has on so many occasions been fully discussed. Nor shall I, for the same reason, undertake to show that a far greater portion of the revenue has been disbursed at the North, than its due share; and that the joint effect of these causes has been, to transfer a vast amount from South to North, which, under an equal system of revenue and disbursements, would not have been lost to her. If to this be added, that many of the duties were imposed, not for revenue, but for protection, — that is, intended to put money, not in the treasury, but directly into the pocket of the manufacturers, — some conception may be formed of the immense amount which, in the long course of sixty years, has been transferred from South to North. There are no data by which it can be estimated with any certainty; but it is safe to say, that it amounts to hundreds of millions of dollars. Under the most moderate estimate, it would be sufficient to add greatly to the wealth of the North, and thus greatly increase her population by attracting emigration from all quarters to that section.

This, combined with the great primary cause, amply explains why the North has acquired a preponderance in every department of the Government by its disproportionate increase of population and States. The former, as has been shown, has increased, in fifty years, 2,400,000 over that of the South. This increase of population, during so long a period, is satisfactorily accounted for, by the number of emigrants, and the increase of their descendants, which have been attracted to the Northern section from Europe and the South, in consequence of the advantages derived from the causes assigned. If they had not existed — if the South had retained all the capital which has been extracted from her by the fiscal action of the Government; and, if it had not been excluded by the ordinance of 1787 and the Missouri compromise, from the region lying between the Ohio and the Mississippi rivers, and between the Mississippi and the Rocky Mountains north of 36° 30′ — it scarcely admits of a doubt, that it would have divided the emigration with the North, and by retaining her own people, would have at least equalled the North in population under the census of 1840, and probably under that about to be taken. She would also, if she had retained her equal rights in those territories, have maintained an equality in the number of States with the North, and have preserved the equilibrium between the two sections that existed at the commencement of the Government. The loss, then, of the equilibrium is to be attributed to the action of this Government.

But while these measures were destroying the equilibrium between the two sections, the action of the Government was leading to a radical change in its character, by concentrating all the power of the system in itself. The occasion will not permit me to trace the measures by which this great change has been consummated. If it did, it would not be difficult to show that the process commenced at an early period of the Government; and that it proceeded, almost without interruption, step by step, until it absorbed virtually its entire powers; but without going through the whole process to establish the fact, it may be done satisfactorily by a very short statement.

That the Government claims, and practically maintains the right to decide in the last resort, as to the extent of its powers, will scarcely be denied by any one conversant with the political history of the country. That it also claims the right to resort to force to maintain whatever power it claims, against all opposition, is equally certain. Indeed it is apparent, from what we daily hear, that this has become the prevailing and fixed opinion of a great majority of the community. Now, I ask, what limitation can possibly be placed upon the powers of a government claiming and exercising such rights? And, if none can be, how can the separate governments of the States maintain and protect the powers reserved to them by the constitution — or the people of the several States maintain those which are reserved to them, and among others, the sovereign powers by which they ordained and established, not only their separate State Constitutions and Governments, but also the Constitution and Government of the United States? But, if they have no constitutional means of maintaining them against the right claimed by this Government, it necessarily follows, that they hold them at its pleasure and discretion, and that all the powers of the system are in reality concentrated in it. It also follows, that the character of the Government has been changed in consequence, from a federal republic, as it originally came from the hands of its framers, into a great national consolidated democracy. It has indeed, at present, all the characteristics of the latter, and not one of the former, although it still retains its outward form.

The result of the whole of these causes combined is — that the North has acquired a decided ascendancy over every department of this Government, and through it a control over all the powers of the system. A single section governed by the will of the numerical majority, has now, in fact, the control of the Government and the entire powers of the system. What was once a constitutional federal republic, is now converted, in reality, into one as absolute as that of the Autocrat of Russia, and as despotic in its tendency as any absolute government that ever existed.

As, then, the North has the absolute control over the Government, it is manifest, that on all questions between it and the South, where there is a diversity of interests, the interest of the latter will be sacrificed to the former, however oppressive the effects may be; as the South possesses no means by which it can resist, through the action of the Government. But if there was no question of vital importance to the South, in reference to which there was a diversity of views between the two sections, this state of things might be endured, without the hazard of destruction to the South. But such is not the fact. There is a question of vital importance to the Southern section, in reference to which the views and feelings of the two sections are as opposite and hostile as they can possibly be.

I refer to the relation between the two races in the Southern section, which constitutes a vital portion of her social organization. Every portion of the North entertains views and feelings more or less hostile to it. Those most opposed and hostile, regard it as a sin, and consider themselves under the most sacred obligation to use every effort to destroy it. Indeed, to the extent that they conceive they have power, they regard themselves as implicated in the sin, and responsible for not suppressing it by the use of all and every means. Those less opposed and hostile, regard it as a crime — an offence against humanity, as they call it; and, although not so fanatical, feel themselves bound to use all efforts to effect the same object; while those who are least opposed and hostile, regard it as a blot and a stain on the character of what they call the Nation, and feel themselves accordingly bound to give it no countenance or support. On the contrary, the Southern section regards the relation as one which cannot be destroyed without subjecting the two races to the greatest calamity, and the section to poverty, desolation, and wretchedness; and accordingly they feel bound, by every consideration of interest and safety, to defend it.

This hostile feeling on the part of the North towards the social organization of the South long lay dormant, but it only required some cause to act on those who felt most intensely that they were responsible for its continuance, to call it into action. The increasing power of this Government, and of the control of the Northern section over all its departments, furnished the cause. It was this which made an impression on the minds of many, that there was little or no restraint to prevent the Government from doing whatever it might choose to do. This was sufficient of itself to put the most fanatical portion of the North in action, for the purpose of destroying the existing relation between the two races in the South.

The first organized movement towards it commenced in 1835. Then, for the first time, societies were organized, presses established, lecturers sent forth to excite the people of the North, and incendiary publications scattered over the whole South, through the mail. The South was thoroughly aroused. Meetings were held every where, and resolutions adopted, calling upon the North to apply a remedy to arrest the threatened evil, and pledging themselves to adopt measures for their own protection, if it was not arrested. At the meeting of Congress, petitions poured in from the North, calling upon Congress to abolish slavery in the District of Columbia, and to prohibit, what they called, the internal slave trade between the States — announcing at the same time, that their ultimate object was to abolish slavery, not only in the District, but in the States and throughout the Union. At this period, the number engaged in the agitation was small, and possessed little or no personal influence.

Neither party in Congress had, at that time, any sympathy with them or their cause. The members of each party presented their petitions with great reluctance. Nevertheless, small and contemptible as the party then was, both of the great parties of the North dreaded them. They felt, that though small, they were organized in reference to a subject which had a great and a commanding influence over the Northern mind. Each party, on that account, feared to oppose their petitions, lest the opposite party should take advantage of the one who might do so, by favoring them. The effect was, that both united in insisting that the petitions should be received, and that Congress should take jurisdiction over the subject. To justify their course, they took the extraordinary ground, that Congress was bound to receive petitions on every subject, however objectionable they might be, and whether they had, or had not, jurisdiction over the subject. These views prevailed in the House of Representatives, and partially in the Senate; and thus the party succeeded in their first movements, in gaining what they proposed — a position in Congress, from which agitation could be extended over the whole Union. This was the commencement of the agitation, which has ever since continued, and which, as is now acknowledged, has endangered the Union itself.

As for myself, I believed at that early period, if the party who got up the petitions should succeed in getting Congress to take jurisdiction, that agitation would follow, and that it would in the end, if not arrested, destroy the Union. I then so expressed myself in debate, and called upon both parties to take grounds against assuming jurisdiction; but in vain. Had my voice been heeded, and had Congress refused to take jurisdiction, by the united votes of all parties, the agitation which followed would have been prevented, and the fanatical zeal that gives impulse to the agitation, and which has brought us to our present perilous condition, would have become extinguished, from the want of fuel to feed the flame. That was the time for the North to have shown her devotion to the Union; but, unfortunately, both of the great parties of that section were so intent on obtaining or retaining party ascendancy, that all other considerations were overlooked or forgotten.

What has since followed are but natural consequences. With the success of their first movement, this small fanatical party began to acquire strength; and with that, to become an object of courtship to both the great parties. The necessary consequence was, a further increase of power, and a gradual tainting of the opinions of both of the other parties with their doctrines, until the infection has extended over both; and the great mass of the population of the North, who, whatever may be their opinion of the original abolition party, which still preserves its distinctive organization, hardly ever fail, when it comes to acting, to co-operate in carrying out their measures. With the increase of their influence, they extended the sphere of their action. In a short time after the commencement of their first movement, they had acquired sufficient influence to induce the legislatures of most of the Northern States to pass acts, which in effect abrogated the clause of the constitution that provides for the delivery up of fugitive slaves. Not long after, petitions followed to abolish slavery in forts, magazines, and dockyards, and all other places where Congress had exclusive power of legislation. This was followed by petitions and resolutions of legislatures of the Northern States, and popular meetings, to exclude the Southern States from all territories acquired, or to be acquired, and to prevent the admission of any State hereafter into the Union, which, by its constitution, does not prohibit slavery. And Congress is invoked to do all this, expressly with the view to the final abolition of slavery in the States. That has been avowed to be the ultimate object from the beginning of the agitation until the present time; and yet the great body of both parties of the North, with the full knowledge of the fact, although disavowing the abolitionists, have co-operated with them in almost all their measures.

Such is a brief history of the agitation, as far as it has yet advanced. Now I ask, Senators, what is there to prevent its further progress, until it fulfills the ultimate end proposed, unless some decisive measure should be adopted to prevent it? Has any one of the causes, which has added to its increase from its original small and contemptible beginning until it has attained its present magnitude, diminished in force? Is the original cause of the movement — that slavery is a sin, and ought to be suppressed — weaker now than at the commencement? Or is the abolition party less numerous or influential, or have they less influence with, or control over the two great parties of the North in elections? Or has the South greater means of influencing or controlling the movements of this Government now, than it had when the agitation commenced? To all these questions but one answer can be given: No — no — no. The very reverse is true. Instead of being weaker, all the elements in favor of agitation are stronger now than they were in 1835, when it first commenced, while all the elements of influence on the part of the South are weaker. Unless something decisive is done, I again ask, what is to stop this agitation, before the great and final object at which it aims — the abolition of slavery in the States — is consummated? Is it, then, not certain, that if something is not done to arrest it, the South will be forced to choose between abolition and secession? Indeed, as events are now moving, it will not require the South to secede, in order to dissolve the Union. Agitation will of itself effect it, of which its past history furnishes abundant proof — as I shall next proceed to show.

It is a great mistake to suppose that disunion can be effected by a single blow. The cords which bound these States together in one common Union, are far too numerous and powerful for that. Disunion must be the work of time. It is only through a long process, and successively, that the cords can be snapped, until the whole fabric falls asunder. Already the agitation of the slavery question has snapped some of the most important, and has greatly weakened all the others, as I shall proceed to show.

The cords that bind the States together are not only many, but various in character. Some are spiritual or ecclesiastical; some political; others social. Some appertain to the benefit conferred by the Union, and others to the feeling of duty and obligation.

The strongest of those of a spiritual and ecclesiastical nature, consisted in the unity of the great religious denominations, all of which originally embraced the whole Union. All these denominations, with the exception, perhaps, of the Catholics, were organized very much upon the principle of our political institutions. Beginning with smaller meetings, corresponding with the political divisions of the country, their organization terminated in one great central assemblage, corresponding very much with the character of Congress. At these meetings the principal clergymen and lay members of the respective denominations, from all parts of the Union, met to transact business relating to their common concerns. It was not confined to what appertained to the doctrines and discipline of the respective denominations, but extended to plans for disseminating the Bible — establishing missions, distributing tracts — and of establishing presses for the publication of tracts, newspapers, and periodicals, with a view of diffusing religious information — and for the support of their respective doctrines and creeds. All this combined contributed greatly to strengthen the bonds of the Union. The ties which held each denomination together formed a strong cord to hold the whole Union together; but, powerful as they were, they have not been able to resist the explosive effect of slavery agitation.

The first of these cords which snapped, under its explosive force, was that of the powerful Methodist Episcopal Church. The numerous and strong ties which held it together, are all broken, and its unity gone. They now form separate churches; and, instead of that feeling of attachment and devotion to the interests of the whole church which was formerly felt, they are now arrayed into two hostile bodies, engaged in litigation about what was formerly their common property.

The next cord that snapped was that of the Baptists — one of the largest and most respectable of the denominations. That of the Presbyterian is not entirely snapped, but some of its strands have given way. That of the Episcopal Church is the only one of the four great Protestant denominations which remains unbroken and entire.

The strongest cord, of a political character, consists of the many and powerful ties that have held together the two great parties which have, with some modifications, existed from the beginning of the Government. They both extended to every portion of the Union, and strongly contributed to hold all its parts together. But this powerful cord has fared no better than the spiritual. It resisted, for a long time, the explosive tendency of the agitation, but has finally snapped under its force — if not entirely, in a great measure. Nor is there one of the remaining cords which has not been greatly weakened. To this extent the Union has already been destroyed by agitation, in the only way it can be, by sundering and weakening the cords which bind it together.

If the agitation goes on, the same force, acting with increased intensity, as has been shown, will finally snap every cord, when nothing will be left to hold the States together except force. But, surely, that can, with no propriety of language, be called a Union, when the only means by which the weaker is held connected with the stronger portion is force. It may, indeed, keep them connected; but the connection will partake much more of the character of subjugation, on the part of the weaker to the stronger, than the union of free, independent, and sovereign States, in one confederation, as they stood in the early stages of the Government, and which only is worthy of the sacred name of Union.

Having now, Senators, explained what it is that endangers the Union, and traced it to its cause, and explained its nature and character, the question again recurs — How can the Union be saved? To this I answer, there is but one way by which it can be — and that is — by adopting such measures as will satisfy the States belonging to the Southern section, that they can remain in the Union consistently with their honor and their safety. There is, again, only one way by which this can be effected, and that is — by removing the causes by which this belief has been produced. Do *this*, and discontent will cease — harmony and kind feelings between the sections be restored — and every apprehension of danger to the Union removed. The question, then, is — How can this be done? But, before I undertake to answer this question, I propose to show by what the Union cannot be saved.

It cannot, then, be saved by eulogies on the Union, however splendid or numerous. The cry of "Union, Union — the glorious Union!" can no more prevent disunion than the cry of "Health, health — glorious health!" on the part of the physician, can save a patient lying dangerously ill. So long as the Union, instead of being regarded as a protector, is regarded in the opposite character, by not much less than a majority of the States, it will be in vain to attempt to conciliate them by pronouncing eulogies on it.

Besides this cry of Union comes commonly from those whom we cannot believe to be sincere. It usually comes from our assailants. But we cannot believe them to be sincere; for, if they loved the Union, they would necessarily be devoted to the constitution. It made the Union, — and to destroy the constitution would be to destroy the Union. But the only reliable and certain evidence of devotion to the constitution is, to abstain, on the one hand, from violating it, and to repel, on the other, all attempts to violate it. It is only by faithfully performing these high duties that the constitution can be preserved, and with it the Union.

But how stands the profession of devotion to the Union by our assailants, when brought to this test? Have they abstained from violating the constitution? Let the many acts passed by the Northern States to set aside and annul the clause of the constitution providing for the delivery up of fugitive slaves answer. I cite this, not that it is the only instance (for there are many others), but because the violation in this particular is too notorious and palpable to be denied. Again: have they stood forth faithfully to repel violations of the constitution? Let their course in reference to the agitation of the slavery question, which was commenced and has been carried on for fifteen years, avowedly for the purpose of abolishing slavery in the States — an object all acknowledged to be unconstitutional — answer. Let them show a single instance, during this long period, in which they have denounced the agitators or their attempts to effect what is admitted to be unconstitutional, or a single measure which they have brought forward for that purpose. How can we, with all these facts before us, believe that they are sincere in their profession of devotion to the Union, or avoid believing their profession is but intended to increase the vigor of their assaults and to weaken the force of our resistance?

Nor can we regard the profession of devotion to the Union, on the part of those who are not our assailants, as sincere, when they pronounce eulogies upon the Union, evidently with the intent of charging us with disunion, without uttering one word of denunciation against our assailants. If friends of the Union, their course should be to unite with us in repelling these assaults, and denouncing the authors as enemies of the Union. Why they avoid this, and pursue the course they do, it is for them to explain.

Nor can the Union be saved by invoking the name of the illustrious Southerner whose mortal remains repose on the western bank of the Potomac. He was one of us — a slaveholder and a planter. We have studied his history, and find nothing in it to justify submission to wrong. On the contrary, his great fame rests on the solid foundation, that, while he was careful to avoid doing wrong to others, he was prompt and decided in repelling wrong. I trust that, in this respect, we profited by his example.

Nor can we find any thing in his history to deter us from seceding from the Union, should it fail to fulfill the objects for which it was instituted, by being permanently and hopelessly converted into the means of oppressing instead of protecting us. On the contrary, we find much in his example to encourage us, should we be forced to the extremity of deciding between submission and disunion.

There existed then, as well as now, a union — that between the parent country and her then colonies. It was a union that had much to endear it to the people of the colonies. Under its protecting and superintending care, the colonies were planted and grew up and prospered, through a long course of years, until they became populous and wealthy. Its benefits were not limited to them. Their extensive agricultural and other productions, gave birth to a flourishing commerce, which richly rewarded the parent country for the trouble and expense of establishing and protecting them. Washington was born and grew up to manhood under that union. He acquired his early distinction in its service, and there is every reason to believe that he was devotedly attached to it. But his devotion was a rational one. He was attached to it, not as an end, but as a means to an end. When it failed to fulfill its end, and, instead of affording protection, was converted into the means of oppressing the colonies, he did not hesitate to draw his sword, and head the great movement by which that union was for ever severed, and the independence of these States established. This was the great and crowning glory of his life, which has spread his fame over the whole globe, and will transmit it to the latest posterity.

Nor can the plan proposed by the distinguished Senator from Kentucky, nor that of the administration save the Union. I shall pass by, without remark, the plan proposed by the Senator, and proceed directly to the consideration of that of the administration. I however assure the distinguished and able Senator, that, in taking this course, no disrespect whatever is intended to him or his plan. I have adopted it, because so many Senators of distinguished abilities, who were present when he delivered his speech, and explained his plan, and who were fully capable to do justice to the side they support, have replied to him.

The plan of the administration cannot save the Union, because it can have no effect whatever, towards satisfying the States composing the southern section of the Union, that they can, consistently with safety and honor, remain in the Union. It is, in fact, but a modification of the Wilmot Proviso. It proposes to effect the same object, — to exclude the South from all territory acquired by the Mexican treaty. It is well known that the South is united against the Wilmot Proviso, and has committed itself by solemn resolutions, to resist, should it be adopted. Its opposition *is not to the name*, but that which it *proposes to effect*. That, the Southern States hold to be unconstitutional, unjust, inconsistent with their equality as members of the common Union, and calculated to destroy irretrievably the equilibrium between the two sections. These objections equally apply to what, for brevity, I will call the Executive Proviso. There is no difference between it and the Wilmot, except in the mode of effecting the object; and in that respect, I must say, that the latter is much the least objectionable. It goes to its object openly, boldly, and distinctly. It claims for Congress unlimited power over the territories, and proposes to assert it over the territories acquired from Mexico, by a positive prohibition of slavery. Not so the Executive Proviso. It takes an indirect course, and in order to elude the Wilmot Proviso, and thereby avoid encountering the united and determined resistance of the South, it denies, by implication, the authority of Congress to legislate for the territories, and claims the right as belonging exclusively to the inhabitants of the territories. But to effect the object of excluding the South, it takes care, in the mean time, to let in emigrants freely from the Northern States and all other quarters, except from the South, which it takes special care to exclude by holding up to them the danger of having their slaves liberated under the Mexican laws. The necessary consequence is to exclude the South from the territory, just as effectually as would the Wilmot Proviso. The only difference in this respect is, that what one proposes to effect directly and openly, the other proposes to effect indirectly and covertly.

But the Executive Proviso is more objectionable than the Wilmot, in another and more important particular. The latter, to effect its object, inflicts a dangerous wound upon the constitution, by depriving the Southern States, as joint partners and owners of the territories, of their rights in them; but it inflicts no greater wound than is absolutely necessary to effect its object. The former, on the contrary, while it inflicts the same wound, inflicts others equally great, and, if possible, greater, as I shall next proceed to explain.

In claiming the right for the inhabitants, instead of Congress, to legislate for the territories, the Executive Proviso, assumes that the sovereignty over the territories is vested in the former: or to express it in the language used in a resolution offered by one of the Senators from Texas (General Houston, now absent), they have "the same inherent right of self-government as the people in the States." The assumption is utterly unfounded, unconstitutional, without example, and contrary to the entire practice of the Government, from its commencement to the present time, as I shall proceed to show.

The recent movement of individuals in California to form a constitution and a State government, and to appoint Senators and Representatives, is the first fruit of this monstrous assumption. If the individuals who made this movement had gone into California as adventurers, and if, as such, they had conquered the territory and established their independence, the sovereignty of the country would have been vested in them, as a separate and independent community. In that case, they would have had the right to form a constitution, and to establish a government for themselves; and if, afterwards, they thought proper to apply to Congress for admission into the Union as a sovereign and independent State, all this would have been regular, and according to established principles. But such is not the case. It was the United States who conquered California and finally acquired it by treaty. The sovereignty, of course, is vested in them, and not in the individuals who have attempted to form a constitution and a State without their consent. All this is clear, beyond controversy unless it can be shown that they have since lost or been divested of their sovereignty.

Nor is it less clear, that the power of legislating over the acquired territory is vested in Congress, and not, as is assumed, in the inhabitants of the territories. None can deny that the Government of the United States has the power to acquire territories, either by war or treaty; but if the power to acquire exists, it belongs to

Congress to carry it into execution. On this point there can be no doubt, for the constitution expressly provides, that Congress shall have power "to make all laws which shall be necessary and proper to carry into execution the foregoing powers" (those vested in Congress), "and all other powers vested by this constitution in the Government of the United States, or in any department or officer thereof." It matters not, then, where the power is vested; for, if vested at all in the Government of the United States, or any of its departments, or officers, the power of carrying it into execution is clearly vested in Congress. But this important provision, while it gives to Congress the power of legislating over territories, imposes important limitations on its exercise, by restricting Congress to passing laws necessary and proper for carrying the power into execution. The prohibition extends, not only to all laws not suitable or appropriate to the object of the power, but also to all that are unjust, unequal, or unfair, — for all such laws would be unnecessary and improper, and, therefore, unconstitutional.

Having now established, beyond controversy, that the sovereignty over the territories is vested in the United States, — that is, in the several States composing the Union, — and that the power of legislating over them is expressly vested in Congress, it follows, that the individuals in California who have undertaken to form a constitution and a State, and to exercise the power of legislating without the consent of Congress, have usurped the sovereignty of the State and the authority of Congress, and have acted in open defiance of both. In other words, what they have done is revolutionary and rebellious in its character, anarchical in its tendency, and calculated to lead to the most dangerous consequences. Had they acted from premeditation and design, it would have been, in fact, actual rebellion; but such is not the case. The blame lies much less upon them than upon those who have induced them to take a course so unconstitutional and dangerous. They have been led into it by language held here, and the course pursued by the Executive branch of the Government.

I have not seen the answer of the Executive to the calls made by the two Houses of Congress for information as to the course which it took, or the part which it acted, in reference to what was done in California. I understand the answers have not yet been printed. But there is enough known to justify the assertion, that those who profess to represent and act under the authority of the Executive, have advised, aided, and encouraged the movement, which terminated in forming, what they call a constitution and a State. General Riley, who professed to act as civil Governor, called the convention — determined on the number, and distribution of the delegates — appointed the time and place of its meeting — was present during the session — and gave its proceedings his approbation and sanction. If he acted without authority, he ought to have been tried, or at least reprimanded, and his course disavowed. Neither having been done, the presumption is, that his course has been approved. This, of itself, is sufficient to identify the Executive with his acts, and to make it responsible for them. I touch not the question, whether General Riley was appointed, or received the instructions under which he professed to act from the present Executive, or its predecessor. If from the former, it would implicate the preceding, as well as the present administration. If not, the responsibility rests exclusively on the present.

It is manifest from this statement, that the Executive Department has undertaken to perform acts preparatory to the meeting of the individuals to form their so-called constitution and government, which appertain exclusively to Congress. Indeed, they are identical, in many respects, with the provisions adopted by Congress, when it gives permission to a territory to form a constitution and government, in order to be admitted as a State into the Union.

Having now shown that the assumption upon which the Executive, and the individuals in California, acted throughout this whole affair, is unfounded, unconstitutional, and dangerous; it remains to make a few remarks, in order to show that what has been done, is contrary to the entire practice of the Government, from the commencement to the present time.

From its commencement until the time that Michigan was admitted, the practice was uniform. Territorial governments were first organized by Congress. The Government of the United States appointed the governors, judges, secretaries, marshals, and other officers; and the inhabitants of the territory were represented by legislative bodies, whose acts were subject to the revision of Congress. This state of things continued until the government of a territory applied to Congress to permit its inhabitants to form a constitution and government, preparatory to admission into the Union. The act preliminary to giving permission was, to ascertain whether the inhabitants were sufficiently numerous to authorize them to be formed into a State. This was done by taking a census. That being done, and the number proving sufficient, permission was granted. The act granting it, fixed all the preliminaries — the time and place of holding the convention; the qualification of the voters; establishment of its boundaries, and all other measures necessary to be settled previous to admission. The act giving permission necessarily withdraws the sovereignty of the United States, and leaves the inhabitants of the incipient State as free to form their constitution and government as were the original States of the Union after they had declared their independence. At this stage, the inhabitants of the territory became, for the first time, a people, in legal and constitutional language. Prior to this, they were, by the old acts of Congress, called inhabitants, and not people. All this is perfectly consistent with the sovereignty of the United States, with the powers of Congress, and with the right of a people to self-government.

Michigan was the first case in which there was any departure from the uniform rule of acting. Hers was a very slight departure from established usage. The ordinance of 1787 secured to her the right of becoming a State, when she should have 60,000 inhabitants. Owing to some neglect, Congress delayed taking the census. In the mean time her population increased, until it clearly exceeded more than twice the number which entitled her to admission. At this stage, she formed a constitution and government, without a census being taken by the United States, and Congress waived the omission, as there was no doubt she had more than a sufficient number to entitle her to admission. She was not admitted at the first session she applied, owing to some difficulty respecting the boundary between her and Ohio. The great irregularity, as to her admission, took place at the next session — but on a point which can have no possible connection with the case of California.

The irregularities in all other cases that have since occurred, are of a similar nature. In all, there existed territorial governments established by Congress, with officers appointed by the United States. In all, the territorial government took the lead in calling conventions, and fixing the preliminaries preparatory to the formation of a constitution and admission into the Union. They all recognized the sovereignty of the United States, and the authority of Congress over the territories; and wherever there was any departure from established usage, it was done on the presumed consent of Congress, and not in defiance of its authority, or the sovereignty of the United States over the territories. In this respect California stands alone, without usage or a single example to cover her case.

It belongs now, Senators, to you to decide what part you will act in reference to this unprecedented transaction. The Executive has laid the paper purporting to be the Constitution of California before you, and asks you to admit her into the Union as a State; and the question is, will you or will you not admit her? It is a grave question, and there rests upon you a heavy responsibility. Much, very much, will depend upon your decision. If you admit her, you indorse and give your sanction to all that has been done. Are you prepared to do so? Are you prepared to surrender your power of legislation for the territories — a power expressly vested in Congress by the constitution, as has been fully established? Can you, consistently with your oath to support the constitution, surrender the power? Are you prepared to admit that the inhabitants of the territories possess the sovereignty over them, and that any number, more or less, may claim any extent of territory they please; may form a constitution and government, and erect it into a State, without asking your permission? Are you prepared to surrender the sovereignty of the United States over whatever territory may be hereafter acquired to the first adventurers who may rush into it? Are you prepared to surrender virtually to the Executive Department all the powers which you have heretofore exercised over the territories? If not, how can you, consistently with your duty and your oaths to support the constitution, give your assent to the admission of California as a State, under a pretended constitution and government? Again, can you believe that the project of a constitution which they have adopted has the least validity? Can you believe that there is such a State in reality as the State of California? No; there is no such State. It has no legal or constitutional existence. It has no validity, and can have none, without your sanction. How, then, can you admit it as a State, when, according to the provision of the constitution, your power is limited to admitting new States. To be admitted, it must be a State, — and an existing State, independent of your sanction, before you can admit it. When you give your permission to the inhabitants of a territory to form a constitution and a State, the constitution and State they form, derive their authority from the people, and not from you. The State, before it is admitted is actually a State, and does not become so by the *act of admission*, as would be the case with California, should you admit her contrary to the constitutional provisions and established usage heretofore.

The Senators on the other side of the Chamber must permit me to make a few remarks in this connection particularly applicable to them, — with the exception of a few Senators from the South, sitting on the other side of the Chamber. — When the Oregon question was before this body, not two years since, you took (if I mistake not) universally the ground, that Congress had the sole and absolute power of legislating for the territories. How, then, can you now, after the short interval which has elapsed, abandon the ground which you took, and thereby virtually admit that the power of legislating, instead of being in Congress, is in the inhabitants of the territories? How can you justify and sanction by your votes the acts of the Executive, which are in direct derogation of what you then contended for? But to approach still nearer to the present time, how can you, after condemning, little more than a year since, the grounds taken by the party which you defeated at the last election, wheel round and support by your votes the grounds which, as explained recently on this floor by the candidate of the party in the last election, are identical with those on which the Executive has acted in reference to California? What are we to understand by all this? Must we conclude that there is no sincerity, no faith in the acts and declarations of public men, and that all is a mere acting or hollow profession? Or are we to conclude that the exclusion of the South from the territory acquired from Mexico is an object of so paramount a character in your estimation, that right, justice, constitution and consistency must all yield, when they stand in the way of our exclusion?

But, it may be asked, what is to be done with California, should she not be admitted? I answer, remand her back to the territorial condition, as was done in the case of Tennessee, in the early stage of the Government. Congress, in her case, had established a territorial government in the usual form, with a governor, judges, and other officers, appointed by the United States. She was entitled, under the deed of cession, to be admitted into the Union as a State as soon as she had sixty thousand inhabitants. The territorial government, believing it had that number, took a census, by which it appeared it exceeded it. She then formed a constitution, and applied for admission. Congress refused to admit her, on the ground that the census should be taken by the United States, and that Congress had not determined whether the territory should be formed into one or two States, as it was authorized to do under the cession. She returned quietly to her territorial condition. An act was passed to take a census by the United States, containing a provision that the territory should form one State. All afterwards was regularly conducted, and the territory admitted as a State in due form. The irregularities in the case of California are immeasurably greater, and offer much stronger reasons for pursuing the same course. But, it may be said, California may not submit. That is not probable; but if she should not, when she refuses, it will then be time for us to decide what is to be done.

Having now shown what cannot save the Union, I return to the question with which I commenced, How can the Union be saved? There is but one way by which it can with any certainty; and that is, by a full and final settlement, on the principle of justice, of all the questions at issue between the two sections. The South asks for justice, simple justice, and less she ought not to take. She has no compromise to offer, but the constitution; and no concession or surrender to make. She has already surrendered so much that she has little left to surrender. Such a settlement would go to the root of the evil, and remove all cause of discontent, by satisfying the South, she could remain honorably and safely in the Union, and thereby restore the harmony and fraternal feelings between the sections, which existed anterior to the Missouri agitation. Nothing else can, with any certainty, finally and for ever settle the questions at issue, terminate agitation, and save the Union.

But can this be done? Yes, easily; not by the weaker party, for it can of itself do nothing — not even protect itself — but by the stronger. The North has only to will it to accomplish it — to do justice by conceding to the South an equal right in the acquired territory, and to do her duty by causing the stipulations relative to fugitive slaves to be faithfully fulfilled — to cease the agitation of the slave question, and to provide for the insertion of a provision in the constitution, by an amendment, which will restore to the South, in substance, the power she possessed of protecting herself, before the equilibrium between the sections was destroyed by the action of this Government. There will be no difficulty in devising such a provision — one that will protect the South, and which, at the same time, will improve and strengthen the Government, instead of impairing and weakening it.

But will the North agree to this? It is for her to answer the question. But, I will say, she cannot refuse, if she has half the love of the Union which she professes to have, or without justly exposing herself to the charge that her love of power and aggrandizement is far greater than her love of the Union. At all events, the responsibility of saving the Union rests on the North, and not on the South. The South cannot save it by any act of hers, and the North may save it without any sacrifice whatever, unless to do justice, and to perform her duties under the constitution, should be regarded by her as a sacrifice.

It is time, Senators, that there should be an open and manly avowal on all sides, as to what is intended to be done. If the question is not now settled, it is uncertain whether it ever can hereafter be; and we, as the representatives of the States of this Union, regarded as governments, should come to a distinct understanding as to our respective views, in order to ascertain whether the great questions at issue can be settled or not. If you, who represent the stronger portion, cannot agree to settle them on the broad principle of justice and duty, say so; and let the States we both represent agree to separate and part in peace. If you are unwilling we should part in peace, tell us so, and we shall know what to do, when you reduce the question to submission or resistance. If you remain silent, you will compel us to infer by your acts what you intend. In that case, California will become the test question. If you admit her, under all the difficulties that oppose her admission, you compel us to infer that you intend to exclude us from the whole of the acquired territories, with the intention of destroying, irretrievably, the equilibrium between the two sections. We would be blind not to perceive in that case, that your real objects are power and aggrandizement, and infatuated not to act accordingly.

I have now, Senators, done my duty in expressing my opinions fully, freely, and candidly, on this solemn occasion. In doing so, I have been governed by the motives which have governed me in all the stages of the agitation of the slavery question since its commencement. I have exerted myself, during the whole period, to arrest it, with the intention of saving the Union, if it could be done; and if it could not, to save the section where it has pleased Providence to cast my lot, and which I sincerely believe has justice and the constitution on its side. Having faithfully done my duty to the best of my ability, both to the Union and my section, throughout this agitation, I shall have the consolation, let what will come, that I am free from all responsibility.

DANIEL WEBSTER

(1782-1852)

Consistently counted among the world's great orators and generally regarded as America's greatest orator, Daniel Webster excelled in all types of speaking. He was equally at home in the Senate chamber, in front of a jury, or before a popular audience at some significant public gathering. He was not, however, considered "a man of the people" as was Henry Clay. Aristocratic in appearance and bearing, Webster, in contrast to Clay, spoke with grave deliberation and gave the impression of wishing to appeal more directly to the intellect than to the emotions. According to William Mathews,

> Webster's manner in speaking was usually calm, quite the opposite of Clay's or Calhoun's. He was the most deliberate of our great orators, expressing himself in measured sentences with great economy of words. . . . Except in moments of high excitement, he had little action, — an occasional gesture with the right hand being all. . . . The vast mass of the man did much to make his words impressive. "He carried men's minds, and overwhelmingly pressed his thought upon them, with the immense current of his physical energy." [1]

In his "Discourse on the Death of Daniel Webster," Theodore Parker described him in these words:

> . . . a great man, a man of the largest mould, a great body and a great brain, he seemed made to last a hundred years. . . . In the Senate of the United States, he looked an emperor in that council.

[1] Oratory and Orators, p. 332.

Even the majestic Calhoun seemed common compared with him. Clay looked vulgar, and Van Buren but a fox. . . . His face was rugged with volcanic fires, great passions, and great thoughts.

Oliver Dyer's portrait too adds to our understanding of Webster's oratorical effectiveness:

He was godlike in appearance and in power. He was not so tall as Clay, but he was much larger and more massive in every way. He had broad shoulders, a deep chest, and a large frame. . . . Webster's head was phenomenal in size, and beauty of outline, and grandeur of appearance. . . . His brow was so protuberant that his eyes, though unusually large, seemed sunken, and were likened unto "great burning lamps set deep in the mouths of caves." . . . The head, the face, the whole presence of Webster, was kingly, majestic, godlike. And when one heard him speak, he found that Webster's voice was just exactly the kind of voice that such a looking man ought to have. It was deep, resonant, mellow, sweet, with a thunder roll in it which, when let out to its full power, was awe inspiring. In ordinary speech its magnificent bass notes rolled forth like the rich tones of a deep-voiced organ; but when he chose to do so, he could elevate his voice in ringing, clarion, tender tones of thrilling power. He also had a faculty of magnifying a word into such prodigious volume and force that it would drop from his lips as a great boulder might drop through the ceiling, and jar the Senate chamber like a clap of thunder.[2]

Aside from his physical impressiveness and tremendous intellect, Webster's great strength as an orator was his manner of presentation; he was a master of prose style. His speeches, unlike those of Clay's, are read as a permanent and deserved part of American political literature. With an ear sensitive to nuances of language rhythm and balance, Webster developed a style of deceptive simplicity, yet one of exquisite richness and beauty.

In his renowned speech of March 7, 1850, Webster came to Clay's assistance and argued magnificently in behalf of compromise with the South, although personally he abhorred the slave system. In this, his last outstanding Senate address, Webster's urgent theme was the maintenance of the Union whatever the cost. Many in the North, however, charged that Webster had betrayed them, and the vituperation loosed upon him was awesome indeed. But actually

2 *Great Senators,* pp. 251-253.

Webster was reiterating a thesis that he had expounded through-out his career: the Constitution and the Union must be preserved, or — in his own sublime utterance — "Liberty and Union, now and forever, one and inseparable." Regrettably and understandably, Webster never really recovered politically or personally from the volume and character of the abuse showered upon him by the North. Politically, his hope for the Whig Presidential nomination in 1852 was shattered; personally, his heart literally was broken by those in the North who labeled him a political charlatan. Eventually he retired to the seclusion of his home in Marshfield where he died in October, 1852, the last of the illustrious Trium-virate to pass from the American scene.

On the day of Webster's scheduled remarks to the Senate, the Congressional Globe records the following observation:

> At an early hour this morning, the Senate chamber was completely occupied by ladies and such few gentlemen as had been able to obtain admittance, who endured several hours patient possession of seats, and even of the floor, that they might hear the long-expected speech of the Senator from Massachusetts.

With the start of the day's business, Senator Walker rose and said: "Mr. President, this vast audience has not come together to hear me, and there is but one man, in my opinion, who can assemble such an audience. They expect to hear him, and I feel it to be my duty, therefore, as it is my pleasure, to give the floor to the Senator from Massachusetts."

COMPROMISE SPEECH OF 1850

by

Daniel Webster

Delivered in the United States Senate on March 7, 1850.

MR. PRESIDENT, — I WISH TO speak to-day, not as a Massachusetts man, nor as a Northern man, but as an American, and a member of the Senate of the United States. It is fortunate that there is a Senate of the United States; a body not yet moved from its propriety, not lost to a just sense of its own dignity and its own high responsibilities, and a body to which the country looks, with confidence, for wise, moderate, patriotic, and healing counsels. It is not to be denied that we live in the midst of strong agitations, and are surrounded by very considerable dangers to our institutions and government. The imprisoned winds are let loose. The East, the North, and the stormy South combine to throw the whole sea into commotion, to toss its billows to the skies, and disclose its profoundest depths. I do not affect to regard myself, Mr. President, as holding, or as fit to hold, the helm in this combat with the political elements; but I have a duty to perform, and I mean to perform it with fidelity, not without a sense of existing dangers, but not without hope. I have a part to act, not for my own security or safety, for I am looking out for no fragment upon which to float away from the wreck, if wreck there must be, but for the good of the whole, and the preservation of all; and there is that which will keep me to my duty during this struggle, whether the sun and the stars shall appear, or shall not appear for many days. I speak to-day for the preservation of the Union. "Hear me for my cause." I speak to-day, out of a solicitous and anxious heart, for the restoration to the country of that quiet and that harmony which make the blessings of this Union so rich, and so dear to us all. These are the topics that I propose to myself to discuss; these are the motives, and the sole motives, that influence me in the wish to communicate my opinions to the Senate and the country; and if I can do any thing, however little, for the promotion of these ends, I shall have accomplished all that I expect.

Mr. President, it may not be amiss to recur very briefly to the events which, equally sudden and extraordinary, have brought the country into its present political condition. In May, 1846, the United States declared war against Mexico. Our armies, then on the frontiers, entered the provinces of that republic, met and defeated all her troops, penetrated her mountain passes, and occupied her capital. The marine force of the United States took possession of her forts and her towns, on the Atlantic and on the Pacific. In less than two years a treaty was negotiated, by which Mexico ceded to the United States a vast territory, extending seven or eight hundred miles along the shores of the Pacific, and reaching back over the mountains, and across the desert, until it joins the frontier of the State of Texas. It so happened, in the distracted and feeble condition of the Mexican government, that, before the declaration of war by the United States against Mexico had become known in California, the people of California, under the lead of American officers, overthrew the existing Mexican provincial government, and raised an independent flag. When the news arrived at San Francisco that war had been declared by the United States against Mexico, this independent flag was pulled down, and the stars and stripes of this Union hoisted in its stead. So, sir, before the war was over, the forces of the United States, military and naval, had possession of San Francisco and Upper California, and a great rush of emigrants from various parts of the world took place into California in 1846 and 1847. But now behold another wonder.

In January of 1848, a party of Mormons made a discovery of an extraordinarily rich mine of gold, or rather of a great quantity of gold, hardly proper to be called a mine, for it was spread near the surface, on the lower part of the south, or American, branch of the Sacramento. They attempted to conceal their discovery for some time; but soon another discovery of gold, perhaps of greater importance, was made, on another part of the American branch of the Sacramento, and near Sutter's Fort, as it is called. The fame of these discoveries spread far and wide. They inflamed more and more the spirit of emigration towards California, which had already been excited; and adventurers crowded into the country by hundreds, and flocked towards the Bay of San Francisco. This, as I have said, took place in the winter and spring of 1848. The digging commenced in the spring of that year, and from that time to this the work of searching for gold has been prosecuted with a success not heretofore known in the history of this globe. You recollect, sir, how incredulous at first the American public was at the accounts which reached us of these discoveries; but we all know, now, that these accounts received, and continue to receive, daily confirmation, and down to the present moment I suppose the assurance is as strong, after the experience of these several months, of the existence of deposits of gold apparently inexhaustible in the regions near San Francisco, in California, as it was at any period of the earlier dates of the accounts.

It so happened, sir, that although, after the return of peace, it became a very important subject for legislative consideration and legislative decision to provide a proper territorial government for California, yet differences of opinion between the two houses of Congress prevented the establishment of any such territorial government at the last session. Under this state of things, the inhabitants of California, already amounting to a considerable number, thought it to be their duty, in the summer of last year, to establish a local government. Under the proclamation of General Riley, the people chose delegates to a convention, and that convention met at Monterey. It formed a constitution for the State of California, which, being referred to the people, was adopted by them in their primary assemblages. Desirous of immediate connection with the United States, its Senators were appointed and representatives chosen, who have come hither, bringing with them the authentic constitution of the State of California; and they now present themselves, asking, in behalf of their constituents, that it may be admitted into this Union as one of the United States. This constitution, sir, contains an express prohibition of slavery, or involuntary servitude, in the State of California. It is said, and I suppose truly, that, of the members who composed that convention, some sixteen were natives of, and had been residents in, the slave-holding States, about twenty-two were from the non-slave-holding States, and the remaining ten members were either native Californians or old settlers in that country. This prohibition of slavery, it is said, was inserted with entire unanimity.

It is this circumstance, sir, the prohibition of slavery, which has contributed to raise, I do not say it has wholly raised, the dispute as to the propriety of the admission of California into the Union under this constitution. It is not to be denied, Mr. President, nobody thinks of denying, that, whatever reasons were assigned at the commencement of the late war with Mexico, it was prosecuted for the purpose of the acquisition of territory, and under the alleged argument that the cession of territory was the only form in which proper compensation could be obtained by the United States from Mexico, for the various claims and demands which the people of this country had against that government. At any rate, it will be found that President Polk's message, at the commencement of the session of December, 1847, avowed that the war was to be prosecuted until some acquisition of territory should be made. As the acquisition was to be south of the line of the United States, in warm climates and countries, it was naturally, I suppose, expected by the South, that whatever acquisitions were made in that region would be added to the slave-holding portion of the United States. Very little of accurate information was possessed of the real physical character, either of California or New Mexico, and events have not turned out as was expected. Both California and New Mexico are likely to come in as free States; and therefore some degree of disappointment and surprise has resulted. In other words, it is obvious that the question which has so long harassed the country, and at some times very seriously alarmed the minds of wise and good men, has come upon us for a fresh discussion; the question of slavery in these United States.

Now, sir, I propose, perhaps at the expense of some detail and consequent detention of the Senate, to review historically this question, which, partly in consequence of its own importance, and partly, perhaps mostly, in consequence of the manner in which it has been discussed in different portions of the country, has been a source of so much alienation and unkind feeling between them.

We all know, sir, that slavery has existed in the world from time immemorial. There was slavery, in the earliest periods of history, among the Oriental nations. There was slavery among the Jews; the theocratic government of that people issued no injunction against it. There was slavery among the Greeks; and the ingenious philosophy of the Greeks found, or sought to find, a justification for it exactly upon the grounds which have been assumed for such a justification in this country; that is, a natural and original difference among the races of mankind, and the inferiority of the black or colored race to the white. The Greeks justified their system of slavery upon that idea, precisely. They held the African and some of the Asiatic tribes to be inferior to the white race; but they did not show, I think, by any close process of logic, that, if this were true, the more intelligent and the stronger had therefore a right to subjugate the weaker.

The more manly philosophy and jurisprudence of the Romans placed the justification of slavery on entirely different grounds. The Roman jurists, from the first and down to the fall of the empire, admitted that slavery was against the natural law, by which, as they maintained, all men, of whatsoever clime, color, or capacity, were equal; but they justified slavery, first, upon the ground and authority of the law of nations, arguing, and arguing truly, that at that day the conventional law of nations admitted that captives in war, whose lives, according to the notions of the times, were at the absolute disposal of the captors, might, in exchange for exemption from death, be made slaves for life, and that such servitude might descend to their posterity. The jurists of Rome also maintained, that, by the civil law, there might be servitude or slavery, personal and hereditary; first, by the voluntary act of an individual, who might sell himself into slavery; secondly, by his being reduced into a state of slavery by his creditors, in satisfaction of his debts; and, thirdly, by being placed in a state of servitude or slavery for crime. At the introduction of Christianity, the Roman world was full of slaves, and I suppose there is to be found no injunction against that relation between man and man in the teachings of the Gospel of Jesus Christ or any of his Apostles. The object of the instruction imparted to mankind by the founder of Christianity was to touch the heart, purify the soul, and improve the lives of individual men. That object went directly to the first fountain of all the political and social relations of the human race, as well as of all true religious feeling, the individual heart and mind of man.

Now, sir, upon the general nature and influence of slavery there exists a wide difference of opinion between the northern portion of this country and the southern. It is said on the one side, that, although not the subject of any injunction or direct prohibition in the New Testament, slavery is a wrong; that it is founded merely in the right of the strongest; and that it is an oppression, like unjust wars, like all those conflicts by which a powerful nation subjects a weaker to its will; and that, in its nature, whatever may be said of it in the modifications which have taken place, it is not according to the meek spirit of the Gospel. It is not "kindly affectioned"; it does not "seek another's, and not its own"; it does not "let the oppressed go free." These are sentiments that are cherished, and of late with greatly augmented force, among the people of the Northern States. They have taken hold of the religious sentiment of that part of the country, as they have, more or less, taken hold of the religious feelings of a considerable portion of mankind. The South, upon the other side, having been accustomed to this relation between the two races all their lives, from their birth, having been taught, in general, to treat the subjects of this bondage with care and kindness, and I believe, in general, feeling great kindness for them, have not taken the view of the subject which I have mentioned. There are thousands of religious men, with consciences as tender as any of their brethren at the North, who do not see the unlawfulness of slavery; and there are more thousands, perhaps, that, whatsoever they may think of it in its origin, and as a matter depending upon natural right, yet take things as they are, and, finding slavery to be an established relation of the society in which they live, can see no way in which, let their opinions on the abstract question be what they may, it is in the power of the present generation to relieve themselves from this relation. And candor obliges me to say, that I believe they are just as conscientious, many of them, and the religious people, all of them, as they are at the North who hold different opinions.

The honorable Senator from South Carolina the other day alluded to the separation of that great religious community, the Methodist Episcopal Church. That separation was brought about by differences of opinion upon this particular subject of slavery. I felt great concern, as that dispute went on, about the result. I was in hopes that the difference of opinion might be adjusted, because I looked upon that religious denomination as one of the great props of religion and morals throughout the whole country, from Maine to Georgia, and westward to our utmost western boundary. The result was against my wishes and against my hopes. I have read all their proceedings and all their arguments; but I have never yet been able to come to the conclusion that there was any real ground for that separation; in other words, that any good could be produced by that separation. I must say I think there was some want of candor and charity. Sir, when a question of this kind seizes on the religious sentiments of mankind, and comes to be discussed in religious assemblies of the clergy and laity, there is always to be expected, or always to be feared, a great degree of excitement. It is in the nature of man, manifested by his whole history, that religious disputes are apt to become warm in proportion to the strength of the convictions which men entertain of the magnitude of the questions at issue. In all such disputes, there will sometimes be found men with whom every thing is absolute; absolutely wrong, or absolutely right. They see the right clearly; they think others ought to see it, and they are disposed to establish a broad line of distinction between what is right and what is wrong. They are not seldom willing to establish that line upon their own convictions of truth and justice; and are ready to mark and guard it by placing along it a series of dogmas, as lines of boundary on the earth's surface are marked by posts and stones. There are men who, with clear perceptions, as they think, of their own duty, do not see how too eager a pursuit of one duty may involve them in the violation of others, or how too warm an embracement of one truth may lead to a disregard of other truths equally important. As I heard it stated strongly, not many days ago, these persons are disposed to mount upon some particular duty, as upon a war-horse, and to drive furiously on and upon and over all other duties that may stand in the way. There are men who, in reference to disputes of that sort, are of opinion that human duties may be ascertained with the exactness of mathematics. They deal with morals as with mathematics; and they think what is right may be distinguished from what is wrong with the precision of an algebraic equation. They have, therefore, none too much charity towards others who differ from them. They are apt, too, to think that nothing is good but what is perfect, and that there are no compromises or modifications to be made in consideration of difference of opinion or in deference to other men's judgment. If their perspicacious vision enables them to detect a spot on the face of the sun, they think that a good reason why the sun should be struck down from heaven. They prefer the chance of running into utter darkness to living in heavenly light, if that heavenly light be not absolutely without any imperfection. There are impatient men; too impatient always to give heed to the admonition of St. Paul, that we are not to "do evil that good may come"; too impatient to wait for the slow progress of moral causes in the improvement of mankind. They do not remember that the doctrines and the miracles of Jesus Christ have, in eighteen hundred years, converted only a small portion of the human race; and among the nations that are converted to Christianity, they forget how many vices and crimes, public and private, still prevail, and that many of them, public crimes especially, which are so clearly offences against the Christian religion, pass without exciting particular indignation. Thus wars are waged, and unjust wars. I do not deny that there may be just wars. There certainly are; but it was the remark of an eminent person, not many years ago, on the other side of the Atlantic, that it is one of the greatest reproaches to human nature that wars are sometimes just. The defence of nations sometimes causes a just war against the injustice of other nations. In this state of sentiment upon the general nature of slavery lies the cause of a great part of those unhappy divisions, exasperations, and reproaches which find vent and support in different parts of the Union.

But we must view things as they are. Slavery does exist in the United States. It did exist in the States before the adoption of this Constitution, and at that time. Let us, therefore, consider for a moment what was the state of sentiment, North and South, in regard to slavery, at the time this Constitution was adopted. A remarkable change has taken place since; but what did the wise and great men of all parts of the country think of slavery then? In what estimation did they hold it at the time when this Constitution was adopted? It will be found, sir, if we will carry ourselves by historical research back to that day, and ascertain men's opinions by authentic records still existing among us, that there was then no diversity of opinion between the North and South upon the subject of slavery. It will be found that both parts of the country held it equally an evil, a moral and political evil. It will not be found that, either at the North or at the South, there was much, though there was some, invective against slavery as inhuman and cruel. The great ground of objection to it was political; that it weakened the social fabric; that, taking the place of free labor, society became less strong and labor less productive; and therefore we find from all the eminent men of the time the clearest expression of their opinion that slavery is an evil. They ascribed its existence here, not without truth, and not without some acerbity of temper and force of language, to the injurious policy of the mother country, who, to favor the navigator, had entailed these evils upon the Colonies. I need hardly refer, sir, particularly to the publications of the day. They are matters of history on the record. The eminent men, the most eminent men, and nearly all the conspicuous politicians of the South, held the same sentiments; that slavery was an evil, a blight, a scourge, and a curse. There are no terms of reprobation of slavery so vehement in the North at that day as in the South. The North was not so much excited against it as the South; and the reason is, I suppose, that there was much less of it at the North, and the people did not see, or think they saw, the evils so prominently as they were seen, or thought to be seen, at the South.

Then, sir, when this Constitution was framed, this was the light in which the Federal Convention viewed it. That body reflected the judgment and sentiments of the great men of the South. A member of the other house, whom I have not the honor to know, has, in a recent speech, collected extracts from these public documents. They prove the truth of what I am saying, and the question then was, how to deal with it, and how to deal with it as an evil. They came to this general result. They thought that slavery could not be continued in the country if the importation of slaves were made to cease, and therefore they provided that, after a certain period, the importation might be prevented by the act of the new government. The period of twenty years was proposed by some gentleman from the North, I think, and many members of the Convention from the South opposed it as being too long. Mr. Madison especially was somewhat warm against it. He said it would bring too much of this mischief into the country to allow the importation of slaves for such a period. Because we must take along with us, in the whole of this discussion, when we are considering the sentiments and opinions in which the constitutional provision originated, that the conviction of all men was, that, if the importation of slaves ceased, the white race would multiply faster than the black race, and that slavery would therefore gradually wear out and expire. It may not be improper here to allude to that, I had almost said, celebrated opinion of Mr. Madison. You observe, sir, that the term *slave*, or *slavery*, is not used in the Constitution. The Constitution does not require that "fugitive slaves" shall be delivered up. It requires that persons held to service in one State, and escaping into another, shall be delivered up. Mr. Madison opposed the introduction of the term *slave*, or *slavery*, into the Constitution; for he said that he did not wish to see it recognized by the Constitution of the United States of America that there could be property in men.

Now, sir, all this took place in the Convention in 1787; but connected with this, concurrent and contemporaneous, is another important transaction, not sufficiently attended to. The Convention for framing this Constitution assembled in Philadelphia in May, and sat until September, 1787. During all that time the Congress of the United States was in session at New York. It was a matter of design, as we know, that the Convention should not assemble in the same city where Congress was holding its sessions. Almost all the public men of the country, therefore, of distinction and eminence, were in one or the other of these two assemblies; and I think it happened, in some instances, that the same gentlemen were members of both bodies. If I mistake not, such was the case with Mr. Rufus King, then a member of Congress from Massachusetts. Now, at the very time when the Convention in Philadelphia was framing this Constitution, the Congress in New York was framing the Ordinance of 1787, for the organization and government of the territory northwest of the Ohio. They passed that Ordinance on the 13th of July, 1787, at New York, the very month, perhaps the very day, on which these questions about the importation of slaves and the character of slavery were debated in the Convention at Philadelphia. So far as we can now learn, there was a perfect concurrence of opinion between these two bodies; and it resulted in this Ordinance of 1787, excluding slavery from all the territory over which the Congress of the United States had jurisdiction, and that was all the territory northwest of the Ohio. Three years before, Virginia and other States had made a cession of that great territory to the United States; and a most munificent act it was. I never reflect upon it without a disposition to do honor and justice, and justice would be the highest honor, to Virginia, for the cession of her northwestern territory. I will say, sir, it is one of her fairest claims to the respect and gratitude of the country, and that, perhaps, it is only second to that other claim which belongs to her; that from her counsels, and from the intelligence and patriotism of her leading statesmen, proceeded the first idea put into practice of the formation of a general constitution of the United States. The Ordinance of 1787 applied to the whole territory over which the Congress of the United States had jurisdiction. It was adopted two years before the Constitution of the United States went into operation; because the Ordinance took effect immediately on its passage, while the Constitution of the United States, having been framed, was to be sent to the States to be adopted by their Conventions; and then a government was to be organized under it. This Ordinance, then, was in operation and force when the Constitution was adopted, and the government put in motion, in April, 1789.

Mr. President, three things are quite clear as historical truths. One is, that there was an expectation that, on the ceasing of the importation of slaves from Africa, slavery would begin to run out here. That was hoped and expected. Another is, that, as far as there was any power in Congress to prevent the spread of slavery in the United States, that power was executed in the most absolute manner, and to the fullest extent. An honorable member,* whose health does not allow him to be here to-day —

(A SENATOR. *He is here.*)

I am very happy to hear that he is; may he long be here, and in the enjoyment of health to serve his country! The honorable member said, the other day, that he considered this Ordinance as the first in the series of measures calculated to enfeeble the South, and deprive them of their just participation in the benefits and privileges of this government. He says, very properly, that it was enacted under the old Confederation, and before this Constitution went into effect; but my present purpose is only to say, Mr. President, that it was established with the entire and unanimous concurrence of the whole South. Why, there it stands! The vote of every State in the Union was unanimous in favor of the Ordinance, with the exception of a single individual vote, and that individual vote was given by a Northern man. This Ordinance prohibiting slavery for ever northwest of the Ohio has the hand and seal of every Southern member in Congress. It was therefore no aggression of the North on the South. The other and third clear historical truth is, that the Convention meant to leave slavery in the States as they found it, entirely under the authority and control of the States themselves.

This was the state of things, sir, and this the state of opinion, under which those very important matters were arranged, and those three important things done; that is, the establishment of the Constitution of the United States with a recognition of slavery as it existed in the States; the establishment of the ordinance for the government of the Northwestern Territory, prohibiting, to the full extent of all territory owned by the United States, the introduction of slavery into that territory, while leaving to the States all power over slavery in their own limits; and creating a power, in the new government, to put an end to the importation of slaves, after a limited period. There was entire coincidence and concurrence of sentiment between the North and the South, upon all these questions, at the period of the adoption of the Constitution. But opinions, sir, have changed, greatly changed; changed North and

Editor's Note: Mr. Calhoun.

changed South. Slavery is not regarded in the South now as it was then. I see an honorable member of this body paying me the honor of listening to my remarks; he brings to my mind, sir, freshly and vividly, what I have learned of his great ancestor, so much distinguished in his day and generation, so worthy to be succeeded by so worthy a grandson, and of the sentiments he expressed in the Convention in Philadelphia.

Here we may pause. There was, if not an entire unanimity, a general concurrence of sentiment running through the whole community, and especially entertained by the eminent men of all parts of the country. But soon a change began, at the North and the South, and a difference of opinion showed itself; the North growing much more warm and strong against slavery, and the South growing much more warm and strong in its support. Sir, there is no generation of mankind whose opinions are not subject to be influenced by what appear to them to be their present emergent and exigent interests. I impute to the South no particularly selfish view in the change which has come over her. I impute to her certainly no dishonest view. All that has happened has been natural. It has followed those causes which always influence the human mind and operate upon it. What, then, have been the causes which have created so new a feeling in favor of slavery in the South, which have changed the whole nomenclature of the South on that subject, so that, from being thought and described in the terms I have mentioned and will not repeat, it has now become an institution, a cherished institution, in that quarter; no evil, no scourge, but a great religious, social, and moral blessing, as I think I have heard it latterly spoken of? I suppose this, sir, is owing to the rapid growth and sudden extension of the COTTON plantations of the South. So far as any motive consistent with honor, justice, and general judgment could act, it was the COTTON interest that gave a new desire to promote slavery, to spread it, and to use its labor. I again say that this change was produced by causes which must always produce like effects. The whole interest of the South became connected, more or less, with the extension of slavery. If we look back to the history of the commerce of this country in the early years of this government, what were our exports? Cotton was hardly, or but to a very limited extent, known. In 1791 the first parcel of cotton of the growth of the United States was exported, and amounted only to 19,200 pounds. It has gone on increasing rapidly, until the whole crop may now, perhaps, in a season of great product and high prices, amount to a hundred millions of dollars. In the years I have mentioned, there was more of wax, more of indigo, more of rice, more of almost every article of export from the South, than of cotton. When Mr. Jay negotiated the treaty of 1794 with England, it is evident from the twelfth article of the treaty, which was suspended by the Senate, that he did not know that cotton was exported at all from the United States.

Well, sir, we know what followed. The age of cotton became the golden age of our Southern brethren. It gratified their desire for improvement and accumulation, at the same time that it excited it. The desire grew by what it fed upon, and there soon came to be an eagerness for other territory, a new area or new areas for the cultivation of the cotton crop; and measures leading to this result were brought about rapidly, one after another, under the lead of Southern men at the head of the government, they having a majority in both branches of Congress to accomplish their ends. The honorable member from South Carolina observed that there has been a majority all along in favor of the North. If that be true, sir, the North has acted either very liberally and kindly, or very weakly; for they never exercised that majority efficiently five times in the history of the government, when a division or trial of strength arose. Never. Whether they were out-generalled, or whether it was owing to other causes, I shall not stop to consider; but no man acquainted with the history of the Union can deny that the general lead in the politics of the country, for three fourths of the period that has elapsed since the adoption of the Constitution, has been a Southern lead.

In 1802, in pursuit of the idea of opening a new cotton region, the United States obtained a cession from Georgia of the whole of her western territory, now embracing the rich and growing States of Alabama and Mississippi. In 1803 Louisiana was purchased from France, out of which the States of Louisiana, Arkansas, and Missouri have been framed, as slave-holding States. In 1819 the cession of Florida was made, bringing in another region adapted to cultivation by slaves. Sir, the honorable member from South Carolina thought he saw in certain operations of the government, such as the manner of collecting the revenue, and the tendency of measures calculated to promote emigration into the country, what accounts for the more rapid growth of the North than the South. He ascribes that more rapid growth, not to the operation of time, but to the system of government and administration established under this Constitution. That is a matter of opinion. To a certain extent it may be true; but it does seem to me that, if any operation of the government can be shown in any degree to have promoted the population, and growth, and wealth of the North, it is much more sure that there are sundry important and distinct operations of the government, about which no man can doubt, tending to promote, and which absolutely have promoted, the increase of the slave interest and the slave territory of the South. It was not time that brought in Louisiana; it was the act of men. It was not time that brought in Florida; it was the act of men. And lastly, sir, to complete those acts of legislation which have contributed so much to enlarge the area of the institution of slavery, Texas, great and vast and illimitable Texas, was added to the Union as a slave State in 1845; and that, sir, pretty much closed the whole chapter, and settled the whole account.

That closed the whole chapter and settled the whole account, because the annexation of Texas, upon the conditions and under the guaranties upon which she was admitted, did not leave within the control of this government an acre of land, capable of being cultivated by slave labor, between this Capitol and the Rio Grande or the Nueces, or whatever is the proper boundary of Texas; not an acre. From that moment, the whole country, from this place to the western boundary of Texas, was fixed, pledged, fastened, decided, to be slave territory for ever, by the solemn guaranties of law. And I now say, sir, as the proposition upon which I stand this day, and upon the truth and firmness of which I intend to act until it is overthrown, that there is not at this moment within the United States, or any territory of the United States, a single foot of land, the character of which, in regard to its being free territory or slave territory, is not fixed by some law, and some irrepealable law, beyond the power of the action of the government. Is it not so with respect to Texas? It is most manifestly so. The honorable member from South Carolina, at the time of the admission of Texas, held an important post in the executive department of the government; he was Secretary of State. Another eminent person of great activity and adroitness in affairs, I mean the late Secretary of the Treasury, was a conspicuous member of this body, and took the lead in the business of annexation, in coöperation with the Secretary of State; and I must say that they did their business faithfully and thoroughly; there was no botch left in it. They rounded it off, and made as close joiner-work as ever was exhibited. Resolutions of annexation were brought into Congress, fitly joined together, compact, efficient, conclusive upon the great object which they had in view, and those resolutions passed.

Allow me to read a part of these resolutions. It is the third clause of the second section of the resolution of the 1st of March, 1845, for the admission of Texas, which applies to this part of the case. That clause is as follows: —

New States, of convenient size, not exceeding four in number, in addition to said State of Texas, and having sufficient population, may hereafter, by the consent of said State, be formed out of the territory thereof, which shall be entitled to admission under the provisions of the Federal Constitution. And such States as may be formed out of that portion of said territory lying south of thirty-six degrees thirty minutes north latitude, commonly known as the Missouri Compromise line, shall be admitted into the Union with or without slavery, as the people of each State asking admission may desire; and in such State or States as shall be formed out of said territory north of said Missouri Compromise line, slavery or involuntary servitude (except for crime) shall be prohibited.

Now, what is here stipulated, enacted, and secured? It is, that all Texas south of 36° 30′, which is nearly the whole of it, shall be admitted into the Union as a slave State. It was a slave State, and therefore came in as a slave State; and the guaranty is, that new States shall be made out of it, to the number of four, in addition to the State then in existence and admitted at that time by these resoluions, and that such States as are formed out of that portion of Texas lying south of 36° 30′ may come in as slave States. I know no form of legislation which can strengthen this. I know no mode of recognition that can add a tittle of weight to it. I listened respectfully to the resolutions of my honorable friend from Tennessee. He proposed to recognize that stipulation with Texas. But any additional recognition would weaken the force of it; because it stands here on the ground of a contract, a thing done for a consideration. It is a law founded on a contract with Texas, and designed to carry that contract into effect. A recognition now, founded not on any consideration or any contract, would not be so strong as it now stands on the face of the resolution. I know no way, I candidly confess, in which this government, acting in good faith, as I trust it always will, can relieve itself from that stipulation and pledge, by any honest course of legislation whatever. And therefore I say again, that, so far as Texas is concerned, in the whole of that State south of 36° 30', which, I suppose, embraces all the territory capable of slave cultivation, there is no land, not an acre, the character of which is not established by law; a law which cannot be repealed without the violation of a contract, and plain disregard of the public faith.

I hope, sir, it is now apparent that my proposition, so far as it respects Texas, has been maintained, and that the provision in this article is clear and absolute; and it has been well suggested by my friend from Rhode Island, that that part of Texas which lies north of 36° 30' of north latitude, and which may be formed into free States, is dependent, in like manner, upon the consent of Texas, herself a slave State.

Now, sir, how came this? How came it to pass that within these walls, where it is said by the honorable member from South Carolina that the free States have always had a majority, this resolution of annexation, such as I have described it, obtained a majority in both houses of Congress? Sir, it obtained that majority by the great number of Northern votes added to the entire Southern vote, or at least nearly the whole of the Southern vote. The aggregate was made up of Northern and Southern votes. In the House of Representatives there were about eighty Southern votes and about fifty Northern votes for the admission of Texas. In the Senate the vote for the admission of Texas was twenty-seven, and twenty-five against it; and of those twenty-seven votes, constituting the majority, no less than thirteen came from the free States, and four of them were from New England. The whole of these thirteen Senators, constituting within a fraction, you see, one half of all the votes in this body for the admission of this immeasurable extent of slave territory, were sent here by free States.

Sir, there is not so remarkable a chapter in our history of political events, political parties, and political men as is afforded by this admission of a new slave-holding territory, so vast that a bird cannot fly over it in a week. New England, as I have said, with some of her own votes, supported this measure. Three fourths of the votes of liberty-loving Connecticut were given for it in the other house, and one half here. There was one vote for it from Maine, but, I am happy to say, not the vote of the honorable member who addressed the Senate the day before yesterday, and who was then a Representative from Maine in the House of Representatives; but there was one vote from Maine, ay, and there was one vote for it from Massachusetts, given by a gentleman then representing, and now living in, the district in which the prevalence of Free Soil sentiment for a couple of years or so has defeated the choice of any member to represent it in Congress. Sir, that body of Northern and Eastern men who gave those votes at that time are now seen taking upon themselves, in the nomenclature of politics, the appellation of the Northern Democracy. They undertook to wield the destinies of this empire, if I may give that name to a republic, and their policy was, and they persisted in it, to bring into this country and under this government all the territory they could. They did it, in the case of Texas, under pledges, absolute pledges, to the slave interest, and they afterwards lent their aid in bringing in these new conquests, to take their chance for slavery or freedom. My honorable friend from Georgia, in March, 1847, moved the Senate to declare that the war ought not to be prosecuted for the conquest of territory, or for the dismemberment of Mexico. The whole of the Northern Democracy voted against it. He did not get a vote from them. It suited the patriotic and elevated sentiments of the Northern Democracy to bring in a world from among the mountains and valleys of California and New Mexico, or any other part of Mexico, and then quarrel about it; to bring it in, and then endeavor to put upon it the saving grace of the Wilmot Proviso. There were two eminent and highly respectable gentlemen from the North and East, then leading gentlemen in the Senate, (I refer, and I do so with entire respect, for I entertain for both of those gentlemen, in general, high regard, to Mr. Dix of New York and Mr. Niles of Connecticut,) who both voted for the admission of Texas. They would not have that vote any other way than as it stood; and they would have it as it did stand. I speak of the vote upon the annexation of Texas. Those two gentlemen would have the resolution of annexation just as it is, without amendment; and they voted for it just as it is, and their eyes were all open to its true character. The honorable member from South Carolina who addressed us the

other day was then Secretary of State. His correspondence with
Mr. Murphy, the Chargé d'Affaires of the United States in Texas,
had been published. That correspondence was all before those
gentlemen, and the Secretary had the boldness and candor to avow
in that correspondence, that the great object sought by the annexation of Texas was to strengthen the slave interest of the
South. Why, sir, he said so in so many words ——

(MR. CALHOUN. *Will the honorable Senator permit me to interrupt him for a moment?*

MR. WEBSTER. *Certainly.*

MR. CALHOUN. *I am very reluctant to interrupt the honorable
gentleman; but, upon a point of so much importance, I deem it
right to put myself rectus in curia. I did not put it upon the
ground assumed by the Senator. I put it upon this ground: that
Great Britain had announced to this country, in so many words,
that her object was to abolish slavery in Texas, and, through Texas,
to accomplish the abolition of slavery in the United States and the
world. The ground I put it on was, that it would make an exposed
frontier, and, if Great Britain succeeded in her object, it would
be impossible that that frontier could be secured against the aggressions of the Abolitionists; and that this government was
bound, under the guaranties of the Constitution, to protect us
against such a state of things.*

MR. WEBSTER. *That comes, I suppose, sir, to exactly the same
thing. It was, that Texas must be obtained for the security of the
slave interest of the South.*

MR. CALHOUN. *Another view is very distinctly given.*

MR. WEBSTER. *That was the object set forth in the correspondence of a worthy gentleman not now living, who preceded the
honorable member from South Carolina in the Department of
State. There repose on the files of the Department, as I have
occasion to know, strong letters from Mr. Upshur to the United
States minister in England, and I believe there are some to the
same minister from the honorable Senator himself, asserting to
this effect the sentiments of this government; namely, that Great
Britain was expected not to interfere to take Texas out of the
hands of its then existing government and make it a free country.
But my argument, my suggestion, is this; that those gentlemen
who composed the Northern Democracy when Texas was brought*

into the Union saw clearly that it was brought in as a slave country, and brought in for the purpose of being maintained as slave territory, to the Greek Kalends. I rather think the honorable gentleman who was then Secretary of State might, in some of his correspondence with Mr. Murphy, have suggested that it was not expedient to say too much about this object, lest it should create some alarm. At any rate, Mr. Murphy wrote to him that England was anxious to get rid of the constitution of Texas, because it was a constitution establishing slavery; and that what the United States had to do was to aid the people of Texas in upholding their constitution; but that nothing should be said which should offend the fanatical men of the North. But, sir, the honorable member did avow this object himself, openly, boldly and manfully; he did not disguise his conduct or his motives.

MR. CALHOUN. Never, never.

MR. WEBSTER. What he means he is very apt to say.

MR. CALHOUN. Always, always.

MR. WEBSTER. And I honor him for it.)

This admission of Texas was in 1845. Then, in 1847, flagrante bello between the United States and Mexico, the proposition I have mentioned was brought forward by my friend from Georgia, and the Northern Democracy voted steadily against it. Their remedy was to apply to the acquisitions, after they should come in, the Wilmot Proviso. What follows? These two gentlemen, worthy and honorable and influential men, (and if they had not been they could not have carried the measure,) these two gentlemen, members of this body, brought in Texas, and by their votes they also prevented the passage of the resolution of the honorable member from Georgia, and then they went home and took the lead in the Free Soil party. And there they stand, sir! They leave us here, bound in honor and conscience by the resolutions of annexation; they leave us here, to take the odium of fulfilling the obligations in favor of slavery which they voted us into, or else the greater odium of violating those obligations, while they are at home making capital and rousing speeches for free soil and no slavery. And therefore I say, sir, that there is not a chapter in our history, respecting public measures and public men, more full of what would create surprise, more full of what does create, in my mind, extreme mortification, than that of the conduct of the Northern Democracy on this subject.

Mr. President, sometimes, when a man is found in a new relation to things around him and to other men, he says the world has changed, and that he has not changed. I believe, sir, that our self-respect leads us often to make this declaration in regard to ourselves when it is not exactly true. An individual is more apt to change, perhaps, than all the world around him. But, under the present circumstances, and under the responsibility which I know I incur by what I am now stating here, I feel at liberty to recur to the various expressions and statements, made at various times, of my own opinions and resolutions respecting the admission of Texas, and all that has followed. Sir, as early as 1836, or in the early part of 1837, there was conversation and correspondence between myself and some private friends on this project of annexing Texas to the United States; and an honorable gentleman with whom I have had a long acquaintance, a friend of mine, now perhaps in this chamber, I mean General Hamilton, of South Carolina, was privy to that correspondence. I had voted for the recognition of Texan independence, because I believed it to be an existing fact, surprising and astonishing as it was, and I wished well to the new republic; but I manifested from the first utter opposition to bringing her, with her slave territory, into the Union. I happened, in 1837, to make a public address to political friends in New York, and I then stated my sentiments upon the subject. It was the first time that I had occasion to advert to it; and I will ask a friend near me to have the kindness to read an extract from the speech made by me on that occasion. It was delivered in Niblo's Garden, in 1837.

(MR. GREENE then read the following extract from the speech of Mr. Webster to which he referred: —

Gentlemen, we all see that, by whomsoever possessed, Texas is likely to be a slave-holding country; and I frankly avow my entire unwillingness to do any thing which shall extend the slavery of the African race on this continent, or add other slave-holding States to the Union. When I say that I regard slavery in itself as a great moral, social, and political evil, I only use language which has been adopted by distinguished men, themselves citizens of slave-holding States. I shall do nothing, therefore, to favor or encourage its further extension. We have slavery already amongst us. The Constitution found it in the Union; it recognized it, and gave it solemn guaranties. To the full extent of these guaranties we are all bound, in honor, in justice, and by the Constitution. All the stipulations contained in the Constitution in favor of the slave-holding States which are already in the Union ought to be fulfilled, and, so far as depends on me, shall be fulfilled, in the fulness of their spirit, and to the exactness of their letter. Slavery, as it exists in the States, is beyond the reach of Congress. It is a concern of the States themselves; they have never submitted it to Congress, and Congress has no rightful power over it. I shall concur, therefore, in no act, no measure, no menace, no indication of purpose, which shall interfere or threaten to interfere with the exclusive authority of the several States over the subject of slavery as it exists within their respective limits. All this appears to me to be matter of plain and imperative duty.

But when we come to speak of admitting new States, the subject assumes an entirely different aspect. Our rights and our duties are then both different. . . .

I see, therefore, no political necessity for the annexation of Texas to the Union; no advantages to be derived from it; and objections to it of a strong, and, in my judgment, decisive character.)

I have nothing, sir, to add to, or to take from, those sentiments. That speech, the Senate will perceive, was made in 1837. The purpose of immediately annexing Texas at that time was abandoned or postponed; and it was not revived with any vigor for some years. In the mean time it happened that I had become a member of the executive administration, and was for a short period in the Department of State. The annexation of Texas was a subject of conversation, not confidential, with the President and heads of departments, as well as with other public men. No serious attempt was then made, however, to bring it about. I left the Department of State in May, 1843, and shortly after I learned, though by means which were no way connected with official information, that a design had been taken up of bringing Texas, with her slave territory and population, into this Union. I was in Washington at the time, and persons are now here who will remember that we had an arranged meeting for conversation upon it. I went home to Massachusetts and proclaimed the existence of that purpose, but I could get no audience and but little attention. Some did not believe it, and some were too much engaged in their own pursuits to give it any heed. They had gone to their farms or to their merchandise, and it was impossible to arouse any feeling in New England, or in Massachusetts, that should combine the two great political parties against this annexation; and, indeed, there was no hope of bringing the Northern Democracy into that view, for their leaning was all the other way. But, sir, even with Whigs, and leading Whigs, I am ashamed to say, there was a great indifference towards the admission of Texas, with slave territory, into the Union.

The project went on. I was then out of Congress. The annexation resolutions passed on the 1st of March, 1845; the legislature of Texas complied with the conditions and accepted the guaranties; for the language of the resolution is, that Texas is to come in "upon the conditions and under the guaranties herein prescribed." I was returned to the Senate in March, 1845, and was here in December following, when the acceptance by Texas of the conditions proposed by Congress was communicated to us by the President, and an act for the consummation of the union was laid before the two houses. The connection was then not completed. A final law, doing the deed of annexation ultimately, had not been passed; and when it was put upon its final passage here, I expressed my opposition to it, and recorded my vote in the negative; and there that vote stands, with the observations that I made upon that occasion. Nor is this the only occasion on which I have expressed myself to the same effect. It has happened that, between 1837 and this time, on various occasions, I have expressed my entire opposition to the admission of slave States, or the acquisition of new slave territories, to be added to the United States. I know, sir, no change in my own sentiments, or my own purposes, in that respect. I will now ask my friend from Rhode Island to read another extract from a speech of mine made at a Whig Convention in Springfield, Massachusetts, in the month of September, 1847.

(MR. GREENE *here read the following extract:* —

We hear much just now of a *panacea* for the dangers and evils of slavery and slave annexation, which they call the "Wilmot Proviso." That certainly is a just sentiment, but it is not a sentiment to found any new party upon. It is not a sentiment on which Massachusetts Whigs differ. There is not a man in this hall who holds to it more firmly than I do, nor one who adheres to it more than another.

I feel some little interest in this matter, sir. Did not I commit myself in 1837 to the whole doctrine, fully, entirely? And I must be permitted to say that I cannot quite consent that more recent discoverers should claim the merit and take out a patent.

I deny the priority of their invention. Allow me to say, sir, it is not their thunder. . . .

We are to use the first and the last and every occasion which offers to oppose the extension of slave power.

But I speak of it here, as in Congress, as a political question, a question for statesmen to act upon. We must so regard it. I certainly do not mean to say that it is less important in a moral point of view, that it is not more important in many other points of view; but as a legislator, or in any official capacity, I must look at it, consider it, and decide it as a matter of political action.)

On other occasions, in debates here, I have expressed my determination to vote for no acquisition, or cession, or annexation, north or south, east or west. My opinion has been, that we have territory enough, and that we should follow the Spartan maxim, "Improve, adorn what you have," seek no further. I think that it was in some observations that I made on the three-million loan bill that I avowed this sentiment. In short, sir, it has been avowed quite as often, in as many places, and before as many assemblies, as any humble opinions of mine ought to be avowed.

But now that, under certain conditions, Texas is in the Union, with all her territory, as a slave State, with a solemn pledge, also, that, if she shall be divided into many States, those States may come in as slave states south of 36° 30', how are we to deal with this subject? I know no way of honest legislation, when the proper time comes for the enactment, but to carry into effect all that we have stipulated to do. I do not entirely agree with my honorable friend from Tennessee, that, as soon as the time comes when she is entitled to another representative, we should create a new State. On former occasions, in creating new States out of territories, we have generally gone upon the idea that, when the population of the territory amounts to about sixty thousand, we would consent to its admission as a State. But it is quite a different thing when a State is divided, and two or more States made out of it. It does not follow in such a case that the same rule of apportionment should be applied. That, however, is a matter for the consideration of Congress, when the proper time arrives. I may not then be here; I may have no vote to give on the occasion; but I wish it to be distinctly understood, that, according to my view of the matter, this government is solemnly pledged, by law and contract, to create new States out of Texas, with her consent, when her population shall justify and call for such a proceeding, and, so far as such States are formed out of Texan territory lying south of 36° 30', to let them come in as slave States. That is the meaning of the contract which our friends, the Northern Democracy, have left us to fulfil; and I, for one, mean to fulfil it, because I will not violate the faith of the government. What I mean to say is, that the time for the admission of new States formed out of Texas, the number of such States, their boundaries, the requisite amount of population, and all other things connected with the admission, are in the free discretion of Congress, except this; to wit, that, when new States formed out of Texas are to be admitted, they have a right, by legal stipulation and contract, to come in as slave States.

Now, as to California and New Mexico, I hold slavery to be excluded from those territories by a law even superior to that which admits and sanctions it in Texas. I mean the law of nature, of physical geography, the law of the formation of the earth. That law settles for ever, with a strength beyond all terms of human enactment, that slavery cannot exist in California or New Mexico. Understand me, sir; I mean slavery as we regard it; the slavery of the colored race as it exists in the Southern States. I shall not discuss the point, but leave it to the learned gentlemen who have undertaken to discuss it; but I suppose there is no slavery of that description in California now. I understand that peonism, a sort of penal servitude, exists there, or rather a sort of voluntary sale of a man and his offspring for debt, an arrangement of a peculiar nature known to the law of Mexico. But what I mean to say is, that it is as impossible that African slavery, as we see it among us, should find its way, or be introduced, into California and New Mexico, as any other natural impossibility. California and New Mexico are Asiatic in their formation and scenery. They are composed of vast ridges of mountains, of great height, with broken ridges and deep valleys. The sides of these mountains are entirely barren; their tops capped by perennial snow. There may be in California, now made free by its constitution, and no doubt there are, some tracts of valuable land. But it is not so in New Mexico. Pray, what is the evidence which every gentleman must have obtained on this subject, from information sought by himself or communicated by others? I have inquired and read all I could find, in order to acquire information on this important subject. What is there in New Mexico that could, by any possibility, induce any body to go there with slaves? There are some narrow strips of tillable land on the borders of the rivers; but the rivers themselves dry up before midsummer is gone. All that the people can do in that region is to raise some little articles, some little wheat for their *tortillas*, and that by irrigation. And who expects to see a hundred black men cultivating tobacco, corn, cotton, rice, or any thing else, on lands in New Mexico, made fertile only by irrigation?

I look upon it, therefore, as a fixed fact, to use the current expression of the day, that both California and New Mexico are destined to be free, so far as they are settled at all, which I believe, in regard to New Mexico, will be but partially for a great length of time; free by the arrangement of things ordained by the Power above us. I have therefore to say, in this respect also, that this country is fixed for freedom, to as many persons as shall ever live in it, by a less repealable law than that which attaches to the right of holding slaves in Texas; and I will say further, that, if a resolution or a bill were now before us, to provide a territorial government for New Mexico, I would not vote to put any prohibition into it whatever. Such a prohibition would be idle, as it respects any effect it would have upon the territory; and I would not take pains uselessly to reaffirm an ordinance of nature, nor to reënact the will of God. I would put in no Wilmot Proviso for the mere purpose of a taunt or a reproach. I would put into it no evidence of the votes of superior power, exercised for no purpose but to wound the pride, whether a just and a rational pride, or an irrational pride, of the citizens of the Southern States. I have no such object, no such purpose. They would think it a taunt, an indignity; they would think it to be an act taking away from them what they regard as a proper equality of privilege. Whether they expect to realize any benefit from it or not, they would think it at least a plain theoretic wrong; that something more or less derogatory to their character and their rights had taken place. I propose to inflict no such wound upon any body, unless something essentially important to the country, and efficient to the preservation of liberty and freedom, is to be effected. I repeat, therefore, sir, and, as I do not propose to address the Senate often on this subject, I repeat it because I wish it to be distinctly understood, that, for the reasons stated, if a proposition were now here to establish a government for New Mexico, and it was moved to insert a provision for a prohibition of slavery, I would not vote for it.

Sir, if we were now making a government for New Mexico, and any body should propose a Wilmot Proviso, I should treat it exactly as Mr. Polk treated that provision for excluding slavery from Oregon. Mr. Polk was known to be in opinion decidedly averse to the Wilmot Proviso; but he felt the necessity of establishing a government for the Territory of Oregon. The proviso was in the bill, but he knew it would be entirely nugatory; and, since it must be entirely nugatory, since it took away no right, no describable, no tangible, no appreciable right of the South, he said he would sign the bill for the sake of enacting a law to form a government in that Territory, and let that entirely useless, and, in that connection, entirely senseless, proviso remain. Sir, we hear occasionally of the annexation of Canada; and if there be any man, any of the Northern Democracy, or any one of the Free Soil party, who supposes it necessary to insert a Wilmot Proviso in a territorial government for New Mexico, that man would of course be of opinion that it is necessary to protect the everlasting snows of Canada from the foot of slavery by the same overspreading wing of an act of Congress. Sir, wherever there is a substantive good to be done, wherever there is a foot of land to be prevented from becoming slave territory, I am ready to assert the principle of the exclusion of slavery. I am pledged to it from the year 1837; I have been pledged to it again and again; and I will perform those pledges; but I will not do a thing unnecessarily that wounds the feelings of others, or that does discredit to my own understanding.

Now, Mr. President, I have established, so far as I proposed to do so, the proposition with which I set out, and upon which I intend to stand or fall; and that is, that the whole territory within the former United States, or in the newly acquired Mexican provinces, has a fixed and settled character, now fixed and settled by law which cannot be repealed; in the case of Texas without a violation of public faith, and by no human power in regard to California or New Mexico; that, therefore, under one or other of these laws, every foot of land in the States or in the Territories has already received a fixed and decided character.

Mr. President, in the excited times in which we live, there is found to exist a state of crimination and recrimination between the North and South. There are lists of grievances produced by each; and those grievances, real or supposed, alienate the minds of one portion of the country from the other, exasperate the feelings, and subdue the sense of fraternal affection, patriotic love, and mutual regard. I shall bestow a little attention, sir, upon these various grievances existing on the one side and on the other. I begin with complaints of the South. I will not answer, further than I have, the general statements of the honorable Senator from South Carolina, that the North has prospered at the expense of the South in consequence of the manner of administering this government, in the collecting of its revenues, and so forth. These are disputed topics, and I have no inclination to enter into them. But I will allude to other complaints of the South, and especially to one which has in my opinion just foundation; and that is, that there has been found at the North, among individuals and among legislators, a disinclination to perform fully their constitutional duties in regard to the return of persons bound to service who have escaped into the free States. In that respect, the South, in my judgment, is right, and the North is wrong. Every member of every Northern legislature is bound by oath, like every other officer in the country, to support the Constitution of the United States; and the article of the Constitution which says to these States that they shall deliver up fugitives from service is as binding in honor and conscience as any other article. No man fulfils his duty in any legislature who sets himself to find excuses, evasions, escapes from this constitutional obligation. I have always thought that the Constitution addressed itself to the legislatures of the States or to the States themselves. It says that those persons escaping to other States "shall be delivered up," and I confess I have always been of the opinion that it was an injunction upon the States themselves. When it is said that a person escaping into another State, and coming therefore within the jurisdiction of that State, shall be delivered up, it seems to me the import of the clause is, that the State itself, in obedience to the Constitution, shall cause him to be delivered up. That is my judgment. I have always entertained that opinion, and I entertain it now. But when the subject, some years ago, was before the Supreme Court of the United States, the majority of the judges held that the power to cause fugitives from service to be delivered up was a power to be exercised under the authority of this government. I do not know, on the whole, that it may not have been a fortunate decision. My habit is to respect the result of judicial deliberations and the solemnity of judicial decisions. As it now stands, the business of seeing that these fugitives are delivered up resides in the power of Congress and the national judicature, and my friend at the head of the Judiciary Committee has a bill on the subject now before the Senate, which, with some amendments to it, I propose to support, with all its provisions, to the fullest extent. And I desire to call the attention of all sober-minded men at the North, of all conscientious men, of all men who are not carried away by some fanatical idea or some false impression, to their constitutional obligations. I put it to all the sober and sound minds at the North as a question of morals and a question of conscience. What right have they, in their legislative capacity or any other capacity, to endeavor to get round this Constitution, or to embarrass the free exercise of the rights secured by the Constitution to the persons whose slaves escape from them? None at all; none at all. Neither in the forum of conscience, nor before the face of the Constitution, are they, in my opinion, justified in such an attempt. Of course it is a matter for their consideration. They probably, in the excitement of the times, have not stopped to consider of this. They have followed what seemed to be the current of thought and of motives, as the occasion arose, and they have neglected to investigate fully the real question, and to consider their constitutional obligations; which, I am sure, if they did consider, they would fulfil with alacrity. I repeat, therefore, sir, that here is a well-founded ground of complaint against the North, which ought to be removed, which it is now in the power of the different departments of this government to remove; which calls for the enactment of proper laws authorizing the judicature of this government, in the several States, to do all that is necessary for the recapture of fugitive slaves and for their restoration to those who claim them. Wherever I go, and whenever I speak on the subject, and when I speak here I desire to speak to the whole North, I say that the South has been injured in this respect, and has a right to complain; and the North has been too careless of what I think the Constitution peremptorily and emphatically enjoins upon her as a duty.

Complaint has been made against certain resolutions that emanate from legislatures at the North, and are sent here to us, not only on the subject of slavery in this District, but sometimes recommending Congress to consider the means of abolishing slavery in the States. I should be sorry to be called upon to present any resolutions here which could not be referable to any committee or any power in Congress; and therefore I should be unwilling to receive from the legislature of Massachusetts any instructions to present resolutions expressive of any opinion whatever on the subject of slavery, as it exists as the present moment in the States, for two reasons: first, because I do not consider that the legislature of Massachusetts has any thing to do with it; and next, because I do not consider that I, as her representative here, have any thing to do with it. It has become, in my opinion, quite too common; and if the legislatures of the States do not like that opinion, they have a great deal more power to put it down than I have to uphold it; it has become, in my opinion, quite too common a practice for the State legislatures to present resolutions here on all subjects and to instruct us on all subjects. There is no public man that requires instruction more than I do, or who requires information more than I do, or desires it more heartily; but I do not like to have it in too imperative a shape. I took notice, with pleasure, of some remarks made upon this subject, the other day, in the Senate of Massachusetts, by a young man of talent and character, of whom the best hopes may be entertained. I mean Mr. Hillard. He told the Senate of Massachusetts that he would vote for no instructions whatever to be forwarded to members of Congress, nor for any resolutions to be offered expressive of the sense of Massachusetts as to what her members of Congress ought to do. He said that he saw no propriety in one set of public servants giving instructions and reading lectures to another set of public servants. To his own master each of them must stand or fall, and that master is his constituents. I wish these sentiments could become more common. I have never entered into the question, and never shall, as to the binding force of instructions. I will, however, simply say this: if there be any matter pending in this body, while I am a member of it, in which Massachusetts has an interest of her own not adverse to the general interests of the country, I shall pursue her instructions with gladness of heart and with all the efficiency which I can bring to the occasion. But if the question be one which affects her interest, and at the same time equally affects the interests of all the other States, I shall no more regard her particular wishes or instructions than I should regard the wishes of a man who might appoint me an arbitrator or referee to decide some question of important private right between him and his neighbor, and then *instruct* me to decide in his favor. If ever there was a government upon earth it is this government, if ever there was a body upon earth it is this body, which should consider itself as composed by agreement of all, each member appointed by some, but organized by the general consent of all, sitting here, under the solemn obligations of oath and conscience, to do that which they think to be best for the good of the whole.

Then, sir, there are the Abolition societies, of which I am unwilling to speak, but in regard to which I have very clear notions and opinions. I do not think them useful. I think their operations for the last twenty years have produced nothing good or valuable. At the same time, I believe thousands of their members to be honest and good men, perfectly well-meaning men. They have excited feelings; they think they must do something for the cause of liberty; and, in their sphere of action, they do not see what else they can do than to contribute to an Abolition press, or an Abolition society, or to pay an Abolition lecturer. I do not mean to impute gross motives even to the leaders of these societies, but I am not blind to the consequences of their proceedings. I cannot but see what mischiefs their interference with the South has produced. And is it not plain to every man? Let any gentleman who entertains doubts on this point recur to the debates in the Virginia House of Delegates in 1832, and he will see with what freedom a proposition made by Mr. Jefferson Randolph for the gradual abolition of slavery was discussed in that body. Every one spoke of slavery as he thought; very ignominious and disparaging names and epithets were applied to it. The debates in the House of Delegates on that occasion, I believe, were all published. They were read by every colored man who could read, and to those who could not read, those debates were read by others. At that time Virginia was not unwilling or afraid to discuss this question, and to let that part of her population know as much of the discussion as they could learn. That was in 1832. As has been said by the honorable member from South Carolina, these Abolition societies commenced their course of action in 1835. It is said, I do not know how true it may be, that they sent incendiary publications into the slave States; at any rate, they attempted to arouse, and did arouse, a very strong feeling; in other words, they created great agitation in the North against Southern slavery. Well, what was the result? The bonds of the slaves were bound more firmly than before, their rivets were more strongly fastened. Public opinion, which in Virginia had begun to be exhibited against slavery, and was opening out for the discussion of the question, drew back and shut itself up in its castle. I wish to know whether any body in Virginia can now talk openly as Mr. Randolph, Governor McDowell, and others talked in 1832, and sent their remarks to the press? We all know the fact, and we all know the cause; and every thing that these agitating people have done has been, not to enlarge, but to restrain, not to set free, but to bind faster, the slave population of the South.

Again, sir, the violence of the Northern press is complained of. The press violent! Why, sir, the press is violent everywhere. There are outrageous reproaches in the North against the South, and there are reproaches as vehement in the South against the North. Sir, the extremists of both parts of this country are violent; they mistake loud and violent talk for eloquence and for reason. They think that he who talks loudest reasons best. And this we must expect, when the press is free, as it is here, and I trust always will be; for, with all its licentiousness and all its evil, the entire and absolute freedom of the press is essential to the preservation of government on the basis of a free constitution. Wherever it exists there will be foolish and violent paragraphs in the newspapers, as there are, I am sorry to say, foolish and violent speeches in both houses of Congress. In truth, sir, I must say that, in my opinion, the vernacular tongue of the country has become greatly vitiated, depraved, and corrupted by the style of our Congressional debates. And if it were possible for those debates to vitiate the principles of the people as much as they have depraved their tastes, I should cry out, "God save the Republic!"

Well, in all this I see no solid grievance, no grievance presented by the South, within the redress of the government, but the single one to which I have referred; and that is, the want of a proper regard to the injunction of the Constitution for the delivery of fugitive slaves.

There are also complaints of the North against the South. I

need not go over them particularly. The first and gravest is, that the North adopted the Constitution, recognizing the existence of slavery in the States, and recognizing the right, to a certain extent, of the representation of slaves in Congress, under a state of sentiment and expectation which does not now exist; and that, by events, by circumstances, by the eagerness of the South to acquire territory and extend her slave population, the North finds itself, in regard to the relative influence of the South and the North, of the free States and the slave States, where it never did expect to find itself when they agreed to the compact of the Constitution. They complain, therefore, that, instead of slavery being regarded as an evil, as it was then, an evil which all hoped would be extinguished gradually, it is now regarded by the South as an institution to be cherished, and preserved, and extended; an institution which the South has already extended to the utmost of her power by the acquisition of new territory.

Well, then, passing from that, every body in the North reads; and every body reads whatsoever the newspapers contain; and the newspapers, some of them, especially those presses to which I have alluded, are careful to spread about among the people every reproachful sentiment uttered by any Southern man bearing at all against the North; every thing that is calculated to exasperate and to alienate; and there are many such things, as every body will admit, from the South, or some portion of it, which are disseminated among the reading people; and they do exasperate, and alienate, and produce a most mischievous effect upon the public mind at the North. Sir, I would not notice things of this sort appearing in obscure quarters; but one thing has occurred in this debate which struck me very forcibly. An honorable member from Louisiana addressed us the other day on this subject. I suppose there is not a more amiable and worthy gentleman in this chamber, nor a gentleman who would be more slow to give offence to any body, and he did not mean in his remarks to give offence. But what did he say? Why, sir, he took pains to run a contrast between the slaves of the South and the laboring people of the North, giving the preference, in all points of condition, and comfort, and happiness, to the slaves of the South. The honorable member, doubtless, did not suppose that he gave any offence, or did any injustice. He was merely expressing his opinion. But does he know how remarks of that sort will be received by the laboring people of the North? Why, who are the laboring people of the North? They are the whole North. They are the people who till their own farms with their own hands; freeholders, educated men, independent men. Let me say, sir, that five sixths of the whole property of the North is in the hands of the laborers of the North; they cultivate their farms, they educate their children, they provide the means of independence. If they are not freeholders, they earn wages; these wages accumulate, are turned into capital, into new freeholds, and small capitalists are created. Such is the case, and such the course of things, among the industrious and frugal. And what can these people think when so respectable and worthy a gentleman as the member from Louisiana undertakes to prove that the absolute ignorance and the abject slavery of the South are more in conformity with the high purposes and destiny of immortal, rational human beings, than the educated, the independent free labor of the North?

There is a more tangible and irritating cause of grievance at the North. Free blacks are constantly employed in the vessels of the North, generally as cooks or stewards. When the vessel arrives at a Southern port, these free colored men are taken on shore, by the police or municipal authority, imprisoned, and kept in prison till the vessel is again ready to sail. This is not only irritating, but exceedingly unjustifiable and oppressive. Mr. Hoar's mission, some time ago, to South Carolina, was a well-intended effort to remove this cause of complaint. The North thinks such imprisonments illegal and unconstitutional; and as the cases occur constantly and frequently, they regard it as a great grievance.

Now, sir, so far as any of these grievances have their foundation in matters of law, they can be redressed, and ought to be redressed; and so far as they have their foundation in matters of opinion, in sentiment, in mutual crimination and recrimination, all that we can do is to endeavor to allay the agitation, and cultivate a better feeling and more fraternal sentiments between the South and the North.

Mr. President, I should much prefer to have heard from every member on this floor declarations of opinion that this Union could never be dissolved, than the declaration of opinion by any body, that, in any case, under the pressure of any circumstances, such a dissolution was possible. I hear with distress and anguish the word "secession," especially when it falls from the lips of those who are patriotic, and known to the country, and known all over the world, for their political services. Secession! Peaceable secession! Sir, your eyes and mine are never destined to see that miracle. The dismemberment of this vast country without convulsion! The breaking up of the fountains of the great deep without ruffling the surface! Who is so foolish, I beg every body's pardon, as to expect to see any such thing? Sir, he who sees these States, now revolving in harmony around a common centre, and expects to see them quit their places and fly off without convulsion, may look the next hour to see the heavenly bodies rush from their spheres, and jostle against each other in the realms of space, without causing the wreck of the universe. There can be no such thing as a peaceable secession. Peaceable secession is an utter impossibility. Is the great Constitution under which we live, covering this whole country, is it to be thawed and melted away by secession, as the snows on the mountain melt under the influence of a vernal sun, disappear almost unobserved, and run off? No, sir! No, sir! I will not state what might produce the disruption of the Union; but, sir, I see as plainly as I see the sun in heaven what that disruption itself must produce; I see that it must produce war, and such a war as I will not describe, *in its twofold character.*

Peaceable secession! Peaceable secession! The concurrent agreement of all the members of this great republic to separate! A voluntary separation, with alimony on one side and on the other. Why, what would be the result? Where is the line to be drawn? What States are to secede? What is to remain American? What am I to be? An American no longer? Am I to become a sectional man, a local man, a separatist, with no country in common with the gentlemen who sit around me here, or who fill the other house of Congress? Heaven forbid! Where is the flag of the republic to remain? Where is the eagle still to tower? or is he to cower, and shrink, and fall to the ground? Why, sir, our ancestors, our fathers and our grandfathers, those of them that are yet living amongst us with prolonged lives, would rebuke and reproach us; and our children and our grandchildren would cry out shame upon us, if we of this generation should dishonor these ensigns of the power of the government and the harmony of that Union which is every day felt among us with so much joy and gratitude. What is to become of the army? What is to become of the navy? What is to become of the public lands? How is each of the thirty States to defend itself? I know, although the idea has not been stated distinctly, there is to be, or it is supposed possible that there will be, a Southern Confederacy. I do not mean, when I allude to this statement, that any one seriously contemplates such a state of things. I do not mean to say that it is true, but I have heard it suggested elsewhere, that the idea has been entertained, that, after the dissolution of this Union, a Southern Confederacy might be formed. I am sorry, sir, that it has ever been thought of, talked of, or dreamed of, in the wildest flights of human imagination. But the idea, so far as it exists, must be of a separation, assigning the slave States to one side and the free States to the other. Sir, I may express myself too strongly, perhaps, but there are impossibilities in the natural as well as in the physical world, and I hold the idea of a separation of these States, those that are free to form one government, and those that are slave-holding to form another, as such an impossibility. We could not separate the States by any such line, if we were to draw it. We could not sit down here to-day and draw a line of separation that would satisfy any five men in the country. There are natural causes that would keep and tie us together, and there are social and domestic relations which we could not break if we would, and which we should not if we could.

Sir, nobody can look over the face of this country at the present moment, nobody can see where its population is the most dense and growing, without being ready to admit, and compelled to admit, that ere long the strength of America will be in the Valley of the Mississippi. Well, now, sir, I beg to inquire what the wildest enthusiast has to say on the possibility of cutting that river in two, and leaving free States at its source and on its branches, and slave States down near its mouth, each forming a separate government? Pray, sir, let me say to the people of this country, that these things are worthy of their pondering and of their consideration. Here, sir, are five millions of freemen in the free States north of the river Ohio. Can any body suppose that this population can be severed, by a line that divides them from the territory of a foreign and an alien government, down somewhere, the Lord knows where, upon the lower banks of the Mississippi? What would become of Missouri? Will she join the *arrondissement* of the slave States? Shall the man from the Yellow Stone and the Platte be connected, in the new republic, with the man who lives on the southern extremity of the Cape of Florida? Sir, I am ashamed to pursue this line of remark. I dislike it, I have an utter disgust for it. I would rather hear of natural blasts and mildews, war, pestilence, and famine, than to hear gentlemen talk of secession. To break up this great government! to dismember this glorious country! to astonish Europe with an act of folly such as Europe for two centuries has never beheld in any government or any people! No, sir! no, sir! There will be no secession! Gentlemen are not serious when they talk of secession.

Sir, I hear there is to be a convention held at Nashville. I am bound to believe that, if worthy gentlemen meet at Nashville in convention, their object will be to adopt conciliatory counsels; to advise the South to forbearance and moderation, and to advise the North to forbearance and moderation; and to inculcate principles of brotherly love and affection, and attachment to the Constitution of the country as it now is. I believe, if the convention meet at all, it will be for this purpose; for certainly, if they meet for any purpose hostile to the Union, they have been singularly inappropriate in their selection of a place. I remember, sir, that, when the treaty of Amiens was concluded between France and England, a sturdy Englishman and a distinguished orator, who regarded the conditions of the peace as ignominious to England, said in the House of Commons, that, if King William could know the terms of that treaty, he would turn in his coffin! Let me commend this saying of Mr. Windham, in all its emphasis and in all its force, to any persons who shall meet at Nashville for the purpose of concerting measures for the overthrow of this Union over the bones of Andrew Jackson!

Sir, I wish now to make two remarks, and hasten to a conclusion. I wish to say, in regard to Texas, that if it should be hereafter, at any time, the pleasure of the government of Texas to cede to the United States a portion, larger or smaller, of her territory which lies adjacent to New Mexico, and north of 36° 30' of north latitude, to be formed into free States, for a fair equivalent in money or in the payment of her debt, I think it an object well worthy the consideration of Congress, and I shall be happy to concur in it myself, if I should have a connection with the government at that time.

I have one other remark to make. In my observations upon slavery as it has existed in this country, and as it now exists, I have expressed no opinion of the mode of its extinguishment or melioration. I will say, however, though I have nothing to propose, because I do not deem myself so competent as other gentlemen to take any lead on this subject, that if any gentleman from the South shall propose a scheme, to be carried on by this government upon a large scale, for the transportation of free colored people to any colony or any place in the world, I should be quite disposed to incur almost any degree of expense to accomplish that object. Nay, sir, following an example set more than twenty years ago by a great man, then a Senator from New York, I would return to Virginia, and through her to the whole South, the money received from the lands and territories ceded by her to this government, for any such purpose as to remove, in whole or in part, or in any way to diminish or deal beneficially with, the free colored population of the Southern States. I have said that I honor Virginia for her cession of this territory. There have been received into the treasury of the United States eighty millions of dollars, the proceeds of the sales of the public lands ceded by her. If the residue should be sold at the same rate, the whole aggregate will exceed two hundred millions of dollars. If Virginia and the South see fit to adopt any proposition to relieve themselves from the free people of color among them, or such as may be made free, they have my full consent that the government shall pay them any sum of money out of the proceeds of that cession which may be adequate to the purpose.

And now, Mr. President, I draw these observations to a close. I have spoken freely, and I meant to do so. I have sought to make no display. I have sought to enliven the occasion by no animated discussion, nor have I attempted any train of elaborate argument. I have wished only to speak my sentiments, fully and at length, being desirous, once and for all, to let the Senate know, and to let the country know, the opinions and sentiments which I entertain on all these subjects. These opinions are not likely to be suddenly changed. If there be any future service that I can render to the country, consistently with these sentiments and opinions, I shall cheerfully render it. If there be not, I shall still be glad to have had an opportunity to disburden myself from the bottom of my heart, and to make known every political sentiment that therein exists.

And now, Mr. President, instead of speaking of the possibility or utility of secession, instead of dwelling in those caverns of darkness, instead of groping with those ideas so full of all that is horrid and horrible, let us come out into the light of day; let us enjoy the fresh air of Liberty and Union; let us cherish those hopes which belong to us; let us devote ourselves to those great objects that are fit for our consideration and our action; let us raise our conceptions to the magnitude and the importance of the duties that devolve upon us; let our comprehension be as broad as the country for which we act, our aspirations as high as its certain destiny; let us not be pigmies in a case that calls for men. Never did there devolve on any generation of men higher trusts than now devolve upon us, for the preservation of this Constitution and the harmony and peace of all who are destined to live under it. Let us make our generation one of the strongest and brightest links in that golden chain which is destined, I fondly believe, to grapple the people of all the States to this Constitution for ages to come. We have a great, popular, constitutional government, guarded by law and by judicature, and defended by the affections of the whole people. No monarchical throne presses these States together, no iron chain of military power encircles them; they live and stand under a government popular in its form, representative in its character, founded upon principles of equality, and so constructed, we hope, as to last for ever. In all its history it has been beneficent; it has trodden down no man's liberty; it has crushed no State. Its daily respiration is liberty and patriotism; its yet youthful veins are full of enterprise, courage, and honorable love of glory and renown. Large before, the country has now, by recent events, become vastly larger. This republic now extends, with a vast breadth, across the whole continent. The two great seas of the world wash the one and the other shore. We realize, on a mighty scale, the beautiful description of the ornamental border of the buckler of Achilles: —

> Now, the broad shield complete, the artist crowned
> With his last hand, and poured the ocean round;
> In living silver seemed the waves to roll,
> And beat the buckler's verge, and bound the whole.

STEPHEN A. DOUGLAS

(1813-1861)

The decade 1850-1860 was one of the most crucial in our country's history, and possibly the most active and famous political figure of most of that decade was the Democratic senator from Illinois, Stephen A. Douglas. The vivid description of the man recorded by Carl Schurz is especially good:

> He was a man of low stature, but broad-shouldered and big-chested. His head, sitting upon a stout, strong neck, was the very incarnation of forceful combativeness; a square jaw and broad chin; a rather large, firm-set mouth, the nose straight and somewhat broad; quick, piercing eyes with a deep, dark, scowling, menacing horizontal wrinkle between them; a broad forehead and an abundance of dark hair which at that period he wore rather long and which, when in excitement, he shook and tossed defiantly like a lion's mane. The whole figure was compact and strongly knit and muscular, as if made for constant fight. He was not inaptly called "the little giant" by his partisans.[1]

Although some biographers and historians attribute nothing to Douglas but the loftiest of motives, while others attribute nothing to him but the most partisan and selfish, practically all acknowledge his ability as an orator. In My Diary North and South, W. H. Russell writes that "few men speak better than Senator Douglas . . . words are well chosen, the flow of his ideas even and constant . . . thoughts well cut, precise, and vigorous . . ." Though not at all kindly disposed toward Douglas, Harriet Beecher Stowe concedes that he has "two requisites of a debater — a melodious voice and a sharply-defined enunciation." Schurz, too, testifies to the effectiveness of Douglas as a speaker:

[1] Reminiscences, II, 30.

His sentences were clear-cut, direct, positive. They went straight to the mark like bullets, and sometimes like cannonballs, tearing and crushing. There was nothing ornate, nothing imaginative in his language, no attempt at "beautiful speaking." But it would be difficult to surpass his clearness and force of statement when his position was right. . . .[2]

On January 23, 1854, Chairman Douglas of the Committee on Territories reported a bill to organize the Territory of Nebraska which differed from the original bill in two respects: (1) it divided the territory into Kansas and Nebraska, and (2) it expressly declared that that provision in the Missouri Act of 1820 which forever prohibited slavery north of 36° 30' latitude (except the state of Missouri itself) was no longer operative; it had been replaced by a fundamental principle established by the Compromise Measures of 1850. In brief, this principle would allow the people of a territory to decide the slavery question for themselves without congressional interference. What in effect was the direct repeal of the Missouri Compromise, long regarded as a sacred compact, unleashed a furious storm of protest from the antislavery elements who were firmly convinced that Douglas had "sold out" to the South in return for its support in his bid for the Presidential nomination at the next Democratic national convention.

Holding steadfast to his doctrine of "popular sovereignty," Douglas rose to close the debate on the measure at about 11:30 in the evening of March 3. His intention was not to help secure a favorable vote in the Senate since that was already assured. But rather his purpose was to justify himself and his proposal to the people of the North who by now were violently opposed to him and to the legislation he had authored. The speech that followed is one of the most masterful persuasive efforts ever heard in the halls of Congress. Despite the fact that he spoke until daybreak, the Senator from Illinois never once lost command of the situation. The warmth of his argument and the courtesy extended to his opponents in the debate once caused Seward to exclaim, "I have never had so much respect for the senator as I have tonight." Although polite in yielding the floor, Douglas was devastating in his replies. Seward, Chase, and Sumner were no match for "the Little Giant" in the thrust and parry of parliamentary debate. Even Rhodes, generally unfavorable to Douglas, comments that

[2] Ibid.

"always a splendid fighter, he seemed this night like a gladiator who contended against great odds." Great odds they were since practically the whole North was at war with Douglas. As he himself remarked, he "could travel from Boston to Chicago by the light of his own effigies."

Though Douglas that night won a victory for popular sovereignty, that victory carried the seeds of its own destruction. The bloody civil strife that followed in Kansas between proslavery and antislavery factions was but the prelude to the Civil War itself which finally brought an end to slavery in the United States. Senator Chase, Douglas' chief opponent in the debate, had the gift of prophecy that fateful March morning. According to Rhodes:

> As the senators went home this sombre March morning, they heard the boom of the cannon from the navy-yard proclaiming the triumph of what Douglas called popular sovereignty. Chase and Sumner, who were devoted friends, walked down the steps of the Capitol together, and as they heard the thunders of victory, Chase exclaimed: "They celebrate a present victory, but the echoes they awake will never rest until slavery itself shall die." [3]

THE KANSAS-NEBRASKA BILL

by
Stephen A. Douglas

Delivered in the United States Senate on March 3 and 4, 1854.*

IT has been urged in debate that there is no necessity for these Territorial organizations; and I have been called upon to point out

[3] *History of the United States*, I, 476.

*Editors' Note: Senator Douglas began his speech late on the night of March 3, 1854, and finished at daybreak on March 4. Time after time he was interrupted by such distinguished Senators as Sumner, Seward, Everett, and Chase, to name only a few. These constant interruptions make Douglas' prepared text difficult to follow and therefore the editors felt an abridgment was necessary. The version given here, that of Johnston and Woodburne in *American Oratory* (Vol. 3), faithfully reproduces the tone and substance of the speech.

any public and national considerations which require action at this time. Senators seem to forget that our immense and valuable possessions on the Pacific are separated from the States and organized Territories on this side of the Rocky Mountains by a vast wilderness, filled by hostile savages — that nearly a hundred thousand emigrants pass through this barbarous wilderness every year, on their way to California and Oregon — that these emigrants are American citizens, our own constituents, who are entitled to the protection of law and government, and that they are left to make their way, as best they may, without the protection or aid of law or government. The United States mails for New Mexico and Utah, and official communications between this Government and the authorities of those Territories, are required to be carried over these wild plains, and through the gorges of the mountains, where you have made no provisions for roads, bridges, or ferries to facilitate travel, or forts or other means of safety to protect life. As often as I have brought forward and urged the adoption of measures to remedy these evils, and afford security against the damages to which our people are constantly exposed, they have been promptly voted down as not being of sufficient importance to command the favorable consideration of Congress. Now, when I propose to organize the Territories, and allow the people to do for themselves what you have so often refused to do for them, I am told that there are not white inhabitants enough permanently settled in the country to require and sustain a government. True; there is not a very large population there, for the very reason that your Indian code and intercourse laws exclude the settlers, and forbid their remaining there to cultivate the soil. You refuse to throw the country open to settlers, and then object to the organization of the Territories, upon the ground that there is not a sufficient number of inhabitants. . . .

I will now proceed to the consideration of the great principle involved in the bill, without omitting, however, to notice some of those extraneous matters which have been brought into this discussion with the view of producing another anti-slavery agitation. We have been told by nearly every Senator who has spoken in opposition to this bill, that at the time of its introduction the people were in a state of profound quiet and repose, that the anti-slavery agitation had entirely ceased, and that the whole country was acquiescing cheerfully and cordially in the compromise measures of 1850 as a final adjustment of this vexed question. Sir, it is truly refreshing to hear Senators, who contested every inch of ground in opposition to those measures, when they were under discussion, who predicted all manner of evils and calamities from their adoption, and who raised the cry of appeal, and even resistance, to their execution, after they had become the laws of the land — I say it is really refreshing to hear these same Senators now bear their united testimony to the wisdom of those measures, and to the patriotic motives which induced us to pass them in defiance of their threats and resistance, and to their beneficial effects in restoring peace, harmony, and fraternity to a distracted country. These are precious confessions from the lips of those who stand pledged never to assent to the propriety of those measures, and to make war upon them, so long as they shall remain upon the statute-book. I well understand that these confessions are now made, not with the view of yielding their assent to the propriety of carrying those enactments into faithful execution, but for the purpose of having a pretext for charging upon me, as the author of this bill, the responsibility of an agitation which they are striving to produce. They say that I, and not they, have revived the agitation. What have I done to render me obnoxious to this charge? They say that I wrote and introduced this Nebraska bill. That is true; but I was not a volunteer in the transaction. The Senate, by a unanimous vote, appointed me chairman of the Territorial Committee, and associated five intelligent and patriotic Senators with me, and thus made it our duty to take charge of all Territorial business. In like manner, and with the concurrence of these complaining Senators, the Senate referred to us a distinct proposition to organize this Nebraska Territory, and required us to report specifically upon the question. I repeat, then, we were not volunteers in this business. The duty was imposed upon us by the Senate. We were not unmindful of the delicacy and responsibility of the position. We were aware that, from 1820 to 1850, the abolition doctrine of Congressional interference with slavery in the Territories and new States had so far prevailed as to keep up an incessant slavery agitation in Congress, and throughout the country, whenever any new Territory was to be acquired or organized. We were also aware that, in 1850, the right of the people to decide this question for themselves, subject only to the

Constitution, was submitted for the doctrine of Congressional intervention. This first question, therefore, which the committee were called upon to decide, and indeed the only question of any material importance in framing this bill, was this: Shall we adhere to and carry out the principle recognized by the compromise measures of 1850, or shall we go back to the old exploded doctrine of Congressional interference, as established in 1820, in a large portion of the country, and which it was the object of the Wilmot proviso to give a universal application, not only to all the territory which we then possessed, but all which we might hereafter acquire? There are no alternatives. We were compelled to frame the bill upon the one or the other of these two principles. The doctrine of 1820 or the doctrine of 1850 must prevail. In the discharge of the duty imposed upon us by the Senate, the committee could not hesitate upon this point, whether we consulted our own individual opinions and principles, or those which were known to be entertained and boldly avowed by a large majority of the Senate. The two great political parties of the country stood solemnly pledged before the world to adhere to the compromise measures of 1850, "in principle and substance." A large majority of the Senate — indeed, every member of the body, I believe, except the two avowed Abolitionists [Mr. Chase and Mr. Sumner] — profess to belong to one or the other of these parties, and hence were supposed to be under a high moral obligation to carry out "the principle and substance" of those measures in all new Territorial organizations. The report of the committee was in accordance with this obligation. I am arraigned, therefore, for having endeavored to represent the opinions and principles of the Senate truly — for having performed my duty in conformity with parliamentary law — for having been faithful to the trust imposed in me by the Senate. Let the vote this night determine whether I have thus faithfully represented your opinions. When a majority of the Senate shall have passed the bill — when the majority of the States shall have endorsed it through their representatives upon this floor — when a majority of the South and a majority of the North shall have sanctioned it — when a majority of the Whig party and a majority of the Democratic party shall have voted for it — when each of these propositions shall be demonstrated by the vote this night on the final passage of the bill, I shall be willing to submit the question to the country, whether, as the organ of the committee, I performed my duty in the report and bill which have called down upon my head so much denunciation and abuse.

Mr. President, the opponents of this measure have had much to say about the mutations and modifications which this bill has undergone since it was first introduced by myself, and about the alleged departure of the bill, in its present form, from the principle laid down in the original report of the committee as a rule of action in all future Territorial organizations. Fortunately there is no necessity, even if your patience would tolerate such a course of argument at this late hour of the night, for me to examine these speeches in detail, and reply to each charge separately. Each speaker seems to have followed faithfully in the footsteps of his leader in the path marked out by the Abolition confederates in their manifesto, which I took occasion to expose on a former occasion. You have seen them on their winding way, meandering the narrow and crooked path in Indian file, each treading close upon the heels of the other, and neither venturing to take a step to the right or left, or to occupy one inch of ground which did not bear the footprint of the Abolition champion. To answer one, therefore, is to answer the whole. The statement to which they seem to attach the most importance, and which they have repeated oftener, perhaps, than any other, is, that, pending the compromise measures of 1850, no man in or out of Congress ever dreamed of abrogating the Missouri compromise; that from that period down to the present session nobody supposed that its validity had been impaired, or any thing done which rendered it obligatory upon us to make it inoperative hereafter; that at the time of submitting the report and bill to the Senate, on the fourth of January last, neither I nor any member of the committee ever thought of such a thing; and that we could never be brought to the point of abrogating the eighth section of the Missouri act until after the Senator from Kentucky introduced his amendment to my bill.

Mr. President, before I proceed to expose the many misrepresentations contained in this complicated charge, I must call the attention of the Senate to the false issue which these gentlemen are endeavoring to impose upon the country, for the purpose of diverting public attention from the real issue contained in the bill. They wish to have the people believe that the abrogation of what they call the Missouri compromise was the main object and aim of the bill, and that the only question involved is, whether the prohibition of slavery north of 36° 30′ shall be repealed or not? That which is a mere incident they choose to consider the principle. They make war on the means by which we propose to accomplish an object, instead of openly resisting the object itself. The principle which we propose to carry into effect by the bill is this: *That Congress shall neither legislate slavery into any Territories or State, nor out of the same; but the people shall be left free to regulate their domestic concerns in their own way, subject only to the Constitution of the United States.*

In order to carry this principle into practical operation, it becomes necessary to remove whatever legal obstacles might be found in the way of its free exercise. It is only for the purpose of carrying out this great fundamental principle of self-government that the bill renders the eighth section of the Missouri act inoperative and void.

Now, let me ask, will these Senators who have arraigned me, or any one of them, have the assurance to rise in his place and declare that this great principle was never thought of or advocated as applicable to Territorial bills, in 1850; that from that session until the present, nobody ever thought of incorporating this principle in all new Territorial organizations; that the Committee on Territories did not recommend it in their report; and that it required the amendment of the Senator from Kentucky to bring us up to that point? Will any one of my accusers dare to make this issue, and let it be tried by the record? I will begin with the compromises of 1850. Any Senator who will take the trouble to examine our journals, will find that on the 25th of March of that year I reported from the Committee on Territories two bills including the following measures; the admission of California, a Territorial government for New Mexico, and the adjustment of the Texas boundary. These bills proposed to leave the people of Utah and New Mexico free to decide the slavery question for themselves, *in the precise language of the Nebraska bill now under discussion.* A few weeks afterward the committee of thirteen took those two bills and put a wafer between them, and reported them back to the Senate as one bill, with some slight amendments. One of these amendments was, that the Territorial Legislatures should not legislate upon the subject of African slavery. I objected to that provision upon the ground that it subverted the great principle of self-government upon which the bill had been originally framed by the Territorial Committee. On the first trial, the Senate refused to strike it out, but subsequently did so, after full debate, in order to establish that principle as the rule of action in Territorial organizations. . . . But my accusers attempt to raise up a false issue, and thereby divert public attention from the real one, by the cry that the Missouri compromise is to be repealed or violated by the passage of this bill. Well, if the eighth section of the Missouri act, which attempted to fix the destinies of future generations in those Territories for all time to come, in utter disregard of the rights and wishes of the people when they should be received into the Union as States, be inconsistent with the great principles of self-government and the Constitution of the United States, it ought to be abrogated. The legislation of 1850 abrogated the Missouri compromise, so far as the country embraced within the limits of Utah and New Mexico was covered by the slavery restriction. It is true, that those acts did not in terms and name repeal the act of 1820, as originally adopted, or as extended by the resolutions annexing Texas in 1845, any more than the report of the Committee on Territories proposed to repeal the same acts this session. But the acts of 1850 did authorize the people of those Territories to exercise "all rightful powers of legislation consistent with the Constitution," not excepting the question of slavery; and did provide that, when those Territories should be admitted into the Union, they should be received with or without slavery as the people thereof might determine at the date of their admission. These provisions were in direct conflict with a clause in the former enactment, declaring that slavery should be forever prohibited in any portion of said Territories, and hence rendered such clause inoperative and void to the extent of such conflict. This was an inevitable consequence, resulting from the provisions in those acts, which gave the people the right to decide the slavery question for themselves, in conformity with the Constitution. It was not necessary to go further and declare that certain previous enactments, which were incompatible with the exercise of the powers conferred in the bills, are hereby repealed. The very act of granting those powers and rights has the legal effect of removing all obstructions to the exercise of them by the people, as prescribed in those Territorial bills. Following that example, the Committee on Territories did not consider it necessary to declare the eighth section of the Missouri act repealed. We were content to organize Nebraska in the precise language of the Utah and New Mexico bills. Our object was to leave the people entirely free to form and regulate their domestic institutions and internal concerns in their own way, under the Constitution; and we deemed it wise to accomplish that object in the exact terms in which the same thing had been done in Utah and New Mexico by the acts of 1850. This was the principle upon which the committee voted; and our bill was supposed, and is now believed, to have been in accordance with it. When doubts were raised whether the bill did fully carry out the principle laid down in the report, amendments were made from time to time, in order to avoid all misconstruction, and make the true intent of the act more explicit. The last of these amendments was adopted yesterday, on the motion of the distinguished Senator from North Carolina [Mr. Badger], in regard to the revival of any laws or regulations which may have existed prior to 1820. That amendment was not intended to change the legal effect of the bill. Its object was to repel the slander which had been propogated by the enemies of the measure in the North — that the Southern supporters of the bill desired to legislate slavery into these Territories. The South denies the right of Congress either to legislate slavery into any Territory or State, or out of any Territory or State. Non-intervention by Congress with slavery in the States or Territories is the doctrine of the bill, and all the amendments which have been agreed to have been made with the view of removing all doubt and cavil as to the true meaning and object of the measure. . . .

Well, sir, what is this Missouri compromise, of which we have heard so much of late? It has been read so often that it is not necessary to occupy the time of the Senate in reading it again. It was an act of Congress, passed on the 6th of March, 1820, to authorize the people of Missouri to form a constitution and a State government, preparatory to the admission of such State into the Union. The first section provided that Missouri should be received into the Union "on an equal footing with the original States in all respects whatsoever." The last and eighth section provided that slavery should be "forever prohibited" in all the territory which had been acquired from France north of 36° 30', and not included within the limits of the State of Missouri. There is nothing in the terms of the law that purports to be a compact, or indicates that it was any thing more than an ordinary act of legislation. To prove that it was more than it purports to be on its face, gentlemen must produce other evidence, and prove that there was such an understanding as to create a moral obligation in the nature of a compact. Have they shown it?

Now, if this was a compact, let us see how it was entered into. The bill originated in the House of Representatives, and passed that body without a Southern vote in its favor. It is proper to remark, however, that it did not at that time contain the eighth section, prohibiting slavery in the Territories; but in lieu of it, contained a provision prohibiting slavery in the proposed State of Missouri. In the Senate, the clause prohibiting slavery in the State was stricken out, and the eighth section added to the end of the bill, by the terms of which slavery was to be forever prohibited in the territory not embraced in the State of Missouri north of 36° 30′. The vote on adding this section stood in the Senate, 34 in the affirmative, and 10 in the negative. Of the Northern Senators, 20 voted for it, and 2 against it. On the question of ordering the bill to a third reading as amended, which was the test vote on its passage, the vote stood 24 yeas and 20 nays. Of the Northern Senators, 4 only voted in the affirmative, and 18 in the negative. Thus it will be seen that if it was intended to be a compact, the North never agreed to it. The Northern Senators voted to insert the prohibition of slavery in the Territories; and then, in the proportion of more than four to one, voted against the passage of the bill. The North, therefore, never signed the compact, never consented to it, never agreed to be bound by it. This fact becomes very important in vindicating the character of the North for repudiating this alleged compromise a few months afterward. The act was approved and became a law on the 6th of March, 1820. In the summer of that year, the people of Missouri formed a constitution and State government preparatory to admission into the Union in conformity with the act. At the next session of Congress the Senate passed a joint resolution declaring Missouri to be one of the States of the Union, on an equal footing with the original States. This resolution was sent to the House of Representatives, where it was rejected by Northern votes, and thus Missouri was voted out of the Union, instead of being received into the Union under the act of the 6th of March, 1820, now known as the Missouri compromise. Now, sir, what becomes of our plighted faith, if the act of the 6th of March, 1820, was a solemn compact, as we are now told? They have all rung the changes upon it, that it was a sacred and irrevocable compact, binding in honor, in conscience, and morals, which could not be violated or repudiated without perfidy and dishonor! . . . Sir, if this was a compact, what must be thought of those who violated it almost immediately after it was formed? I say it is a calumny upon the North to say that it was a compact. I should feel a flush of shame upon my cheek, as a Northern man, if I were to say that it was a compact, and that the section of the country to which I belong received the consideration, and then repudiated the obligation in eleven months after it was entered into. I deny that it was a compact, in any sense of the term. But if it was, the record proves that faith was not observed — that the contract was never carried into effect — that after the North had procured the passage of the act prohibiting slavery in the Territories, with a majority in the House large enough to prevent its repeal, Missouri was refused admission into the Union as a slave-holding State, in conformity with the act of March 6, 1820. If the proposition be correct, as contended for by the opponents of this bill — that there was a solemn compact between the North and the South that, in consideration of the prohibition of slavery in the Territories, Missouri was to be admitted into the Union, in conformity with the act of 1820 — that compact was repudiated by the North, and rescinded by the joint action of the two parties within twelve months from its date. Missouri was never admitted under the act of the 6th of March, 1820. She was refused admission under that act. She was voted out of the Union by Northern votes, notwithstanding the stipulation that she should be received; and, in consequence of these facts, a new compromise was rendered necessary, by the terms of which Missouri was to be admitted into the Union conditionally — admitted on a condition not embraced in the act of 1820, and, in addition, to a full compliance with all the provisions of said act. If, then, the act of 1820, by the eighth section of which slavery was prohibited in Missouri, was a compact, it is clear to the comprehension of every fair-minded man that the refusal of the North to admit Missouri, in compliance with its stipulations, and without further conditions, imposes upon us a high, moral obligation to remove the prohibition of slavery in the Territories, since it has been shown to have been procured upon a condition never performed. . . .

Mr. President, I did not wish to refer to these things. I did not understand them fully in all their bearings at the time I made my first speech on this subject; and, so far as I was familiar with them, I made as little reference to them as was consistent with my duty; because it was a mortifying reflection to me, as a Northern man, that we had not been able, in consequence of the abolition excitement at the time, to avoid the appearance of bad faith in the observance of legislation, which has been denominated a compromise. There were a few men then, as there are now, who had the moral courage to perform their duty to the country and the Constitution, regardless of consequences personal to themselves. There were ten Northern men who dared to perform their duty by voting to admit Missouri into the Union on an equal footing with the original States, and with no other restriction than that imposed by the Constitution. I am aware that they were abused and denounced as we are now — that they were branded as dough-faces — traitors to freedom, and to the section of country whence they came. . . .

I think I have shown that if the act of 1820, called the Missouri compromise, was a compact, it was violated and repudiated by a solemn vote of the House of Representatives in 1821, within eleven months after it was adopted. It was repudiated by the North by a majority vote, and that repudiation was so complete and successful as to compel Missouri to make a new compromise, and she was brought into the Union under the new compromise of 1821, and not under the act of 1820. This reminds me of another point made in nearly all the speeches against this bill, and, if I recollect right, was alluded to in the abolition manifesto; to which, I regret to say, I had occasion to refer so often. I refer to the significant hint that Mr. Clay was dead before any one dared to bring forward a proposition to undo the greatest work of his hands. The Senator from New York [Mr. Seward] has seized upon this insinuation and elaborated, perhaps, more fully than his compeers; and now the Abolition press, suddenly, and, as if by miraculous conversion, teems with eulogies upon Mr. Clay and his Missouri compromise of 1820.

Now, Mr. President, does not each of these Senators know that Mr. Clay was not the author of the act of 1820? Do they not know that he disclaimed it in 1850 in this body? Do they not know that the Missouri restriction did not originate in the House, of which he was a member? Do they not know that Mr. Clay never came into the Missouri controversy as a compromiser until after the compromise of 1820 was repudiated, and it became necessary to make another? I dislike to be compelled to repeat what I have conclusively proven, that the compromise which Mr. Clay effected was the act of 1821, under which Missouri came into the Union, and not the act of 1820. Mr. Clay made that compromise after you had repudiated the first one. How, then, dare you call upon the spirit of that great and gallant statesman to sanction your charge of bad faith against the South on this question? . . .

Now, Mr. President, as I have been doing justice to Mr. Clay on this question, perhaps I may as well do justice to another great man, who was associated with him in carrying through the great measures of 1850, which mortified the Senator from New York so much, because they defeated his purpose of carrying on the agitation. I allude to Mr. Webster. The authority of his great name has been quoted for the purpose of proving that he regarded the Missouri act as a compact, an irrepealable compact. Evidently the distinguished Senator from Massachusetts [Mr. Everett] supposed he was doing Mr. Webster entire justice when he quoted the passage which he read from Mr. Webster's speech of the 7th of March, 1850, when he said that he stood upon the position that every part of the American continent was fixed for freedom or for slavery by irrepealable law. The Senator says that by the expression "irrepealable law," Mr. Webster meant to include the compromise of 1820. Now, I will show that that was not Mr. Webster's meaning — that he was never guilty of the mistake of saying that the Missouri act of 1820 was an irrepealable law. Mr. Webster said in that speech that every foot of territory in the United States was fixed as to its character for freedom or slavery by an irrepealable law. He then inquired if it was not so in regard to Texas? He went on to prove that it was; because, he said, there was a compact in express terms between Texas and the United States. He said the parties were capable of contracting and that there was a valuable consideration; and hence, he contended, that in that case there was a contract binding in honor and morals and law; and that it was irrepealable without a breach of faith.

He went on to say:

Now, as to California and New Mexico, I hold slavery to be excluded from these Territories by a law even superior to that which admits and sanctions it in Texas — I mean the law of nature — of physical geography — the law of the formation of the earth.

That was the irrepealable law which he said prohibited slavery in the Territories of Utah and New Mexico. He went on to speak of the prohibition of slavery in Oregon, and he said it was an "entirely useless and, in that connection, senseless proviso."

He went further, and said:

That the whole territory of the States of the United States, or in the newly-acquired territory of the United States, has a fixed and settled character, now fixed and settled by law, which cannot be repealed in the case of Texas without a violation of public faith, and cannot be repealed by any human power in regard to California or New Mexico; that, under one or other of these laws, every foot of territory in the States or in the Territories has now received a fixed and decided character.

What irrepealable laws? "One or the other" of those which he had stated. One was the Texas compact; the other, the law of nature and physical geography; and he contended that one or the other fixed the character of the whole American continent for freedom or for slavery. He never alluded to the Missouri compromise, unless it was by the allusion to the Wilmot proviso in the Oregon bill, and therein said it was a useless and, in that connection, senseless thing. Why was it a useless and senseless thing? Because it was re-enacting the law of God; because slavery had already been prohibited by physical geography. Sir, that was the meaning of Mr. Webster's speech. . . .

Mr. President, I have occupied a good deal of time in exposing the cant of these gentlemen about the sanctity of the Missouri compromise, and the dishonor attached to the violation of plighted faith. I have exposed these matters in order to show that the object of these men is to withdraw from public attention the real principle involved in the bill. They well know that the abrogation of the Missouri compromise is the incident and not the principle of the bill. They well understand that the report of the committee and the bill propose to establish the principle in all Territorial organizations, that the question of slavery shall be referred to the people to regulate for themselves, and that such legislation should be had as was necessary to remove all legal obstructions to the free exercise of this right by the people. The eighth section of the Missouri act standing in the way of this great principle must be rendered inoperative and void, whether expressly repealed or not, in order to give the people the power of regulating their own domestic institutions in their own way, subject only to the Constitution.

Now, sir, if these gentlemen have entire confidence in the correctness of their own position, why do they not meet the issue boldly and fairly, and controvert the soundness of this great principle of popular sovereignty in obedience to the Constitution? They know full well that this was the principle upon which the colonies separated from the crown of Great Britain, the principle upon which the battles of the Revolution were fought, and the principle upon which our republican system was founded. They cannot be ignorant of the fact that the Revolution grew out of the assertion of the right on the part of the imperial Government to interfere with the internal affairs and domestic concerns of the colonies. . . .

The Declaration of Independence had its origin in the violation of that great fundamental principle which secured to the colonies the right to regulate their own domestic affairs in their own way; and the Revolution resulted in the triumph of that principle, and the recognition of the right asserted by it. Abolitionism proposes to destroy the right and extinguish the principle for which our forefathers waged a seven years' bloody war, and upon which our whole system of free government is founded. They not only deny the application of this principle to the Territories, but insist upon fastening the prohibition upon all the States to be formed out of those Territories. Therefore, the doctrine of the Abolitionists — the doctrine of the opponents of the Nebraska and Kansas bill, and the advocates of the Missouri restriction — demands Congressional interference with slavery not only in the Territories, but in all the new States to be formed therefrom. It is the same doctrine, when applied to the Territories and new States of this Union, which the British Government attempted to enforce by the sword upon the American colonies. It is this fundamental principle of self-government which constitutes the distinguishing feature of the Nebraska bill. The opponents of the principle are consistent in opposing the bill. I do not blame them for their opposition. I only ask them to meet the issue fairly and openly, by acknowledging that they are opposed to the principle which it is the object of the bill to carry into operation. It seems that there is no power on earth, no intellectual power, no mechanical power, that can bring them to a fair discussion of the true issue. If they hope to delude the people and escape detection for any considerable length of time under the catch-words "Missouri compromise" and "faith of compacts," they will find that the people of this country have more penetration and intelligence than they have given them credit for.

Mr. President, there is an important fact connected with this slavery regulation, which should never be lost sight of. It has always arisen from one and the same cause. Whenever that cause has been removed, the agitation has ceased; and whenever the cause has been renewed, the agitation has sprung into existence. That cause is, and ever has been, the attempt on the part of Congress to interfere with the question of slavery in the Territories and new States formed therefrom. Is it not wise then to confine our action within the sphere of our legitimate duties, and leave this vexed question to take care of itself in each State and Territory, according to the wishes of the people thereof, in conformity to the forms, and in subjection to the provisions, of the Constitution?

The opponents of the bill tell us that agitation is no part of their policy; that their great desire is peace and harmony; and they complain bitterly that I should have disturbed the repose of the country by the introduction of this measure! Let me ask these professed friends of peace, and avowed enemies of agitation, how the issue could have been avoided. They tell me that I should have let the question alone; that is, that I should have left Nebraska unorganized, the people unprotected, and the Indian barrier in existence, until the swelling tide of emigration should burst through, and accomplish by violence what it is the part of wisdom and statesmanship to direct and regulate by law. How long could you have postponed action with safety? How long could you maintain that Indian barrier, and restrain the onward march of civilization, Christianity, and free government by a barbarian wall? Do you suppose that you could keep that vast country a howling wilderness in all time to come, roamed over by hostile savages, cutting

off all safe communication between our Atlantic and Pacific possessions? I tell you that the time for action has come, and cannot
be postponed. It is a case in which the "let-alone" policy would
precipitate a crisis which must inevitably result in violence, anarchy, and strife.

You cannot fix bounds to the onward march of this great and
growing country. You cannot fetter the limbs of the young giant.
He will burst all your chains. He will expand, and grow, and increase, and extend civilization, Christianity, and liberal principles.
Then, sir, if you cannot check the growth of the country in that
direction, is it not the part of wisdom to look the danger in the
face, and provide for an event which you cannot avoid? I tell you,
sir, you must provide for lines of continuous settlement from the
Mississippi valley to the Pacific ocean. And in making this provision, you must decide upon what principles the Territories shall
be organized; in other words, whether the people shall be allowed
to regulate their domestic institutions in their own way, according
to the provisions of this bill, or whether the opposite doctrine of
Congressional interference is to prevail. Postpone it, if you will;
but whenever you do act, this question must be met and decided.

The Missouri compromise was interference; the compromise of
1850 was non-interference, leaving the people to exercise their
rights under the Constitution. The Committee on Territories were
compelled to act on this subject. I, as their chairman, was bound
to meet the question. I chose to take the responsibility regardless
of consequences personal to myself. I should have done the same
thing last year, if there had been time; but we know, considering
the late period at which the bill then reached us from the House,
that there was not sufficient time to consider the question fully,
and to prepare a report upon the subject. I was, therefore, persuaded by my friends to allow the bill to be reported to the Senate,
in order that such action might be taken as should be deemed
wise and proper. The bill was never taken up for action — the last
night of the session having been exhausted in debate on a motion
to take up the bill. This session, the measure was introduced by
my friend from Iowa [Mr. Dodge], and referred to the Territorial
Committee during the first week of the session. We have abundance of time to consider the subject; it is a matter of pressing
necessity, and there was no excuse for not meeting it directly and
fairly. We were compelled to take our position upon the doctrine

either of intervention or non-intervention. We chose the latter for two reasons: first, because we believed that the principle was right; and, second, because it was the principle adopted in 1850, to which the two great political parties of the country were solemnly pledged.

There is another reason why I desire to see this principle recognized as a rule of action in all time to come. It will have the effect to destroy all sectional parties and sectional agitations. If, in the language of the report of the committee, you withdraw the slavery question from the halls of Congress and the political arena, and commit it to the arbitrament of those who are immediately interested in and alone responsible for its consequences, there is nothing left out of which sectional parties can be organized. It never was done, and never can be done on the bank, tariff, distribution, or any party issue which has existed, or may exist, after this slavery question is withdrawn from politics. On every other political question these have always supporters and opponents in every portion of the Union — in each State, county, village, and neighborhood — residing together in harmony and good fellowship, and combating each other's opinions and correcting each other's errors in a spirit of kindness and friendship. These differences of opinion between neighbors and friends, and the discussions that grow out of them, and the sympathy which each feels with the advocates of his own opinions in every portion of this widespread Republic, add an overwhelming and irresistible moral weight to the strength of the Confederacy. Affection for the Union can never be alienated or diminished by any other party issues than those which are joined upon sectional or geographical lines. When the people of the North shall all be rallied under one banner, and the whole South marshalled under another banner, and each section excited to frenzy and madness by hostility to the institutions of the other, then the patriot may well tremble for the perpetuity of the Union. Withdraw the slavery question from the political arena, and remove it to the States and Territories, each to decide for itself, such a catastrophe can never happen. Then you will never be able to tell, by any Senator's vote for or against any measure, from what State or section of the Union he comes.

Why then, can we not withdraw this vexed question from politics? Why can we not adopt the principle of this bill as a rule of action in all new Territorial organizations? Why can we not deprive these agitators of their vocation and render it impossible for Senators to come here upon bargains on the slavery question? I believe that the peace, the harmony, and perpetuity of the Union require us to go back to the doctrines of the Revolution, to the principles of the Constitution, to the principles of the Compromise of 1850, and leave the people, under the Constitution, to do as they may see proper in respect to their own internal affairs.

Mr. President, I have not brought this question forward as a Northern man or as a Southern man. I am unwilling to recognize such divisions and distinctions. I have brought it forward as an American Senator, representing a State which is true to this principle, and which has approved of my action in respect to the Nebraska bill. I have brought it forward not as an act of justice to the South more than to the North. I have presented it especially as an act of justice to the people of those Territories and of the States to be formed therefrom, now and in all time to come. I have nothing to say about Northern rights or Southern rights. I know of no such divisions or distinctions under the Constitution. The bill does equal and exact justice to the whole Union, and every part of it; it violates the right of no State or Territory; but places each on a perfect equality, and leaves the people thereof to the free enjoyment of all their rights under the Constitution.

Now, sir, I wish to say to our Southern friends that if they desire to see this great principle carried out; now is their time to rally around it, to cherish it, preserve it, make it the rule of action in all future time. If they fail to do it now, and thereby allow the doctrine of interference to prevail, upon their heads the consequences of that interference must rest. To our Northern friends, on the other hand, I desire to say, that from this day henceforward they must rebuke the slander which has been uttered against the South, that they desire to legislate slavery into the Territories. The South has vindicated her sincerity, her honor, on that point by bringing forward a provision negativing, in express terms, any such effect as a result of this bill. I am rejoiced to know that while the proposition to abrogate the eighth section of the Missouri act comes from a free State, the proposition to negative the conclusion that slavery is thereby introduced, comes from a slave-holding State. Thus, both sides furnish conclusive evidence that they go for the principle, and the principle only, and desire to take no advantage of any possible misconstruction.

Mr. President, I feel that I owe an apology to the Senate for having occupied their attention so long, and a still greater apology for having discussed the question in such an incoherent and desultory manner. But I could not forbear to claim the right of closing this debate. I thought gentlemen would recognize its propriety when they saw the manner in which I was assailed and misrepresented in the course of this discussion, and especially by assaults still more disreputable in some portions of the country. These assaults have had no other effect upon me than to give me courage and energy for a still more resolute discharge of duty. I say frankly that, in my opinion, this measure will be as popular at the North as at the South, when its provisions and principles shall have been fully developed, and become well understood. The people at the North are attached to the principles of self-government, and you cannot convince them that that is self-government which deprives a people of the right of legislating for themselves, and compels them to receive laws which are forced upon them by a Legislature in which they are not represented. We are willing to stand upon this great principle of self-government everywhere; and it is to us a proud reflection that, in this whole discussion, no friend of the bill has urged an argument in its favor which could not be used with the same propriety in a free State as in a slave State, and vice versâ. No enemy of the bill has used an argument which would bear repetition one mile across Mason and Dixon's line. Our opponents have dealt entirely in sectional appeals. The friends of the bill have discussed a great principle of universal application, which can be sustained by the same reasons, and the same arguments, in every time and in every corner of the Union.

ABRAHAM LINCOLN

(1809-1865)

In the estimation of those who saw and heard Lincoln speak, he
lacked the so-called "oratorical graces." His voice tended to be
thin in tone and high in pitch; his posture was ungainly, his gestures awkward. Despite such handicaps of voice and appearance,
he went on to gain universal recognition as one of America's truly
distinguished orators. How did he manage to attain such recognition? The essential and enduring distinction between the true
and the pseudo orator is expressed well by Robert G. Ingersoll:

> If you wish to know the difference between an orator and an
> elocutionist — between what is felt and what is said — between
> what the heart and brain can do together and what the brain can
> do alone — read Lincoln's wondrous words at Gettysburg, and then
> the speech of Edward Everett. The oration of Lincoln will never be
> forgotten. It will live until languages are dead and lips are dust.
> The speech of Everett will never be read. The elocutionists believe
> in the virtue of voice, the sublimity of syntax, the majesty of long
> sentences, and the genius of gesture. The orator loves the real,
> the simple, the natural. He places the thought above all.[1]

A similar opinion of Lincoln's eloquence is voiced by General
Sherman:

> I have seen and heard many of the famous orators of our country,
> but Lincoln's unstudied speeches surpassed all that I ever heard. I
> have never seen them equaled, or even imitated. It was not scholar-
> ship; it was not rhetoric; it was not elocution; it was the unaffected
> and spontaneous eloquence of the heart.[2]

[1] Works of Ingersoll, III, 169-170.
[2] The Independent 47:448 (Ap 4, 1895)

Lincoln's avoidance of sham is further attested to by *Carl Schurz* who witnessed Lincoln's opening of the Quincy debate with Douglas and who later remarked that "there was . . . in all he said, a tone of earnest truthfulness, of elevated, noble sentiment, and of kindly sympathy, which added greatly to the strength of his argument. . . ." Lincoln's natural energy, his directness of communication, and his shunning of the artificial are graphically pointed up in the following description by his friend and law partner, *William Herndon*:

When he began speaking, his voice was shrill, piping, and unpleasant. His manner, his attitude, his dark, yellow face, wrinkled and dry, his oddity of pose, his diffident movements — everything seemed to be against him, but only for a short time. After having arisen, he generally placed his hands behind him, the back of his left hand in the palm of his right, the thumb and fingers of his right hand clasped around the left arm at the wrist. For a few moments he played the combination of awkwardness, sensitiveness, and diffidence. As he proceeded he became somewhat animated, and to keep in harmony with his growing warmth his hands relaxed their grasp and fell to his side. Presently he clasped them in front of him, interlocking his fingers, one thumb meanwhile chasing another. His speech now requiring more emphatic utterance, his fingers unlocked and his hands fell apart. His left arm was thrown behind, the back of his hand resting against his body, his right hand seeking his side. By this time he had gained sufficient composure, and his real speech began. He did not gesticulate as much with his hands as with his head. He used the latter frequently, throwing it with vim this way and that. This movement was a significant one when he sought to enforce his statement. . . . He never sawed the air nor rent space into tatters and rags as some do. He never acted for stage effect. He was cool, considerate, reflective — in time self-possessed and self-reliant. His style was clear, terse, and compact. In argument he was logical, demonstrative, and fair. He was careless of his dress, and his clothes, instead of fitting neatly as did the garments of Douglas on the latter's well-rounded form, hung loosely on his giant frame. As he moved along in his speech he became freer and less uneasy in his movements; to that extent he was graceful. He had a perfect naturalness, a strong individuality; and to that extent he was dignified. . . . He spoke with effectiveness and to move the judgment as well as the emotions of men. There was a world of meaning and emphasis in the long, bony finger of his right hand as he dotted the ideas on the minds of his hearers.

Sometimes, to express joy or pleasure, he would raise both hands at an angle of about fifty degrees, the palms upward, as if desirous of embracing the spirit of that which he loved. If the sentiment was one of detestation — denunciation of slavery, for example — both arms, thrown upward and fists clenched, swept through the air, and he expressed an execration that was truly sublime. This was one of his most effective gestures, and signified most vividly a fixed determination to drag down the object of his hatred and trample it in the dust. He always stood squarely on his feet, toe even with toe; that is, he never put one foot before the other. He neither touched nor leaned on anything for support. He made but few changes in his positions and attitudes. He never ranted, never walked backward and forward on the platform. . . . As he proceeded with his speech the exercise of his vocal organs altered somewhat the tone of his voice. It lost in a measure its former acute and shrilling pitch, and mellowed into a more harmonious and pleasant sound. His form expanded, and, not withstanding the sunken breast, he rose up a splendid and imposing figure. . . . Such was Lincoln the orator.[3]

Lincoln's deserved reputation as one of our foremost orators rests upon a combination of factors: (1) his meticulous preparation, (2) his ability to reason lucidly and cogently, (3) his genuine humility and utter sincerity and earnestness, (4) his stand upon ideals of the highest order and of universal appeal, and (5) his remarkable talent for expressing lofty sentiments in language magnificent in its beauty and rhythm. As an example of this talent, note the closing words of his Second Inaugural:

With malice toward none; with charity for all; with firmness in the right, as God gives us to see the right, let us strive on to finish the work we are in: to bind up the nation's wounds; to care for him who shall have borne the battle, and for his widow, and his orphan — to do all which may achieve and cherish a just and lasting peace among ourselves, and with all nations.

On the rainy evening of February 27, 1860, William Cullen Bryant introduced Lincoln to an audience of distinguished people at Cooper Institute in New York City. The next day the New York Tribune reported that "since the days of Clay and Webster

[3] Herndon and Weik, *Abraham Lincoln*, II, 75-77.

no man has spoken to a larger assemblage of the intellect and mental culture of our city." The Tribune further commented:

> Mr. Lincoln is one of nature's orators, using his rare powers solely to elucidate and convince, though their inevitable effect is to delight and electrify as well. . . . The vast assemblage frequently rang with cheers and shouts of applause, which were prolonged and intensified at the close. No man ever before made such an impression on his first appeal to a New York audience.

Herndon declared:

> . . . the speech was devoid of all rhetorical imagery, with a marked suppression of the pyrotechnics of stump oratory. It was constructed with a view to accuracy of statement, simplicity of language, and unity of thought. In some respects like a lawyer's brief, it was logical, temperate in tone, powerful — irresistably driving conviction home to men's reasons and their souls. No former effort in the line of speech-making had cost Lincoln so much time and thought as this one.[4]

Nicolay and Hay remarked as follows:

> If any part of the audience came with the expectation of hearing the rhetorical fire-works of a Western stump-speaker of the "half-horse, half-alligator" variety, they met novelty of an unlooked for kind. In Lincoln's entire address he neither introduced an anecdote nor essayed a witticism; and the first half of it does not contain even an illustrative figure or poetical fancy. It was the quiet, searching exposition of the historian, and the terse, compact reasoning of the statesman, about an abstract principle of legislation, in language well-nigh as restrained and colorless as he would have employed in arguing a case before a court. Yet such was the apt choice of words, the easy precision of sentences, the simple strength of proposition, the fairness of every point he assumed, and the force of every conclusion he drew, that his listeners followed him with the interest and delight a child feels in its easy mastery of a plain sum in arithmetic.[5]

At Cooper Institute, Lincoln made a brilliant and definitive statement of the antislavery position and his efforts on that occa-

4 Ibid., 165–166.
5 Abraham Lincoln, II, 20.

sion made him famous in the East. This fame, in the minds of many, did much to pave Lincoln's way to the White House. As final testimony to the impact achieved by this political lecture, Horace Greeley, writing some years later in Century Magazine (July, 1892) stated:

> . . . I do not hesitate to pronounce Mr. Lincoln's speech at Cooper Institute in the spring of 1860 the very best political address to which I ever listened, and I have heard some of Webster's finest. As a literary effort, it would not of course bear comparison with many of Webster's speeches; but regarded as an effort to convince the largest possible number that they ought to be on the speaker's side, not the other, I do not hesitate to pronounce it unsurpassed.

THE COOPER INSTITUTE ADDRESS

by

Abraham Lincoln

Delivered in New York City on February 27, 1860.

MR. PRESIDENT AND FELLOW-CITIZENS OF NEW YORK: The facts with which I shall deal this evening are mainly old and familiar; nor is there anything new in the general use I shall make of them. If there shall be any novelty, it will be in the mode of presenting the facts, and the inferences and observations following that presentation. In his speech last autumn at Columbus, Ohio, as reported in the New York Times, Senator Douglas said: —

> Our fathers, when they framed the government under which we live, understood this question just as well, and even better, than we do now.

I fully endorse this, and I adopt it as a text for this discourse. I so adopt it because it furnishes a precise and an agreed starting-point for a discussion between Republicans and that wing of the Democracy headed by Senator Douglas. It simply leaves the inquiry: What was the understanding those fathers had of the question mentioned?

What is the frame of government under which we live? The answer must be, "The Constitution of the United States." That Constitution consists of the original, framed in 1787, and under which the present government first went into operation, and twelve subsequently framed amendments, the first ten of which were framed in 1789.

Who were our fathers that framed the Constitution? I suppose the "thirty-nine" who signed the original instrument may be fairly called our fathers who framed that part of the present government. It is almost exactly true to say they framed it, and it is altogether true to say they fairly represented the opinion and sentiment of the whole nation at that time. Their names, being familiar to nearly all, and accessible to quite all, need not now be repeated.

I take these "thirty-nine," for the present, as being "our fathers who framed the government under which we live." What is the question which, according to the text, those fathers understood "just as well, and even better, than we do now"?

It is this: Does the proper division of local from Federal authority, or anything in the Constitution, forbid our Federal Government to control as to slavery in our Federal Territories?

Upon this, Senator Douglas holds the affirmative, and Republicans the negative. This affirmation and denial form an issue; and this issue — this question — is precisely what the text declares our fathers understood "better than we." Let us now inquire whether the "thirty-nine," or any of them, ever acted upon this question; and if they did, how they acted upon it — how they expressed that better understanding. In 1784, three years before the Constitution, the United States then owning the Northwestern Territory, and no other, the Congress of the Confederation had before them the question of prohibiting slavery in that Territory, and four of the "thirty-nine" who afterward framed the Constitution were in that Congress, and voted on that question. Of these, Roger Sherman, Thomas Mifflin, and Hugh Williamson voted for the prohibition, thus showing that, in their understanding, no line dividing local from Federal authority, nor anything else, properly forbade the Federal Government to control as to slavery in Federal territory. The other of the four, James McHenry, voted against the prohibition, showing that for some cause he thought it improper to vote for it.

In 1787, still before the Constitution, but while the convention was in session framing it, and while the Northwestern Territory still was the only Territory owned by the United States, the same question of prohibiting slavery in the Territory again came before the Congress of the Confederation; and two more of the "thirty-nine" who afterward signed the Constitution were in that Congress, and voted on the question. They were William Blount and William Few; and they both voted for the prohibition — thus showing that in their understanding no line dividing local from Federal authority, nor anything else, properly forbade the Federal Government to control as to slavery in Federal territory. This time the prohibition became a law, being part of what is now well known as the Ordinance of '87.

The question of Federal control of slavery in the Territories seems not to have been directly before the convention which framed the original Constitution; and hence it is not recorded that the "thirty-nine," or any of them, while engaged on that instrument, expressed any opinion on that precise question.

In 1789, by the first Congress which sat under the Constitution, an act was passed to enforce the Ordinance of '87, including the prohibition of slavery in the Northwestern Territory. The bill for this act was reported by one of the "thirty-nine" — Thomas Fitzsimmons, then a member of the House of Representatives from Pennsylvania. It went through all its stages without a word of opposition, and finally passed both branches without ayes and nays, which is equivalent to a unanimous passage. In this Congress there were sixteen of the thirty-nine fathers who framed the original Constitution. They were John Langdon, Nicholas Gilman, Wm. S. Johnson, Roger Sherman, Robert Morris, Thomas Fitzsimmons, Abraham Baldwin, William Few, Rufus King, William Patterson, George Clymer, Richard Bassett, George Read, Pierce Butler, Daniel Carroll, and James Madison.

This shows that, in their understanding, no line dividing local from Federal authority, nor anything in the Constitution, properly forbade Congress to prohibit slavery in the Federal territory; else both their fidelity to correct principle, and their oath to support the Constitution, would have constrained them to oppose the prohibition.

Again, George Washington, another of the "thirty-nine," was then President of the United States, and as such approved and signed the bill, thus completing its validity as a law, and thus showing that, in his understanding, no line dividing local from Federal authority, nor anything in the Constitution, forbade the Federal Government to control as to slavery in Federal territory.

No great while after the adoption of the original Constitution, North Carolina ceded to the Federal Government the country now constituting the State of Tennessee; and a few years later Congress ceded that which now constitutes the States of Mississippi and Alabama. In both deeds of cession it was made a condition by the ceding States that the Federal Government should not prohibit slavery in the ceded country. Besides this, slavery was then actually in the ceded country. Under these circumstances, Congress, on taking charge of these countries, did not absolutely prohibit slavery within them. But they did interfere with it — take control of it — even there, to a certain extent. In 1798 Congress organized the Territory of Mississippi. In the act of organization they prohibited the bringing of slaves into the Territory from any place without the United States, by fine, and giving freedom to slaves so brought. This act passed both branches of Congress without yeas and nays. In that Congress were three of the "thirty-nine" who framed the original Constitution. They were John Langdon, George Read, and Abraham Baldwin. They all probably voted for it. Certainly they would have placed their opposition to it upon record if, in their understanding, any line dividing local from Federal authority, or anything in the Constitution, properly forbade the Federal Government to control as to slavery in Federal Territory.

In 1803, the Federal Government purchased the Louisiana country. Our former territorial acquisitions came from certain of our own States; but this Louisiana country was acquired from a foreign nation. In 1804, Congress gave a territorial organization to that part of it which now constitutes the State of Louisiana. New Orleans, lying within that part, was an old and comparatively large city. There were other considerable towns and settlements, and slavery was extensively and thoroughly intermingled with the people. Congress did not, in the Territorial Act, prohibit slavery;

but they did interfere with it — take control of it — in a more marked and extensive way than they did in the case of Mississippi. The substance of the provision therein made in relation to slaves was:

1st. That no slave should be imported into the Territory from foreign parts.

2d. That no slave should be carried into it who had been imported into the United States since the first day of May, 1798.

3d. That no slave should be carried into it, except by the owner, and for his own use as a settler; the penalty in all cases being a fine upon the violator of the law, and freedom to the slave.

This act also was passed without ayes or nays. In the Congress which passed it there were two of the "thirty-nine." They were Abraham Baldwin and Jonathan Dayton. As stated in the case of Mississippi, it is probable they both voted for it. They would not have allowed it to pass without recording their opposition to it if, in their understanding, it violated either the line properly dividing local from Federal authority, or any provision of the Constitution.

In 1819-20 came and passed the Missouri question. Many votes were taken, by yeas and nays, in both branches of Congress, upon the various phases of the general question. Two of the "thirty-nine" — Rufus King and Charles Pinckney — were members of that Congress. Mr. King steadily voted for slavery prohibition and against all compromises, while Mr. Pinckney as steadily voted against slavery prohibition and against all compromises. By this, Mr. King showed that, in his understanding, no line dividing local from Federal authority, nor anything in the Constitution, was violated by Congress prohibiting slavery in Federal territory; while Mr. Pinckney, by his votes, showed that, in his understanding, there was some sufficient reason for opposing such prohibition in that case.

The cases I have mentioned are the only acts of the "thirty-nine," or of any one of them, upon the direct issue, which I have been able to discover.

To enumerate the persons who thus acted as being four in 1784, two in 1787, seventeen in 1789, three in 1798, two in 1804, and two in 1819-20, there would be thirty of them. But this would be counting John Langdon, Roger Sherman, William Few, Rufus King, and George Read each twice, and Abraham Baldwin three times. The true number of those of the "thirty-nine" whom I have shown to have acted upon the question which, by the text, they understood better than we, is twenty-three, leaving sixteen not shown to have acted upon it in any way.

Here, then, we have twenty-three out of our thirty-nine fathers "who framed the government under which we live," who have, upon their official responsibility and their corporal oaths, acting upon the very question which the text affirms they "understood just as well, and even better, than we do now"; and twenty-one of them — a clear majority of the whole "thirty-nine" — so acting upon it as to make them guilty of gross political impropriety and wilful perjury if, in their understanding, any proper division between local and Federal authority, or anything in the Constitution they had made themselves, and sworn to support, forbade the Federal Government to control as to slavery in the Federal Territories. Thus the twenty-one acted; and, as actions speak louder than words, so actions under such responsibility speak still louder.

Two of the twenty-three voted against Congressional prohibition of slavery in the Federal Territories, in the instances in which they acted upon the question. But for what reasons they so voted is not known. They may have done so because they thought a proper division of local from Federal authority, or some provision or principle of the Constitution, stood in the way; or they may, without any such question, have voted against the prohibition on what appeared to them to be sufficient grounds of expediency. No one who has sworn to support the Constitution can conscientiously vote for what he understands to be an unconstitutional measure, however expedient he may think it; but one may and ought to vote against a measure which he deems constitutional if, at the same time, he deems it inexpedient. It, therefore, would be unsafe to set down even the two who voted against the prohibition as having done so because, in their understanding, any proper division of local from Federal authority, or anything in the Constitution, forbade the Federal Government to control as to slavery in Federal territory.

The remaining sixteen of the "thirty-nine," so far as I have discovered, have left no record of their understanding upon the direct question of Federal control of slavery in the Federal Territories. But there is much reason to believe that their understanding upon that question would not have appeared different from that of their twenty-three compeers, had it been manifested at all.

For the purpose of adhering rigidly to the text, I have purposely omitted whatever understanding may have been manifested by any person, however distinguished, other than the thirty-nine fathers who framed the original Constitution; and, for the same reason, I have also omitted whatever understanding may have been manifested by any of the "thirty-nine" even on any other phase of the general question of slavery. If we should look into their acts and declarations on those other phases, as the foreign slave-trade, and the morality and policy of slavery generally, it would appear to us that on the direct question of Federal control of slavery in Federal Territories, the sixteen, if they had acted at all, would probably have acted just as the twenty-three did. Among that sixteen were several of the most noted anti-slavery men of those times — Dr. Franklin, Alexander Hamilton, and Gouverneur Morris — while there was not one now known to have been otherwise, unless it may be John Rutledge, of South Carolina.

The sum of the whole is that of our thirty-nine fathers who framed the original Constitution, twenty-one — a clear majority of the whole — certainly understood that no proper division of local from Federal authority, nor any part of the Constitution, forbade the Federal Government to control slavery in the Federal Territories; while all the rest had probably the same understanding. Such, unquestionably, was the understanding of our fathers who framed the original Constitution; and the text affirms that they understood the question "better than we."

But, so far, I have been considering the understanding of the question manifested by the framers of the original Constitution. In and by the original instrument, a mode was provided for amending it; and, as I have already stated, the present frame of "the government under which we live" consists of that original, and twelve amendatory articles framed and adopted since. Those who now insist that Federal control of slavery in Federal Territories violates the Constitution, point us to the provisions which they suppose it thus violates; and, as I understand, they all fix upon provisions in these amendatory articles, and not in the original instrument. The Supreme Court, in the Dred Scott case, plant themselves upon the fifth amendment, which provides that no person shall be deprived of "life, liberty, or property without due process of law"; while Senator Douglas and his peculiar adherents plant themselves upon the tenth amendment, providing that "the powers not delegated to the United States by the Constitution" "are reserved to the States respectively, or to the people."

Now it so happens that these amendments were framed by the first Congress which sat under the Constitution — the identical Congress which passed the act, already mentioned, enforcing the prohibition of slavery in the Northwestern Territory. Not only was it the same Congress, but they were the identical, same individual men who, at the same session, and at the same time within the session, had under consideration, and in progress toward maturity, these constitutional amendments, and this act prohibiting slavery in all the territory the nation then owned. The constitutional amendments were introduced before, and passed after the act enforcing the Ordinance of '87; so that, during the whole pendency of the act to enforce the Ordinance, the constitutional amendments were also pending.

The seventy-six members of that Congress, including sixteen of the framers of the original Constitution, as before stated, were preëminently our fathers who framed that part of "the government under which we live," which is now claimed as forbidding the Federal Government to control slavery in the Federal Territories.

Is it not a little presumptuous in anyone at this day to affirm that the two things which that Congress deliberately framed, and carried to maturity at the same time, are absolutely inconsistent with each other? And does not such affirmation become impudently absurd when coupled with the other affirmation, from the same mouth, that those who did the two things alleged to be inconsistent, understood whether they really were inconsistent better than we — better than he who affirms that they are inconsistent?

It is surely safe to assume that the thirty-nine framers of the original Constitution, and the seventy-six members of the Congress which framed the amendments thereto, taken together, do certainly include those who may be fairly called "our fathers who framed the government under which we live." And so assuming, I defy any man to show that any one of them ever, in his whole life, declared that, in his understanding, any proper division of local from Federal authority, or any part of the Constitution, forbade the Federal Government to control as to slavery in the Federal Territories. I go a step further. I defy anyone to show that any living man in the world ever did, prior to the beginning of the present century (and I might almost say prior to the beginning of the last half of the present century), declare that, in his understanding, any proper division of local from Federal authority, or any part of the Constitution, forbade the Federal Government to control as to slavery in the Federal Territories. To those who now so declare I give not only "our fathers who framed the government under which we live," but with them all other living men within the century in which it was framed, among whom to search, and they shall not be able to find the evidence of a single man agreeing with them.

Now, and here, let me guard a little against being misunderstood. I do not mean to say we are bound to follow implicitly in whatever our fathers did. To do so would be to discard all the lights of current experience — to reject all progress, all improvement. What I do say is that if we would supplant the opinions and policy of our fathers in any case, we should do so upon evidence so conclusive, and argument so clear, that even their great authority, fairly considered and weighed, cannot stand; and most surely not in a case whereof we ourselves declare they understood the question better than we.

If any man at this day sincerely believes that a proper division of local from Federal authority, or any part of the Constitution, forbids the Federal Government to control as to slavery in the Federal Territories, he is right to say so, and to enforce his position by all truthful evidence and fair argument which he can. But he has no right to mislead others, who have less access to history, and less leisure to study it, into the false belief that "our fathers who framed the government under which we live" were of the same opinion — thus substituting falsehood and deception for truthful evidence and fair argument. If any man at this day sincerely believes "our fathers who framed the government under which we live" used and applied principles, in other cases, which ought to have led them to understand that a proper division of local from Federal authority, or some part of the Constitution, forbids the Federal Government to control as to slavery in the Federal Territories, he is right to say so. But he should, at the same time, brave the responsibility of declaring that, in his opinion, he understands their principles better than they did themselves; and especially should he not shirk that responsibility by asserting that they "understood the question just as well, and even better, than we do now."

But enough! Let all who believe that "our fathers who framed the government under which we live understood this question just as well, and even better, than we do now," speak as they spoke, and act as they acted upon it. This is all Republicans ask — all Republicans desire — in relation to slavery. As those fathers marked it, so let it be again marked, as an evil not to be extended, but to be tolerated and protected only because of and so far as its actual presence amongst us makes that toleration and protection a necessity. Let all the guaranties those fathers gave it be not grudgingly, but fully and fairly maintained. For this Republicans contend, and with this, so far as I know or believe, they will be content.

And now, if they would listen — as I suppose they will not — I would address a few words to the Southern people.

I would say to them: You consider yourselves a reasonable and a just people; and I consider that in the general qualities of reason and justice you are not inferior to any other people. Still, when you speak of us Republicans, you do so only to denounce us as reptiles, or, at the best, as no better than outlaws. You will grant a hearing to pirates or murderers, but nothing like it to "Black Republicans." In all your contentions with one another, each of you deems an unconditional condemnation of "Black Republicanism," as the first thing to be attended to. Indeed, such condemnation of us seems to be an indispensable prerequisite — license, so to speak — among you to be admitted or permitted to speak at all. Now can you or not be prevailed upon to pause and to consider whether this is quite just to us, or even to yourselves? Bring forward your charges and specifications, and then be patient long enough to hear us deny or justify.

You say we are sectional. We deny it. That makes an issue: and the burden of proof is upon you. You produce your proof; and what is it? Why, that our party has no existence in your section — gets no votes in your section. The fact is substantially true; but does it prove the issue? If it does, then in case we should, without change of principle, begin to get votes in your section, we should thereby cease to be sectional. You cannot escape this conclusion; and yet, are you willing to abide by it? If you are, you will probably soon find that we have ceased to be sectional, for we shall get votes in your section this very year. You will then begin to discover, as the truth plainly is, that your proof does not touch the issue. The fact that we get no votes in your section is a fact of your making, and not of ours. And if there be fault in that fact, that fault is primarily yours, and remains so until you show that we repel you by some wrong principle or practice. If we do repel you by any wrong principle or practice, the fault is ours; but this brings you to where you ought to have started — to a discussion of the right or wrong of our principle. If our principle, put in practice, would wrong your section for the benefit of ours, or for any other object, then our principle, and we with it, are sectional, and are justly opposed and denounced as such. Meet us, then, on the question of whether our principle, put in practice, would wrong your section; and so meet us as if it were possible that something may be said on your side. Do you accept the challenge? No! Then you really believe that the principle which "our fathers who framed the government under which we live" thought so clearly right as to adopt it, and indorse it again and again, upon their official oaths, is in fact so clearly wrong as to demand your condemnation without a moment's consideration.

Some of you delight to flaunt in our faces the warning against sectional parties given by Washington in his Farewell Address. Less than eight years before Washington gave that warning, he had, as President of the United States, approved and signed an act of Congress enforcing the prohibition of slavery in the Northwestern Territory, which act embodied the policy of the government upon that subject up to and at the very moment he penned that warning; and about one year after he penned it, he wrote Lafayette that he considered that prohibition a wise measure, expressing in the same connection his hope that we should at some time have a confederacy of free States.

Bearing this in mind, and seeing that sectionalism has since arisen upon this same subject, is that warning a weapon in your hands against us, or in our hands against you? Could Washington himself speak, would he cast the blame of that sectionalism upon us, who sustain his policy, or upon you, who repudiate it? We respect that warning of Washington, and we commend it to you, together with his example pointing to the right application of it.

But you say you are conservative — eminently conservative — while we are revolutionary, destructive, or something of the sort. What is conservatism? Is it not adherence to the old and tried, against the new and untried? We stick to, contend for, the identical old policy on the point in controversy which was adopted by

"our fathers who framed the government under which we live";
while you with one accord reject, and scout, and spit upon that
old policy, and insist upon substituting something new. True, you
disagree among yourselves as to what that substitute shall be. You
are divided on new propositions and plans, but you are unanimous
in rejecting and denouncing the old policy of the fathers. Some of
you are for reviving the foreign slave-trade; some for a Congressional slave code for the Territories; some for Congress forbidding
the Territories to prohibit slavery within their limits; some for
maintaining slavery in the Territories through the judiciary; some
for the "gur-reat pur-rinciple" that "if one man would enslave another, no third man should object," fantastically called "popular
sovereignty," but never a man among you is in favor of Federal
prohibition of slavery in Federal Territories, according to the practice of "our fathers who framed the government under which we
live." Not one of all your various plans can show a precedent or
an advocate in the century within which our government originated. Consider, then, whether your claim of conservatism for
yourselves, and your charge of destructiveness against us, are based
on the most clear and stable foundations.

And again, you say we have made the slavery question more
prominent than it formerly was. We deny it. We admit that it
is more prominent, but we deny that we made it so. It was not we,
but you, who discarded the old policy of the fathers. We resisted,
and still resist, your innovation; and thence comes the greater
prominence of the question. Would you have that question reduced to its former proportions? Go back to that old policy. What
has been will be again, under the same conditions. If you would
have the peace of the old times, re-adopt the precepts and policy
of the old times.

You charge that we stir up insurrections among your slaves. We
deny it; and what is your proof? Harper's Ferry! John Brown!!
John Brown was no Republican; and you have failed to implicate a
single Republican in his Harper's Ferry enterprise. If any member
of our party is guilty in that matter, you know it or you do not
know it. If you do know it, you are inexcusable for not designating
the man and proving the fact. If you do not know it, you are inexcusable for asserting it, and especially for persisting in the assertion
after you have tried and failed to make the proof. You need not

be told that persisting in a charge which one does not know to be true is simply malicious slander.

Some of you admit that no Republican designedly aided or encouraged the Harper's Ferry affair, but still insist that our doctrines and declarations necessarily lead to such results. We do not believe it. We know we hold no doctrine, and make no declaration which were not held to and made by "our fathers who framed the government under which we live." You never dealt fairly by us in relation to this affair. When it occurred, some important State elections were near at hand, and you were in evident glee with the belief that, by charging the blame upon us, you could get an advantage of us in those elections. The elections came, and your expectations were not quite fulfilled. Every Republican man knew that, as to himself at least, your charge was a slander, and he was not much inclined by it to cast his vote in your favor. Republican doctrines and declarations are accompanied with a continual protest against any interference whatever with your slaves, or with you about your slaves. Surely this does not encourage them to revolt. True, we do, in common with "our fathers who framed the government under which we live," declare our belief that slavery is wrong; but the slaves do not hear us declare even this. For anything we say or do, the slaves would scarcely know there is a Republican party. I believe they would not, in fact, generally know it but for your misrepresentations of us in their hearing. In your political contests among yourselves each faction charges the other with sympathy with Black Republicanism; and then, to give point to the charge, defines Black Republicanism to simply be insurrection, blood, and thunder among the slaves.

Slave insurrections are no more common now than they were before the Republican party was organized. What induced the Southampton insurrection, twenty-eight years ago, in which at least three times as many lives were lost as at Harper's Ferry? You can scarcely stretch your very elastic fancy to the conclusion that Southampton was "got up by Black Republicanism." In the present state of things in the United States, I do not think a general, or even a very extensive, slave insurrection is possible. The indispensable concert of action cannot be attained. The slaves have no means of rapid communication; nor can incendiary freeman, black or white, supply it. The explosive materials are everywhere in parcels; but there neither are, nor can be supplied, the indispensable connecting trains.

Much is said by Southern people about the affection of slaves for their masters and mistresses; and a part of it, at least, is true. A plot for an uprising could scarcely be devised and communicated to twenty individuals before some one of them, to save the life of a favorite master or mistress, would divulge it. This is the rule; and the slave revolution in Hayti was not an exception to it, but a case occurring under peculiar circumstances. The Gunpowder Plot of British history, though not connected with slaves, was more in point. In that case, only about twenty were admitted to the secret; and yet one of them, in his anxiety to save a friend, betrayed the plot to that friend, and, by consequence, averted the calamity. Occasional poisonings from the kitchen, and open or stealthy assassinations in the field, and local revolts extending to a score or so, will continue to occur as the natural results of slavery; but no general insurrection of slaves, as I think, can happen in this country for a long time. Whoever much fears, or much hopes for, such an event will be alike disappointed.

In the language of Mr. Jefferson, uttered many years ago, "It is still in our power to direct the process of emancipation and deportation peaceably, and in such slow degrees as that the evil will wear off insensibly; and their places be, pari passu, filled up by free white laborers. If, on the contrary, it is left to force itself on, human nature must shudder at the prospect held up."

Mr. Jefferson did not mean to say, nor do I, that the power of emancipation is in the Federal Government. He spoke of Virginia; and, as to the power of emancipation, I speak of the slaveholding States only. The Federal Government, however, as we insist, has the power of restraining the extension of the institution — the power to insure that a slave insurrection shall never occur on any American soil which is now free from slavery.

John Brown's effort was peculiar. It was not a slave insurrection. It was an attempt by white men to get up a revolt among slaves, in which the slaves refused to participate. In fact, it was so absurd that the slaves, with all their ignorance, saw plainly enough it could not succeed. That affair, in its philosophy, corresponds with the many attempts, related in history, at the assassination of kings and emperors. An enthusiast broods over the oppression of a people till he fancies himself commissioned by Heaven to liberate them.

He ventures the attempt, which ends in little else than his own execution. Orsini's attempt on Louis Napoleon, and John Brown's attempt at Harper's Ferry, were, in their philosophy, precisely the same. The eagerness to cast blame on old England in the one case, and on New England in the other, does not disprove the sameness of the two things.

And how much would it avail you, if you could, by the use of John Brown, Helper's book, and the like, break up the Republican organization? Human action can be modified to some extent, but human nature cannot be changed. There is a judgment and a feeling against slavery in this nation, which cast at least a million and a half of votes. You cannot destroy that judgment and feeling — that sentiment — by breaking up the political organization which rallies around it. You can scarcely scatter and disperse an army which has been formed into order in the face of your heaviest fire; but if you could, how much would you gain by forcing the sentiment which created it out of the peaceful channel of the ballot-box into some other channel? What would that other channel probably be? Would the number of John Browns be lessened or enlarged by the operation?

But you will break up the Union rather than submit to a denial of your constitutional rights.

That has a somewhat reckless sound; but it would be palliated, if not fully justified, were we proposing, by the mere force of numbers, to deprive you of some right plainly written down in the Constitution. But we are proposing no such thing.

When you make these declarations, you have a specific and well-understood allusion to an assumed constitutional right of yours to take slaves into the Federal Territories, and to hold them there as property. But no such right is specially written in the Constitution. That instrument is literally silent about any such right. We, on the contrary, deny that such a right has any existence in the Constitution, even by implication.

Your purpose, then, plainly stated, is that you will destroy the government, unless you be allowed to construe and force the Constitution as you please, on all points in dispute between you and us. You will rule or ruin in all events.

This, plainly stated, is your language. Perhaps you will say the Supreme Court has decided the disputed constitutional question in your favor. Not quite so. But, waiving the lawyer's distinction between dictum and decision, the court has decided the question for you in a sort of way. The court has substantially said, it is your constitutional right to take slaves into the Federal Territories, and to hold them there as property. When I say the decision was made in a sort of way, I mean it was made in a divided court, by a bare majority of the judges, and they not quite agreeing with one another in the reasons for making it; that it is so made as that its avowed supporters disagree with one another about its meaning, and that it was mainly based upon a mistaken statement of fact — the statement in the opinion that "the right of property in a slave is distinctly and expressly affirmed in the Constitution."

An inspection of the Constitution will show that the right of property in a slave is not "distinctly and expressly affirmed" by it. Bear in mind, the judges do not pledge their judicial opinion that such right is impliedly affirmed in the Constitution; but they pledge their veracity that it is "distinctly and expressly" affirmed there — "distinctly," that is, not mingled with anything else — "expressly," that is, in words meaning just that, without the aid of any inference, and susceptible of no other meaning.

If they had only pledged their judicial opinion that such right is affirmed in the instrument by implication, it would be open to others to show that neither the word "slave" nor "slavery" is to be found in the Constitution, nor the word "property" even, in any connection with language alluding to the thing slave or slavery; and that wherever in that instrument the slave is alluded to, he is called a "person"; and wherever his master's legal right in relation to him is alluded to, it is spoken of as "service or labor which may be due" — as a debt payable in service or labor. Also it would be open to show, by contemporaneous history, that this mode of alluding to slaves and slavery, instead of speaking of them, was employed on purpose to exclude from the Constitution the idea that there could be property in man.

To show all this is easy and certain.

When this obvious mistake of the judges shall be brought to their notice, is it not reasonable to expect that they will withdraw the mistaken statement, and reconsider the conclusion based upon it?

And then it is to be remembered that "our fathers who framed the government under which we live" — the men who made the Constitution — decided this same constitutional question in our favor long ago; decided it without division among themselves when making the decision; without division among themselves about the meaning of it after it was made, and, so far as any evidence is left, without basing it upon any mistaken statement of facts.

Under all these circumstances, do you really feel yourselves justified to break up this government unless such a court decision as yours is shall be at once submitted to as a conclusive and final rule of political action? But you will not abide the election of a Republican president! In that supposed event, you say, you will destroy the Union; and then, you say, the great crime of having destroyed it will be upon us! That is cool. A highwayman holds a pistol to my ear, and mutters through his teeth, "Stand and deliver, or I shall kill you, and then you will be a murderer!"

To be sure, what the robber demanded of me — my money — was my own; and I had a clear right to keep it; but it was no more my own than my vote is my own; and the threat of death to me, to extort my money, and the threat of destruction to the Union, to extort my vote, can scarcely be distinguished in principle.

A few words now to Republicans. It is exceedingly desirable that all parts of this great Confederacy shall be at peace, and in harmony one with another. Let us Republicans do our part to have it so. Even though much provoked, let us do nothing through passion and ill temper. Even though the Southern people will not so much as listen to us, let us calmly consider their demands, and yield to them if, in our deliberate view of our duty, we possibly can. Judging by all they say and do, and by the subject and nature of their controversy with us, let us determine, if we can, what will satisfy them.

Will they be satisfied if the Territories be unconditionally surrendered to them? We know they will not. In all their present complaints against us, the Territories are scarcely mentioned. Invasions and insurrections are the rage now. Will it satisfy them if, in the future, we have nothing to do with invasions and insurrections? We know it will not. We so know, because we know we never had anything to do with invasions and insurrections; and yet this total abstaining does not exempt us from the charge and the denunciation.

The question recurs, What will satisfy them? Simply this: we must not only let them alone, but we must somehow convince them that we do let them alone. This, we know by experience, is no easy task. We have been so trying to convince them from the very beginning of our organization, but with no success. In all our platforms and speeches we have constantly protested our purpose to let them alone; but this has had no tendency to convince them. Alike unavailing to convince them is the fact that they have never detected a man of us in any attempt to disturb them.

These natural and apparently adequate means all failing, what will convince them? This, and this only: cease to call slavery wrong, and join them in calling it right. And this must be done thoroughly — done in acts as well as words. Silence will not be tolerated — we must place ourselves avowedly with them. Senator Douglas's new sedition law must be enacted and enforced, suppressing all declarations that slavery is wrong, whether made in politics, in presses, in pulpits, or in private. We must arrest and return their fugitive slaves with greedy pleasure. We must pull down our free State constitutions. The whole atmosphere must be disinfected from all taint of opposition to slavery, before they will cease to believe that all their troubles proceed from us.

I am quite aware they do not state their case precisely in this way. Most of them would probably say to us, "Let us alone; do nothing to us, and say what you please about slavery." But we do let them alone — have never disturbed them — so that, after all, it is what we say which dissatisfies them. They will continue to accuse us of doing, until we cease saying.

I am also aware they have not as yet in terms demanded the overthrow of our free State constitutions. Yet those constitutions declare the wrong of slavery with more solemn emphasis than do all other sayings against it; and when all these other sayings shall have been silenced, the overthrow of these constitutions will be demanded, and nothing be left to resist the demand. It is nothing to the contrary that they do not demand the whole of this just now. Demanding what they do, and for the reason they do, they can voluntarily stop nowhere short of this consummation. Holding, as they do, that slavery is morally right and socially elevating, they cannot cease to demand a full national recognition of it as a legal right and a social blessing.

Nor can we justifiably withhold this on any ground save our conviction that slavery is wrong. If slavery is right, all words, acts, laws, and constitutions against it are themselves wrong, and should be silenced and swept away. If it is right, we cannot justly object to its nationality — its universality; if it is wrong, they cannot justly insist upon its extension — its enlargement. All they ask we could readily grant, if we thought slavery right; all we ask they could as readily grant, if they thought it wrong. Their thinking it right and our thinking it wrong is the precise fact upon which depends the whole controversy. Thinking it right, as they do, they are not to blame for desiring its full recognition as being right; but thinking it wrong, as we do, can we yield to them? Can we cast our votes with their view, and against our own? In view of our moral, social, and political responsibilities, can we do this?

Wrong as we think slavery is, we can yet afford to let it alone where it is, because that much is due to the necessity arising from its actual presence in the nation; but can we, while our votes will prevent it, allow it to spread into the national Territories, and to overrun us here in these free States? If our sense of duty forbids this, then let us stand by our duty fearlessly and effectively. Let us be diverted by none of those sophistical contrivances wherewith we are so industriously plied and belabored — contrivances such as groping for some middle ground between the right and the wrong: vain as the search for a man who should be neither a living man nor a dead man; such as a policy of "don't care" on a question about which all true men do care; such as Union appeals beseeching true Union men to yield to Disunionists, reversing the divine rule, and calling, not the sinners, but the righteous to repentance: such as invocations to Washington, imploring men to unsay what Washington said and undo what Washington did.

Neither let us be slandered from our duty by false accusations against us, nor frightened from it by menaces of destruction to the government, nor of dungeons to ourselves. Let us have faith that right makes might, and in that faith let us to the end dare to do our duty as we understand it.

HENRY W. GRADY

(1850-1889)

Henry W. Grady, managing editor and part owner of the Atlanta
Constitution, literally became nationally famous overnight. His
masterful twenty-minute address to the New England Society in
New York City on December 22, 1886, on "The New South" received nationwide acclaim and made its author one of the most
sought-after speakers in the country. That speech also made Grady
the acknowledged spokesman of "the New South," a South that
sorely needed an eloquent spokesman like Grady to help effect
and sustain friendly feelings between the North and the South.
In two ways, principally, Grady hoped to cement peaceful relations
between the two sections: (1) by demonstrating to the North that
the South actually was taking positive steps to ameliorate the condition of the Negro, and (2) by pointing out and emphasizing to
Northern capitalists the natural advantages of the South for industrial development and expansion. From 1886 to 1889 (the year
of his death) Grady dedicated himself to this awesome task of
placating the North and uplifting the pride and economy of the
South. His magnificent speech efforts in behalf of these goals have
permanently established Henry W. Grady as one of the most gifted
and effective orators in our history.

Essentially, Grady's style was ornate and emotional rather than
unadorned and logically precise; it was a style of speaking tremendously moving and stimulating. One listener characterized Grady's
speaking as "a cannon ball in full flight fringed with flowers";
another noted that "Grady makes you feel like you want to be
an angel and with the angels stand." The man was a master word
painter and created verbal images that were virtually impossible to
resist. "No man," recorded the New York Evangelist, "could take

156

an audience from the first sentence, and hold it to the last, more perfectly than he." In addition, Grady exuded a powerful personal magnetism, an outgrowth of the complete sincerity and sparkling humor of the man. The Nashville American paid him this tribute:

> He was intensely, almost devoutly Southern, but he had always the respectful attention of the North when he spoke for the land of his nativity. There was the ring of sincerity in his fervid utterances, and his audiences, whether in the North or in the South, felt that every word came hot from the Heart.

Not only was Grady deadly in earnest, he also had something to say. "His word," observed the Boston Post, "brought conviction as his glowing phrases stirred the sentiment of his hearers, and amid all the embellishments of oratory there was presented the substantial fabric of fact."

Invited to be guest speaker of the evening at the annual meeting of the Boston Merchants Association on December 13, 1889, Grady painstakingly prepared his speech on "The Race Problem in the South." Fully aware that his words would be widely reported in the press, he could not afford to antagonize the North, and did not wish to offend the South. The times were critical in terms of good will between North and South, since Congressman Henry Cabot Lodge was determined to get legislation through Congress authorizing the Federal Government to supervise polling places in the South during national elections in order to safeguard the Negro vote. On December 3, 1889, even President Harrison urged that such a "force bill" (as the South termed it) should be passed. Rightfully disturbed at the prospects of renewed sectional strife, Grady was apprehensive lest he should inadvertently fan the flames of ill feeling. But in speaking to the some four hundred persons crowded into the dining hall of the Hotel Vendome, Grady was frank, bold, imaginative, optimistic, and reached what Joel Chandler Harris called "the high-water mark of modern oratory." The Boston Advertiser considered the address "superior to that which he delivered in New York and which won for him a national reputation. . . . It was, in fact, one of the finest specimens of elegant and fervid oratory which this generation has heard."

Ten days later, however, Grady was dead of pneumonia, and the voice of a rare and truly inspirational leader suddenly and tragically was silenced. Such a man was able to inspire men because of his deep and abiding faith in the promise of what tomorrow held. "He was," as Harris puts it, "the embodiment . . . of that smiling faith in the future that brings happiness and contentment, and he had the faculty of imparting his faith to other people. For him the sun was always shining, and he tried to make it shine for other men."

THE RACE PROBLEM IN THE SOUTH

by

Henry W. Grady

Delivered in Boston at the Hotel Vendome on December 13, 1889.

MR. PRESIDENT: BIDDEN BY your invitation to a discussion of the race problem — forbidden by occasion to make a political speech — I appreciate, in trying to reconcile orders with propriety, the perplexity of the little maid, who, bidden to learn to swim, was yet adjured, "Now, go, my darling; hang your clothes on a hickory limb, and don't go near the water."

The stoutest apostle of the Church, they say, is the missionary, and the missionary, wherever he unfurls his flag, will never find himself in deeper need of unction and address than I, bidden tonight to plant the standard of a Southern Democrat in Boston's banquet hall, and to discuss the problem of the races in the home of Phillips and of Sumner. But, Mr. President, if a purpose to speak in perfect frankness and sincerity; if earnest understanding of the vast interests involved; if a consecrating sense of what disaster may follow further misunderstanding and estrangement; if these may be counted to steady undisciplined speech and to strengthen an untried arm — then, sir, I shall find the courage to proceed.

Happy am I that this mission has brought my feet at last to press New England's historic soil and my eyes to the knowledge of her beauty and her thrift. Here within touch of Plymouth Rock and Bunker Hill — where Webster thundered and Longfellow sang, Emerson thought and Channing preached — here, in the cradle of American letters and almost of American liberty, I hasten to make the obeisance that every American owes New England when first he stands uncovered in her mighty present. Strange apparition! This stern and unique figure — carved from the ocean and the wilderness — its majesty kindling and growing amid the storms of winter and of wars — until at last the gloom was broken, its beauty disclosed in the sunshine, and the heroic workers rested at its base — while startled kings and emperors gazed and marveled that from the rude touch of this handful cast on a bleak and unknown shore should have come the embodied genius of human government and the perfected model of human liberty! God bless the memory of those immortal workers, and prosper the fortunes of their living sons — and perpetuate the inspiration of their handiwork.

Two years ago, sir, I spoke some words in New York that caught the attention of the North. As I stand here to reiterate, as I have done everywhere, every word I then uttered — to declare that the sentiments I then avowed were universally approved in the South — I realize that the confidence begotten by that speech is largely responsible for my presence here to-night. I should dishonor myself if I betrayed that confidence by uttering one insincere word, or by withholding one essential element of the truth. Apropos of this last, let me confess, Mr. President, before the praise of New England has died on my lips, that I believe the best product of her present life is the procession of seventeen thousand Vermont Democrats that for twenty-two years, undiminished by death, unrecruited by birth or conversion, have marched over their rugged hills, cast their Democratic ballots and gone back home to pray for their unregenerate neighbors, and awake to read the record of twenty-six thousand Republican majority. May the God of the helpless and the heroic help them, and may their sturdy tribe increase.

Far to the South, Mr. President, separated from this section by a line — once defined in irrepressible difference, once traced in fratricidal blood, and now, thank God, but a vanishing shadow — lies the fairest and richest domain of this earth. It is the home of a brave and hospitable people. There is centered all that can please or prosper humankind. A perfect climate above a fertile soil yields to the husbandman every product of the temperate zone. There, by night the cotton whitens beneath the stars, and by day the wheat locks the sunshine in its bearded sheaf. In the same field the clover steals the fragrance of the wind, and tobacco catches the quick aroma of the rains. There are mountains stored with exhaustless treasures; forests — vast and primeval; and rivers that, tumbling or loitering, run wanton to the sea. Of the three essential items of all industries — cotton, iron and wood — that region has easy control. In cotton, a fixed monopoly — in iron, proven supremacy — in timber, the reserve supply of the Republic. From this assured and permanent advantage, against which artificial conditions cannot much longer prevail, has grown an amazing system of industries. Not maintained by human contrivance of tariff or capital, afar off from the fullest and cheapest source of supply, but resting in divine assurance, within touch of field and mine and forest — not set amid costly farms from which competition has driven the farmer in despair, but amid cheap and sunny lands, rich with agriculture, to which neither season nor soil has set a limit — this system of industries is mounting to a splendor that shall dazzle and illumine the world. That, sir, is the picture and the promise of my home — a land better and fairer than I have told you, and yet but fit setting in its material excellence for the loyal and gentle quality of its citizenship. Against that, sir, we have New England recruiting the Republic from its sturdy loins, shaking from its overcrowded hives new swarms of workers, and touching this land all over with its energy and its courage. And yet — while in the Eldorado of which I have told you but fifteen per cent of its lands are cultivated, its mines scarcely touched, and its population so scant that, were it set equidistant, the sound of the human voice could not be heard from Virginia to Texas — while on the threshold of nearly every house in New England stands a son, seeking, with troubled eyes, some new land in which to carry his modest patrimony, the strange fact remains that in 1880 the South had fewer northern-born citizens than she had in 1870 — fewer in '70 than in '60. Why is this? Why is it, sir, though the section line be now but a mist that the breath may dispel, fewer men of the North have crossed it over to the South, than when it was crimson with the best blood of the Republic, or even when the slaveholder stood guard every inch of its way?

There can be but one answer. It is the very problem we are now to consider. The key that opens that problem will unlock to the world the fairest half of this Republic, and free the halted feet of thousands whose eyes are already kindling with its beauty. Better than this, it will open the hearts of brothers for thirty years estranged, and clasp in lasting comradeship a million hands now withheld in doubt. Nothing, sir, but this problem and the suspicions it breeds, hinders a clear understanding and a perfect union. Nothing else stands between us and such love as bound Georgia and Massachusetts at Valley Forge and Yorktown, chastened by the sacrifices of Manassas and Gettysburg, and illumined with the coming of better work and a nobler destiny than was ever wrought with the sword or sought at the cannon's mouth.

If this does not invite your patient hearing to-night — hear one thing more. My people, your brothers in the South — brothers in blood, in destiny, in all that is best in our past and future — are so beset with this problem that their very existence depends on its right solution. Nor are they wholly to blame for its presence. The slave-ships of the Republic sailed from your ports, the slaves worked in our fields. You will not defend the traffic, nor I the institution. But I do here declare that in its wise and humane administration in lifting the slave to heights of which he had not dreamed in his savage home, and giving him a happiness he has not yet found in freedom, our fathers left their sons a saving and excellent heritage. In the storm of war this institution was lost. I thank God as heartily as you do that human slavery is gone forever from American soil. But the free man remains. With him, a problem without precedent or parallel. Note its appalling conditions. Two utterly dissimilar races on the same soil — with equal political and civil rights — almost equal in numbers, but terribly unequal in intelligence and responsibility — each pledged against fusion — one for a century in servitude to the other, and freed at last by a desolating war, the experiment sought by neither but approached by both with doubt — these are the conditions. Under these, adverse at every point, we are required to carry these two races in peace and honor to the end.

Never, sir, has such a task been given to mortal stewardship. Never before in this Republic has the white race divided on the rights of an alien race. The red man was cut down as a weed because he hindered the way of the American citizen. The yellow man was shut out of this Republic because he is an alien, and inferior. The red man was owner of the land — the yellow man was highly civilized and assimilable — but they hindered both sections and are gone! But the black man, affecting but one section, is clothed with every privilege of government and pinned to the soil, and my people commanded to make good at any hazard, and at any cost, his full and equal heirship of American privilege and prosperity. It matters not that every other race has been routed or excluded without rime or reason. It matters not that wherever the whites and the blacks have touched, in any era or in any clime, there has been an irreconcilable violence. It matters not that no two races, however similar, have lived anywhere, at any time, on the same soil with equal rights in peace! In spite of these things we are commanded to make good this change of American policy which has not perhaps changed American prejudice — to make certain here what has elsewhere been impossible between whites and blacks — and to reverse, under the very worst conditions, the universal verdict of racial history. And driven, sir, to this superhuman task with an impatience that brooks no delay — a rigor that accepts no excuse — and a suspicion that discourages frankness and sincerity. We do not shrink from this trial. It is so interwoven with our industrial fabric that we cannot disentangle it if we would — so bound up in our honorable obligation to the world, that we would not if we could. Can we solve it? The God who gave it into our hands, He alone can know. But this the weakest and wisest of us do know: we cannot solve it with less than your tolerant and patient sympathy — with less than the knowledge that the blood that runs in your veins is our blood — and that, when we have done our best, whether the issue be lost or won, we shall feel your strong arms about us and hear the beating of your approving hearts!

The resolute, clear-headed, broad-minded men of the South — the men whose genius made glorious every page of the first seventy years of American history — whose courage and fortitude you tested in five years of the fiercest war — whose energy has made bricks without straw and spread splendor amid the ashes of their war-wasted homes — these men wear this problem in their hearts and brains, by day and by night. They realize, as you cannot, what this problem means — what they owe to this kindly and dependent race — the measure of their debt to the world in whose despite they defended and maintained slavery. And though their feet are hindered in its undergrowth, and their march cumbered with its burdens, they have lost neither the patience from which comes clearness, nor the faith from which comes courage. Nor, sir, when in passionate moments is disclosed to them that vague and awful shadow, with its lurid abysses and its crimson stains, into which I pray God they may never go, are they struck with more of apprehension than is needed to complete their consecration!

Such is the temper of my people. But what of the problem itself? Mr. President, we need not go one step further unless you concede right here that the people I speak for are as honest, as sensible and as just as your people, seeking as earnestly as you would in their place to rightly solve the problem that touches them at every vital point. If you insist that they are ruffians, blindly striving with bludgeon and shotgun to plunder and oppress a race, then I shall sacrifice my self-respect and tax your patience in vain. But admit that they are men of common sense and common honesty, wisely modifying an environment they cannot wholly disregard — guiding and controlling as best they can the vicious and irresponsible of either race — compensating error with frankness, and retrieving in patience what they lost in passion — and conscious all the time that wrong means ruin — admit this, and we may reach an understanding to-night.

The President of the United States, in his late message to Congress, discussing the plea that the South should be left to solve this problem, asks: "Are they at work upon it? What solution do they offer? When will the black man cast a free ballot? When will he have the civil rights that are his?" I shall not here protest against a partizanry that, for the first time in our history, in time of peace, has stamped with the great seal of our government a stigma upon the people of a great and loyal section; though I gratefully remember that the great dead soldier, who held the helm of State for the eight stormiest years of reconstruction, never found need for such a step; and though there is no personal sacrifice I would not make to remove this cruel and unjust imputation on my people from the archives of my country! But, sir, backed by a record, on every page of which is progress, I venture to make earnest and respectful answer to the questions that are asked. We give to the world this year a crop of 7,500,000 bales of cotton, worth $450,000,000, and its cash equivalent in grain, grasses and fruit. This enormous crop could not have come from the hands of sullen and discontented labor. It comes from peaceful fields, in which laughter and gossip rise above the hum of industry, and contentment runs with the singing plow. It is claimed that this ignorant labor is defrauded of its just hire. I present the tax books of Georgia, which show that the negro, twenty-five years ago a slave, has in Georgia alone $10,000,000 of assessed property, worth twice that much. Does not that record honor him and vindicate his neighbors?

What people, penniless, illiterate, has done so well? For every Afro-American agitator, stirring the strife in which alone he prospers, I can show you a thousand negroes, happy in their cabin homes, tilling their own land by day, and at night taking from the lips of their children the helpful message their State sends them from the schoolhouse door. And the schoolhouse itself bears testimony. In Georgia we added last year $250,000 to the school fund, making a total of more than $1,000,000 — and this in the face of prejudice not yet conquered — of the fact that the whites are assessed for $368,000,000, the blacks for $10,000,000, and yet forty-nine per cent. of the beneficiaries are black children; and in the doubt of many wise men if education helps, or can help, our problem. Charleston, with her taxable values cut half in two since 1860, pays more in proportion for public schools than Boston. Although it is easier to give much out of much than little out of little, the South, with one-seventh of the the taxable property of the country, with relatively larger debt, having received only one-twelfth as much of public lands, and having back of its tax books none of the $500,000,000 of bonds that enrich the North — and though it pays annually $26,000,000 to your section as pensions — yet gives nearly one-sixth to the public school fund. The South since 1865 has spent $122,000,000 in education, and this year is pledged to $32,000,000 more for State and city schools, although the blacks, paying one-thirtieth of the taxes, get nearly one-half of the fund. Go into our fields and see whites and blacks working side by side. On our buildings in the same squad. In our shops at the same forge. Often the blacks crowd the whites from work, or lower wages by their greater need and simpler habits, and yet are permitted, because we want to bar them from no avenue in which their feet are fitted to tread. They could not there be elected orators of white universities, as they have been here, but they do enter there a hundred useful trades that are closed against them here. We hold it better and wiser to tend the weeds in the garden than to water the exotic in the window.

In the South there are negro lawyers, teachers, editors, dentists, doctors, preachers, multiplying with the increasing ability of their race to support them. In villages and towns they have their military companies equipped from the armories of the State, their churches and societies built and supported largely by their neighbors. What is the testimony of the courts? In penal legislation we have steadily reduced felonies to misdemeanors, and have led the world in mitigating punishment for crime, that we might save, as far as possible, this dependent race from its own weakness. In our penitentiary record sixty per cent. of the prosecutors are negroes, and in every court the negro criminal strikes the colored juror, that white men may judge his case.

In the North, one negro in every 185 is in jail — in the South, only one in 446. In the North the percentage of negro prisoners is six times as great as that of native whites; in the South, only four times as great. If prejudice wrongs him in Southern courts, the record shows it to be deeper in Northern courts. I assert here, and a bar as intelligent and upright as the bar of Massachusetts will solemnly indorse my assertion, that in the Southern courts, from highest to lowest, pleading for life, liberty or property, the negro has distinct advantage because he is a negro, apt to be overreached, oppressed — and that this advantage reaches from the juror in making his verdict to the judge in measuring his sentence.

Now, Mr. President, can it be seriously maintained that we are terrorizing the people from whose willing hands comes every year $1,000,000,000 of farm crops? Or have robbed a people who, twenty-five years from unrewarded slavery, have amassed in one State $20,000,000 of property? Or that we intend to oppress the people we are arming every day? Or deceive them, when we are educating them to the utmost limit of our ability? Or outlaw them, when we work side by side with them? Or reënslave them under legal forms, when for their benefit we have even imprudently narrowed the limit of felonies and mitigated the severity of law? My fellow-countrymen, as you yourselves may sometimes have to appeal at the bar of human judgment for justice and for right, give to my people to-night the fair and unanswerable conclusion of these incontestable facts.

But it is claimed that under this fair seeming there is disorder and violence. This I admit. And there will be until there is one ideal community on earth after which we may pattern. But how widely is it misjudged? It is hard to measure with exactness whatever touches the negro. His helplessness, his isolation, his century of servitude, — these dispose us to emphasize and magnify his wrongs. This disposition, inflamed by prejudice and partizanry, has led to injustice and delusion. Lawless men may ravage a county in Iowa and it is accepted as an incident — in the South, a drunken row is declared to be the fixed habit of the community. Regulators may whip vagabonds in Indiana by platoons and it scarcely arrests attention — a chance collision in the South among relatively the same classes is gravely accepted as evidence that one race is destroying the other. We might as well claim that the Union was ungrateful to the colored soldier who followed its flag because a Grand Army post in Connecticut closed its doors to a negro veteran as for you to give racial significance to every incident in the South, or to accept exceptional grounds as the rule of our society. I am not one of those who becloud American honor with the parade of the outrages of either section, and belie American character by declaring them to be significant and representative. I prefer to maintain that they are neither, and stand for nothing but the passion and sin of our poor fallen humanity. If society, like a machine, were no stronger than its weakest part, I should despair of both sections. But, knowing that society, sentient and responsible in every fiber, can mend and repair until the whole has the strength of the best, I despair of neither. These gentlemen who come with me here, knit into Georgia's busy life as they are, never saw, I dare assert, an outrage committed on a negro! And if they did, no one of you would be swifter to prevent or punish. It is through them, and the men and women who think with them — making nine-tenths of every Southern community — that these two races have been carried thus far with less of violence than would have been possible anywhere else on earth. And in their fairness and courage and steadfastness — more than in all the laws that can be passed, or all the bayonets that can be mustered — is the hope of our future.

When will the blacks cast a free ballot? When ignorance anywhere is not dominated by the will of the intelligent; when the laborer anywhere casts a vote unhindered by his boss; when the vote of the poor anywhere is not influenced by the power of the rich; when the strong and the steadfast do not everywhere control the suffrage of the weak and shiftless — then, and not till then, will the ballot of the negro be free. The white people of the South are banded, Mr. President, not in prejudice against the blacks — not in sectional estrangement— not in the hope of political dominion — but in a deep and abiding necessity. Here is this vast ignorant and purchasable vote — clannish, credulous, impulsive, and passionate — tempting every art of the demagogue, but insensible to the appeal of the statesman. Wrongly started, in that it was led into alienation from its neighbor and taught to rely on the protection of an outside force, it cannot be merged and lost in the two great parties through logical currents, for it lacks political conviction and even that information on which conviction must be based. It must remain a faction — strong enough in every community to control on the slightest division of the whites. Under that division it becomes the prey of the cunning and unscrupulous of both parties. Its credulity is imposed upon, its patience inflamed, its cupidity tempted, its impulses misdirected — and even its superstition made to play its part in a campaign in which every interest of society is jeopardized and every approach to the ballot-box debauched. It is against such campaigns as this — the folly and the bitterness and the danger of which every Southern community has drunk deeply — that the white people of the South are banded together. Just as you are in Massachusetts would be banded if 300,000 men, not one in a hundred able to read his ballot — banded in race instinct holding against you the memory of a century of slavery, taught by your late conquerors to distrust and oppose you, had already travestied legislation from your State House, and in every species of folly or villainy had wasted your substance and exhausted your credit.

But admitting the right of the whites to unite against this tremendous menace, we are challenged with the smallness of our vote. This has long been flippantly charged to be evidence and has now been solemnly and officially declared to be proof of political turpitude and baseness on our part. Let us see. Virginia — a state now under fierce assault for this alleged crime — cast in 1888 seventy-five per cent. of her vote; Massachusetts, the State in which I speak, sixty per cent. of her vote. Was it suppression in Virginia and natural causes in Massachusetts? Last month Virginia cast sixty-nine per cent. of her vote; and Massachusetts, fighting in every district, cast only forty-nine per cent. of hers. If Virginia is condemned because thirty-one per cent. of her vote was silent, how shall this State escape, in which fifty-one per cent. was dumb? Let us enlarge this comparison. The sixteen Southern States in '88 cast sixty-seven per cent. of their total vote — the six New England States but sixty-three per cent. of theirs. By what fair rule shall the stigma be put upon one section while the other escapes? A congressional election in New York last week, with the polling place in touch of every voter, brought out only 6,000 votes of 28,000 — and the lack of opposition is assigned as the natural cause. In a district in my State, in which an opposition speech has not been heard in ten years and the polling places are miles apart — under the unfair reasoning of which my section has been a constant victim — the small vote is charged to be proof of forcible suppression. In Virginia an average majority of 12,000, unless hopeless division of the minority, was raised to 42,000; in Iowa, in the same election, a majority of 32,000 was wiped out and an opposition majority of 8,000 was established. The change of 40,000 votes in Iowa is accepted as political revolution — in Virginia an increase of 30,000 on a safe majority is declared to be proof of political fraud.

It is deplorable, sir, that in both sections a larger percentage of the vote is not regularly cast. But more inexplicable that this should be so in New England than in the South. What invites the negro to the ballot-box? He knows that of all men it has promised him most and yielded him least. His first appeal to suffrage was the promise of "forty acres and a mule"; his second, the threat that Democratic success meant his reënslavement. Both have been proved false in his experience. He looked for a home, and he got the Freedman's Bank. He fought under promise of the loaf, and in victory was denied the crumbs. Discouraged and deceived, he has realized at last that his best friends are his neighbors with whom his lot is cast, and whose prosperity is bound up in his — and that he has gained nothing in politics to compensate the loss of their confidence and sympathy, that is at last his best and enduring hope. And so, without leaders or organization — and lacking the resolute heroism of my party friends in Vermont that make their hopeless march over the hills a high and inspiring pilgrimage — he shrewdly measures the occasional agitator, balances his little account with politics, touches up his mule, and jogs down the furrow, letting the mad world wag as it will!

The negro voter can never control in the South, and it would be well if partizans at the North would understand this. I have seen the white people of a State set about by black hosts until their fate seemed sealed. But, sir, some brave men, banding them together, would rise as Elisha rose in beleaguered Samaria, and, touching their eyes with faith, bid them look abroad to see the very air "filled with the chariots of Israel and the horsemen thereof." If there is any human force that cannot be withstood, it is the power of the banded intelligence and responsibility of a free community. Against it, numbers and corruption cannot prevail. It cannot be forbidden in the law, or divorced in force. It is the inalienable right of every free community — the just and righteous safeguard against an ignorant or corrupt suffrage. It is on this, sir, that we rely in the South. Not the cowardly menace of mask or shotgun, but the peaceful majesty of intelligence and responsibility, massed and unified for the protection of its homes and the preservation of its liberty. That, sir, is our reliance and our hope, and against it all the powers of earth shall not prevail. It is just as certain that Virginia would come back to the unchallenged control of her white race — that before the moral and material power of her people once more unified, opposition would crumble until its last desperate leader was left alone, vainly striving to rally his disordered hosts — as that night should fade in the kindling glory of the sun. You may pass force bills, but they will not avail. You may surrender your own liberties to federal election law; you may submit, in fear of a necessity that does not exist, that the very form of this govern‐ ment may be changed; you may invite federal interference with the New England town meeting, that has been for a hundred years the guarantee of local government in America — this old State which holds in its charter the boast that it "is a free and independ‐ ent commonwealth" — it may deliver its election machinery into the hands of the government it helped to create — but never, sir, will a single State of this Union, North or South, be delivered again to the control of an ignorant and inferior race. We wrested our state governments from negro supremacy when the Federal drum‐ beat rolled closer to the ballot-box, and Federal bayonets hedged it deeper about than will ever again be permitted in this free govern‐ ment. But, sir, though the cannon of this Republic thundered in every voting district in the South, we still should find in the mercy of God the means and the courage to prevent its reëstablishment.

I regret, sir, that my section, hindered with this problem, stands in seeming estrangement to the North. If, sir, any man will point out to me a path down which the white people of the South, divided, may walk in peace and honor, I will take that path, though I take it alone — for at its end, and nowhere else, I fear, is to be found the full prosperity of my section and the full restoration of this Union. But, sir, if the negro had not been enfranchised the South would have been divided and the Republic united. His enfranchisement — against which I enter no protest — holds the South united and compact. What solution, then, can we offer for the problem? Time alone can disclose it to us. We simply report progress, and ask your patience. If the problem be solved at all — and I firmly believe it will, though nowhere else has it been — it will be solved by the people most deeply bound in interest, most deeply pledged in honor to its solution. I had rather see my people render back this question rightly solved than to see them gather all the spoils over which faction has contended since Cataline conspired and Cæsar fought. Meantime we treat the negro fairly, measuring to him justice in the fullness the strong should give to the weak, and leading him in the steadfast ways of citizenship, that he may no longer be the prey of the unscrupulous and the sport of the thoughtless. We open to him every pursuit in which he can prosper, and seek to broaden his training and capacity. We seek to hold his confidence and friendship — and to pin him to the soil with ownership, that he may catch in the fire of his own hearthstone that sense of responsibility the shiftless can never know. And we gather him into that alliance of intelligence and responsibility that, though it now runs close to racial lines, welcomes the responsible and intelligent of any race. By this course, confirmed in our judgment, and justified in the progress already made, we hope to progress slowly but surely to the end.

The love we feel for that race, you cannot measure nor comprehend. As I attest it here, the spirit of my old black mammy, from her home up there, looks down to bless, and through the tumult of this night steals the sweet music of her croonings as thirty years ago she held me in her black arms and led me smiling to sleep. This scene vanishes as I speak, and I catch a vision of an old Southern home with its lofty pillars and its white pigeons fluttering down through the golden air. I see women with strained and anxious faces, and children alert yet helpless. I see night come down with its dangers and its apprehensions, and in a big homely room I feel on my tired head the touch of loving hands — now worn and wrinkled, but fairer to me yet than the hands of mortal woman, and stronger yet to lead me than the hands of mortal man — as they lay a mother's blessing there, while at her knees — the truest altar I yet have found — I thank God that she is safe in her sanctuary, because her slaves, sentinel in the silent cabin, or guard at her chamber door, puts a black man's loyalty between her and danger.

I catch another vision. The crisis of battle — a soldier, struck, staggering, fallen. I see a slave, scuffling through the smoke, winding his black arms about the fallen form, reckless of hurtling death — bending his trusty face to catch the words that tremble on the stricken lips, so wrestling meantime with agony that he would lay down his life in his master's stead. I see him by the weary bedside, ministering with uncomplaining patience, praying with all his humble heart that God will lift his master up, until death comes in mercy and in honor to still the soldier's agony and seal the soldier's life. I see him by the open grave — mute, motionless, uncovered, suffering for the death of him who in life fought against his freedom. I see him, when the mold is heaped and the great drama of his life is closed, turn away and with downcast eyes and uncertain step start out into new and strange fields, faltering, struggling, but moving on, until his shambling figure is lost in the light of this better and brighter day. And from the grave comes a voice, saying, "Follow him! put your arms about him in his need, even as he put his about me. Be his friend as he was mine." And out into this new world — strange to me as to him, dazzling, bewildering both — I follow! And may God forget my people — when they forget these!

Whatever the future may hold for them, whether they plod along in the servitude from which they have been listed since the Cyrenian was laid hold upon by the Roman soldiers, and made to bear the cross of the fainting Christ— whether they find homes again in Africa, and thus hasten the prophecy of the psalmist, who said, "And suddenly Ethiopia shall hold out her hands unto God" — whether forever dislocated and separate, they remain a weak people, beset by stronger, and exist, as the Turk, who lives in the jealousy rather than in the conscience of Europe — or whether in this miraculous Republic they break through the caste of twenty centuries and, belying universal history, reach the full stature of citizenship, and in peace maintain it — we shall give them uttermost justice and abiding friendship. And whatever we do, into whatever seeming estrangement we may be driven, nothing shall disturb the love we bear this Republic, or mitigate our consecration to its service. I stand here, Mr. President, to profess no new loyalty. When General Lee, whose heart was the temple of our hopes, and whose arm was clothed with our strength, renewed his allegiance to this Government at Appomattox, he spoke from a heart too great to be false, and he spoke for every honest man from Maryland to Texas. From that day to this Hamilcar has nowhere in the South sworn young Hannibal to hatred and vengeance, but everywhere to loyalty and to love. Witness the veteran standing at the base of a Confederate monument, above the graves of his comrades, his empty sleeve tossing in the April wind, adjuring the young men about him to serve as earnest and loyal citizens the Government against which their fathers fought. This message, delivered from that sacred presence, has gone home to the hearts of my fellows! And, sir, I declare here, if physical courage be always equal to human aspiration, that they would die, sir, if need be, to restore this Republic their fathers fought to dissolve.

Such, Mr. President, is this problem as we see it, such is the temper in which we approach it, such the progress made. What do we ask of you? First, patience; out of this alone can come perfect work. Second, confidence; in this alone can you judge fairly. Third, sympathy; in this you can help us best. Fourth, give us your sons as hostages. When you plant your capital in millions, send your sons that they may know how true are our hearts and may help to swell the Caucasian current until it can carry with danger this black infusion. Fifth, loyalty to the Republic — for there is sectionalism in loyalty as in estrangement. This hour little needs the loyalty that is loyal to one section and yet holds the other in enduring suspicion and estrangement. Give us the broad and perfect loyalty that loves and trusts Georgia alike with Massachusetts — that knows no South, no North, no East, no West, but endears with equal and patriotic love every foot of our soil, every State of our Union.

A mighty duty, sir, and a mighty inspiration impels everyone of us to-night to lose in patriotic consecration whatever estranges, whatever divides. We, sir, are Americans — and we stand for human liberty! The uplifting force of the American idea is under every throne on earth. France, Brazil — these are our victories. To redeem the earth from king-craft and oppression — this is our mission! And we shall not fail. God has sown in our soil the seed of His millennial harvest, and He will not lay the sickle to the ripening crop until His full and perfect day has come. Our history, sir, has been a constant and expanding miracle, from Plymouth Rock and Jamestown, all the way — aye, even from the hour when from the voiceless and traceless ocean a new world rose to the sight of the inspired sailor. As we approach the fourth centennial of that stupendous day — when the old world will come to marvel and to learn amid our gathering treasures — let us resolve to crown the miracles of our past with the spectacle of a Republic, compact, united, indissoluble in the bonds of love — loving from the Lakes to the Gulf — the wounds of war healed in every heart as on every hill, serene and resplendent at the summit of human achievement and earthly glory, blazing out the path and making clear the way up which all the nations of the earth must come in God's appointed time!

PART TWO

The Dawn of the Twentieth Century: American Nationalism and Expansion

The decade immediately preceding and the one immediately following the dawn of the twentieth century combine to form an almost unbelievable period in American history. During this wild, unrestrained, turbulent era the United States surged from a second-rate to a first-rate power. This country's explosive economic and industrial expansion amounted, in the opinion of some, to a revolution. In international affairs, the United States became a young and sometimes rash world power. It attracted the persecuted and the downtrodden to its shores, and the population grew rapidly with a complex mixture of nationalities. This sudden emergence of a modern and powerful America brought with it serious economic, social, and governmental problems. The controversies were violent, and no matter what their nature, the stronger man won and the weaker man lost. It was not a time when human kindness and lofty moral standards directed human behavior.

It was against this background of chaotic growth and vehement controversy that some of our greatest speakers met the challenge of their time. This was the era which marked the eloquence of

Theodore Roosevelt, William Jennings Bryan, Albert J. Beveridge, Carl Schurz, Robert Ingersoll, George Frisbie Hoar, Jonathan P. Dolliver, Joseph B. Foraker, Joseph H. Choate, William Bourke Cockran, Chauncey M. Depew, and others equally distinguished. In this era, too, began the early careers of Robert M. LaFollette, Henry Cabot Lodge, William Howard Taft, William E. Borah, Charles Evans Hughes, and others who were to become famous in American history.

The phenomenal economic growth of the period sprang from factors too numerous and complex to be detailed here. But the following are among the more obvious of the principal contributing causes. New processes were discovered for the mining and processing of iron and copper; as a result, huge industries grew up throughout the country. The first automobile show was held in 1900, and in a few short years the Model T was in mass production. The air-brake and other inventions built nation-wide railroad systems. The electric light came into general use. Meat-packing became a mass production industry.

With this economic revolution came many abuses — many of which were economic, others social. The rich man swallowed up the poor man. The big corporation swallowed up the little one. The natural resources of the country — forests, oil, iron, and copper — were pillaged. Wealth concentrated in industrial areas, and the agricultural sections suffered. Industrial, racial, and social violence was rampant.

From such backgrounds came the speeches of the period. Never has there been such a diversity of issues. Seldom has there been such violent argument.

One of the paramount issues of the time was the controversy on whether or not the silver standard should supplant the gold standard as the basis of our currency. Wealth had settled in the

175

industrial East, and poverty had settled in the agricultural West. As a cure for his ills the farmer urged the free coinage of silver. Rarely has a problem brought forth greater eloquence. William Jennings Bryan led the fight for the free coinage of silver. Supporting him were such orators as Senators John W. Daniel of Virginia, Ben Tillman of South Carolina, Henry M. Teller of Colorado, and Governor John P. Altgeld of Illinois. Against Bryan and his supporters were arrayed such stalwarts as Robert G. Ingersoll, William Bourke Cockran, and Carl Schurz. Three of these speeches, all given in 1896, have become a definite part of the literature of the period. In rather quick succession came Bryan's "Cross of Gold Speech," Cockran's "Answering Mr. Bryan," and Ingersoll's "Chicago and New York Gold Speech." The speeches of Bryan and Ingersoll are printed in this section.

Also illustrative of the controversies of the time was the debate on the Pure Food and Drug Act in 1905. The act was introduced in the Senate in December by Senator W. B. Heybrun of Idaho at the request of President Theodore Roosevelt. The bill aimed to protect the public from alarming health conditions arising from contaminated food and dangerous patent medicines. Republican leaders who represented big business tried to defeat the bill. Senator Nelson W. Aldrich, Republican from Rhode Island, contended that the act put the "liberty of the people in jeopardy." Senator J. C. Spooner of Wisconsin and Senator Orville H. Platt of Connecticut made the same contention. But Senator Porter J. McComber replied "that a man may determine for himself what he will eat and what he will not eat." Great pressure for passage of the act came from powerful newspapers who were shocked by Upton Sinclair's description of conditions in the meat-packing industry in his book, The Jungle. Finally, on February 15, 1906, all opposition collapsed and the act was passed.

Other stirring arguments on important issues concerned the protective tariff, anti-trust regulation, the income tax, labor laws, conservation of natural resources, railroad legislation, laws to curb crime, health and personal safety legislation. These and many other such topics furnished dramatic speech occasions in Congress and on the public platform. Typical of such speech situations is Theodore Roosevelt's "The Man with the Muck Rake," offered in this collection.

This, too, was the era of American imperialism: the acquisition of Hawaii, the Philippines, Cuba, Puerto Rico, and other far-flung possessions; the beginning of work on the Panama Canal; the reaffirmation of the Monroe Doctrine; and the dispatch of the American fleet around the world in a show of power. Many political leaders cheered this rapid ascendancy to world power; many looked upon it as a national calamity. Throughout this debate over imperialism, Roosevelt, Lodge, Beveridge, and Foraker — the pro-imperialists — matched their talents against such protagonists as Bryan, Schurz, and Hoar.

The intensity and richness of the eloquence of the period can perhaps best be related by listing a few of the speeches that were delivered in the year 1899. On February 15 Beveridge made a great pro-imperialist speech in Philadelphia entitled "The Republic That Never Retreats." Bryan presented an anti-imperialist speech in reply in Washington on February 22 entitled "America's Mission." Roosevelt in turn answered Bryan's speech with an address in Chicago on April 10 called "The Strenuous Life." Carl Schurz responded with an anti-imperialist speech in Chicago on October 17 on the topic, "The Policy of Imperialism." Representative of this period of imperialism, this section offers Beveridge's "The Star of Empire, or America a World Republic" and Schurz's "The Policy of Imperialism."

The dawn of the twentieth century brought many critical issues, and it produced some of the best speakers in our history. It is regrettable that only a few of the speeches of this interesting period can be given in this book.

WILLIAM JENNINGS BRYAN

(1860-1925)

No speaker in American history ever spoke face to face to so many people as did William Jennings Bryan. Probably no man was ever more eloquent. His name actually was synonymous with platform skill. During half a century thousands of men with quaking knees have prefaced incoherent speech efforts by saying, "Well, I am no William Jennings Bryan."

Bryan was a colorful and controversial figure in American political life for a quarter of a century. Three times he was the defeated Democratic candidate for President of the United States, and he was Secretary of State for a short time in the cabinet of Woodrow Wilson. Born in Salem, Illinois, and graduated from Illinois College and Union College of Law, he practiced law in Lincoln, Nebraska, for a few years and began his public career with his election to Congress. The causes which he espoused and the vigor with which he spoke for them won him many enthusiastic followers and brought him as well many bitter opponents. Some of the explosive causes Bryan championed were the free coinage of silver, sweeping anti-trust legislation, national prohibition, and a graduated federal income tax. He vehemently denounced American imperialism and military preparedness, and because of his belief that the United States should maintain "peace at any price," he resigned from the Wilson cabinet.

The sources of Bryan's great speaking ability cannot be reviewed adequately in the short space available for a brief evaluation. However, a few reasons for his power should be pointed out. In the first place, he presented a fine physical appearance — he was large of stature, graceful, and impressive. His head was massive, and his features were sharply chiseled and handsome; his eyes flashed when he spoke. Certainly his platform power was no accident. As the New York Sun for July 10, 1896, observed, "Mr. Bryan is a smooth-faced man of early middle life and his dark hair is long and wavy. . . . His rhetoric and English and his oratorical gestures were almost superb. . . ."

Another source of power was his rich, resonant voice that had a range capable of every delicate inflection. So clearly and forcefully did he speak that he could be heard distinctly by everyone in his audience in the largest halls and in the sprawling expanses of open air meetings. Mark Sullivan said in Our Times:

> This account of Bryan's "Cross of Gold" speech fails to give adequate emphasis to his voice. Ex-Senator Thomas of Colorado speaks of it as "glorious," and the use of that word means much from a man who is austerely intellectual on all subjects, and as to Bryan is even a little cynical. It was not merely that Bryan's was the first voice that day to be able to fill the big hall. The music of it was memorable. Years afterward, men who were there talked of Bryan's speech in ways that showed it was a high spot in their emotional experiences. It was as an emotional experience that it was remembered, like hearing Patti or Jenny Lind. Ex-Senator Thomas says that Bryan brought tears to the eyes of men and caused women in the gallery to become hysterical.[1]

While Bryan was endowed by nature with an excellent voice and an imposing physique, for many years he studied how to use his powers most effectively. He rehearsed many of his speeches down to their smallest details. No one can deny that he used his speech faculties with consummate skill.

Finally, he was the master of language. He used words that were instantly comprehensible to his audience, and the thought pattern was simple. He had, furthermore, a gift for the colorful word and the apt figure of speech. Because the ordinary man loved him for his charm and his speaking, he was affectionately known as the "Great Commoner."

One criticism frequently leveled at Bryan was that he offered little factual evidence and argument in his speeches. His critics pointed to this characteristic in his speaking as proof of his shallowness and unreliability. His supporters, on the other hand, said he preferred to give his audiences sound conclusions rather than

[1] I, 124-25, published by Charles Scribner's Sons.

argumentative details. Wilson John Abbot, writing in the Review of Reviews for August, 1896, said:

> Personal observation of the man justifies the assertion that he is a deep student of the economic issues involved in political contests in the United States, but study of his speeches must convince his closest friends that he seldom employs the information he has dug out. Doubtless this is done from shrewd calculation. To the average audience in a political campaign a conclusion, stated in picturesque phrase, supported by apt illustration and urged with flowery or with impassioned rhetoric, appeals with far more force than the most concise and clear statement of the processes by which that conclusion has been obtained.[2]

The "Cross of Gold" speech was William Jennings Bryan's most famous speech. Never in the history of American public address was the maxim that true eloquence must exist in the man, in the subject, and in the occasion so dramatically demonstrated as in this speech which has become one of the most startling platform events within the memory of contemporary political observers.

The occasion was the Democratic National Convention meeting in Chicago on July 9, 1896. The subject was the plank in the party platform proposing a coinage of silver. The man was William Jennings Bryan, who had been selected to conclude the debate. The story is told vividly by Harry Thurston Peck in his Twenty Years of the Republic:

> Until now there had spoken no man, to whom that riotous assembly would listen with respect. But at this moment there appeared upon the platform Mr. William Jennings Bryan, of Nebraska. . . . As he confronted the 20,000 yelling, cursing, shouting men before him, they felt at once that indescribable, magnetic thrill which beasts and men alike experience in the presence of a master. Serene and self-possessed, and with a smile upon his lips, he faced the roaring multitude with a splendid consciousness of power. Before a single word had been uttered by him, the pandemonium sank to an inarticulate murmur, and when he began to speak, even this was hushed to the profoundest silence. A mellow, penetrating voice, that reached, apparently without the slightest effort, to the farthermost recesses of that enormous hall, gave utterance to a brief exordium. . . . The repose and graceful dignity of his manner, the

[2] P. 171.

courteous reference to his opponents, and the perfect clearness and simplicity of his language, riveted the attention of every man and woman in the convention hall. . . . He spoke with the utmost deliberation, so that every word was driven home to each hearer's consciousness and yet with an ever-increasing force, which found fit expression in the wonderful harmony and power of his voice. His sentences rang out, now with an accent of superb disdain, and now with the stirring challenge of a bugle call. . . . The great hall seemed to rock and sway with the fierce energy of the shout that ascended from twenty thousand throats. . . . The leaderless Democracy of the West was leaderless no more. Throughout the latter part of his address, a crash of applause had followed every sentence; but now the tumult was like that of a great sea thundering against the dikes. Twenty thousand men and women went mad with an irresistible enthusiasm. This orator had met their mood to the very full. He had found magic words for the feeling which they had been unable to express. And so he had played at will upon their very heart-strings, until the full tide of their emotion was let loose in one tempestuous roar of passion. . . .[3]

William Allen White, one of the outstanding journalists of the time, was critical of the speech and did not share Peck's enthusiasm. Although he fully recognized its amazing effectiveness, White thought the consequences were catastrophic. Writing in McClure's Magazine for July, 1900, he said:

No fluttering wings of doubt, that would have brushed by another man's eyes and made him stammer and hesitate in his climaxes, disturbed Bryan. His magnificent earnestness was hypnotic. Because he lost no force of his eloquence convincing himself, the weight of all his rhetoric, of his splendid magnetic presence, of his resonant voice, fell upon the delegates and filled them with the frenzy that has made every reckless mob of history. Bryan's supremacy in the Chicago Convention was as inevitable as Robespierre's in the Assembly. And he did even more than hypnotize the delegates. Through the nerves of the telegraph that speech thrilled a continent, and for a day a nation was in a state of mental and moral catalepsy.

If the election had been held that July day, Bryan would have been chosen President. Indeed, all his opponents did in the three

---

[3] Reprinted by permission of Dodd, Mead & Company from *Twenty Years of the Republic* by Harry Thurston Peck. Copyright 1906, 1934, by Constance Peck Beatty.

months following this speech was to arouse the people from their trance. It took much shaking up to break the spell, much marching of the patient up and down the land under torches and to martial music to revive him and restore him to his natural faculties. It is not fair, therefore, to say that the man who put the moral and mental faculties of the nation to sleep is not a strong man. He may not be particularly wise, for wisdom and oratorical strength are not inseparably allied.[4]

No matter what one's personal opinions may be about the ideas which were expressed and the speech methods employed, he will agree that the speech was one of the most dramatic in the history of American public address.

THE CROSS OF GOLD SPEECH

by

William Jennings Bryan

Delivered in Chicago at the Democratic Convention on July 9, 1896.

I WOULD BE presumptuous, indeed, to present myself against the distinguished gentlemen to whom you have listened if this were a mere measuring of abilities; but this is not a contest between persons. The humblest citizen in all the land, when clad in the armor of a righteous cause, is stronger than all the hosts of error. I come to speak to you in defense of a cause as holy as the cause of liberty — the cause of humanity.

When this debate is concluded, a motion will be made to lay upon the table the resolution offered in commendation of the administration, and also the resolution offered in condemnation of the administration. We object to bringing this question down to the level of persons. The individual is but an atom; he is born,

4 P. 234.

he acts, he dies; but principles are eternal; and this has been a contest over a principle.

Never before in the history of this country has there been witnessed such a contest as that through which we have just passed. Never before in the history of American politics has a great issue been fought out as this issue has been, by the voters of a great party. On the fourth of March, 1895, a few Democrats, most of them members of Congress, issued an address to the Democrats of the nation, asserting that the money question was the paramount issue of the hour; declaring that a majority of the Democratic party had the right to control the action of the party on this paramount issue; and concluding with the request that the believers in the free coinage of silver in the Democratic party should organize, take charge of, and control the policy of the Democratic party. Three months later, at Memphis, an organization was perfected, and the silver Democrats went forth openly and courageously proclaiming their belief, and declaring that, if successful, they would crystallize into a platform the declaration which they had made. Then began the conflict. With a zeal approaching the zeal which inspired the Crusaders who followed Peter the Hermit, our silver Democrats went forth from victory unto victory until they are now assembled, not to discuss, not to debate, but to enter up the judgement already rendered by the plain people of this country. In this contest brother has been arrayed against brother, father against son. The warmest ties of love, acquaintance and association have been disregarded; old leaders have been cast aside when they have refused to give expression to the sentiments of those whom they would lead, and new leaders have sprung up to give direction to this cause of truth. Thus has the contest been waged, and we have assembled here under as binding and solemn instructions as were ever imposed upon representatives of the people.

We do not come as individuals. As individuals we might have been glad to compliment the gentleman from New York [Senator Hill], but we know that the people for whom we speak would never be willing to put him in a position where he could thwart the will of the Democratic party. I say it was not a question of persons, it was a question of principle, and it is not with gladness, my friends, that we find ourselves brought into conflict with those who are now arrayed on the other side.

The gentleman who preceded me [ex-Governor Russell] spoke

of the State of Massachusetts; let me assure him that not one present in all this convention entertains the least hostility to the people of the State of Massachusetts, but we stand here representing the people who are the equals, before the law, of the greatest citizens in the State of Massachusetts. When you [*turning to the gold delegates*] come before us and tell us that we are about to disturb your business interests, we reply that you have disturbed our business interests by your course.

We say to you that you have made the definition of a business man too limited in its application. The man who is employed for wages is as much a business man as his employer, the attorney in a country town is as much a business man as the corporation counsel in a great metropolis; the merchant at the cross-roads store is as much a business man as the merchant of New York; the farmer who goes forth in the morning and toils all day — who begins in the spring and toils all summer — and who by the application of brain and muscle to the natural resources of the country creates wealth, is as much a business man as the man who goes upon the board of trade and bets upon the price of grain; the miners who go down a thousand feet into the earth, or climb two thousand feet upon the cliffs, and bring forth from their hiding places the precious metals to be poured into the channels of trade are as much business men as the few financial magnates who, in a back room, corner the money of the world. We come to speak for this broader class of business men.

Ah, my friends, we say not one word against those who live upon the Atlantic coast, but the hardy pioneers who have braved all the dangers of the wilderness, who have made the desert to blossom as the rose — the pioneers away out there [*pointing to the West*], who rear their children near to Nature's heart, where they can mingle their voices with the voices of the birds — out there where they have erected school houses for the education of their young, churches where they praise their Creator, and cemeteries where rest the ashes of their dead — these people, we say, are as deserving of the consideration of our party as any people in this country. It is for these that we speak. We do not come as aggressors. Our war is not a war of conquest; we are fighting in the defense of our homes, our families, and posterity. We have petitioned, and our petitions have been scorned; we have entreated, and our entreaties have been disregarded; we have begged, and they have mocked when our calamity came. We beg no longer; we petition no more. We defy them.

The gentleman from Wisconsin has said that he fears a Robespierre. My friends, in this land of the free you need not fear that a tyrant will spring up from among the people. What we need is an Andrew Jackson to stand, as Jackson stood, against the encroachments of organized wealth.

They tell us that this platform was made to catch votes. We reply to them that changing conditions make new issues, that the principles on which Democracy rests are as everlasting as the hills, but that they must be applied to new conditions as they arise. Conditions have arisen, and we are here to meet those conditions. They tell us that the income tax ought not be brought in here; that it is a new idea. They criticize us for our criticism of the Supreme Court of the United States. My friends, we have not criticized; we have simply called attention to what you already know. If you want criticisms, read the dissenting opinions of the court. There you will find criticisms. They say that we passed an unconstitutional law; we deny it. The income tax law was not unconstitutional when it was passed; it was not unconstitutional when it went before the Supreme Court for the first time; it did not become unconstitutional until one of the judges changed his mind, and we cannot be expected to know when a judge will change his mind. The income tax is just. It simply intends to put the burdens of government upon the backs of the people. I am in favor of an income tax. When I find a man who is not willing to bear his share of the burdens of the government which protects him, I find a man who is unworthy to enjoy the blessings of a government like ours.

They say that we are opposing national bank currency; it is true. If you will read what Thomas Benton said, you will find he said that, in searching history, he could find but one parallel to Andrew Jackson; that was Cicero, who destroyed the conspiracy of Cataline and saved Rome. Benton said that Cicero only did for Rome what Jackson did for us when he destroyed the bank conspiracy and saved America. We say in our platform that we believe that the right to coin and issue money is a function of government. We believe it. We believe that it is a part of sovereignty, and can no more with safety be delegated to private individuals than we could afford to delegate to private individuals the power to make penal statutes or levy taxes. Mr. Jefferson, who was once regarded as good Democratic authority, seems to have differed in opinion from the gentleman who has addrest us on the part of the minority. Those who are opposed to this proposition tell us that the issue of paper money is a function of the bank, and that the Government ought to go out of the banking business. I stand with Jefferson rather than with them, and tell them, as he did, that the issue of money is a function of government, and that banks ought to go out of the governing business.

They complain about the plank which declares against life tenure in office. They have tried to strain it to mean that which it does not mean. What we oppose by that plank is the life tenure which is being built up in Washington, and which excludes from participation in official benefits the humbler members of society.

Let me call your attention to two or three important things. The gentleman from New York says that he will propose an amendment to the platform providing that the proposed change in our monetary system shall not affect contracts already made. Let me remind you that there is no intention of affecting those contracts which according to present laws are made payable in gold; but if he means to say that we cannot change our monetary system without protecting those who have loaned money before the change was made, I desire to ask him where, in law or in morals, he can find justification for not protecting the debtors when the act of 1873 was passed, if he now insists that we must protect the creditors.

He says he will also propose an amendment which will provide for the suspension of free coinage if we fail to maintain the parity within a year. We reply that when we advocate a policy which we believe will be successful, we are not compelled to raise a doubt as to our own sincerity by suggesting what we shall do if we fail. I ask him, if he would apply his logic to us, why he does not apply it to himself. He says he wants this country to try to secure an international agreement. Why does he not tell us what he is going to do if he fails to secure an international agreement? There is more reason for him to do that than there is for us to provide against the failure to maintain the parity. Our opponents have tried for twenty years to secure an international agreement, and those are waiting for it most patiently who do not want it at all.

And now, my friends, let me come to the paramount issue. If

they ask us why it is that we say more on the money question than we say upon the tariff question, I reply that, if protection has slain its thousands, the gold standard has slain its tens of thousands. If they ask us why we do not embody in our platform all the things that we believe in, we reply that when we have restored the money of the Constitution all other necessary reforms will be possible; but that until this is done there is no other reform that can be accomplished.

Why is it that within three months such a change has come over the country? Three months ago, when it was confidently asserted that those who believe in the gold standard would frame our platform and nominate our candidate, even the advocates of the gold standard did not think that we could elect a President. And they had good reason for their doubt, because there is scarcely a State here today asking for the gold standard which is not in the absolute control of the Republican party. But note the change. Mr. McKinley was nominated at St. Louis upon a platform which declared for the maintenance of the gold standard until it can be changed into bimetalism by international agreement. Mr. McKinley was the most popular man among the Republicans, and three months ago everybody in the Republican party prophesied his election. How is it to-day? Why, the man who was once pleased to think that he looked like Napoleon — that man shudders to-day when he remembers that he was nominated on the anniversary of the battle of Waterloo. Not only that, but as he listens he can hear with ever-increasing distinctness the sounds of the waves as they beat upon the lonely shores of St. Helena.

Why this change? Ah, my friends, is not the reason for the change evident to any one who will look at the matter? No private character, however pure, no personal popularity, however great, can protect from the avenging wrath of an indignant people a man who will declare that he is in favor of fastening the gold standard upon this country, or who is willing to surrender the right of self-government and place the legislative control of our affairs in the hands of foreign potentates and powers.

We go forth confident that we shall win. Why? Because upon the paramount issue of this campaign there is not a spot of ground upon which the enemy will dare to challenge battle. If they tell us that the gold standard is a good thing, we shall point to their platform and tell them that their platform pledges the party to get rid of the gold standard and substitute bimetalism. If the gold standard is a good thing, why try to get rid of it? I call your attention to the fact that some of the very people who are in this convention to-day and who tell us that we ought to declare in favor of international bimetalism — thereby declaring that the gold standard is wrong and that the principle of bimetalism is better — these very people four months ago were open and avowed advocates of the gold standard, and were then telling us that we could not legislate two metals together, even with the aid of all the world. If the gold standard is a good thing, we ought to declare in favor of its retention and not in favor of abandoning it; and if the gold standard is a bad thing, why should we wait until other nations are willing to help us to let go? Here is the line of battle, and we care not upon which issue they force the fight; we are prepared to meet them on either issue or on both. If they tell us that the gold standard is the standard of civilization, we reply to them that this, the most enlightened of all the nations of the earth, has never declared for a gold standard and that both the great parties this year are declaring against it. If the gold standard is the standard of civilization, why, my friends, should we not have it? If they come to meet us on that issue we can present the history of our nation. More than that; we can tell them that they will search the pages of history in vain to find a single instance where the common people have ever declared themselves in favor of the gold standard. They can find where the holders of fixt investments have declared for a gold standard, but not where the masses have.

Mr. Carlisle said in 1878 that this was a struggle between "the idle holders of idle capital" and "the struggling masses, who produce the wealth and pay the taxes of the country"; and, my friends, the question we are to decide is: Upon which side will the Democratic party fight; upon the side of "the idle holders of idle capital" or upon the side of "the struggling masses"? That is the question which the party must answer first, and then it must be answered by each individual hereafter. The sympathies of the Democratic party, as shown by the platform, are on the side of the struggling masses who have ever been the foundation of the Democratic party. There are two ideas of government. There are those who believe that, if you will only legislate to make the well-to-do prosperous, their prosperity will leak through on those below. The

Democratic idea, however, that if you legislate to make the masses prosperous, their prosperity will find its way up through every class which rests upon them.

You come to us and tell us that the great cities are in favor of the gold standard; we reply that the great cities rest upon our broad and fertile prairies. Burn down your cities and leave our farms, and your cities will spring up again as if by magic; but destroy our farms and the grass will grow in the streets of every city in the country.

My friends, we declare that this nation is able to legislate for its own people on every question, without waiting for the aid or consent of any other nation on earth; and upon that issue we expect to carry every State in the Union. I shall not slander the inhabitants of the fair State of Massachusetts nor the inhabitants of the State of New York by saying that, when they are confronted with the proposition, they will declare that this nation is not able to attend to its own business. It is the issue of 1776 over again. Our ancestors, when but three millions in number, had the courage to declare their political independence of every other nation; shall we, their descendants, when we have grown to seventy millions, declare that we are less independent than our forefathers? No, my friends, that will never be the verdict of our people. Therefore we care not upon what lines the battle is fought. If they say bimetalism is good, but that we cannot have it until the other nations help us, we reply that, instead of having a gold standard because England has, we will restore bimetalism, and then let England have bimetalism because the United States has it. If they dare to come out in the open field and defend the gold standard as a good thing, we will fight them to the uttermost. Having behind us the producing masses of this nation and the world, supported by the commercial interests, the laboring interests, and the toilers everywhere, we will answer their demand for a gold standard by saying to them: You shall not press down upon the brow of labor this crown of thorns, you shall not crucify mankind upon a cross of gold.

ROBERT G. INGERSOLL

(1833-1899)

Called the world's greatest orator by Henry Ward Beecher, Robert G. Ingersoll as a speaker was both versatile and popular: a resourceful and inventive trial lawyer, a much sought-after political campaign speaker, a master hand at eulogy, and a highly successful public lecturer. His unusual power and influence as a speaker derive generally from three principal characteristics of the man. First of all, he was always terribly in earnest — he flatly refused to utter what he did not honestly subscribe to. He thus managed to convey a convincing impression of a man who firmly believed his cause to be a just one. In the second place, he possessed what Herman Kittredge, in his biography of Ingersoll, referred to as "that indefinable thing called presence." This matter of "presence" was the substance of an observation recorded by Hamlin Garland, who at the age of sixteen first heard Ingersoll deliver one of his famous lectures.

He came on the vast stage alone . . . a large man in evening dress, quite bald and smoothly shaven. He began to speak almost before he left the wings, addressing himself to us with colloquial, unaffected directness. . . . He appeared to be speaking to each one of us individually. His tone was confidential, friendly, and yet authoritative. . . . The stage was bare and he had no manuscript. Standing with his hands clasped behind his back, and speaking without effort, he made his words clear to every auditor. . . . I enjoyed the beauty of his phrasing and the almost unequaled magic of his voice. He was a master of colloquial speech. . . . He bantered us, challenged us, electrified us. At times his eloquence held us silent as images and then some witty turn, some humorous phrase, brought roars of applause. . . . His power over his auditors was absolute. . . . [1]

1 Roadside Meetings, pp. 44-45.

190

Finally, Ingersoll was a master of imagery and prose rhythm; Kittredge, in fact, refers to him as "the Michaelangelo of words." Ingersoll's vision at Napoleon's tomb related in his lecture on "The Liberty of Man, Woman, and Child" aptly illustrates his genius at constructing measured, rhythmical sentences aimed at evoking vivid mental images.

A little while ago, I stood by the grave of the old Napoleon — a magnificent tomb of gilt and gold, fit almost for a dead deity — and gazed upon the sarcophagus of rare and nameless marble, where rest at last the ashes of that restless man. . . .

I thought of the orphans and widows he had made — of the tears that had been shed for his glory, and of the only woman who ever loved him, pushed from his heart by the cold hand of ambition. And I said I would rather have been a French peasant and worn wooden shoes. I would rather have lived in a hut with a vine growing over the door, and the grapes growing purple in the kisses of the autumn sun. I would rather have been that poor peasant with my loving wife by my side, knitting as the day died out of the sky — with my children upon my knees and their arms about me — I would rather have been that man gone down to the tongueless silence of the dreamless dust, than to have been that imperial impersonation of force and murder, known as "Napoleon the Great."

Although perhaps best known for his lectures opposing orthodox religion, Ingersoll was highly regarded as a vigorous, colorful political orator. While devoting his energies to the Republican cause during the 1896 Presidential campaign, Colonel Ingersoll delivered his celebrated "Chicago and New York Gold Speech." On October 8 in Chicago he addressed a capacity crowd of some twenty thousand jammed into a huge tent set up near Sacramento Avenue and Lake Street. His sarcasm and wit were frequently directed at William Jennings Bryan, who was the Democratic nominee running against McKinley. Typical was his comment that Bryan's "brain was an insane asylum without a keeper." The Chicago Inter-Ocean of October 9 had this to say about the purpose and effect of the speech.

He came to the ground floor of human existence and talked as man to man. His patriotism, be it religion, sentiment, or that lofty spirit inseparable from man's soul, is his life. Last night he sought to inspire those who heard him with the same loyalty, and he succeeded.

Those passionate outbursts of eloquence, the wit that fairly scintillated, the logic as inexorable as heaven's decrees, his rich rhetoric and immutable facts driven straight to his hearers with the strength of bullets, aroused applause that came as spontaneous as sunlight.

Now eliciting laughter, now silence, now cheers, the great orator, with the singular charm of presence, manner and voice, swayed his immense audience at his own volition. Packed with potency was every sentence, each word a living thing, and with them he flayed financial heresy, laid bare the dire results of free trade, and exposed the dangers of Populism.

This same speech delivered in New York on October 29 was the last speech he intended to make in the campaign and, as it turned out, was the last political address that Ingersoll ever gave. The New York Tribune of October 30, 1896, provides a colorful description of the occasion.

The final rally of the McKinley League for the present campaign, was held last night in Carnegie Music Hall, and the orator chosen to present the doctrines of the Republican party was Robert G. Ingersoll. . . . The great hall was filled. . . . It was crowded from the rear of the stage to the last row of seats in the gallery. . . . The audience was a very fashionable and exclusive one, for admission was only to be had by ticket, and tickets were hard to get. . . . Flags hung from all the gallery rails, and the whole scheme of decoration was consistent and beautiful. At 8:30 o'clock Mr. John E. Milholland appeared upon the stage followed by Col. Ingersoll.

Without any delay Mr. Milholland was presented as the chairman of the meeting. He spoke briefly of the purpose of the party and then said: "There is no intelligent audience under the flag or in any civilized country to whom it would be necessary for me to introduce Robert G. Ingersoll." And the cheers with which the audience greeted the orator proved the truth of his words.

Col. Ingersoll rose impressively and advanced to the front of the stage, from which the speaker's desk had been removed in order to allow him full opportunity to indulge in his habit of walking to and fro as he talked. He was greeted with tremendous applause. . . . He was able to secure instant command of his audience, and while the applause was wildest, he waved his hand, and the gesture was followed by a silence that was oppressive. Still the speaker waited. He did not intend to waste any of his ammunition. Then, convinced that every eye was centered upon him, he spoke, declaring "this is our country." The assembly was his from that instant.

When Ingersoll finished his speech that evening, according to Cameron Rogers, "the thousands who had listened, in their eyes the fixed and stubborn expression of people who intend to shout until their vocal cords . . . force them to silence, cheered till they seemed hypnotized by their own voices."[2] Rogers believes that he made "perhaps the most effective political speech of his life."[3]

THE CHICAGO AND NEW YORK GOLD SPEECH

by

Robert G. Ingersoll

Delivered in Chicago in a special tent near Sacramento Avenue and Lake Street on October 8, 1896, and in New York in Carnegie Hall on October 29, 1896.

LADIES AND GENTLEMEN: This is our country. The legally expressed will of the majority is the supreme law of the land. We are responsible for what our Government does. We cannot excuse ourselves because of the act of some king, or the opinions of nobles. We are the kings. We are the nobles. We are the aristocracy of America, and when our Government does right we are honored, and when our Government does wrong the brand of shame is on the American brow.

Again we are on the field of battle, where thought contends with thought, the field of battle where facts are bullets and arguments are swords.

[2] *Colonel Bob Ingersoll*, p. 283.
[3] *Ibid.*

To-day there is in the United States a vast congress consisting of the people, and in that congress every man has a voice, and it is the duty of every man to inquire into all questions presented, to the end that he may vote as a man and as a patriot should.

No American should be dominated by prejudice. No man standing under our flag should follow after the fife and drum of a party. He should say to himself: "I am a free man, and I will discharge the obligations of an American citizen with all the intelligence I possess."

I love this country because the people are free; and if they are not free it is their own fault.

To-night I am not going to appeal to your prejudices, if you have any. I am going to talk to the sense that you have. I am going to address myself to your brain and to your heart. I want nothing of you except that you will preserve the institutions of the Republic; that you will maintain her honor unstained. That is all I ask.

I admit that all the parties who disagree with me are honest. Large masses of mankind are always honest, the leader not always, but the mass of people do what they believe to be right. Consequently there is no argument in abuse, nothing calculated to convince in calumny. To be kind, to be candid, is far nobler, far better, and far more American. We live in a Democracy, and we admit that every other human being has the same right to think, the same right to express his thought, the same right to vote that we have, and I want every one who hears me to vote in exact accord with his sense, to cast his vote in accordance with his conscience. I want every one to do the best he can for the great Republic, and no matter how he votes, if he is honest, I shall find no fault.

But the great thing is to understand what you are going to do; the great thing is to use the little sense that we have. In most of us the capital is small, and it ought to be turned often. We ought to pay attention, we ought to listen to what is said and then think, think for ourselves.

Several questions have been presented to the American people for their solution, and I propose to speak a little about those questions, and I do not want you to pretend to agree with me. I want no applause unless you honestly believe I am right.

Three great questions are presented: First, as to money; second, as to the tariff, and third, whether this Government has the right of self-defence. Whether this is a Government of law, or whether there shall be an appeal from the Supreme Court to a mob. These are the three questions to be answered next Tuesday by the American people.

First, let us take up this money question. Thousands and thousands of speeches have been made on the subject. Pamphlets thick as the leaves of autumn have been scattered from one end of the Republic to the other, all about money, as if it were an exceedingly metaphysical question, as though there were something magical about it.

What is money? Money is a product of nature. Money is a part of nature. Money is something that man cannot create. All the legislatures and congresses of the world cannot by any possibility create one dollar, any more than they could suspend the attraction of gravitation or hurl a new constellation into the concave sky. Money is not made. It has to be found. It is dug from the crevices of rocks, washed from the sands of streams, from the gravel of ancient valleys; but it is not made. It cannot be created. Money is something that does not have to be redeemed. Money is the redeemer. And yet we have a man running for the presidency on three platforms with two Vice-Presidents, who says that money is the creature of law. It may be that law sometimes is the creature of money, but money was never the creature of law.

A nation can no more create money by law than it can create corn and wheat and barley by law, and the promise to pay money is no nearer money than a warehouse receipt is grain, or a bill of fare is a dinner. If you can make money by law, why should any nation be poor?

The supply of law is practically unlimited. Suppose one hundred people should settle on an island, form a government, elect a legislature. They would have the power to make law, and if law can make money, if money is the creature of law, why should not these one hundred people on the island be as wealthy as Great Britain? What is to hinder? And yet we are told that money is the creature of law. In the financial world that is as absurd as perpetual motion in mechanics; it is as absurd as the fountain of eternal youth, the philosopher's stone, or the transmutation of metals.

What is a dollar? People imagine that a piece of paper with pictures on it, with signatures, is money. The greenback is not money — never was; never will be. It is a promise to pay money; not money. The note of the nation is no nearer money than the note of an individual. A bank note is not money. It is a promise to pay money; that is all.

Well, what is a dollar? In the civilized world it is twenty-three grains and twenty-two one hundredths of pure gold. That is a dollar. Well, cannot we make dollars out of silver? Yes, I admit it, but in order to make a silver dollar you have got to put a dollar's worth of silver in the silver dollar, and you have to put as much silver in it as you can buy for twenty-three grains and twenty-two one-hundredths of a grain of pure gold. It takes a dollar's worth of silver to make a dollar. It takes a dollar's worth of paper to make a paper dollar. It takes a dollar's worth of iron to make an iron dollar; and there is no way of making a dollar without the value.

And let me tell you another thing. You do not add to the value of gold by coining it any more than you add to the value of wheat by measuring it; any more than you add to the value of coal by weighing it. Why do you coin gold? Because every man cannot take a chemist's outfit with him. He cannot carry a crucible and retort, scales and acids, and so the Government coins it, simply to certify how much gold there is in the piece.

Ah, but, says this same gentleman, what gives our money — our silver — its value? It is because it is a legal tender, he says. Nonsense; nonsense. Gold was not given value by being made a legal tender, but being valuable it was made a legal tender. And gold gets no value to-day from being a legal tender. I not only say that, but I will prove it; and I will not only prove it, but I will demonstrate it. Take a twenty dollar gold piece, hammer it out of shape, mar the Goddess of Liberty, pound out the United States of America and batter the eagle, and after you get it pounded how much is it worth?

It is worth exactly twenty dollars. Is it a legal tender? No. Has its value been changed? No. Take a silver dollar. It is a legal tender; now pound it into a cube, and how much is it worth? A little less than fifty cents. What gives it the value of a dollar? The fact that it is a legal tender? No; but the promise of the Government to keep it on an equality with gold. I will not only say this, but I will demonstrate it. I do not ask you to take my word; just use the sense you have.

The Mexican silver dollar has a little more silver in it than one of our dollars, and the Mexican silver dollar is a legal tender in Mexico. If there is any magic about legal tender it ought to work as well in Mexico as in the United States. I take an American silver dollar and I go to Mexico. I buy a dinner for a dollar and I give to the Mexican the American dollar and he gives me a Mexican dollar in change. Yet both of the dollars are legal tender. Why is it that the Mexican dollar is worth only fifty cents? Because the Mexican Government has not agreed to keep it equal with gold; that is all, that is all.

We want the money of the civilized world, and I will tell you now that in the procession of nations every silver nation lags behind — every one. There is not a silver nation on the globe where decent wages are paid for human labor — not one. The American laborer gets ten times as much here in gold as a laborer gets in China in silver, twenty times as much as a laborer does in India, four times as much as a laborer gets in Russia; and yet we are told that the man who will "follow England" with the gold standard lacks patriotism and manhood. What then shall we say of the man that follows China, that follows India in the silver standard?

Does that require patriotism?

It certainly requires self-denial.

And yet these gentlemen say that our money is too good. They might as well say the air is too pure; they might as well say the soil is too rich. How can money be too good? Mr. Bryan says that it is so good, people hoard it; and let me tell him they always will. Mr. Bryan wants money so poor that everybody will be anxious to spend it. He wants money so poor that the rich will not have it. Then he thinks the poor can get it. We are willing to toil for good money. Good money means the comforts and luxuries of life. Real money is always good. Paper promises and silver substitutes may be poor; words and pictures may be cheap and may fade to worthlessness — but gold shines on.

In Chicago, many years ago, there was an old colored man at the Grand Pacific. I met him one morning, and he looked very sad, and I said to him, "Uncle, what is the matter?" "Well," he said, "my wife ran away last night. Pretty good looking woman; a good deal younger than I am; but she has run off." And he says: "Colonel, I want to give you my idea about marriage. If a man wants to marry a woman and have a good time, and be satisfied and secure in his mind, he wants to marry some woman that no other man on God's earth would have.",

That is the kind of money these gentlemen want in the United States. Cheap money. Do you know that the words cheap money are a contradiction in terms? Cheap money is always discounted when people find out that it is cheap. We want good money, and I do not care how much we get. But we want good money. Men are willing to toil for good money; willing to work in the mines; willing to work in the heat and glare of the furnace; willing to go to the top of the mast on the wild sea; willing to work in tenements; women are willing to sew with their eyes filled with tears for the sake of good money. And if anything is to be paid in good money, labor is that thing. If any man is entitled to pure gold, it is the man who labors. Let the big fellows take cheap money. Let the men living next the soil be paid in gold. But I want the money of this country as good as that of any other country. When our money is below par we feel below par. I want our money, no matter how it is payable, to have the gold behind it. That is the money I want in the United States.

I want to teach the people of the world that a Democracy is honest. I want to teach the people of the world that America is not only capable of self-government, but that it has the self-denial, the courage, the honor, to pay its debts to the last farthing.

Mr. Bryan tells the farmers who are in debt that they want cheap money. What for? To pay their debts. And he thinks that is a compliment to the tillers of the soil. The statement is an insult to the farmers, and the farmers of Maine and Vermont have answered him.

And if the farmers of those States with their soil can be honest, I think a farmer in Illinois has no excuse for being a rascal. I regard the farmers as honest men, and when the sun shines and the rains fall and the frosts wait, they will pay their debts. They are good men, and I want to tell you to-night that all the stories that have been told about farmers being Populists are not true.

You will find the Populists in the towns, in the great cities, in the villages. All the failures, no matter for what reason, are on the Populist's side. They want to get rich by law. They are tired of work.

And yet Mr. Bryan says vote for cheap money so that you can

pay your debts in fifty cent dollars. Will an honest man do it?

Suppose a man has borrowed a thousand bushels of wheat of his neighbor, of sixty pounds to the bushel, and then Congress should pass a law making thirty pounds of wheat a bushel. Would that farmer pay his debt with five hundred bushels and consider himself an honest man?

Mr. Bryan says, "Vote for cheap money to pay your debts," and thereupon the creditor says, "What is to become of me?" Mr. Bryan says, "We will make it one dollar and twenty-nine cents an ounce, and make it of the ratio of sixteen to one, make it as good as gold." And thereupon the poor debtor says, "How is that going to help me?" And in nearly all the speeches that this man has made he has taken the two positions, first, that we want cheap money to pay debts, and second, that the money would be just as good as gold for creditors.

Now, the question is: Can Congress make fifty cents' worth of silver worth one dollar? That is the question, and if Congress can, then I oppose the scheme on account of its extravagance. What is the use of wasting all that silver? Think about it. If Congress can make fifty cents' worth of silver worth a dollar by law, why can it not make one cent's worth of silver worth a dollar by law. Let us save the silver and use it for forks and spoons. The supply even of silver is limited — the supply of law is inexhaustible. Do not waste silver, use more law. You cannot fix values by law any more than you can make cooler summers by shortening thermometers.

There is another trouble. If Congress, by the free coinage of silver, can double its value, why should we allow an Englishman with a million dollars' worth of silver bullion at the market price, to bring it to America, have it coined free of charge, and make it exactly double the value? Why should we put a million dollars in his pocket? That is too generous. Why not buy the silver from him in the open market and let the Government make the million dollars? Nothing is more absurd; nothing is more idiotic. I admit that Mr. Bryan is honest. I admit it. If he were not honest his intellectual pride would not allow him to make these statements.

Well, another thing says our friend, "Gold has been cornered"; and thousands of people believe it. You have no idea of the credulity of some folks. I say that it has not been cornered, and I will not only prove it, I will demonstrate it. Whenever the Stock

Exchange or some of the members have a corner on stocks, that stock goes up, and if it does not, that corner bursts. Whenever gentlemen in Chicago get up a corner on wheat in the Produce Exchange, wheat goes up or the corner bursts. And yet they tell me there has been a corner in gold for all these years, yet since 1873 to the present time the rate of interest has steadily gone down.

If there had been a corner the rate of interest would have steadily advanced. There is a demonstration. But let me ask, for my own information, if they corner gold what will prevent their cornering silver? Or are you going to have it so poor that it will not be worth cornering?

Then they say another thing, and that is that the demonetization of silver is responsible for all the hardships we have endured, for all the bankruptcy, for all the panics. That is not true, and I will not only prove it, but I will demonstrate it. The poison of demonetization entered the American veins, as they tell us, in 1873, and has been busy in its hellish work from that time to this; and yet, nineteen years after we were vaccinated, 1892, was the most prosperous year ever known by this Republic. All the wheels turning, all the furnaces aflame, work at good wages, everybody prosperous. How, Mr. Bryanite, how do you account for that? Just be honest a minute and think about it.

Then there is another thing. In 1816 Great Britain demonetized silver, and that wretched old government has had nothing but gold from that day to this as a standard. And to show you the frightful results of that demonetization, that government does not own now above one-third of the globe, and all the winds are busy floating her flags. There is a demonstration.

Mr. Bryan tells us that free coinage will bring silver 16 to 1. What is the use of stopping there? Why not make it 1 to 1? Why not make it equal with gold and be done with it? And why should it stop at exactly one dollar and twenty-nine cents? I do not know. I am not well acquainted with all the facts that enter into the question of value, but why should it stop at exactly one dollar and twenty-nine cents? I do not know. And I guess if he were cross-examined along toward the close of the trial he would admit that he did not know.

And yet this statesman calls this silver the money of our fathers. Well, let us see. Our fathers did some good things. In 1792 they made gold and silver the standards, and at a ratio of 15 to 1. But where you have two metals and endeavor to make a double standard it is very hard to keep them even. They vary, and, as old Dogberry says, "An two men ride of a horse, one must ride behind." They made the ratio 15 to 1, and who did it? Thomas Jefferson and Alexander Hamilton. Jefferson, the greatest man, with one exception, that ever sat in the presidential chair. With one exception. (A VOICE: "Who was that?") Abraham Lincoln. Alexander Hamilton, with more executive ability than any other man that ever stood under the flag. And how did they fix the ratio? They found the commercial value in the market; that is how they did it. And they went on and issued American dollars 15 to 1; and in 1806, when Jefferson was President, the coinage was stopped. Why? There was too much silver in the dollars, and people instead of passing them around put them aside and sold them to the silversmiths.

Then in 1834 the ratios changed; not quite sixteen to one. That was based again on the commercial value, and instead of sixteen to one they went into the thousands in decimals. It was not quite sixteen to one. They wanted to fix it absolutely on the commercial value. Then a few more dollars were coined; and our fathers coined of these sacred dollars up to 1873, eight millions, and seven millions had been melted.

In 1853 the gold standard was in fact adopted, and, as I have told you, from 1792 to 1873 only eight millions of silver had been coined.

What have the "enemies of silver" done since that time? Under the act of 1878 we have coined over four hundred and thirty millions of these blessed dollars. We bought four million ounces of silver in the open market every month, and in spite of the vast purchases silver continued to go down. We are coining about two millions a month now, and silver is still going down. Even the expectation of the election of Bryan cannot add the tenth of one per cent. to the value of silver bullion. It is going down day by day.

But what I want to say to-night is, if you want silver money, measure it by the gold standard.

I wish every one here would read the speech of Senator Sherman, delivered at Columbus a little while ago, in which he gives the history of American coinage, and every man who will read it will find that silver was not demonetized in 1873. You will find that it was demonetized in 1853, and if he will read back he will find that the apostles of silver now were in favor of the gold standard in 1873. Senator Jones of Nevada in 1873 voted for the law of 1873. He said from his seat in the Senate, that God had made gold the standard. He said that gold was the mother of civilization. Whether he has heard from God since or not I do not know. But now he is on the other side. Senator Stewart of Nevada was there at the time; he voted for the act of 1873, and said that gold was the only standard. He has changed his mind. So they have said of me that I used to talk another way, and they have published little portions of speeches, without publishing all that was said. I want to tell you to-night that I have never changed on the money question.

On many subjects I have changed. I am very glad to feel that I have grown a little in the last forty or fifty years. And a man should allow himself to grow, to bud and blossom and bear new fruit, and not be satisfied with the rotten apples under the tree.

But on the money question I have not changed. Sixteen years ago in this city at Cooper Union, in 1880, in discussing this precise question, I said that I wanted gold and silver and paper; that I wanted the paper issued by the General Government, and back of every paper dollar I wanted a gold dollar or a silver dollar worth a dollar in gold. I said then, "I want that silver dollar worth a dollar in gold if you have to make it four feet in diameter." I said then, "I want our paper so perfectly secure that when the savage in Central Africa looks upon a Government bill of the United States his eyes will gleam as though he looked at shining gold." I said then, "I want every paper dollar of the Union to be able to hold up its hand and swear, 'I know that my Redeemer liveth.'" I said then, "The Republic cannot afford to debase money; cannot afford to be a clipper of coin; an honest nation, honest money; for nations as well as individuals, honesty is the best policy everywhere and forever." I have not changed on that subject. As I told a gentleman the other day, "I am more for silver than you are because I want twice as much of it in a dollar as you do."

Ah, but they say, "free coinage would bring prosperity." I do not believe it, and I will tell you why. Elect Bryan, come to the silver standard, and what would happen? We have in the United States about six hundred million dollars in gold. Every dollar would instantly go out of circulation. Why? No man will use the best money when he can use cheaper. Remember that. No carpenter will use mahogany when his contract allows pine. Gold will go out of circulation, and what next would happen? All the greenbacks would fall to fifty cents on the dollar. The only reason they are worth a dollar now is because the Government has agreed to pay them in gold. When you come to a silver basis they fall to fifty cents. What next? All the national bank notes would be cut square in two. Why? Because they are secured by United States bonds, and when we come to a silver basis, United States bonds would be paid in silver, fifty cents on the dollar. And what else would happen? What else? These sacred silver dollars would instantly become fifty cent pieces, because they would no longer be redeemable in gold; because the Government would no longer be under obligation to keep them on a parity with gold. And how much currency and specie would that leave for us in the United States? In value three hundred and fifty million dollars. That is five dollars per capita. We have twenty dollars per capita now, and yet they want to go to five dollars for the purpose of producing prosperous times!

What else would happen? Every human being living on an income would lose just one-half. Every soldiers' pension would be cut in two. Every human being who has a credit in the savings bank would lose just one-half. All the life insurance companies would pay just one-half. All the fire insurance companies would pay just one-half, and leave you the ashes for the balance. That is what they call prosperity.

And what else? The Republic would be dishonored. The believers in monarchy — in the divine right of kings —the aristocracies of the Old World — would say, "Democracy is a failure, freedom is a fraud, and liberty is a liar;" and we would be compelled to admit the truth. No; we want good, honest money. We want money that will be good when we are dead. We want money that will keep the wolf from the door, no matter what Congress does. We want money that no law can create; that is what we want. There was a time when Rome was mistress of the world, and there was a time when the arch of the empire fell, and the empire was buried in the dust of oblivion; and before those days the Roman people coined gold, and one of those coins is as good to-night as when Julius Cæsar rode at the head of his legions. That is the money we want. We want money that is honest.

But Mr. Bryan hates the bondholders. Who are the bondholders? Let us be honest; let us have some sense. When this Government was in the flame of civil war it was compelled to sell bonds, and everybody who bought a bond bought it because he believed the great Republic would triumph at last. Every man who bought a bond was our friend, and every bond that he purchased added to the chances of our success. They were our friends, and I respect them all. Most of them are dead, and the bonds they bought have been sold and resold maybe hundreds of times, and the men who have them now paid a hundred and twenty in gold, and why should they not be paid in gold? Can any human being think of any reason? And yet Mr. Bryan says that the debt is so great that it cannot be paid in gold. How much is the Republic worth? Let me tell you? This Republic to-day — its lands in cultivation, its houses, railways, canals, and money — is worth seventy thousand million dollars. And what do we owe? One billion five hundred million dollars, and what is the condition of the country? It is the condition of a man who has seventy dollars and owes one dollar and a half. This is the richest country on the globe. Have we any excuse for being thieves? Have we any excuse for failing to pay the debt? No, sir; no, sir. Mr. Bryan hates the bondholders of the railways. Why? I do not know. What did those wretches do? They furnished the money to build the one hundred and eighty thousand miles of railway in the United States; that is what they did.

They paid the money that threw up the road-bed, that shoveled the gravel; they paid the men that turned the ore into steel and put it in form for use; they paid the men that cut down the trees and made the ties, that manufactured the locomotives and the cars. That is what they did. No wonder that a presidential failure hates them.

So this man hates bankers. Now, what is a banker? Here is a little town of five thousand people, and some of them have a little money. They do not want to keep it in the house because some Bryan man might find it; I mean if it were silver. So one citizen buys a safe and rents a room and tells all the people, "You deposit the overplus with me to hold it subject to your order upon your orders signed as checks;" and so they do, and in a little while he finds that he has on hand continually about one hundred thousand dollars more than is called for, and thereupon he loans it to the fellow who started the livery stable and to the chap that opened the grocery and to the fellow with the store, and he makes this idle money work for the good and prosperity of the town. And that is all he does. And these bankers now, if Mr. Bryan becomes President, can pay the depositors in fifty cent dollars; and yet they are such rascally wretches that they say, "We prefer to pay back gold." You can see how mean they are.

Mr. Bryan hates the rich. Would he like to be rich? He hates the bondholders. Would he like to have a million? He hates the successful man. Does he want to be a failure? If he does, let him wait until the third day of November. We want honest money because we are honest people; and there never was any real prosperity for a nation or an individual without honesty, without integrity, and it is our duty to preserve the reputation of the great Republic.

Better be an honest bankrupt than a rich thief. Poverty can hold in its hand the jewel, honor — a jewel that outshines all other gems. A thousand times better be poor and noble than rich and fraudulent.

Then there is another question — the question of the tariff. I admit that there are a great many arguments in favor of free trade, but I assert that all the facts are the other way. I want American people as far as possible to manufacture everything that Americans use.

The more industries we have the more we will develop the American brain, and the best crop you can raise in every country is a crop of good men and good women — of intelligent people. And another thing, I want to keep this market for ourselves. A nation that sells raw material will grow ignorant and poor; a nation that manufactures will grow intelligent and rich. It only takes muscle to dig ore. It takes mind to manufacture a locomotive, and only that labor is profitable that is mixed with thought. Muscle must be in partnership with brain. I am in favor of keeping this market for ourselves, and yet some people say: "Give us the market of the world." Well, why don't you take it? There is no export duty on anything. You can get things out of this country cheaper than from any other country in the world. Iron is as cheap here in the ground, so are coal and stone, as any place on earth. The timber is as cheap in the forest. Why don't you make things and sell them in Central Africa, in China and Japan? Why don't you do it? I will tell you why. It is because labor is too high; that is all. Almost the entire value is labor. You make a ton of steel rails worth twenty-five dollars; the ore in the ground is worth only a few cents, the coal in the earth only a few cents, the lime in the cliff only a few cents — altogether not one dollar and fifty cents; but the ton is worth twenty-five dollars; twenty-three dollars and fifty cents labor! That is the trouble. The steamship is worth five hundred thousand dollars, but the raw material is not worth ten thousand dollars. The rest is labor. Why is labor higher here than in Europe? Protection. And why do these gentlemen ask for the trade of the world? Why do they ask for free trade? Because they want cheaper labor. That is all; cheaper labor. The markets of the world! We want our own markets. I would rather have the market of Illinois than all of China with her four hundred millions. I would rather have the market of one good county in New York than all of Mexico. What do they want in Mexico? A little red calico, a few sombreros and some spurs. They make their own liquor and they live on red pepper and beans. What do you want of their markets? We want to keep our own. In other words, we want to pursue the policy that has given us prosperity in the past. We tried a little bit of free trade in 1892 when we were all prosperous. I said then: "If Grover Cleveland is elected it will cost the people five hundred million dollars." I am no prophet, nor the son of a prophet, nor a profitable son, but I placed the figure too low. His election has cost a thousand million dollars. There is an old song, "You Put the Wrong Man off at Buffalo;" we took the wrong man on at Buffalo. We tried just a little of it, not much. We tried the Wilson bill — a bill, according to Mr. Cleveland, born of perfidy and dishonor — a bill that he was not quite foolish enough to sign and not brave enough to veto. We tried it and we are tired of it, and if experience is a teacher the American people know a little more than they did. We want to do our own work, and we want to mingle our thought with our labor. We are the most inventive of all the peoples. We sustain the same relation to invention that the ancient Greeks did to sculpture. We want to develop the brain; we want to cultivate the imagination, and we want to cover our land with happy homes. A thing is worth sometimes the thought that is in it, sometimes the genius. Here is a man buys a little piece of linen for twenty-five cents, he buys a few paints for fifteen cents, and a few brushes, and he paints a picture; just a little one; a picture, maybe, of a cottage with a dear old woman, white hair, serene forehead and satisfied eyes; at the corner a few hollyhocks in bloom — may be a tree in blossom, and as you listen you seem to hear the songs of birds — the hum of bees, and your childhood all comes back to you as you look. You feel the dewy grass beneath your bare feet once again, and you go back in your mind until the dear old woman on the porch is once more young and fair. There is a soul there. Genius has done its work. And the little picture is worth five, ten, may be fifty thousand dollars. All the result of labor and genius.

And another thing we want is to produce great men and great women here in our own country; then again we want business. Talk about charity, talk about the few dollars that fall unconsciously from the hand of wealth, talk about your poorhouses and your sewing societies and your poor little efforts in the missionary line in the worst part of your town! Ah, there is no charity like business. Business gives work to labor's countless hands; business wipes the tears from the eyes of widows and orphans; business dimples with joy the cheek of sorrow; business puts a roof above the heads of the homeless; business covers the land with happy homes.

We do not want any populistic philanthropy. We want no fiat philosophy. We want no silver swindles. We want business. Wind and wave are our servants; let them work. Steam and electricity are our slaves; let them toil. Let all the wheels whirl; let all the shuttles fly. Fill the air with the echoes of hammer and saw. Fill the furnace with flame; the moulds with liquid iron. Let them glow.

Build homes and palaces of trade. Plow the fields, reap the waving grain. Create all things that man can use. Business will feed the hungry, clothe the naked, educate the ignorant, enrich the world with art — fill the air with song. Give us Protection and Prosperity. Do not cheat us with free trade dreams. Do not deceive us with debased coin. Give us good money — the life blood of business — and let it flow through the veins and arteries of commerce.

And let me tell you to-night the smoke arising from the factories' great plants forms the only cloud on which has ever been seen the glittering bow of American promise. We want work, and I tell you to-night that my sympathies are with the men who work, with the women who weep. I know that labor is the Atlas on whose shoulders rests the great superstructure of civilization and the great dome of science adorned with all there is of art. Labor is the great oak, labor is the great column, and labor, with its deft and cunning hands, has created the countless things of art and beauty. I want to see labor paid. I want to see capital civilized until it will be willing to give labor its share, and I want labor intelligent enough to settle all these questions in the high court of reason. And let me tell the workingman to-night: You will never help yourself by destroying your employer. You have work to sell. Somebody has to buy it, if it is bought, and somebody has to buy it that has the money. Who is going to manufacture something that will not sell. Nobody is going into the manufacturing business through philanthropy, and unless your employer makes a profit, the mill will be shut down and you will be out of work. The interest of the employer and the employed should be one. Whenever the employers of the continent are successful, then the workingman is better paid, and you know it. I have some hope in the future for the workingman. I know what it is to work. I do not think my natural disposition runs in that direction, but I know what it is to work, and I have worked with all my might at one dollar and a half a week. I did the work of a man for fifty cents a day, and I was not sorry for it. In the horizon of my future burned and gleamed the perpetual star of hope. I said to myself: I live in a free country, and I have a chance; I live in a free country, and I have as much liberty as any other man beneath the flag, and I have enjoyed it.

Something has been done for labor. Only a few years ago a man worked fifteen or sixteen hours a day but the hours have been reduced to at least ten and are on the way to still further reduction. And while the hours have been decreased the wages have as certainly been increased. In forty years — in less — the wages of American workingmen have doubled. A little while ago you received an average of two hundred and eighty-five dollars a year; now you receive an average of more than four hundred and ninety dollars; there is the difference. So it seems to me that the star of hope is still in the sky for every workingman. Then there is another thing: every workingman in this country can take his little boy on his knee and say, "John, all the avenues to distinction, wealth, and glory are open to you. There is the free school; take your chances with the rest." And it seems to me that that thought ought to sweeten every drop of sweat that trickles down the honest brow of toil.

So let us have protection! How much? Enough, so that our income at least will equal our outgo. That is a good way to keep house. I am tired of depression and deficit. I do not like to see a President pawning bonds to raise money to pay his own salary. I do not like to see the great Republic at the mercy of anybody, so let us stand by protection.

There is another trouble. The gentleman now running for the presidency — a tireless talker — oh, if he had a brain equal to his vocal chords, what a man! And yet when I read his speeches it seems to me as though he stood on his head and thought with his feet. This man is endeavoring to excite class against class, to excite the poor against the rich. Let me tell you something. We have no classes in the United States. There are no permanent classes here. The millionaire may be a mendicant, the mendicant may be a millionaire. The man now working for the millionaire may employ that millionaire's sons to work for him. There is a chance for us all. Sometimes a numskull is born in the mansion, and a genius rises from the gutter. Old Mother Nature has a queer way of taking care of her children. You cannot tell. You cannot tell. Here we have a free open field of competition, and if a man passes me in the race I say: "Good luck. Get ahead of me if you can, you are welcome."

And why should I hate the rich? Why should I make my heart a den of writhing, hissing snakes of envy? Get rich. I do not care. I am glad I live in a country where somebody can get rich. It is a spur in the flank of ambition. Let them get rich. I have known good men that were quite rich, and I have known some mean men who were in straitened circumstances. So I have known as good men as ever breathed the air, who were poor. We must respect the man; what is inside, not what is outside.

That is why I like this country. That is why I do not want it dishonored. I want no class feeling. The citizens of America should be friends. Where capital is just and labor intelligent, happiness dwells. Fortunate that country where the rich are extravagant and the poor economical. Miserable that country where the rich are economical and the poor are extravagant. A rich spendthrift is a blessing. A rich miser is a curse. Extravagance is a splendid form of charity. Let the rich spend, let them build, let them give work to their fellow-men, and I will find no fault with their wealth, provided they obtained it honestly.

There was an old fellow by the name of Socrates. He happened to be civilized, living in a barbarous time, and he was tried for his life. And in his speech in which he defended himself is a paragraph that ought to remain in the memory of the human race forever.

He said to those judges, "During my life I have not sought ambition, wealth. I have not sought to adorn my body, but I have endeavored to adorn my soul with the jewels of patience and justice, and above all, with the love of liberty." Such a man rises above all wealth.

Why should we envy the rich? Why envy a man who has no earthly needs? Why envy a man that carries a hundred canes? Why envy a man who has that which he cannot use? I know a great many rich men and I have read about a great many others, and I do not envy them. They are no happier than I am. You see, after all, few rich men own their property. The property owns them. It gets them up early in the morning. It will not let them sleep; it makes them suspect their friends. Sometimes they think their children would like to attend a first-class funeral. Why should we envy the rich? They have fear; we have hope. They are on the top of the ladder; we are close to the ground. They are afraid of falling, and we hope to rise.

Why should we envy the rich? They never drank any colder water than I have. They never ate any lighter biscuits or any better corn bread. They never drank any better Illinois wine, or felt better after drinking it, than I have; than you have. They never saw any more glorious sunsets with the great palaces of amethyst and gold, and they never saw the heavens thicker with constellations; they never read better poetry. They know no more about the ecstasies of love than we do. They never got any more pleasure out of courting than I did. Why should we envy the rich? I know as much about the ecstasies of love of wife and child and friends as they. They never had any better weather in June than I have, or you have. They can buy splendid pictures. I can look at them. And who owns a great picture or a great statue? The man who bought it? Possibly, and possibly not. The man who really owns it, is the man who understands it, that appreciates it, the man into whose heart its beauty and genius come, the man who is ennobled and refined and glorified by it.

They have never heard any better music than I have.

When the great notes, winged like eagles, soar to the great dome of sound, I have felt just as good as though I had a hundred million dollars.

Do not try to divide this country into classes. The rich man that endeavors to help his fellow-man deserves the honor and respect of the great Republic. I have nothing against the man that got rich in the free and open field of competition. Where they combine to rob their fellow-men, then I want the laws enforced. That is all. Let them play fair and they are welcome to all they get.

And why should we hate the successful? Why? We cannot all be first. The race is a vast procession; a great many hundred millions are back of the center, and in front there is only one human being; that is all. Shall we wait for the other fellows to catch up? Shall the procession stop? I say, help the fallen, assist the weak, help the poor, bind up the wounds, but do not stop the procession.

Why should we envy the successful? Why should we hate them? And why should we array class against class? It is all wrong. For instance, here is a young man, and he is industrious. He is in love with a girl around the corner. She is in his brain all day — in his heart all night, and while he is working he is thinking. He gets a little ahead, they get married. He is an honest man, he gets credit, and the first thing you know he has a good business of his own and he gets rich; educates his children, and his old age is filled with content and love. Good! His companions bask in the sunshine of idleness. They have wasted their time, wasted their wages in dissipation, and when the winter of life comes, when the snow falls on the barren fields of the wasted days, then shivering with cold, pinched with hunger, they curse the man who has succeeded. Thereupon they all vote for Bryan.

Then there is another question, and that is whether the Government has a right to protect itself? And that is whether the employees of railways shall have a right to stop the trains, a right to prevent interstate commerce, a right to burn bridges and shoot engineers? Has the United States the right to protect commerce between the States? I say, yes.

It is the duty of the President to lay the mailed hand of the

Republic upon the mob. We want no mobs in this country. This is a Government of the people and by the people, a Government of law, and these laws should be interpreted by the courts in judicial calm. We have a supreme tribunal. Undoubtedly it has made some bad decisions, but it has made a vast number of good ones. The judges do the best they can. Of course they are not like Mr. Bryan, infallible. But they are doing the best they can, and when they make a decision that is wrong it will be attacked by reason, it will be attacked by argument, and in time it will be reversed, but I do not believe in attacking it with a torch or by a mob. I hate the mob spirit. Civilized men obey the law. Civilized men believe in order. Civilized men believe that a man that makes property by industry and economy has the right to keep it. Civilized men believe that that man has the right to use it as he desires, and they will judge of his character by the manner in which he uses it. If he endeavors to assist his fellow-man he will have the respect and admiration of his fellow-men. But we want a Government of law. We do not want labor questions settled by violence and blood.

I want to civilize the capitalist so that he will be willing to give what labor is worth. I want to educate the workingman so that he will be willing to receive what labor is worth. I want to civilize them both to that degree that they can settle all their disputes in the high court of reason.

But when you tell me that they can stop the commerce of the Nation, then you preach the gospel of the bludgeon, the gospel of torch and bomb. I do not believe in that religion. I believe in a religion of kindness, reason and law. The law is the supreme will of the supreme people, and we must obey it or we go back to savagery and black night. I stand by the courts. I stand by the President who endeavors to preserve the peace. I am against mobs; I am against lynchings, and I believe it is the duty of the Federal Government to protect all of its citizens at home and abroad; and I want a Government powerful enough to say to the Governor of any State where they are murdering American citizens without process of law — I want the Federal Government to say to the Governor of that State: "Stop; stop shedding the blood of American citizens. And if you cannot stop it, we can." I believe in a Government that will protect the lowest, the poorest and weakest as promptly as the mightiest and strongest. That is my Government. This old doctrine of State Sovereignty perished in the flame of civil war, and I tell you to-night that that infamous lie was surrendered to Grant with Lee's sword at Appomattox.

I believe in a strong Government, not in a Government that can make money, but in a strong Government.

Oh, I forgot to ask the question, "If the Government can make money why should it collect taxes?"

Let us be honest. Here is a poor man with a little yoke of cattle, cultivating forty acres of stony ground, working like a slave in the heat of summer, in the cold blasts of winter, and the Government makes him pay ten dollars taxes, when, according to these gentlemen, it could issue a one hundred thousand dollar bill in a second. Issue the bill and give the fellow with the cattle a rest. Is it possible for the mind to conceive anything more absurd than that the Government can create money?

Now, the next question is, or the next thing is, you have to choose between men. Shall Mr. Bryan be the next President or shall McKinley occupy that chair? Who is Mr. Bryan? He is not a tried man. If he had the capacity to reason, if he had logic, if he could spread the wings of imagination, if there were in his heart the divine flower called pity, he might be an orator, but lacking all these, he is as he is.

When Major McKinley was fighting under the flag, Bryan was in his mother's arms, and judging from his speeches he ought to be there still. What is he? He is a Populist. He voted for General Weaver. Only a little while ago he denied being a Democrat. His mind is filled with vagaries. A fiat money man. His brain is an insane asylum without a keeper.

Imagine that man President. Whom would he call about him? Upon whom would he rely? Probably for Secretary of State he would choose Ignatius Donnelly of Minnesota; for Secretary of the Interior, Henry George; for Secretary of War, Tillman with his pitchforks; for Postmaster-General, Peffer of Kansas. Once somebody said: "If you believe in fiat money, why don't you believe in fiat hay, and you can make enough hay out of Peffer's whiskers to feed all the cattle in the country." For Secretary of the Treasury, Coin Harvey. For Secretary of the Navy, Coxey, and then he could keep off the grass. And then would come the millennium. The great cryptogram and the Bacon cipher; the single tax, State saloons, fiat money, free silver, destruction of banks and credit, bondholders and creditors mobbed, courts closed, debts repudiated and the rest of the folks made rich by law.

And suppose Bryan should die, and then think, think of Thomas Watson sitting in the chair of Abraham Lincoln. That is enough to give a patriot political nightmare.

If McKinley dies there is an honest capable man to take his place. A man who believes in business, in prosperity. A man who knows what money is. A man who would never permit the laying of a land warrant on a cloud. A man of good sense, a man of level head. A man that loves his country, a man that will protect its honor.

And is McKinley a tried man? Honest, candid, level-headed, putting on no airs, saying not what he thinks somebody else thinks, but what he thinks, and saying it in his own honest, forcible way. He has made hundreds of speeches during this campaign, not to people whom he ran after, but to people who came to see him. Not from the tail end of cars, but from the doorstep of his home, and every speech has been calculated to make votes. Every speech has increased the respect of the American people for him, every one. He has never slopped over. Four years ago I read a speech made by him at Cleveland, on the tariff. I tell you to-night that he is the best posted man on the tariff under the flag. I tell you that he knows the road to prosperity. I read that speech. It had foundation, proportion, dome, and he handled his facts as skillfully as Cæsar marshaled his hosts on the fields of war, and ever since I read it I have had profound respect for the intelligence and statesmanship of William McKinley.

He will call about him the best, the wisest, and the most patriotic men, and his cabinet will respect the highest and loftiest interests and aspirations of the American people.

Then you have to make another choice. You have to choose between parties, between the new Democratic and the old Republican. And I want to tell you the new Democratic is worse than the old, and that is a good deal for me to say. In 1861 hundreds and hundreds of thousands of Democrats thought more of country than of party. Hundreds and hundreds of thousands shouldered their muskets, rushed to the rescue of the Republic, and sustained the administration of Abraham Lincoln. With their help the Rebellion was crushed, and now hundreds and hundreds of thousands of Democrats will hold country above party and will join with the Republicans in saving the honor, the reputation, of the United States; and I want to say to all the National Democrats who feel that they cannot vote for Bryan, I want to say to you, vote for McKinley. This is no war for blank cartridges. Your gun makes as much noise, but it does not do as much execution.

If you vote for Palmer it is not to elect him, it is simply to defeat Bryan, and the sure way to defeat Bryan is to vote for McKinley. You have to choose between parties. The new Democratic party, with its allies, the Populists and Socialists and Free Silverites, represents the follies, the mistakes, and the absurdities of a thousand years. They are in favor of everything that cannot be done. Whatever is, is wrong. They think creditors are swindlers, and debtors who refuse to pay their debts are honest men. Good money is bad and poor money is good. A promise is better than a performance. They desire to abolish facts, punish success, and reward failure. They are worse than the old. And yet I want to be honest. I am like the old Dutchman who made a speech in Arkansas. He said: "Ladies and Gentlemen, I must tell you the truth. There are good and bad in all parties except the Democratic party, and in the Democratic party there are bad and worse." The new Democratic party, a party that believes in repudiation, a party that would put the stain of dishonesty on every American brow and that would make this Government subject to the mob.

You have to make your choice. I have made mine. I go with the party that is traveling my way. I do not pretend to belong to anything or that anything belongs to me. When a party goes my way I go with that party and I stick to it as long as it is traveling my road. And let me tell you something. The history of the Republican party is the glory of the United States. The Republican party has the enthusiasm of youth and the wisdom of old age. The Republican party has the genius of administration. The Republican party knows the wants of the people. The Republican party kept this country on the map of the world and kept our flag in the air. The Republican party made our country free, and that one fact fills all the heavens with light. The Republican party is the pioneer of progress; the grandest organization that has ever existed among men. The Republican party is the conscience of the nineteenth century. I am proud to belong to it. Vote the Republican ticket and you will be happy here, and if there is another life you will be happy there.

I had an old friend down in Woodford County, Charley Muli-dore. He won a coffin on Lincoln's election. He took it home and every birthday he called in his friends. They had a little game of "sixty-six" on the coffin lid. When the game was over they opened the coffin and took out the things to eat and drink and had a festival, and the minister in the little town, hearing of it, was scandalized, and he went to Charley Mulidore and he said: "Mr. Mulidore, how can you make light of such awful things?" "What things?" "Why," he said, "Mr. Mulidore, what did you do with that coffin? In a little while you die, and then you come to the day of judgment." "Well, Mr. Preacher, when I come to that day of judgment they will say, 'What is your name?' I will tell them, 'Charley Mulidore.' And they will say, 'Mr. Mulidore, are you a Christian?' 'No, sir, I was a Republican, and the coffin I got out of this morning I won on Abraham Lincoln's election.' And then they will say, 'Walk in, Mr. Mulidore, walk in, walk in; here is your halo and there is your harp.' "

If you want to live in good company vote the Republican ticket. Vote for Black for Governor of the State of New York — a man in favor of protection and honest money; a man that believes in the preservation of the honor of the Nation. Vote for members of Congress that are true to the great principles of the Republican party. Vote for every Republican candidate from the lowest to the highest. This is a year when we mean business. Vote, as I tell you, the Republican ticket if you want good company. If you want to do some good to your fellow-men, if you want to say when you die — when the curtain falls — when the music of the orchestra grows dim — when the lights fade; if you want to live so at that time you can say "the world is better because I lived," vote the Republican ticket in 1896. Vote with the party of Lincoln — greatest of our mighty dead; Lincoln the Merciful. Vote with the party of Grant, the greatest soldier of his century; a man worthy to have been matched against Cæsar for the mastery of the world; as great a general as ever planted on the field of war the torn and tattered flag of victory. Vote with the party of Sherman and Sheridan and Thomas. But the time would fail me to repeat even the names of the philosophers, the philanthropists, the thinkers, the orators, the statesmen, and the soldiers who made the Republican party glorious forever.

We love our country; dear to us for its reputation throughout

the world. We love our country for her credit in all the marts of
the world. We love our country, because under her flag we are
free. It is our duty to hand down the American institutions to
our children unstained, unimpaired. It is our duty to preserve
them for ourselves, for our children, and for their fair children yet
to be.

This is the last speech that I shall make in this campaign, and
to-night there comes upon me the spirit of prophecy. On November 4th you will find that by the largest majorities in our history,
William McKinley has been elected President of the United
States.

ALBERT J. BEVERIDGE

(1862-1927)

Such great public figures and political orators as Bryan, Roosevelt, Lodge, Root, Foraker, Platt, Schurz, and Hoar were firmly established when the twentieth century began. Into this scene stepped Albert J. Beveridge, only thirty-six years of age when he was elected to the Senate in 1899, who was destined to become known as one of the foremost speakers in American history.

To understand his development as a speaker one must recognize a cardinal principle of his speech power. Beveridge himself stated the principle in his brief book, The Art of Public Speaking:

> So, the speaker must master his subject. That means that all facts must be collected, arranged, studied, digested — not only data on one side, but material on the other side and on every side — all of it. And be sure they are facts, not mere assumptions or unproved assertions. Take nothing for granted.
>
> Therefore check up and reverify every item. This means painstaking research, to be sure, but what of it? — are you not proposing to inform, instruct, and advise your fellow citizen? Are you not setting yourself up as a teacher and counselor of the public? [1]

This was the foundation upon which he built his fame as a speaker.

Beveridge's stature as a statesman and his stature as a public speaker grew simultaneously. His greatest successes were both political and oratorical triumphs. Each new recognition of him as a political figure was accompanied by a corresponding new recognition as a platform personality.

On September 16, 1898, in Indianapolis he delivered the remark-

[1] P. 26.

ably eloquent speech, "The March of the Flag," which became an
important campaign document of the Republican party on the
issue of imperialism. The speech began, "The march of the flag.
In 1789, the flag of the Republic waved over four million souls in
thirteen states and their savage territory which stretched to the
Mississippi, to Canada, and to the Floridas. The timid souls of
that day said that no new territory was needed. . . ." Colorfully,
he pursued the doctrine of imperialism until at the end of the
speech, says Bowers, "he sat down in the midst of a remarkable
ovation. Never had Indianapolis been more stirred by campaign
oratory. . . ."[2]

Few people doubt that his election to the United States Senate
by the Indiana State legislature in January, 1899, came as a direct
result of the Indianapolis speech.

Since he could not take his place in the Senate until December,
he made a six months' tour of the Philippines and China to study
the effects of United States foreign policy. When upon his return
he was sworn into office, he was the only member of the Senate
who had seen conditions in the Philippines first hand.

The debate on the Philippines began on December 20, 1899,
when Senator Hoar introduced his resolution that "the United
States abstain from interfering with the freedom and just rights
of other nations or people." Beveridge responded with his resolution that "the Philippine Islands are territory belonging to the
United States, that it is the intention of the United States to retain
them as such" and announced that he would speak on his resolution at noon on Tuesday, January 10.

The speech attracted tremendous interest. His previous speeches
had brought him a reputation for eloquence; his six months in the
Far East had gained him information that people were anxious to
hear; and his flaunting of the tradition that a freshman Senator
should remain silent generated heat to the controversy. When
Tuesday noon came, the floor of the Senate was filled and the
galleries were crowded.

The speech was a great one. Illustrative of the glowing comments was this statement in the Indianapolis Journal:

. . . he won such a triumph as seldom comes to a public man. His
manner was earnest, his delivery graceful, his few gestures, timely

[2] Claude G. Bowers, Beveridge and the Progressive Era, p. 76.

and effective. At intervals he drove home telling points with fervor and dramatic force. . . ."[3]

There was also adverse criticism, but Beveridge emerged as an important political leader and as the most effective speaker of the period. Again, he had achieved simultaneous recognition in government and speech on a single occasion.

For his flaunting of Senate tradition, he received a devastating rebuke when he next rose on March 29, to speak on a bill providing free trade for Puerto Rico. Bowers says, "The galleries were packed when he rose, the Chamber full. . . . But the moment he began to speak, the Senators, with few exceptions, rose and filed into the cloakrooms. . . ."[4] Some months elapsed before Beveridge recovered from this cruel blow.

The summer of 1900 saw the Democratic party again nominate William Jennings Bryan for the Presidency. In his speech of acceptance, Bryan attacked the Republican party for its policy of imperialism. Beveridge, upon the urging of his party, answered the challenge with one of the best speeches of his career. Entitled, "The Star of Empire," it was delivered in Chicago on October 25, 1900, only nine months after his Philippine speech. Because it has striking qualities and because it is less often anthologized than some of his other speeches, "The Star of Empire" is included in this section.

"The Auditorium," says Bowers, "was crowded to hear him open the Illinois campaign with a ringing defense of imperialism, and the applause was almost continuous from the time he came on the stage until he closed. . . ."[5] The Chicago Tribune said:

> Senator Albert J. Beveridge delivered a political address last night in the Auditorium to the largest audience that has greeted a public speaker thus far this campaign. . . . He concluded his speech amid rounds of applause. . . .
>
> As Senator Beveridge concluded his prediction that the war would cease with President McKinley's re-election, the great audience, which had been demonstrative before, completely stopped the speaker with applause.[6]

---

[3] January 10, 1900, p. 1.
[4] Bowers, op cit., p. 128.
[5] Ibid., p. 133.
[6] September 26, 1900, p. 1.

He confidently struck a note for super imperialism as he stated that "Porto Rico is ours, and ours forever; and Cuba ought to have been ours forever . . . and so my answer to Mr. Bryan's comparison is that if we have made a mistake in Cuba we ought not make the same mistake in the Philippines." The speech had the desired effect; according to the Tribune,

> The speech by Senator Beveridge at the Auditorium last evening was a fine specimen of true eloquence, full of fire and force, and as logical as it was powerful. . . . It confirms the brilliant promise of the young Indiana Senator's former utterances on the Philippine issue, and constitutes a crushing and unanswerable reply to the shallow doctrine of Mr. Bryan concerning "imperialism" and "militarism." Mr. Beveridge has shown himself familiar not only with the Philippine situation but with the whole mass of history attending the westward course of civilization.[7]

The effectiveness of this speech, like that of his others, was a product of his vital speech materials which were carefully assembled and arranged. The speech, in accordance with his usual practice, was written out, revised, and finally committed to memory. He spoke rapidly in a clear, distinct voice; he used no notes; and scarcely deviated from his original manuscript. All of his major addresses were given in the same manner, and there is little reason to wonder why he was one of the greatest speakers in our history.

THE STAR OF EMPIRE

by

Albert J. Beveridge

Delivered in Chicago in the Auditorium on September 25, 1900.

"WESTWARD THE STAR OF EMPIRE takes its Way." Not the star of kingly power, for kingdoms are everywhere dissolving in the in-

[7] Ibid., p. 12.

creasing rights of men; not the star of autocratic oppression, for civilization is brightening and the liberties of the people are broadening under every flag. But the star of empire, as Washington used the word, when he called this Republic an "empire"; as Jefferson understood it, when he declared our form of government ideal for extending "our empire"; as Marshall understood it, when he closed a noble period of an immortal constitutional opinion by naming the domain of the American people "our empire."

This is the "empire" of which the prophetic voice declared "Westward the Star of Empire takes its Way" — the star of the empire of liberty and law, of commerce and communication, of social order and the Gospel of our Lord — the star of the empire of the civilization of the world. Westward that star of empire takes its course. And to-day it illumines our path of duty across the Pacific into the islands and lands where Providence has called us.

In that path the American government is marching forward, opposed at every step by those who deny the right of the Republic to plant the institutions of the Flag where Events have planted that Flag itself. For this is our purpose, to perform which the Opposition declares that the Republic has no warrant in the Constitution, in morals or in the rights of man. And I mean to examine to-night every argument they advance for their policy of reaction and retreat.

It is not true, as the Opposition asserts, that every race without instruction and guidance is naturally self-governing. If so, the Indians were capable of self-government. America belonged to them whether they were or were not capable of self-government. If they were capable of self-government it was not only wrong, but it was a crime to set up our independent government on their land without their consent. If this is true, the Puritans, instead of being noble, are despicable characters; and the patriots of 1776, to whom the Opposition compares the Filipinos, were only a swarm of land pirates. If the Opposition is right, the Zulus who owned the Transvaal were capable of self-government, and the Boers who expelled them, according to the Opposition, deserve the abhorrence of righteous men.

But while the Boers took the lands they occupy from the natives who peopled them; while we peopled this country in spite of the Indian who owned it; and while this may be justified by the welfare of the world which those events advanced, that is not what is to be done in the Philippines. The American government, as a government, will not appropriate the Filipinos' land or permit Americans as individuals to seize it. It will protect the Filipinos in their possessions. If any American secures real estate in the Philippines, it will be because he buys it from the owner. Under American administration the Filipino who owns his little plot of ground will experience a security in the possession of his property that he has never known before.

The English in Egypt and India have not taken the land from its owners; they have confirmed the occupants in their ownership. In Hawaii we have not taken the land from its owners; we have secured its owners in their peaceable possession. And our administration in the Philippines will also establish there that same security of property and life which is the very beginning of civilization itself.

If it be said that tropical countries can not be peopled by the Caucasian race, I answer that, even if true, it is no reason why they should not be governed by the Caucasian race. India is a tropical country. India is ruled by England to the advantage of India and England alike. Who denies that India's 300,000,000 are better off under English administration than under the bestial tyranny of native rulers, to whom the agony of their subjects was the highest form of amusement?

Dare Mr. Bryan say that he would have India back to its condition before England took it? If he dare not, he is answered. Dare he say that he would withdraw English rule now? If he dare not, he is answered. Dare he say that he would take the English "residents" from the Malay States and turn them back again to the rule of their burtal lords? If he dare not, he is answered. Dare he say that the Boers should restore the Transvaal to its original owners? If he dare not, he is answered. Dare he deny that the greatest progress shown upon the map of earth to-day is the progress of Egypt during the last twenty years under English rule? If he dare not, he is answered. And he dare not. If he proclaims his faith in the Filipino people, who know not the meaning of self-government, I declare my faith in the American people, who have developed the realities of liberty.

Grant, for the purposes of argument, the Opposition's premise that the white man can not people the Philippines. Grant, also, that the Malays of those islands can not, unaided, establish civilization there; build roads, open mines, erect schools, maintain social order, repress piracy and administer safe government throughout the archipelago. And this must be granted; for they are the same race which inhabits the Malay Peninsula. What, then, is the conclusion demanded by the general welfare of the world?

Surely not that this land, rich in all that civilized man requires, and these people needing the very blessings they ignorantly repel, should be remanded to savagery and the wilderness! If you say this, you say that barbarism and undeveloped resources are better than civilization and the earth's resources developed. What is the conclusion, then, which the logic of civilization compels from these admitted premises? It is that the reign of law must be established throughout these islands, their resources developed and their people civilized by those in whose blood resides the genius of administration.

Such are all Teutonic and Celtic peoples. Such are the Dutch; behold their work in Java. Such are the English; behold their work all around the world. Such the German; behold his advance into the fields of world-regeneration and administration. Such were the French before Napoleon diverted their energies; behold their work in Canada, Louisiana and our great Northwest. And such, more than any people who ever lived, are the Americans, into whose hands God has given the antipodes to develop their resources, to regenerate their people and to establish there the civilization of law-born liberty and liberty-born law.

If the Opposition declares that we ought to set up a separate government over the Philippines because we are setting up a separate government over Cuba, I answer that such an error in Cuba does not justify the same error in the Philippines. I am speaking for myself alone, but speaking thus, I say, that for the good of Cuba more even than for the good of the United States, a separate government over Cuba, uncontrolled by the American Republic, never should have been promised.

Cuba is a mere extension of our Atlantic coast-line. It commands the ocean entrances to the Mississippi and the Isthmian Canal. Jefferson's dearest dream was that Cuba should belong to the United States. To possess this extension of American soil has been the wish of every far-seeing statesman from Jefferson to Blaine. Annexation to the greatest nation the world has ever seen is a prouder Cuban destiny than separate nationality. As an American possession, Cuba might possibly have been fitted for statehood in a period not much longer than that in which Louisiana was prepared for statehood.

Even now the work of regeneration — of cleansing cities, building roads, establishing posts, erecting a system of universal education and the action of all the forces that make up our civilization — is speeding forward faster than at any time or place in human history — American administration! But yesterday there were less than ten thousand Cuban children in school; to-day there are nearly one hundred and fifty thousand Cuban children in school — American administration! But yesterday Havana was the source of our yellow-fever plagues; to-day it is nearly as healthy as New Orleans — American administration!

When we stop this work and withdraw our restraint, revolution will succeed revolution in Cuba, as in the Central and South American countries; Havana again fester with the yellow death; systematic education again degenerate into sporadic instances; and Cuba, which under our control should be a source of profit, power and glory to the Republic and herself, will be a source of irritation and of loss, of danger and disease to both. The United States needs Cuba for our protection; but Cuba needs the United States for Cuba's salvation.

The resolution for Cuban independence, hastily passed by all parties in Congress, at an excited hour, was an error which years of time, propinquity of location, common commerce, mutual interests and similar dangers surely will correct. The President, jealous of American honor, considers that resolution a promise. And American promise means performance. And so the unnatural experiment is to be tried. What war and nature — aye, what God hath joined together — is to be put asunder.

I speak for myself alone, but speaking thus, I say that it will be an evil day for Cuba when the Stars and Stripes come down from Morro Castle. I speak for myself alone, but I believe that in this my voice is the voice of the American millions, as it is the voice of the ultimate future, when I say that Porto Rico is ours and ours for ever; the Philippines are ours and ours for ever; and Cuba ought to have been ours, and by the free choice of her people some day will be ours, and ours for ever.

We have a foreign nation on our north; another on our south-west; and now to permit another foreign nation within cannon shot of our southeast coast, will indeed create conditions which will require that militarism which the Opposition to the Government pretends to fear. Think of Cuba in alliance with England or Germany or France! Think of Cuba a naval station and ally of one of the great foreign powers, every one of whom is a rival of America! And so my answer to Mr. Bryan's comparison is that, if we have made a mistake in Cuba, we ought not to make the same mistake in the Philippines.

I predict that within ten years we shall again be forced to assume the government of Cuba, but only after our commerce has again been paralyzed by revolution, after internal dissension has again spilled Cuban blood, after the yellow fever has threatened our southern coast from its hot-bed in Havana harbor. Cuba independent! Impossible! I predict that at the very next session of Congress we shall pass some kind of law giving this Republic control of Cuba's destiny. If we do not we fail in our duty.

Consider, now, the Opposition's proposed method of procedure in the Philippines: It is to establish a stable government there, turn that government over to the Filipinos, and protect them and their government from molestation by any other nation.

Suppose the Opposition's plan in operation. Suppose a satisfactory government is established, turned over to the Filipinos and American troops withdrawn. The new government must experience feuds, factions and revolution. This is the history of every new government. It was so even with the American people. Witness Shays' Rebellion against the National Government, almost shaking its foundations; witness the Whiskey Rebellion in Pennsylvania, which required the first exercise of armed national power to maintain order with a state of the Union. And we were of a self-governing race — at that period we were almost wholly Anglo-Saxon.

How can we expect the Philippine Malays to escape this common fate of all new governments? Remember that as a race they have not that civil cohesion which binds a people into a nation. Remember that every island is envious of every other one; and that in each island every officer is a "general," jealous of his dignity, intriguing for advancement.

How long would this stable government, which the Opposition asks us to "establish," remain "stable," if we withdrew our forces?

And if resistance broke out in the Visayas, if revolt sprang into flame among the murderous Moros, what would be our duty? It would be to reënter where we had withdrawn and restore the stability of the government which the Opposition declares that we shall establish before we withdraw. And so the Opposition program constantly defeats itself and compels us to do over and over again the work which we must perform at the beginning. And all this without benefit to the Philippine people, without improvement to their lands and with immeasurable loss to ourselves recouped not from a single source of profit. But the American flag floating there for ever means not only established liberty, but permanent stability.

Again governments must have money. That is their first necessity; money for salaries, money for the army, money for public buildings, money for improvements. Before the revenues are established, the government must have money. If the revenues are inadequate, nevertheless the government must have money. Therefore, all governments are borrowers. Even the government of the American people — the richest people of history — is a borrower. Even the government of the British people, who for centuries have been accumulating wealth, must borrow; its bonds are in our own bank vaults. Much more, then, must little governments borrow money.

If, then, we "establish a stable government," as the Opposition demands, and turn that government over to the Filipinos, they also must borrow money. But suppose the Philippine government can not pay its debt when it falls due, as has been the case in many instances on our own continent within the last quarter of a century; as is the case to-day with one of the governments of Central America. If that loan is an English loan, England would seize the revenues of the Philippines for the payment of her debt, as she has done before and is doing now. So would France or Germany or whoever was the creditor nation. Should we have a right to interfere? Of course not, unless we were willing to guarantee the Philippine debt. If, then, the first purpose of the Opposition candidate is carried out, we must:

Keep "stable" the government which we first "establish," or the very purpose of the establishment of that government is defeated.

If the second proposition of the Opposition is performed, we must:

First: Control the finances of the Philippines perpetually; or,

Second: Guarantee the loans the Philippine government makes with other nations; or,

Third: Go to war with those nations to defeat their collection of their just debts.

Is this sound policy? Is it profitable? Is it moral? Is it just to the Filipinos, to the world, to ourselves? Is it humane to the masses of those children who need first of all, and more than all, order, law and peace? Is it prudent, wise, far-seeing statesmanship? And does the adoption of a similar course in Cuba justify it in the Philippines?

No. Here is the program of reason and righteousness, and Time and Events will make it the program of the Republic:

First: We have given Porto Rico such a civil government as her situation demands, under the Stars and Stripes.

Second: We will put down the rebellion and then give the Philippines such a civil government as the situation demands, under the Stars and Stripes.

Third: We are regenerating Cuba, and when our preparatory work is done, we should have given Cuba such a civil government as her situation may demand, under the Stars and Stripes.

The sovereignty of the Stars and Stripes can be nothing but a blessing to any people and to any land.

I do not advocate this course for commercial reasons, though these have their weight. All men who understand production and exchange, understand the commercial advantage resulting from our ownership of these rich possessions. But I waive this large consideration as insignificant, compared with the master argument of the progress of civilization, which under God, the American people are henceforth to lead until our day is done. For henceforward in the trooping of the colors of the nations they shall cluster around and follow the Republic's banner.

The mercantile argument is mighty with Americans in merely mercantile times, and it should be so; but the argument of destiny is the master argument in the hour of destiny, and it should be so. The American people never yet entered on a great movement for merely mercantile reasons. Sentiment and duty have started and controlled every noble current of American history. And at this historic hour, destiny is the controlling consideration in the prophetic statesmanship which conditions require of the American people.

It is destiny that the world shall be rescued from its natural wilderness and from savage men. Civilization is no less an evolution than the changing forms of animal and vegetable life. Surely and steadily the reign of law, which is the very spirit of liberty, takes the place of arbitrary caprice. Surely and steadily the methods of social order are bringing the whole earth under their subjection. And to deny that this is right, is to deny that civilization should increase. In this great work the American people must have their part. They are fitted for the work as no people have ever been fitted; and their work lies before them.

If the Opposition say that they grant this, but that the higher considerations of abstract human rights demand that the Philippines shall have such a government as they wish, regardless of the remainder of the world, I answer that the desire of the Filipinos is not the only factor in determining their government, just as the desire of no individual man is the only factor determining his conduct. It is written in the moral law of individuals that "No man liveth to himself alone"; and it is no less written in the moral law of peoples that "No people liveth to itself alone."

The world is interested in the Philippines, and it has a right to be. The world is interested in India, and it has a right to be. Civilization is interested in China and its government, and that is the duty of civilization. You can not take the Philippines out of the operation of those forces which are binding all mankind into one vast and united intelligence. When Circumstance has raised our flag above them, we dare not turn these misguided children over to destruction by themselves or spoliation by others, and then make answer when the God of nations requires them at our hands, "Am I my brother's keeper?"

If you admit that it is the purpose of that Intelligence that rules the universe to civilize and unify mankind, how is this to be accomplished? If you say that it is by leaving each people to themselves to work out their own salvation, I answer that history shows that civilization has been preserved only by the most superior nations extending it. And the method of extending civilization is by colonization where the superior nation can establish itself among the inferior races; or in place of them, if the inferior races can not exist under civilization, as in New Zealand, Australia and the like.

The method is by administration where the superior nation can not, because of climatic conditions, establish itself among or supplant the inferior races, as in Java, India, and the like. And finally that method is by creating and developing commerce among all the peoples of the world.

It is thus that America itself was discovered; thus that this Republic was builded; thus that South Africa was reclaimed; thus that Australia was recovered from the Bushman and made the home of civilization; thus that Ceylon was taken from wild men and tangled jungle and brought beneath the rule of religion, law and industry. It is thus that Egypt is being redeemed, her deserts fertilized, her starving millions fed, her fellahs made men and the blessings of just government bestowed upon the land of the Pharaohs. It is thus that the regeneration of India has progressed, her cities been cleansed, the reign of hygiene and health gradually established in the very kingdom of pestilence and disease; and the arbitrary and infamous tyranny of petty princes, holding power of life and death over miserable subjects, reduced to the orderly administration of equal and unpurchased justice under equal and impartial laws.

History establishes these propositions;

First: Every people who have become great, have become colonizers or administrators;

Second: Coincident with this colonization and administration, their material and political greatness develops;

Third: Their decline is coincident with the abandonment of the policy of possession and administration, or departure from the true principles thereof.

And as a corollary to these propositions is this self-evident and contemporaneous truth:

Every progressive nation of Europe to-day is seeking lands to colonize and governments to administer.

And can this common instinct of the most progressive peoples of the world — this common conclusion of the ablest statesmen of other nations — be baseless?

If the Opposition asks why this is the mission of the American people now more than heretofore, I answer that before any people assumes these great tasks it goes through a process of consolidation and unification, just as a man achieves maturity before he assumes the tasks of a man. Great Britain never became a colonizing and administering power until the separate peoples of England, Scotland, Ireland and Wales, welded into a single indivisible people, were ready to go forth as a national unit and do the great work to which the world was calling it.

The German people did not embark upon this natural policy until separate duchies, principalities and kingdoms were finally welded by a common war, common blood, and common interests into a great single and indivisible people ready to go forth as a national unit to the great work to which the world was calling it.

The French became colonizers of lands and administrators of governments only when her great statesmen, from Richelieu to Colbert, had knit the separate and divided French people into a national unit and sent it forth to the work to which the world was calling it; and France declined only when she abandoned that natural law of national power and progress, and Napoleon diverted her energies to the internal strifes of Europe. Then her decline began. She lost Canada. The Corsican sold Louisiana to us. And to-day French statesmen at last realize the fatal operation of this law when once disobeyed, and so again are seeking to become one of the colonizing and administering powers of earth.

The American Republic has been going through the process of fitting it for the execution of this natural law of civilization. Hitherto we have had local divisions. The proposition that we were a single people, a national unit, and not a sum of segregated factions, was denied. And it required war and commerce and time — the shedding of blood, the uniting of communities by railroads and telegraphs, the knitting together of the fabric of Nationality by that wonderful loom of human intelligence called the post; and finally, the common and united effort of a foreign war, to bring us to a consciousness of our power as a people. And there is never in nature a power without a corresponding purpose. Shall we now stop this process of nature?

We are this at last, a great national unit ready to carry out that universal law of civilization which requires of every people who have reached our high estate to become colonizers of new lands, administrators of orderly government over savage and senile peoples. And being thus prepared, the lands and peoples needing our administration are delivered to our keeping, not by our design, but by occurrence beyond our control. In the astronomy of Destiny, American Opportunity, American Duty and American Preparedness are in conjunction. Who shall oppose their progress?

These are the laws which history advises are the laws of civilization's growth. These, therefore, are the high ordinances of universal and racial morality which has for its ultimate object "that far-off divine event towards which civilization tends." And it is to this divine order of progress that I appeal in answer to the misapplied individual moralities that would give Australia back to its Bushmen, the United States to its Indians, Ceylon to its natives, and the whole world back to barbarism and night.

If the Opposition says that this program, written not in the statutes of man, but in the nature of things, will smother our institutions with a myriad of soldiers, I answer that the world today demonstrates that it will result in the reverse. If they point to Germany, and other nations with vast military establishments, to prove that colonization and administration over lands held as possessions and dependencies result in the supremacy of the soldiery over the common people, I answer that the examples do not sustain, but destroy the proposition.

Consider Germany. Her standing army in times of peace is 562,000 men. Does colonization cause or require them? No; because she maintained that mighty multitude before the present Emperor and his counsellors developed Germany's progressive colonial and administrative policy. No, again; because, of Germany's standing army of 562,000 men, less than 4,000 are in her possessions, the remainder of her mighty host being stationed within the Empire itself. No, again; because Austria, with no colonies at all, has a standing army in times of peace of over 361,000 men, none of whom is employed in the care of possessions. No, again; because France, a republic, has a standing army in times of peace of 616,000 men, of which less than 10,000 are employed in her colonies and possessions except in Algeria and Tunis, which are considered an immediate part of France. No, again; because Italy, with hardly a colonial possession, maintains a standing army in times of peace of nearly 325,000 men. No, again; because Spain, the world's second largest holder of possessions before we won them, maintained a standing army of less than 100,000 men, of whom less than 10,000 were kept in her misruled and oppressed possessions. No, again; because the greatest colonial power that the world has ever seen, the Empire of Great Britain, has a smaller standing army in times of peace than any power of

Europe — less than half as many as Germany, almost two-thirds less than the soldiers of France, nearly one-third less than Italy, and one-third less than the soldiers maintained by Austria, an absolutely non-colonizing power.

Great Britain's entire standing army of English, Scotch, Welsh and Irish soldiers throughout the entire Empire is only 231,351, of which Ceylon, with a population of 3,500,000, has only one battalion of English infantry and two companies of English artillery. Egypt, with nearly 10,000,000, has less than 6,000 English officers and men; and India, with 300,000,000 population, has less than 75,000 English soldiers. The other soldiers upholding the English flag throughout England's possessions are native soldiers. England has learned the statesmanship of sentiment; and so the people England rules supply the soldiers who defend her flag.

What is it that establishes militarism in Germany? On the west, the immediate proximity of France, her hereditary foe; on the east, the immediate proximity of Russia, her hereditary foe; on the south, the immediate proximity of an heterogeneous empire. What is it that establishes militarism in France? The immediate proximity of Germany on the East, her hereditary foe; the immediate proximity of England on the north, an historic enemy; the immediate proximity of Italy on the south, the third of the Anti-French Dreibund. These are the things which establish militarism in Europe — not colonization, not possessions, not obedience to the great natural law of expansion and growth.

If France, Germany, Italy, Austria, would devote themselves to the world's great work of rescuing the wilderness, of planting civilization, of extending their institutions as England has done, as Germany is beginning to do, as the American Republic, under God, is going to lead the world in doing, the armaments of these European military powers would necessarily dissolve, because there would be no longer occasion for them; and because all their energies would be required in the nobler work to which they would thus set their hands.

To produce the same militarism in America that curses Europe, it would be necessary for Canada on the north to be an equal power with us, hostile with present rivalry and centuries of inherited hatred; and for Mexico to be the same thing on the south. And even then we should have only half the conditions that produce militarism in any European nation. Separate government in

Cuba is the only proposed step that creates conditions of militarism in America. Militarism in extending American authority! No! No! The wider the dominion of the Stars and Stripes, the broader the reign of peace.

If we do our duty in the Philippines, it is admitted that we ought not to govern the Filipinos as fellow-citizens of the Republic. The Platform of the Opposition says that "to make the Filipinos citizens would endanger our civilization." To force upon Malays, who three hundred years ago were savages and who since that time have been schooled only in oppression, that form of self-government exercised by the citizens of the United States, would be to clothe an infant in the apparel of a giant and require of it a giant's strength and tasks. If we govern them, we must govern them with common sense. They must first be made familiar with the simplest principles of liberty — equal obedience to equal laws, impartial justice by unpurchasable courts, protection of property and of the right to labor — in short, with the *substance* of liberty which civilized government will establish among them.

The Filipinos must begin at the beginning and grow in the knowledge of free institutions, and, if possible, into the ultimate practice of free government by observing the operation of those institutions among them and by experiencing their benefits. They have experienced unjust, unequal and arbitrary taxation; this is the result of the institutions of tyranny. They must experience equal, just and scientific taxation; this is the result of free institutions. They have experienced arrest without cause, imprisonment without a hearing, and beheld justice bought and sold; these are the results of the institutions of tyranny. They must experience arrest only for cause publicly made known, conviction only after trial publicly conducted and justice impartial, unpurchasable and speedily administered; these are the results of free institutions.

They have experienced the violation of the home and robbery by public officers; these are the results of the institutions of tyranny. They must experience the sanctity of the fireside, the separation of Church and State, the punishment of soldier or public official practising outrage or extortion upon them; these are the results of free institutions. And these are the results which they will experience under the government of the American Republic. For these are the results of American Institutions, and our *institutions* follow the flag.

The institutions of every nation follow its flag. German institutions follow the flag of the Fatherland. English institutions follow the banner of St. George. French institutions follow the tricolor of France. And just so, American institutions follow the emblem of the Republic. Nay! Our institutions not only follow the flag, *they accompany it*. They troop beneath its fold. Wherever an American citizen goes, he carries the spirit of our institutions. On whatever soil his blood is shed to establish the sovereignty of our flag, there are planted the imperishable seeds of the institutions of our Nation; and there those institutions flourish in proportion as the soil where they are planted is prepared for them.

Free institutions are as definite, certain and concrete as our Constitution itself. Free speech is an institution of liberty. Free schools are an institution of liberty. Freedom of worship is an institution of liberty. Any American school-boy can catalogue free institutions. And as fast as the simplest of these institutions prepares these children Providence has given into our keeping for higher grades, just so fast more complex forms of our institutions will follow as naturally as childhood succeeds infancy, youth succeeds childhood and manhood crowns maturity. Our flag! Our institutions! Our Constitution! This is the immortal order in which American civilization marches.

And so the answer to the politician's battle-cry that "our Constitution follows the flag" is this great truth of popular liberty, OUR INSTITUTIONS FOLLOW THE FLAG.

We are a Nation. We can acquire territory. If we can acquire territory, we can govern it. If we can govern it, we can govern it as its situation may demand. If the Opposition says that power so broad is dangerous to the liberties of the American people, I answer that the American people's liberties can never be endangered at the hands of the American people; and, therefore, that their liberties can not be endangered by the exercise of this power, because this power is power exercised by the American people themselves.

"Congress shall have power to dispose of and make all needful rules and regulations respecting territory belonging to the United States," says the Constitution.

And what is Congress? The agent of the American people. The Constitution created Congress. But who created the Constitution? "We, the people," declares the Constitution itself.

The American people created the Constitution; it is their method. The American people established Congress; it is their instrument. The American people elect the members of Congress; they are the people's servants. Their laws are the people's laws. Their power is the people's power. And if you fear this power, you fear the people. If you want their power restricted, it is because you want the power of the people restricted; and a restriction of their power is a restriction of their liberty. So that the end of the logic of the Opposition is limitation upon the liberties of the American people, for fear that the liberties of the American people will suffer at the hands of the American people — which is absurd.

If the Opposition asserts that the powers which the Constitution gives to the legislative agents of the American people will not be exercised in righteousness, I answer that that can only be because the American people themselves are not righteous. It is the American people, through their agents, who exercise the power; and if those agents do not act as the people would have them, they will discharge those agents and annul their acts. The heart of the whole argument on the constitutional power of the government is faith in the wisdom and virtue of the people; and in that virtue and wisdom I believe, as every man must, who believes in a republic. In the end, the judgment of the masses is right. If this were not so, progress would be impossible, since only through the people is progress achieved.

The Opposition says that American liberties will be lost if we administer the substance of liberty to those children. Does any man believe that the American institution of free schools will be destroyed or impaired because we plant free schools throughout the Philippines? Does any man believe that equal rights will be impaired here, because we establish equal rights there?

The individual rights of Englishmen have not declined since England became an administrator of external governments; on the contrary, as England has extended her colonies, the individual rights of individual Englishmen have increased. The rights of the Crown have not enlarged as England's empire has extended; on the contrary, they have diminished. The period of England's great activity in external government has been precisely the period of the extension of the suffrage in England itself, of the enactment of laws for the protection of labor and the amelioration of all the conditions of life among the common people of England.

The period of England's most active extension of empire has not been the period of her most violent oppression of Ireland; the contrary is true. Ireland's bitterest hour was in Cromwell's day and at Cromwell's hands; and yet England had no definite plan of empire then. Ireland's most progressive period has been within the last quarter of a century, when land laws were enacted by the British Parliament compelling Irish landlords to sell their lands to Irish tenants, and permitting the tenant to purchase his landlord's land by the payment of his rent at a price, fixed not by the landlord, but by the courts and commissions.

Ireland's brightest day has been within the last ten years, in which her people have deposited more money in savings banks than in a century before. And yet the last quarter of a century has been England's most imperial period. The last ten years have witnessed the most systematic work by England in empire building in all her history. And England's experience is not an isolated instance. It would not be isolated even if it were confined to England, since her sway is as wide as the world. But the experience of her people is the experience of every other people who have embarked upon the same great voyage.

This is no unprecedented struggle. It is the ever-old and yet the ever-new, because the ever-elemental contest between the forces of a growing nationality and those who resist it; between the forces of extending dominion and those who oppose it; between the forces that are making us the master people of the world and those who think that our activities should be confined to this continent for ever. It is the eternal duel between the forces of progress and reaction, of construction and disintegration, of growth and of decay.

Both sides are and always have been sincere. Washington was sincere when he advocated the adoption of the Constitution; Patrick Henry was sincere when he resisted it as the death-blow to our liberties. Jefferson was sincere when he acquired the empire of Louisiana; Josiah Quincy was sincere when he declared in Congress that the Louisiana acquisition meant the dissolution of the Union.

Webster was sincere when he asserted the sovereignty of the Nation, the indestructibility of the Union, and declared that the

Constitution could not follow the flag until the American people so decreed; and Calhoun was sincere when he pronounced the doctrine of state sovereignty, the right of nullification, and announced that the Constitution, carrying slavery, followed the flag in spite of the will of the American people. Lincoln was sincere when he proclaimed that the Union was older than the Constitution, that nationality was the indestructible destiny of the American people, and that he would maintain that nationality by arms; and those mistaken ones were sincere who sought to divide the American people and on the field of battle poured out their blood fighting for their faith.

But their sincerity did not make them *right*. Their earnestness, ability, courage could not give them victory. They were struggling against the Fates. They were resisting the onward forces which were making of the American people the master Nation of the world — the forces that established us first as a separate political body, then welded us into a national unit, indivisible; then extended our dominion from ocean to ocean over unexplored wilderness; and now in the ripeness of time fling our authority and unfurl our flag almost around the globe. It is the "divine event" of American principles among the governments of men for which these forces have been working since the Pilgrims landed on the red man's soil. Men — patriotic, brave and wise — have sought to stay that tremendous purpose of destiny, but their opposition was as the feeble finger of a babe against the resistless pour of the Gulf Stream's mighty current.

For God's hand was in it all. His plans were working out their glorious results. And just as futile is resistance to the continuance to-day of the eternal movement of the American people toward the mastery of the world. This is a destiny neither vague nor undesirable. It is definite, splendid and holy.

When nations shall war no more without the consent of the American Republic: what American heart thrills not with pride at that prospect? And yet our interests are weaving themselves so rapidly around the world that that time is almost here.

When governments stay the slaughter of human beings, because the American Republic demands it: what American heart thrills not with pride at that prospect? And yet to-night there sits in Constantinople a sovereign who knows that time is nearly here.

When the commerce of the world on which the world's peace

hangs, traveling every ocean highway of earth, shall pass beneath the guns of the great Republic: what American heart thrills not at that prospect? Yet that time will be here before the first quarter of the twentieth century closes.

When any changing of the map of earth requires a conference of the Powers, and when, at any Congress of the Nations, the American Republic will preside as the most powerful of powers and most righteous of judges; what American heart thrills not at that prospect? And yet, that prospect is in sight, even as I speak.

It is the high and holy destiny of the American people, and from that destiny the American bugles will never sound retreat. "Westward the Star of Empire takes its way!" AMERICAN INSTITUTIONS FOLLOW THE AMERICAN FLAG.

CARL SCHURZ

(1829-1906)

Among the scores of German immigrants who flocked to this country after the unsuccessful Revolution of 1848, there was no reason to single out the name of Carl Schurz for future greatness. True, he had distinguished himself in the Revolution, but America was not Germany, and this immigrant knew but one word of English — beefsteak — when he arrived in New York City in 1852. Yet six years later he was making political speeches on behalf of Lincoln throughout Illinois and Wisconsin. He had studied newspapers and novels until he had attained a mastery of the language. In his fine biography of the man, Claude Fuess points out that Schurz "mastered spoken English very thoroughly, and, by 1860, traces of his German accent were barely perceptible." Fuess adds that it was "through his oratory that Carl Schurz became nationally famous." Mastery of the spoken word helped to carry Schurz to such eminent and responsible public offices as Minister to Spain, United States Senator, and Secretary of the Interior.

As a public speaker, Schurz had few equals for popularity — even though he was physically unimpressive. Fuess describes him as "an awkward looking figure, somewhat over six feet tall, excessively thin of body and rather loose-jointed. . . . Bespectacled and serious of countenance, he looked like an unworldly college professor whose cherished aim was the improvement of his fellow men and women." His complete sincerity, however, won him the admiration and respect of friends and enemies alike. At a celebration given in honor of Mr. Schurz's seventieth birthday, the Honorable Moorfield Storey said:

> The singular clearness of statement, which has never deserted him, his wonderful command of English, the unfailing calmness

and dignity with which he encountered and returned the attacks of his opponents, made him the first debater in the Senate, and an orator second to none. But he never descended to anything unworthy, and you may search his speeches in vain for any appeal to low motive, for any trace of thought for his personal fortunes.[1]

Further evidence of the respect paid Schurz as a speaker is contained in this passage by Bancroft and Dunning from The Reminiscences of Carl Schurz:

. . . the lofty tone of his speeches, emphasized by graceful diction and impressive delivery, at once commanded the close attention of his colleagues on the floor and of large audiences in the galleries. Each formal speech also had much of the literary quality of a well-rounded essay on the subject under discussion; and his argument always appealed to minds capable of grasping the larger aspects of history and philosophy. Although there was no lack of satire and cutting denunciation for false theories and objectionable projects, mere personalities and unreasoned invective were disliked and avoided. Consequently Schurz early won from serious opponents a degree of respectful consideration that Sumner, popularly regarded as the leader of the Senate, had never been able to secure.[2]

Schurz not only was earnest and direct, but also a master of the spoken word. He had the gift of facile expression and ready wit. Fuess characterized him as

. . . a clever extemporaneous speaker, with an easy colloquial style. . . . Only self-restraint kept him from indulging too freely in sarcasm and abuse, which he could on occasions employ with telling effect. . . . In the heat of controversy, he was alert, unperturbed, corrosive, never losing sight of the thread of the argument and always ready with some convincing or withering retort. Unlike Sumner, he was never solemn or pompous, and he did not exaggerate. A gift of crisp and vivid phrasing held the interest of his hearers.[3]

Carl Schurz was seventy years old and in virtual retirement when the proposed annexation of the Philippine Islands by the United States was vigorously protested by various anti-imperialist elements in this country. His age, however, was not enough to keep him from fighting for what he believed was right, and when the Anti-

[1] Edwin D. Shurter, *Masterpieces of Modern Oratory*, p. 295.
[2] III, p. 318.
[3] *Carl Schurz*, p. 172.

Imperialist Convention was held in Chicago on October 17-18, 1899, Carl Schurz was more than willing to make one of the principal addresses. On the night of October 17, Schurz took the platform in Chicago's Central Music Hall, and, with characteristic force and logic, condemned the imperialist policies of the McKinley government. He was wildly cheered by a partisan crowd of some 2,000 people, but the Chicago press was hardly partisan. The Chicago Tribune of October 19 called Schurz's own anti-imperialist policy an "ineffectual, halfway, compromise measure" which was the "statement of mugwumpery." The Chicago Evening Post added that it was

> . . . idle for Mr. Schurz and his sympathizers to assert that the Philippine campaign is immoral and unpopular, to represent it as a campaign of conquest and "criminal aggression." "Peace first," the President has declared, and this is what our soldiers are fighting for in the far East. Ultimate questions of policy have no relation whatever to immediate duty and responsibility.[4]

As always, Carl Schurz had spoken exactly what was on his mind — "Our country, when right to be kept right; when wrong to be put right." But sincerity and patriotism were not enough to win widespread popular support for the cause of anti-imperialism, and the movement died a quiet death. Schurz continued to follow politics and current affairs, but he had made his last great speech. Less than seven years later, the man who had been honored as the greatest German-American of his day was dead.

THE POLICY OF IMPERIALISM

by

Carl Schurz

Delivered in Chicago in the Central Music Hall on October 17, 1899.

MORE THAN EIGHT MONTHS AGO I had the honor of addressing the citizens of Chicago on the subject of American imperialism, mean-

[4] October 18, 1899, p. 4.

ing the policy of annexing to this Republic distant countries and alien populations that will not fit into our democratic system of government. I discussed at that time mainly the baneful effect that the pursuit of an imperialistic policy would produce upon our political institutions. After long silence, during which I have carefully reviewed my own opinions, as well as those of others in the light of the best information I could obtain, I shall now approach the same subject from another point of view.

We all know that the popular mind is much disturbed by the Philippine war, and that, however highly we admire the bravery of our soldiers, nobody professes to be proud of the war itself. There are few Americans who do not frankly admit their regret that this war should ever have happened. I think I risk nothing when I say that it is not merely the bungling conduct of military operations, but a serious trouble of conscience, that disturbs the American heart about this war, and that this trouble of conscience will not be allayed by a more successful military campaign, just as fifty years ago the trouble of conscience about slavery could not be allayed by any compromise.

Many people now, as the slavery compromisers did then, try to ease their minds by saying: "Well, we are in it, and now we must do the best we can." In spite of the obvious futility of this cry in some respects, I will accept it with the one proviso, that we make an honest effort to ascertain what really is the best we can do. To this end let us first clearly remember what has happened.

In April, 1898, we went to war with Spain for the avowed purpose of liberating the people of Cuba, who had long been struggling for freedom and independence. Our object in that war was clearly and emphatically proclaimed by a solemn resolution of Congress repudiating all intention of annexation on our part, and declaring that the Cuban people "are, and of right ought to be, free and independent." This solemn declaration was made to do justice to the spirit of the American people, who were indeed willing to wage a war of liberation, but would not have consented to a war of conquest. It was also to propitiate the opinion of mankind for our action. President McKinley also declared with equal solemnity that annexation by force could not be thought of, because, according to our code of morals, it would be "criminal aggression."

Can it justly be pretended that these declarations referred only to the island of Cuba? What would the American people, what would the world, have said if Congress had resolved that the Cuban people were indeed rightfully entitled to freedom and independence, but that as to the people of other Spanish colonies we recognized no such right; and if President McKinley had declared that the forcible annexation of Cuba would be criminal, but that the forcible annexation of other Spanish colonies would be a righteous act? A general outburst of protest from our own people, and of derision and contempt from the whole world, would have been the answer. No, there can be no cavil — that war was proclaimed to all mankind to be a war of liberation, and not of conquest, and even now our very imperialists are still boasting that the war was prompted by the most unselfish and generous purposes, and that those insult us who do not believe it.

In the course of that war Commodore Dewey, by a brilliant feat of arms, destroyed the Spanish fleet in the harbor of Manila. This did not change the heralded character of the war — certainly not in Dewey's own opinion. The Filipinos, constituting the strongest and foremost tribe of the population of the archipelago, had long been fighting for freedom and independence, just as the Cubans had. The great mass of the other islanders sympathized with them. They fought for the same cause as the Cubans, and they fought against the same enemy — the same enemy against whom we were waging our war of humanity and liberation. They had the same title to freedom and independence which we recognized as "of right" in the Cubans — nay, more; for, as Admiral Dewey telegraphed to our Government, "they are far superior in their intelligence, and more capable of self-government, than the natives of Cuba." The Admiral adds: "I am familiar with both races, and further intercourse with them has confirmed me in this opinion."

Indeed, the mendacious stories spread by our imperialists, which represent those people as barbarians, their doings as "mere savagery" and their chiefs as no better than "cut-throats," have been refuted by such a mass of authoritative testimony, coming in part from men who are themselves imperialists, that their authors should hide their heads in shame; for surely it is not the part of really brave men to calumniate their victims before sacrificing them. We need not praise the Filipinos as in every way the equals of the "embattled farmers" of Lexington and Concord, and Aguinaldo as the peer of Washington; but there is an overwhelming abundance of testimony — some of it unwilling — that the Filipinos are fully the equals, and even the superiors, of the Cubans and the Mexicans. As to Aguinaldo, Admiral Dewey is credited with saying that he is controlled by men abler than himself. The same could be said of more than one of our Presidents. Moreover, it would prove that those are greatly mistaken who predict that the Filipino uprising would collapse were Aguinaldo captured or killed. The old slander that Aguinaldo had sold out the revolutionary movement for a bribe of $400,000 has been so thoroughly exploded by the best authority that it requires uncommon audacity to repeat it.

Now let us see what has happened. Two months before the beginning of our Spanish war, our Consul at Manila reported to the State Department: "Conditions here and in Cuba are practically alike. War exists, battles are of almost daily occurrence. The crown forces have not been able to dislodge a rebel army within ten miles of Manila. A republic is organized here as in Cuba." When, two months later, our war of liberation and humanity began, Commodore Dewey was at Hong Kong with his ships. He received orders to attack and destroy the Spanish fleet in those waters. It was then that our Consul-General at Singapore informed our State Department that he had conferred with General Aguinaldo, then at Singapore, as to the cooperation of the Philippine insurgents, and that he had telegraphed to Commodore Dewey that Aguinaldo was willing to come to Hong Kong to arrange with Dewey for "general cooperation, if desired"; whereupon Dewey promptly answered: "Tell Aguinaldo come soon as possible." The meeting was had. Dewey sailed to Manila to destroy the Spanish fleet, and Aguinaldo was taken to the seat of war on a vessel of the United States. His forces received a supply of arms through Commodore Dewey, and did faithfully and effectively cooperate with our forces against the Spaniards, so effectively, indeed, that soon afterwards by their efforts the Spaniards had lost the whole country, except a few garrisons in which they were practically blockaded.

Now, what were the relations between the Philippine insurgents and this Republic? There is some dispute as to certain agreements, including a promise of Philippine independence, said to have been made between Aguinaldo and our Consul-General at Singapore before Aguinaldo proceeded to cooperate with Dewey. But I lay no stress upon this point. I will let only the record of facts speak. Of these facts the first, of highest importance, is that Aguinaldo was "desired," that is, invited, by officers of the United States to cooperate with our forces. The second is that the Filipino Junta in Hong Kong immediately after these conferences appealed to their countrymen to receive the American fleet, about to sail for Manila, as friends, by a proclamation which had these words: "Compatriots, divine Providence is about to place independence within our reach. The Americans, not from any mercenary motives, but for the sake of humanity, have considered it opportune to extend their protecting mantle to our beloved country. Where you see the American flag flying, assemble in mass. They are our redeemers." With this faith his followers gave Aguinaldo a rapturous greeting upon his arrival at Cavité, where he proclaimed his government and organized his army under Dewey's eyes.

The arrival of our land forces did not at first change these relations. Brigadier-General Thomas M. Anderson, commanding, wrote to Aguinaldo, July 4th, as follows:

> General, I have the honor to inform you that the United States of America, whose land forces I have the honor to command in this vicinity, being at war with the kingdom of Spain, has entire sympathy and most friendly sentiments for the native people of the Philippine Islands. For these reasons I desire to have the most amicable relations with you, and to have you and your people cooperate with us in military operations against the Spanish forces, etc.

Aguinaldo responded cordially, and an extended correspondence followed, special services being asked for by the party of the first part, being rendered by the second and duly acknowledged by the first. All this went on pleasantly until the capture of Manila, in which Aguinaldo effectively cooperated by fighting the Spaniards outside, taking many prisoners from them, and hemming them in. The services they rendered by taking thousands of Spanish prisoners, by harassing the Spaniards in the trenches and by completely blockading Manila on the land side, were amply testified to by our own officers. Aguinaldo was also active on the sea. He had ships which our commanders permitted to pass in and out of Manila Bay, under the flag of the Philippine Republic, on their expeditions against other provinces.

Now, whether there was or not any formal compact of alliance signed and sealed, no candid man who has studied the official documents will deny that in point of fact the Filipinos, having been desired and invited to do so, were, before the capture of Manila, acting, and were practically recognized, as our allies, and that as such they did effective service, which we accepted and profited by. This is an indisputable fact, proved by the record.

It is an equally indisputable fact that during that period the Filipino government constantly and publicly, so that nobody could plead ignorance of it or misunderstand it, informed the world that their object was the achievement of national independence, and that they believed the Americans had come in good faith to help them accomplish that end, as in the case of Cuba. It was weeks after various proclamations and other public utterances of Aguinaldo to that effect that the correspondence between him and General Anderson, which I have quoted, took place, and that the useful services of the Filipinos as our practical allies were accepted. It is, further, an indisputable fact that during this period our Government did not inform the Filipinos that their fond expectations as to our recognition of their independence were mistaken. Our Secretary of State did, indeed, on June 16th write to Mr. Pratt, our Consul-General at Singapore, that our Government knew the Philippine insurgents, not indeed as patriots struggling for liberty, and who, like the Cubans, "are and of right ought to be free and independent," but merely as "discontented and rebellious subjects of Spain," who, if we occupied their country in consequence of the war, would have to yield us due "obedience." And other officers of our Government were instructed not to make any promises to the Filipinos as to the future. But the Filipinos themselves were not so informed. They were left to believe that, while fighting in coöperation with the American forces, they were fighting for their own independence. They could not imagine that the Government of the great American Republic, while boasting of having gone to war with Spain under the banner of liberation and humanity in behalf of Cuba, was capable of secretly plotting to turn that war into one for the conquest and subjugation of the Philippines. Thus the Filipinos went faithfully and bravely on doing for us the service of allies, of brothers in arms, far from dreaming that the same troops with whom they had been asked to coöperate would soon be employed by the great apostle of liberation and humanity to slaughter them for no other reason than that they, the Filipinos, continued to stand up for their own freedom and independence.

But just that was to happen. As soon as Manila was taken and we had no further use for our Filipino allies, they were ordered to fall back and back from the city and its suburbs. Our military commanders treated the Filipinos' country as if it were our own. When Aguinaldo sent one of his aides-de-camp to General Merritt with a request for an interview, General Merritt was "too busy." When our peace negotiations with Spain began, and representatives of the Filipinos asked for audience to solicit consideration of the rights and wishes of their people, the doors were slammed in their faces, in Washington as well as in Paris. And behind those doors the scheme was hatched to deprive the Philippine Islanders of independence from foreign rule, and to make them the subjects of another foreign ruler; and that foreign ruler their late ally, this great Republic which had grandly proclaimed to the world that its war against Spain was not a war of conquest, but a war of liberation and humanity.

Behind those doors which were tightly closed to the people of the Philippines, a treaty was made with Spain, by the direction of President McKinley, which provided for the cession of the Philippine Islands by Spain to the United States for a consideration of $20,000,000. It has been said that this sum was not purchase-money, but a compensation for improvements made by Spain, or a *solatium* to sweeten the pill of cession, or what not. But, stripped of all cloudy verbiage, it was really purchase-money, the sale being made by Spain under duress. Thus Spain sold, and the United States bought, what was called the sovereignty of Spain over the Philippine Islands and their people.

Now look at the circumstances under which that "cession" was made. Spain had lost the possession of the country, except a few isolated and helpless little garrisons, most of which were effectively blockaded by the Filipinos. The American forces occupied Cavité and the harbor and city of Manila, and nothing more. The bulk of the country was occupied and possessed by the people thereof, over whom Spain had, in point of fact, ceased to exercise any sovereignty, the Spanish power having been driven out or destroyed by the Filipino insurrection, while the United States had not acquired, beyond Cavité and Manila, any authority of whatever name by military occupation, nor by recognition on the part of the people. Aguinaldo's army surrounded Manila on the land side, and his government claimed organized control over fifteen provinces. That government was established at Malolos not far from Manila; and a very respectable government, it was. According to Mr. Barrett, our late Minister in Siam, himself an ardent imperialist, who had seen it, it had a well-organized Executive, divided into several departments, ably conducted, and a popular Assembly, a Congress, which would favorably compare with the Parliament of Japan — an infinitely better government than the insurrectionary government of Cuba ever was.

It is said that Aguinaldo's government was in operation among only a part of the people of the islands. This is true. But it is also certain that it was recognized and supported by an immeasurably larger part of the people than Spanish sovereignty, which had practically ceased to exist, and than American rule, which was confined to a harbor and a city, and which was carried on by the exercise of military force under what was substantially martial law over a people that constituted about one-twentieth of the whole population of the islands. Thus, having brought but a very small fraction of the country and its people under our military control, we bought by that treaty the sovereignty over the whole from a Power which had practically lost that sovereignty, and therefore did no longer possess it; and we contemptuously disdained to consult the existing native government, which actually did control a large part of the country and people, and which had been our ally in the war with Spain. The sovereignty we thus acquired may well be defined as Abraham Lincoln once defined the "popular sovereignty" of Senator Douglas's doctrine — as being like a soup made by boiling the shadow of the breastbone of a pigeon that had been starved to death.

No wonder that treaty found opposition in the Senate. Virulent abuse was heaped upon the "statesman who would oppose the ratification of a peace treaty." A peace treaty? This was no peace treaty at all. It was a treaty with half a dozen bloody wars in its belly. It was, in the first place, an open and brutal declaration of war against our allies, the Filipinos, who struggled for freedom and independence from foreign rule. Every man not totally blind could see that. For such a treaty the true friends of peace could, of course, not vote.

But more. Even before that treaty had been assented to by the Senate, that is, even before that ghastly shadow of our Philippine sovereignty had obtained any legal sanction, President McKinley assumed of his own motion the sovereignty of the Philippine Islands by his famous "benevolent assimilation" order of December 21, 1898, through which our military commander at Manila was directed forthwith to extend the military government of the United States over the whole archipelago, and by which the Filipinos were notified that, if they refused to submit, they would be compelled by force of arms. Having bravely fought for their freedom and independence from one foreign rule, they did refuse to submit to another foreign rule, and then the slaughter of our late allies began — the slaughter by American arms of a once friendly and confiding people. And this slaughter has been going on ever since.

This is a grim story. Two years ago the prediction of such a possibility would have been regarded as a hideous nightmare, as the offspring of a diseased imagination. But to-day it is a true tale — a plain recital of facts taken from the official records. These things have actually been done in these last two years by and under the Administration of William McKinley. This is our Philippine war as it stands. Is it a wonder that the American people should be troubled in their consciences? But let us not be too swift in our judgment on the conduct of those in power over us. Let us hear what they have to say in defense of it.

It is pretended that we had a right to the possession of the Philippines, and that self-respect demanded us to enforce that right. What kind of right was it? The right of conquest? Had we really acquired that country by armed conquest, which, as President McKinley has told us, is, according to the American code of morals, "criminal aggression"? But if we had thrown aside our code of morals, we had then not conquered more than the bay and city of Manila. The rest of the country was controlled, if by anybody, by the Filipinos. Or was it the right of possession by treaty? I have already shown that the President ordered the enforcement of our sovereignty over the archipelago before the treaty had by ratification gained legal effect, and also that, in making that treaty, we had bought something called sovereignty which Spain had ceased to possess and could therefore not sell and deliver. But let me bring the matter home to you by a familiar example.

Imagine that in our revolutionary times, France, being at war with England, had brought to this country a fleet and an army, and had, without any definite compact to that effect, cooperated as an ally with our revolutionary forces, permitting all the while the Americans to believe that she did this without any mercenary motive, and that, in case of victory, the American colonies would be free and independent. Imagine then that, after the British surrendered at Yorktown, the King of France had extorted from the British King a treaty ceding, for a consideration of $20,000,000, the sovereignty over the American colonies to France, and that thereupon the King of France had coolly notified the Continental Congress and General Washington that they had to give up their idea of National independence, and to surrender unconditionally to the sovereignty of France, wherefor the French King promised them "benevolent assimilation." Imagine, further, that upon the protest of the Americans that Great Britain, having lost everything in the colonies except New York City and a few other little posts, had no sovereignty to cede, the French King answered that he had bought the Americans at $5 a head, and that if they refused to submit he would give them benevolent assimilation in the shape of bullets. Can there be any doubt that the Continental Congress and General Washington would have retorted that, no matter what the French King might have bought, Great Britain had no sovereignty left to sell; that least of all would the Americans permit themselves to be sold; that the French, in so treating their American allies after such high-sounding professions of friendship and generosity, were a lot of mean, treacherous, contemptible hypocrites, and that the Americans would rather die than submit to such wolves in sheep's clothing? And will any patriotic American now deny that, whatever quibbles of international law about possible cessions of a lost sovereignty might be invented, such conduct of the French would have been simply a shame and that the Americans of that time would have eternally disgraced themselves if they had failed to resist unto death? How, then, can the same patriotic American demand that the Filipinos should surrender and accept American sovereignty under circumstances exactly parallel? And that parallel will not be shaken by any learned international law technicalities, which do not touch the moral element of the subject.

It is also pretended that, whatever our rights, the Filipinos were the original aggressors in the pending fight, and that our troops found themselves compelled to defend their flag against assault.

What are the facts? One evening early in February last some Filipino soldiers entered the American lines without, however, attacking anybody. An American sentry fired, killing one of the Filipinos. Then a desultory firing began at the outposts. It spread until it assumed the proportions of an extensive engagement in which a large number of Filipinos were killed. It is a well-established fact that this engagement could not have been a premeditated affair on the part of the Filipinos, as many of their officers, including Aguinaldo's private secretary, were at the time in the theaters and cafés of Manila. It is further well known that the next day Aguinaldo sent an officer, General Torres, under a flag of truce to General Otis to declare that the fighting had not been authorized by Aguinaldo, but had begun accidentally; that Aguinaldo wished to have it stopped, and proposed to that end the establishment of a neutral zone between the two armies, such as might be agreeable to General Otis; whereupon General Otis curtly answered that the fighting, having once begun, must go on to the grim end. Who was it that really wanted the fight?

But far more important than all this is the fact that President McKinley's "benevolent assimilation" order, which even before the ratification of the treaty demanded that the Philippine Islanders should unconditionally surrender to American sovereignty, in default whereof our military forces would compel them, was really the President's declaration of war against the Filipinos insisting upon independence, however you may quibble about it. When an armed man enters my house under some questionable pretext, and tells me that I must yield to him unconditional control of the premises or he will knock me down — who is the aggressor, no matter who strikes the first blow? No case of aggression can be clearer, shuffle and prevaricate as you will.

Let us recapitulate. We go to war with Spain in behalf of an oppressed colony of hers. We solemnly proclaim this to be a war — not of conquest — God forbid! — but of liberation and humanity. We invade the Spanish colony of the Philippines, destroy the Spanish fleet, and invite the cooperation of the Filipino insurgents against Spain. We accept their effective aid as allies, all the while permitting them to believe that, in case of victory, they will be free and independent. By active fighting they get control of a large part of the interior country, from which Spain is virtually ousted. When we have captured Manila and have no further use for our

Filipino allies, our President directs that, behind their backs, a treaty be made with Spain transferring their country to us; and even before that treaty is ratified, he tells them that, in place of the Spaniards, they must accept us as their masters, and that if they do not, they will be compelled by force of arms. They refuse, and we shoot them down; and, as President McKinley said at Pittsburgh, we shall continue to shoot them down "without useless parley."

I have recited these things in studiously sober and dry matter-of-fact language, without oratorical ornament or appeal. I ask you now what epithet can you find justly to characterize such a course? Happily, you need not search for one, for President McKinley himself has furnished the best when, in a virtuous moment, he said that annexation by force should not be thought of, for, according to the American code of morals, it would be "criminal aggression." Yes, "criminal" is the word. Have you ever heard of any aggression more clearly criminal than this? And in this case there is an element of peculiarly repulsive meanness and treachery. I pity the American who can behold this spectacle without the profoundest shame, contrition and resentment. Is it a wonder, I repeat, that the American people, in whose name this has been done, should be troubled in their consciences?

To justify, or rather to excuse, such things, nothing but a plea of the extremest necessity will avail. Did such a necessity exist? In a sort of helpless way the defenders of this policy ask: "What else could the President have done under the circumstances?" This question is simply childish. If he thought he could not order Commodore Dewey away from Manila after the execution of the order to destroy the Spanish fleet, he could have told the people of the Philippine Islands that this was, on our part, a war not of conquest, but of liberation and humanity; that we sympathized with their desire for freedom and independence, and that we would treat them as we had specifically promised to treat the Cuban people in furthering the establishment of an independent government. And this task would have been much easier than in the case of Cuba, since, according to Admiral Dewey's repeatedly emphatic testimony, the Filipinos were much better fitted for such a government.

Our ingenious Postmaster-General has told us that the President could not have done that because he had no warrant for it, since he did not know whether the American people would wish to keep the Philippine Islands. But what warrant, then, had the President for putting before the Filipinos, by his "benevolent assimilation order," the alternative of submission to our sovereignty or war? Had he any assurance that the American people willed that? If such was his dream, there may be a rude awakening in store for him. But I say that for assenting to the aspiration of the Filipinos to freedom and independence he would have had the fullest possible warrant in the spirit of our institutions and in the resolution of Congress stamping our war against Spain as a war of liberation and humanity. And such a course would surely have been approved by the American people, except perhaps some Jingoes bent upon wild adventure, and some syndicates of speculators unscrupulous in their greed of gain.

There are also some who, with the mysterious mien of a superior sense of responsibility, tell us that the President could not have acted otherwise, because Dewey's victory devolved upon us some grave international or other obligations which would have been disregarded had the President failed to claim sovereignty over the Philippines. What? Did not the destruction of Cervera's fleet and the taking of Santiago devolve the same obligations upon us with regard to Cuba? And who has ever asserted that therefore Cuba must be put under our sovereignty? And did ever anybody pretend that our victories in Mexico fifty years ago imposed upon us international or other obligations which compelled us to assume sovereignty over the Mexican Republic after we had conquered it much more than we have conquered the Philippines? Does not, in the light of history, this obligation-dodge appear as a hollow mockery?

An equally helpless plea is it, that the President could not treat with Aguinaldo and his followers because they did not represent the whole population of the islands. But having an established government and an army of some 25,000 or 30,000 men, and in that army men from various tribes, they represented at least something. They represented at least a large part of the population and a strong nucleus of a national organization. And, as we have to confess that in the Philippines there is no active opposition to the Filipino government except that which we ourselves manage to excite, it may be assumed that they represent the sympathy of practically the whole people.

But, pray, what do we represent there? At first, while the islanders confided in us as their liberators, we represented their hope for freedom and independence. Since we have betrayed that hope and have begun to slaughter them, we represent, as a brute force bent upon subjugating them, only their bitter hatred and detestation. We have managed to turn virtually that whole people, who at first greeted us with childlike trust as their beloved deliverers, into deadly enemies. For it is a notorious fact that those we regard as amigos to-day will to-morrow stand in the ranks of our foes. We have not a true friend left among the islanders unless it be some speculators and the Sultan of Sulu with his harem and his slaves, whose support we have bought with a stipend like that which the Republic in its feeble infancy paid to the pirates of the Barbary States. And even his friendship will hardly last long. Yes, it is a terrible fact that in one year we have made them hate us more, perhaps, than they hated even their Spanish oppressors, who were at least foreign to them, and that the manner in which we are treating them has caused many, if not most, of the Filipinos to wish that they had patiently suffered Spanish tyranny rather than be "liberated" by us.

Thus it appears that we who represent in the Philippines no popular element at all, but are unpopular in the extreme, cannot enter into relations with an established government for the pretended reason that it does not represent all the people, while it does represent a very important part of them, and would probably soon represent them all if we did not constantly throw obstacles in its way — aye, if we did not seek to extinguish it in blood. Was there ever a false pretense more glaring?

But the ghastliest argument of all in defense of the President's course is that he had to extend American sovereignty over the whole archipelago even before the ratification of the treaty, and that he was, and is now, obliged to shoot down the Filipinos, to the end of "restoring order" and "preventing anarchy" in the islands. We are to understand that if our strong armed hand did not restrain them from doing as they pleased — that is, if they were left free and independent — they would quickly begin to cut one another's or other people's throats, and to ravish and destroy one another's or other people's property. We may reasonably assume that if this were sure to be the upshot of their being left free and independent, they would have shown some such tendency where they have actually held sway under their own revolutionary government.

Now for the facts. We have the reports of two naval officers and of two members of the signal corps who travelled extensively behind Aguinaldo's lines through the country controlled by his government. And what did they find? Quiet and orderly rural or municipal communities, in all appearance well organized and governed, full of enthusiasm for their liberty and independence, which they thought secured by the expulsion of the Spaniards, and for their leader Aguinaldo, and at the time — it was before President McKinley had ordered the subjugation of the islands — also for the Americans, whom, with childlike confidence, they still believed friendly to their freedom from all foreign rule. We may be sure that if any anarchical disturbances had happened among them, our imperialists would have eagerly made report. But there has been nothing at all equivalent to such things of our own as the famous "battle of Virden" in Illinois, or the race troubles in our own States, or the numerous lynchings we have witnessed with shame and alarm in various parts of our Republic. The only rumors of so-called "anarchy" have come through a British consul on the island of Borneo, who writes that bloody broils are occurring in some of the southernmost regions of the Philippine archipelago, and that the Americans are wanted there. But the Americans are engaged in killing orderly Filipinos — Filipino soldiers of just that Filipino government which, on its part, would probably soon restore order in the troubled places, if it had not to defend itself against the "criminal aggression" of the Americans.

The imperialists wish us to believe that in the Philippines there is bloody disorder wherever our troops are not. In fact, after the Filipinos had expelled the Spaniards from the interior of their country, bloody disorders began there only when our troops appeared. Here is an example. In December last the city of Iloilo, the second city in commercial importance in the Philippines, was evacuated by the Spaniards and occupied by the Filipinos. General M. P. Miller of our Army was sent in command of an expedition to take possession of it. As he has publicly stated, when he appeared with his ships and soldiers before the city he "received a letter from the business people of Iloilo, principally foreigners, stating that good order was being maintained, life and property being protected, and requesting him not to attack at present."

But soon afterwards he received peremptory orders to attack, and did so; and then the killing and the burning of houses and other work of devastation began. Can it be said that our troops had to go there to "restore order" and prevent bloodshed and devastation? No, order and safety existed there, and it was only with our troops that the bloodshed and devastation came which otherwise might not have occurred.

I am far from meaning to picture the Philippine Islanders as paragons of virtue and gentle conduct. But I challenge the imperialists to show me any instances of bloody disturbance or other savagery among them sufficient to create any necessity for our armed interference to "restore order" or to "save them from anarchy." I ask and demand an answer: Is it not true that, even if there has been such a disorderly tendency, it would have required a long time for it to kill one-tenth as many human beings as we have killed and to cause one-tenth as much devastation as we have caused by our assaults upon them? Is it not true that, instead of being obliged to "restore order," we have carried riot and death and desolation into peaceful communities whose only offense was not that they did not maintain order and safety among themselves, but that they refused to accept us as their rulers? And here is the rub.

In the vocabulary of our imperialists "order" means, above all, submission to their will. Any other kind of order, be it ever so peaceful and safe, must be suppressed with a bloody hand. This "order" is the kind that has been demanded by the despot since the world had a history. Its language has already become dangerously familiar to us — a familiarity which cannot cease too soon.

From all these points of view, therefore, the Philippine war was as unnecessary as it is injust. A wanton, wicked and abominable war — so it is called by untold thousands of American citizens, and so it is at heart felt to be, I have no doubt, by an immense majority of the American people. Aye, as such it is cursed by many of our very soldiers whom our Government orders to shoot down innocent people. And who will deny that this war would certainly have been avoided had the President remained true to the National pledge that the war against Spain should be a war of liberation and humanity and not of conquest? Can there by any doubt that, if the assurance had honestly been given and carried out, we might have had, for the mere asking, all the coaling-stations, and facilities for commercial and industrial enterprise, and freedom for the establishment of schools and churches we might reasonably desire? And what have we now? After eight months of slaughter and devastation, squandered treasure and shame, an indefinite prospect of more and more slaughter, devastation, squandered treasure and shame.

But, we are asked, since we have to deal with a situation not as it might have been, but as it is, what do we propose to do now? We may fairly turn about and say, since not we, but you, have got the country into this frightful mess, what have you to propose? Well, and what is the answer? "No useless parley! More soldiers! More guns! More blood! more devastation! Kill, kill, kill! And when we have killed enough, so that further resistance stops, then we shall see." Translated from smooth phrase into plain English, this is the program. Let us examine it with candor and coolness.

What is the ultimate purpose of this policy? To be perfectly fair, I will assume that the true spirit of American imperialism is represented not by the extremists who want to subjugate the Philippine Islanders at any cost and then exploit the islands to the best advantage of the conquerors, but by the more humane persons who say that we must establish our sovereignty over them to make them happy, to prepare them for self-government, and even recognize their right to complete independence as soon as they show themselves fit for it.

Let me ask these well-meaning citizens a simple question. If you think that the American people may ultimately consent to the independence of those islanders as a matter of right and good policy, why do you insist upon killing them now? You answer: Because they refuse to recognize our sovereignty. Why do they so refuse? Because they think themselves entitled to independence, and are willing to fight and die for it. But if you insist upon continuing to shoot them down for this reason, does not that mean that you want to kill them for demanding the identical thing which you yourself think that you may ultimately find it just and proper to grant them? Would not every drop of blood shed in such a guilty sport cry to Heaven? For you must not forget that establishing our sovereignty in the Philippines means the going on with the work of slaughter and devastation to the grim end, and nobody can tell where that end will be. To kill men in a just war and in obedience to imperative necessity is one thing. To kill men for demanding what you yourself may ultimately have to approve, is another. How can such killing adopted as a policy be countenanced by a man of conscience and humane feelings? And yet, such killing without useless parley is the policy proposed to us.

We are told that we must trust President McKinley and his advisers to bring us out "all right." I should be glad to be able to do so; but I cannot forget that they have got us in all wrong. And here we have to consider a point of immense importance, which I solemnly urge upon the attention of the American people.

It is one of the fundamental principles of our system of democratic government that only the Congress has the power to declare war. What does this signify? That a declaration of war, the initiation of an armed conflict between this Nation and some other Power — the most solemn and responsible act a nation can perform, involving as it does the lives and fortunes of an uncounted number of human beings — shall not be at the discretion of the Executive branch of the Government, but shall depend upon the authority of the legislative representatives of the people — in other words, that, as much as the machinery of government may make such a thing possible, the deliberate will of the people Constitutionally expressed shall determine the awful question of peace or war.

It is true there may be circumstances of foreign aggression or similar emergencies to precipitate an armed conflict without there being a possibility of consulting the popular will beforehand. But, such exceptional cases notwithstanding, the Constitutional principle remains that the question of peace or war is essentially one which the popular will is to decide, and that no possibility should be lost to secure upon it the expression of the popular will through its legislative organs. Whenever such a possibility is wilfully withheld or neglected, and a war has been brought upon the country without every available means being employed thus to consult the popular will upon that question, the spirit of the Constitution is flagrantly violated in one of its most essential principles.

We are now engaged in a war with the Filipinos. You may quibble about it as you will, call it by whatever name you will — it is a war; and a war of conquest on our part at that — a war of barefaced, cynical conquest. Now, I ask any fairminded man whether the President, before beginning that war, or while carrying it on, has ever taken any proper steps to get from the Congress, the representatives of the people, any proper authority for making that war. He issued his famous "benevolent assimilation" order, directing the Army to bring the whole Philippine archipelago as promptly as possible under the military government of the United States, on December 21, 1898, while Congress was in session, and before the treaty with Spain, transferring her shadowy sovereignty over the islands, had acquired any force of law by the assent of the Senate. That was substantially a declaration of war against the Filipinos asserting their independence. He took this step of his own motion. To be sure, he has constantly been telling us that "the whole subject is with Congress," and that "Congress shall direct." But when did he, while Congress was in session, lay a full statement before that body and ask its direction? Why did he not, before he proclaimed that the slaughter must go on without useless parley, call Congress together to consult the popular will in Constitutional form? Why, even in these days, while "swinging around the circle," the President and his Secretaries are speaking of the principal thing, the permanent annexation of the Philippines, not as a question still to be determined, but as a thing done — concluded by the Executive, implying that Congress will have simply to regulate the details.

Now you may bring ever so many arguments to show that the President had technically a right to act as he did, and your reasoning may be ever so plausible — yet the great fact remains that the President did not seek and obtain authority from Congress as to the war to be made, and the policy to be pursued, and that he acted upon his own motion. And this autocratic conduct is vastly aggravated by the other fact that in this democratic Republic, the government of which should be that of an intelligent and well-informed public opinion, a censorship of news has been instituted, which is purposely and systematically seeking to keep the American people in ignorance of the true state of things at the seat of war, and by all sorts of deceitful tricks to deprive them of the knowledge required for the formation of a correct judgment. And this censorship was practised not only in Manila, but directly by the Administration in Washington. Here is a specimen performance revealed by a member of Congress in a public speech: the War Department gave out a despatch from Manila, as follows: "Volunteers willing to remain." The Congressman went to the War Department and asked for the original, which read: "Volunteers unwilling to reënlist, but willing to remain until transports arrive." You will admit that such distortion of official news is a downright swindle upon the people. Does not this give strong color to the charge of the war correspondents that the news is systematically and confessedly so doctored by the officials that it may "help the Administration"?

Those are, therefore, by no means wrong who call this "the President's war." And a war so brought about and so conducted the American people are asked to approve and encourage, simply because "we are in it" — that is, because the President of his own motion has got us into it. Have you considered what this means?

Every man of public experience knows how powerful and seductive precedent is as an argument in the interpretation of laws and of constitutional provisions, or in justification of governmental practices. When a thing, no matter how questionable, has once been done by the government, and approved, or even acquiesced in, by the people, that act will surely be used as a justification of its being done again. In nothing is the authority of precedent more dangerous than in defending usurpations of governmental power. And it is remarkable how prone the public mind is, especially under the influence of party spirit, to accept precedent as a warrant for such usurpations, which, judged upon their own merits, would be sternly condemned. And every such precedent is apt to bring forth a worse one. It is in this way that the most indispensable bulwarks of free government, and of public peace and security, may be undermined. To meet such dangers the American people should, if ever, remember the old saying that "eternal vigilance is the price of liberty."

I am not here as a partisan, but as an American citizen anxious for the future of the Republic. And I cannot too earnestly admonish the American people, if they value the fundamental principles of their government, and their own security and that of their children, for a moment to throw aside all partisan bias and soberly to consider what kind of a precedent they would set, if they consented to, and by consenting approved, the President's management of the Philippine business merely because "we are in it." We cannot expect all our future Presidents to be models of public virtue and wisdom, as George Washington was. Imagine now in the Presidential office a man well-meaning but, it may be, shortsighted and pliable, and under the influence of so-called "friends" who are greedy and reckless speculators, and who would not scruple to push him into warlike complications in order to get great opportunities for profit; or a man of that inordinate ambition which intoxicates the mind and befogs the conscience; or a man of extreme partisan spirit, who honestly believes the victory of his party to be necessary for the salvation of the universe, and may think that a foreign broil would serve the chances of his party; or a man of an uncontrollable combativeness of temperament which might run away with his sense of responsibility — and that we shall have such men in the Presidential chair is by no means unlikely with our loose way of selecting candidates for the Presidency. Imagine, then, a future President belonging to either of these classes to have before him the precedent of Mr. McKinley's management of the Philippine business, sanctioned by the approval or only the acquiescence of the people, and to feel himself permitted — nay, even encouraged — to say to himself that, as this precedent shows, he may plunge the country into warlike conflicts of his own motion, without asking leave of Congress, with only some legal technicalities to cover his usurpation, or, even without such, and that he may, by a machinery of deception called a war-censorship, keep the people in the dark about what is going on; and that into however bad a mess he may have got the country, he may count upon the people, as soon as a drop of blood has been shed, to uphold the usurpation and to cry down everybody who opposes it as a "traitor," and all this because "we are in it"! Can you conceive a more baneful precedent, a more prolific source of danger to the peace and security of the country? Can any sane man deny that it will be all the more prolific of evil if in this way we drift into a foreign policy full of temptation for dangerous adventure?

I say, therefore, that, if we have the future of the Republic at heart, we must not only not uphold the Administration in its course, because "we are in it," but just because we are in it, have been got into it in such a way, the American people should stamp the Administration's proceedings with a verdict of disapproval so clear and emphatic, and "get out of it" in such a fashion, that this will be a solemn warning to future Presidents instead of a seductive precedent.

What, then, to accomplish this end is to be done? Of course, we, as we are here, can only advise. But by calling forth expressions of the popular will by various means of public demonstration, and, if need be, at the polls, we can make that advice so strong that those in power will hardly disregard it. We have often been taunted with having no positive policy to propose. But such a policy has more than once been proposed and I can only repeat it.

In the first place, let it be well understood that those are egregiously mistaken who think that if by a strong military effort the Philippine war be stopped, everything will be right and no more question about it. No, the American trouble of conscience will not be appeased, and the question will be as big and virulent as ever, unless the close of the war be promptly followed by an assurance to the islanders of their freedom and independence, which assurance, if given now, would surely end the war without more fighting.

We propose, therefore, that it be given now. Let there be at once an armistice between our forces and the Filipinos. Let the Philippine Islanders at the same time be told that the American people will be glad to see them establish an independent government, and to aid them in that task as far as may be necessary; that, if the different tribes composing the population of the Philippines are disposed, as at least most of them, if not all, are likely to be, to attach themselves in some way to the government already existing under the Presidency of Aguinaldo, we shall cheerfully accept that solution of the question, and even, if required, lend our good offices to bring it about; and that meanwhile we shall deem it our duty to protect them against interference from other foreign Powers — in other words, that with regard to them we mean honestly to live up to the righteous principles with the profession of which we commended to the world our Spanish war.

And then let us have in the Philippines, to carry out this program, not a small politician, nor a meddlesome martinet, but a statesman of large mind and genuine sympathy who will not merely deal in sanctimonious cant and oily promises with a string to them, but who will prove by his acts that he and we are honest; who will keep in mind that their government is not merely to suit us, but to suit them; that it should not be measured by standards which we ourselves have not been able to reach, but be a government of their own, adapted to their own conditions and notions — whether it be a true republic, like ours, or better, or a dictatorship like that of Porfirio Diaz, in Mexico, or an oligarchy like the one maintained by us in Hawaii, or even something like the boss rule we are tolerating in New York and Pennsylvania.

Those who talk so much about "fitting a people for self-government" often forget that no people were ever made "fit" for self-government by being kept in the leading-strings of a foreign Power. You learn to walk by doing your own crawling and stumbling. Self-government is learned only by exercising it upon one's own responsibility. Of course there will be mistakes, and troubles and disorders. We have had and now have these, too — at the beginning our persecution of the Tories, our flounderings before the Constitution was formed, our Shays's rebellion, our whisky war and various failures and disturbances — among them a civil war that cost us a loss of life and treasure horrible to think of, and the murder of two Presidents. But who will say that on account of these things some foreign Power should have kept the American people in leading-strings to teach them to govern themselves? If the Philippine Islanders do as well as the Mexicans, who have worked their way, since we let them alone after our war of 1847, through many disorders, to an orderly government, who will have a right to find fault with the result? Those who seek to impose upon them an unreasonable standard of excellence in self-government do not seriously wish to let them govern themselves at all. You may take it as a general rule that he who wants to reign over others is solemnly convinced that they are quite unable to govern themselves.

Now, what objection is there to the policy dictated by our fundamental principles and our good faith? I hear the angry cry: "What? Surrender to Aguinaldo? Will not the world ridicule and despise us for such a confession of our incompetency to deal with so feeble a foe? What will become of our prestige?" No, we shall not surrender to Aguinaldo. In giving up a criminal aggression, we shall surrender only to our own consciences, to our own sense of right and justice, to our own understanding of our own true interests and to the vital principles of our own Republic. Nobody will laugh at us whose good opinion we have reason to cherish. There will, of course, be an outcry of disappointment in England. But from whom will it come? From such men as James Bryce or John Morley or any one of those true friends of this Republic who understand and admire and wish to perpetuate and spread the fundamental principles of its vitality? No, not from them. But the outcry will come from those in England who long to see us entangled in complications apt to make this American Republic dependent upon British aid and thus subservient to British interests. They, indeed, will be quite angry. But the less we mind their displeasure as well as their flattery, the better for the safety as well as the honor of our country.

The true friends of this Republic in England, and, indeed, all over the world, who are now grieving to see us go astray, will rejoice, and their hearts will be uplifted with new confidence in our honesty, in our wisdom and in the virtue of democratic institutions when they behold the American people throwing aside all the puerilities of false pride, and returning to the path of their true duty. The world knows how strong we are. It knows full well that if the American people chose to put forth their strength, they could quickly overcome a foe infinitely more powerful than the Filipinos, and that, if we, possessing the strength of the giant, do not use the giant's strength against this feeble foe, it is from the noblest of motives — our love of liberty, our sense of justice and our respect for the rights of others — the respect of the strong for the rights of the weak. The moral prestige which, in fact, we have lost, will be restored, while our prestige of physical prowess and power will certainly not be lessened by showing that we have not only soldiers, guns, ships and money, but also a conscience.

Therefore, the cry is childish, that, unless we take and keep the Philippines, some other Power will promptly grab them. Many a time this cry has been raised to stampede the American people into a policy of annexation — in the San Domingo case, twenty-eight years ago, and more recently in the case of Hawaii — and in neither case was there the slightest danger — not that there were no foreign Powers that would have liked to have those islands, but because they could not have taken them without the risk of grave consequences. Now the old bugbear must do service again. Why should not American diplomacy set about to secure the consent of the Powers most nearly concerned to an agreement to make the Philippine Islands neutral territory, as Belgium and Switzerland are in Europe? Because some of those Powers would like to have the Philippines themselves? Well, are there not among the European Powers some that would like to have Belgium or Switzerland? Certainly; and just because there are several watching each other, the neutrality of those two countries is guaranteed. But even if such an agreement could not be obtained, we may be sure that there is no foreign Power that would lightly risk a serious quarrel with the United States, if this Republic, for the protection of the Philippine Islanders in their effort to build up an independent government, said to the world: "Hands off!" So much for those who think that somebody else might be wicked enough to grab the Philippine Islands, and that, therefore, we must be wicked enough to do the grabbing ourselves.

There are some American citizens who take of this question a purely commercial view. I declare I am ardently in favor of the greatest possible expansion of our trade, and I am happy to say that, according to official statistics, our foreign commerce, in spite of all hindrances raised against it, is now expanding tremendously, owing to the simple rule that the nation offering the best goods at proportionately the lowest prices will have the markets. It will have them without armies, without war fleets, without bloody conquests, without colonies. I confess I am not in sympathy with those, if there be such men among us, who would sacrifice our National honor and the high ideals of the Republic, and who would inflict upon our people the burdens and the demoralizing influences of militarism for a mere matter of dollars and cents. They are among the most dangerous enemies of the public welfare. But as to the annexation of the Philippines, I will, for argument's sake, adopt even their point of view for a moment and ask: Will it pay?

Now, it may well be that the annexation of the Philippines would pay a speculative syndicate of wealthy capitalists, without at the same time paying the American people at large. As to people of our race, tropical countries like the Philippines may be fields of profit for rich men who can hire others to work for them, but not for those who have to work for themselves. Taking a general view of the Philippines as a commercial market for us, I need not again argue against the barbarous notion that in order to have a profitable trade with a country we must own it. If that were true, we should never have had any foreign commerce at all. Neither need I prove that it is very bad policy, when you wish to build up a profitable trade, to ruin your customer first, as you would ruin the Philippines by a protracted war. It is equally needless to show to any well-informed person that the profits of the trade with the islands themselves can never amount to the cost of making and maintaining the conquest of the Philippines.

But there is another point of real importance. Many imperialists admit that our trade with the Philippines themselves will not nearly be worth its cost; but they say that we must have the Philippines as a foothold, a sort of power station, for the expansion of our trade on the Asiatic continent, especially in China. Admitting this, for argument's sake, I ask what kind of a foothold we should really need. Coaling-stations and docks for our fleet, and facilities for the establishment of commercial houses and depots. That is all. And now I ask further, whether we could not easily have had these things if we had, instead of making war upon the Filipinos, favored the independence of the islands. Everybody knows that we could. We might have those things now for the mere asking, if we stopped the war and came to a friendly understanding with the Filipinos to-morrow.

But now suppose we fight on and subjugate the Filipinos and annex the islands — what then? We shall then have of coaling-stations and commercial facilities no more than we would have had in the other case; but the islanders will hate us as their bloody oppressors, and be our bitter and revengeful enemies for generations to come. You may say that this will be of no commercial importance. Let us see. It is by no means impossible, nor even improbable, that, if we are once in the way of extending our commerce with guns behind it, we may get into hot trouble with one or more of our competitors for that Asiatic trade. What then? Then our enemies need only land some Filipino refugees whom we have driven out of their country, and some cargoes of guns and ammunition on the islands, and we shall soon — all the more if we depend on native troops — have a fire in our rear which will oblige us to fight the whole old fight over again. The present subjugation of the Philippines will, therefore, not only not be a help to the expansion of our Asiatic trade, but rather a constant danger and a clog to our feet.

And here a word by the way. A year ago I predicted in an article published in the Century Magazine, that if we turned our war of liberation into a war of conquest, our American sister republics south of us would become distrustful of our intentions with regard to them, and soon begin to form combinations against us, eventually even with European Powers. The newspapers have of late been alive with vague rumors of that sort, so much so that a prominent journal of imperialistic tendency has found it necessary most earnestly to admonish the President, in his next message, to give to the republics south of us the strongest possible assurances of our friendship and good faith. Suppose he does — who will believe him after we have turned our loudly heralded war of liberation into a land-grabbing game — a "criminal aggression"? Nobody will have the slightest trust in our words, be they ever so fair. Drop your conquests, and no assurances of good faith will be required. Keep your conquests, and no such assurances will avail. Our southern neighbors, no less than the Filipinos, will then inevitably distrust our professions, fear our greed and become our secret or open enemies. And who can be foolish enough to believe that this will strengthen our power and help our commerce?

It is useless to say that the subjugated Philippine Islanders will become our friends if we give them good government. However good that government may be, it will, to them, be foreign rule, and foreign rule especially hateful when begun by broken faith, cemented by streams of innocent blood and erected upon the ruins of devastated homes. The American will be and remain to them more a foreigner, an unsympathetic foreigner, than the Spaniard ever was. Let us indulge in no delusion about this. People of our race are but too much inclined to have little tenderness for the rights of what we regard as inferior races, especially those of darker skin. It is of ominous significance that to so many of our soldiers the Filipinos were only "niggers," and that they likened their fights against them to the "shooting of rabbits." And how much good government have we to give them? Are you not aware that our first imperialistic Administration is also the first that, since the enactment of the civil service law, has widened the gates again for a new foray of spoils politics in the public service? What assurance have we that the Philippines, far away from public observation, will not be simply a pasture for needy politicians and for speculating syndicates to grow fat on, without much scruple as to the rights of the despised "natives"? Has it not been so with the British in India, although the British monarchy is much better fitted for imperial rule than our democratic Republic can ever be? True, in the course of time the government of India has been much improved, but it required more than a century of slaughter, robbery, devastation, disastrous blundering, insurrection and renewed bloody subjugation to evolve what there is of good government in India now. And have the populations of India ever become the friends of England? Does not England at heart tremble to-day lest some hostile foreign Power come close enough to throw a firebrand into that fearful mass of explosives?

I ask you, therefore, in all soberness, leaving all higher considerations of justice, morality and principle aside, whether, from a mere business point of view, the killing policy of subjugation is not a colossal, stupid blunder, and whether it would not have been, and would now be, infinitely more sensible to win the confidence and cultivate the friendship of the islanders by recognizing them as of right entitled to their freedom and independence, as we have recognized the Cubans, and thus to obtain from their friendship and gratitude, for the mere asking, all the coaling-stations and commercial facilities we require, instead of getting those things by fighting at an immense cost of blood and treasure, with a probability of having to fight for them again? I put this question to every business man who is not a fool or a reckless speculator. Can there be any doubt of the answer?

A word now on a special point: There are some very estimable men among us who think that even if we concede to the islanders their independence, we should at least keep the city of Manila. I think differently, not from a mere impulse of generosity, but from an entirely practical point of view. Manila is the traditional, if not the natural capital of the archipelago. To recognize the independence of the Philippine Islanders, and at the same time to keep from them Manila, would means as much as to recognize the independence of Cuba and to keep Havana. It would mean to withhold from the islanders their metropolis, that in which they naturally take the greatest pride, that which they legitimately most desire to have, and which, if withheld from them, they would most ardently wish to get back. The withholding of Manila would inevitably leave a sting in their hearts which would never cease to rankle, and might, under critical circumstances, give us as much trouble as the withholding of independence itself. If we wish them to be our friends, we should not do things by halves, but enable them to be our friends without reserve. And I maintain that, commercially as well as politically speaking, the true friendship of the Philippine Islanders will, as to our position in the East, be worth far more to us than the possession of Manila. We can certainly find other points which will give us similar commercial as well as naval advantages without exciting any hostile feeling.

Although I have by no means exhausted this vast subject, discussing only a few phases of it, I have said enough, I think, to show that this policy of conquest is, from the point of view of public morals, in truth "criminal aggression" — made doubly criminal by the treacherous character of it; and that from the point of view of material interest it is a blunder — a criminal blunder, and a blundering crime. I have addressed myself to your reason by sober argument, without any appeal to prejudice or passion. Might we not ask our opponents to answer these arguments, if they can, with equally sober reasoning, instead of merely assailing us with their wild cries of "treason" and "lack of patriotism," and what not? Or do they really feel their cause to be so weak that they depend for its support on their assortment of inarticulate shouts and nebulous phrases?

Here are our "manifest destiny" men who tell us that, whether it be right or not, we must take and keep the Philippines because "destiny" so wills it. We have heard this cry of manifest destiny before, especially when, a half century ago, the slave-power demanded the annexation of Cuba and Central America to strengthen the slave-power. The cry of destiny is most vociferously put forward by those who want to do a wicked thing and to shift the responsibility. The destiny of a free people lies in its intelligent will and its moral strength. When it pleads destiny, it pleads "the baby act." Nay, worse; the cry of destiny is apt to be the refuge of evil intent and of moral cowardice.

Here are our "burden" men, who piously turn up their eyes and tell us, with a melancholy sigh, that all this conquest business may be very irksome, but that a mysterious Providence has put it as a "burden" upon us, which, however sorrowfully, we must bear; that this burden consists in our duty to take care of the poor people of the Philippines; and that in order to take proper care of them we must exercise sovereignty over them; and that if they refuse to accept our sovereignty, we must — alas! alas! — kill them, which makes the burden very solemn and sad.

But cheer up, brethren! We may avoid that mournful way of taking care of them by killing them, if we simply recognize their right to take care of themselves, and gently aid them in doing so. Besides, you may be as much mistaken about the decrees of Providence as before our civil war the Southern Methodist bishops were who solemnly insisted that Providence willed the negroes to remain in slavery.

Next there are our "flag" men, who insist that we must kill the Filipinos fighting for their independence to protect the honor of the stars and stripes. I agree that the honor of our flag sorely needs protection. We have to protect it against desecration by those who are making it an emblem of that hypocrisy which seeks to cover a war of conquest and subjugation with a cloak of humanity and religion; an emblem of that greed which would treat a matter involving our National honor, the integrity of our institutions and the peace and character of the Republic as a mere question of dollars and cents; an emblem of that vulgar lust of war and conquest which recklessly tramples upon right and justice and all our higher ideals; an emblem of the imperialistic ambitions which mock the noblest part of our history and stamp the greatest National heroes of our past as hypocrites or fools. These are the dangers threatening the honor of our flag, against which it needs protection, and that protection we are striving to give it.

Now, a last word to those of our fellow-citizens who feel and recognize as we do that the Philippine war of subjugation is wrong and cruel, and that we ought to recognize the independence of those people, but who insist that, having begun that war, we must continue it until the submission of the Filipinos is complete. I detest, but I can understand, the Jingo whose moral sense is obscured by intoxicating dreams of wild adventure and conquest, and to whom bloodshed and devastation have become a reckless sport. I detest even more, but still I can understand, the cruel logic of those to whom everything is a matter of dollars and cents and whose greed of gain will walk coolly over slaughtered populations. But I must confess I cannot understand the reasoning of those who have moral sense enough to recognize that this war is criminal aggression — who must say to themselves that every drop of blood shed in it by friend or foe is blood wantonly and wickedly shed, and that every act of devastation is barbarous cruelty inflicted upon an innocent people — but who still maintain that we must go on killing, and devastating, and driving our brave soldiers into a fight which they themselves are cursing, because we have once begun it. This I cannot understand. Do they not consider that in such a war, which they themselves condemn as wanton and iniquitous, the more complete our success, the greater will be our disgrace?

What do they fear for the Republic if, before having fully consummated this criminal aggression, we stop to give a people struggling for their freedom what is due them? Will this Republic be less powerful? It will be as strong as ever, nay, stronger, for it will have saved the resources of its power from useless squandering and transformed vindictive enemies into friends. Will it be less respected? Nay, more, for it will have demonstrated its honesty at the sacrifice of false pride. Is this the first time that a powerful nation desisted from the subjugation of a weaker adversary? Have we not the example of England before us, who, after a seven-year war against the American colonists, recognized their independence? Indeed, the example of England teaches us a double lesson. England did not, by recognizing American independence, lose her position in the world and her chances of future greatness; on the contrary, she grew in strength. And secondly, England would have retained, or won anew, the friendship of the Americans, if she had recognized American independence more promptly, before appearing to have been forced to do so by humiliating defeats. Will our friends who are for Philippine independence, but also for continuing to kill those who fight for it, take these two lessons to heart?

Some of them say that we have here to fulfill some of the disagreeable duties of patriotism. Patriotism! Who were the true patriots of England at the time of the American Revolution — King George and Lord North, who insisted upon subjugation; or Lord Chatham and Edmund Burke, who stood up for American rights and American liberty?

Who were the true patriots of France when, recently, that ghastly farce of a military trial was enacted to sacrifice an innocent man for the honor of the French army and the prestige of the French Republic — who were the true French patriots, those who insisted that the hideous crime of an unjust condemnation must be persisted in, or those who bravely defied the cry of "traitor!" and struggled to undo the wrong, and thus to restore the French Republic to the path of justice and to the esteem of the world? Who are the true patriots in America to-day — those who drag our Republic, once so proud of its high principles and ideals, through the mire of broken pledges, vulgar ambitions and vanities and criminal aggressions — those who do violence to their own moral sense by insisting that, like the Dreyfus iniquity, a criminal course once begun must be persisted in, or those who, fearless of the demagogue clamor, strive to make the flag of the Republic once more what it once was — the flag of justice, liberty and true civilization, and to lift up the American people among the nations of the earth to the proud position of the people that have a conscience and obey it?

The country has these days highly and deservedly honored Admiral Dewey as a National hero. Who are his true friends — those who would desecrate Dewey's splendid achievement at Manila by making it the starting-point of criminal aggression, and thus the opening of a most disgraceful and inevitably disastrous chapter of American history, to be remembered with sorrow, or those who strive so to shape the results of that brilliant feat of arms that it may stand in history not as a part of a treacherous conquest, but as a true victory of American good faith in an honest war of liberation and humanity — to be proud of for all time, as Dewey himself no doubt meant it to be?

I know the imperialists will say that I have been pleading here for Aguinaldo and his Filipinos against our Republic. No — not for the Filipinos merely, although as one of those who have grown gray in the struggle for free and honest government, I would never be ashamed to plead for the cause of freedom and independence, even when its banner is carried by dusky and feeble hands. But I am pleading for more. I am pleading for the cause of American honor and self-respect, American interests, American democracy — aye, for the cause of the American people against an administration of our public affairs which has wantonly plunged this country into an iniquitous war; which has disgraced the Republic by a scandalous breach of faith to a people struggling for their freedom whom we had used as allies; which has been systematically seeking to deceive and mislead the public mind by the manufacture of false news; which has struck at the very foundation of our Constitutional government by an Executive usurpation of the war-power; which makes sport of the great principles and high ideals that have been and should ever remain the guiding star of our course; and which, unless stopped in time, will transform this government of the people, for the people and by the people into an imperial government cynically calling itself republican — a government in which the noisy worship of arrogant might will drown the voice of right; which will impose upon the people a burdensome and demoralizing militarism, and which will be driven into a policy of wild and rapacious adventure by the unscrupulous greed of the exploiter — a policy always fatal to democracy.

I plead the cause of the American people against all this, and I here declare my profound conviction that if this administration of our affairs were submitted for judgment to a popular vote on a clear issue, it would be condemned by an overwhelming majority.

I confidently trust that the American people will prove themselves too clear-headed not to appreciate the vital difference between the expansion of the Republic and its free institutions over contiguous territory and kindred populations, which we all gladly welcome if accomplished peaceably and honorably — and imperialism which reaches out for distant lands to be ruled as subject provinces; too intelligent not to perceive that our very first step on the road of imperialism has been a betrayal of the fundamental principles of democracy, followed by disaster and disgrace; too enlightened not to understand that a monarchy may do such things and still remain a strong monarchy, while a democracy cannot do them and still remain a democracy; too wise not to detect the false pride or the dangerous ambitions or the selfish schemes which so often hide themselves under that deceptive cry of mock patriotism: "Our country, right or wrong!" They will not fail to recognize that our dignity, our free institutions and the peace and welfare of this and coming generations of Americans will be secure only as we cling to the watchword of true patriotism: "Our country — when right to be kept right; when wrong to be put right."

THEODORE ROOSEVELT

(1859-1919)

Whether a given age produces its outstanding figures or whether the figures create the age is hard to say, but in any case Theodore Roosevelt and turn-of-the-century America fitted each other perfectly. Our relatively young republic was becoming a great world power, expanding rapidly. It was a hardy, vigorous nation and needed a leader with vigor to match. Theodore Roosevelt was just such a man; a man possessed of an incredible drive and an overwhelming love for his country.

Roosevelt, although he spoke well and often, was never considered to be a polished orator in the sense of a Bryan or a Beveridge. In fact, he himself once said (early in his career) that he "hated public speaking." But he soon overcame this dislike and eventually gained fame as a speaker of the first rank, due in large measure to his friendliness, sincerity, and enthusiasm, all noted here by Richard Murphy:

> Most expressive was the face. The snapping, extended jaw, the flashing teeth, the full moustache gyrating as he exaggerated his diction for full clarity to the crowd, the eyes narrowing in intensity behind the nose glasses — all were trademark features drawn upon by cartoonists. His whole manner was vigorous, suggestive of his moods. He did little prancing about. He shook his fist, but it was at a real or a hypothetical enemy. The movement was not graceful, not Delsartian, but it was excellently coordinated with the thought. Mannerisms which would have seemed burlesque in another, were genuinely expressive of his personality. There is no doubt that a Roosevelt speech gained in its delivery.[1]

[1] "Theodore Roosevelt," Marie K. Hockmuth (ed.), A History and Criticism of American Public Address, III, p. 358.

In essence, his style was simple, direct, yet forceful, and enlivened by such original and memorable phrases as "the square deal," "the strenuous life," "the lunatic fringe," and "speak softly and carry a big stick." Roosevelt's commanding and energetic method of presentation resulted from the fact that he spoke only when he felt he had a message worth communicating.

> The secret of his success as a public speaker lay in the charm and power of his personality, his keen appreciation of the temper of his audience, and, above all, in the fact that he never consented to make an address unless he had something he wanted to say. He was always vitally interested in getting his hearers to see the truth as he saw it, and to take a definite course of action.[2]

If the America of Roosevelt's day was a place of great opportunity, it was a place of great problems as well — trusts, malpractice in industry, "imperialism." Roosevelt was especially concerned about allegedly unsanitary conditions in the packing industry — a concern brought about largely by a reading of Upton Sinclair's book, The Jungle. Criticism, in fact, was flourishing in American magazines, newspapers, and books. Such skilled writers as Ida Tarbell and Ray Stannard Baker were revealing much of the hitherto unknown seamier side of industry in general. No one was happier with this work than Roosevelt, who could not tolerate dishonesty.

But the President was no more tolerant of dishonesty in journalism than he was of dishonesty in industry. The "exposé" movement was rapidly getting out of hand. Criticisms were being written merely for their sensational value, and occasionally even lacked any basis in fact. Roosevelt expressed his feelings on the subject in a letter to Ray Stannard Baker:

> I want to let in light and air but I do not want to let in sewer gas. If a room is fetid and the windows are bolted, I am perfectly willing to knock out the windows, but I would not knock a hole in the drainpipe.[3]

Apparently, Roosevelt's first speech on the subject of irresponsible journalism came as a result of his reading a particularly loose

---

2 William D. Lewis, The Life of Theodore Roosevelt, p. 443.

3 Mark Sullivan, Our Times, III, Charles Scribner's Sons, New York, p. 96.

diatribe in "a certain magazine" just before he was to attend a private dinner of the Gridiron Club on March 17, 1906. At the dinner, he took as his theme a figure from John Bunyan's The Pilgrim's Progress, "The Man with the Muck Rake, the man who could look no way but downward, with the muck rake in his hand; who was offered a celestial crown for his muck rake, but who would neither look up nor regard the crown he was offered, but continued to rake to himself the filth of the floor."

Although the speech, following Gridiron Club tradition, was not published, his allusion soon got around. Roosevelt then realized that he had discovered a potentially valuable figure for a major speech in the person of Bunyan's muckraker. With Roosevelt, "to recognize opportunity was to put both arms around it." It was not long before an occasion for using the figure presented itself.

On April 14, 1906, at the cornerstone laying ceremony for the Congressional Office Building in Washington, D.C., Roosevelt delivered his now famous "Man with the Muck Rake" speech. Before a distinguished assemblage of congressmen, members of the Supreme Court, members of the diplomatic corps and general public, he made his plea for caution and restraint in the campaign of exposure then going on. He was afraid that people would "grow suspicious of the accusation as of the offense" in this carnival of mud-slinging.

His speech was welcomed with open arms by the conservative press. On the other hand, many of the journalists gloried in the title of "muckraker." Certain business interests mistakenly hoped for an indication of the end to Roosevelt's war on big business. Roosevelt himself was concerned with one thing — to stem the tide of yellow journalism. That he was perhaps successful in his aim is suggested by the fact that although sensational exposés continued to be written, the pace slackened off considerably during the following year. The small amount of criticism that Roosevelt received from the press (one paper claimed that his speech would "be a mortification to his friends and a real public misfortune") fazed him not at all. His forthright stand and honesty had won him new friends, who along with many others, would say at his death that he was "the most American of all Americans, a friend of the people, the disciple of righteousness, and the incarnation of the vigorous patriotism that he had preached."

THE MAN WITH THE MUCK RAKE

by

Theodore Roosevelt

Delivered in Washington at the laying of the cornerstone of the Office Building for the House of Representatives on April 14, 1906.

Over a century ago Washington laid the corner-stone of the Capitol in what was then little more than a tract of wooded wilderness here beside the Potomac. We now find it necessary to provide by great additional buildings for the business of the government. This growth in the need for the housing of the government is but a proof and example of the way in which the nation has grown and the sphere of action of the national government has grown. We now administer the affairs of a nation in which the extraordinary growth of population has been outstripped by the growth of wealth and the growth in complex interests. The material problems that face us to-day are not such as they were in Washington's time, but the underlying facts of human nature are the same now as they were then. Under altered external form we war with the same tendencies toward evil that were evident in Washington's time, and are helped by the same tendencies for good. It is about some of these that I wish to say a word to-day.

In Bunyan's "Pilgrim's Progress" you may recall the description of the Man with the Muck Rake, the man who could look no way but downward, with the muck rake in his hand; who was offered a celestial crown for his muck rake, but who would neither look up nor regard the crown he was offered, but continued to rake to himself the filth of the floor.

In "Pilgrim's Progress" the Man with the Muck Rake is set forth as the example of him whose vision is fixed on carnal instead of on spiritual things. Yet he also typifies the man who in this life consistently refuses to see aught that is lofty, and fixes his eyes with solemn intentness only on that which is vile and debasing. Now it is very necessary that we should not flinch from seeing what is vile and debasing. There is filth on the floor, and it must be scraped up with the muck rake; and there are times and places where this service is the most needed of all the services that can be performed. But the man who never does anything else, who never thinks or speaks or writes save of his feats with the muck rake, speedily becomes, not a help to society, not an incitement to good, but one of the most potent forces for evil.

There are, in the body politic, economic and social, many and grave evils, and there is urgent necessity for the sternest war upon them. There should be relentless exposure of and attack upon every evil man, whether politician or business man, every evil practice, whether in politics, in business, or in social life. I hail as a benefactor every writer or speaker, every man who, on the platform, or in book, magazine, or newspaper, with merciless severity makes such attack, provided always that he in his turn remembers that the attack is of use only if it is absolutely truthful. The liar is no whit better than the thief, and if his mendacity takes the form of slander, he may be worse than most thieves. It puts a premium upon knavery untruthfully to attack an honest man, or even with hysterical exaggeration to assail a bad man with untruth. An epidemic of indiscriminate assault upon character does no good, but very great harm. The soul of every scoundrel is gladdened whenever an honest man is assailed, or even when a scoundrel is untruthfully assailed.

Now, it is easy to twist out of shape what I have just said, easy to affect to misunderstand it, and, if it is slurred over in repetition, not difficult really to misunderstand it. Some persons are sincerely incapable of understanding that to denounce mud-slinging does not mean the indorsement of whitewashing; and both the interested individuals who need whitewashing, and those others who practise mud-slinging, like to encourage such confusion of ideas. One of the chief counts against those who make indiscriminate assault upon men in business or men in public life is that they invite a reaction which is sure to tell powerfully in favor of the unscrupulous scoundrel who really ought to be attacked, who ought to be exposed, who ought, if possible, to be put in the penitentiary. If Aristides is praised overmuch as just, people get tired of hearing it; and overcensure of the unjust finally and from similar reasons results in their favor.

Any excess is almost sure to invite a reaction; and, unfortunately, the reaction, instead of taking the form of punishment of those guilty of the excess, is very apt to take the form either of punishment of the unoffending or of giving immunity, and even strength, to offenders. The effort to make financial or political profit out of the destruction of character can only result in public calamity. Gross and reckless assaults on character, whether on the stump or in newspaper, magazine, or book, create a morbid and vicious public sentiment, and at the same time act as a profound deterrent to able men of normal sensitiveness and tend to prevent them from entering the public service at any price. As an instance in point, I may mention that one serious difficulty encountered in getting the right type of men to dig the Panama Canal is the certainty that they will be exposed, both without, and, I am sorry to say, sometimes within, Congress, to utterly reckless assaults on their character and capacity.

At the risk of repetition, let me say again that my plea is not for immunity to, but for the most unsparing exposure of, the politician who betrays his trust, of the big business man who makes or spends his fortune in illegitimate or corrupt ways. There should be a resolute effort to hunt every such man out of the position he has disgraced. Expose the crime, and hunt down the criminal; but remember that even in the case of crime, if it is attacked in sensational, lurid, and untruthful fashion, the attack may do more damage to the public mind than the crime itself. It is because I feel that there should be no rest in the endless war against the forces of evil that I ask that the war be conducted with sanity as well as with resolution. The men with the muck rakes are often indispensable to the well-being of society; but only if they know when to stop raking the muck, and to look upward to the celestial crown above them, to the crown of worthy endeavor. There are beautiful things above and round about them; and if they gradually grow to feel that the whole world is nothing but muck, their power of usefulness is gone. If the whole picture is painted black, there remains no hue whereby to single out the rascals for distinction from their fellows. Such painting finally induces a kind of moral color-blindness; and people affected by it come to the conclusion that no man is really black and no man really white, but that all are gray. In other words, they believe neither in the truth of the attack nor in the honesty of the man who is attacked; they grow as suspicious of the accusation as of the offense; it becomes well-nigh hopeless to stir them either to wrath against wrong-doing or to enthusiasm for what is right; and such a mental attitude in the public gives hope to every knave, and is the despair of honest men.

To assail the great and admitted evils of our political and industrial life with such crude and sweeping generalizations as to include decent men in the general condemnation means the searing of the public conscience. There results a general attitude either of cynical belief in and indifference to public corruption or else of a distrustful inability to discriminate between the good and the bad. Either attitude is fraught with untold damage to the country as a whole. The fool who has not sense to discriminate between what is good and what is bad is well-nigh as dangerous as the man who does discriminate and yet chooses the bad. There is nothing more distressing to every good patriot, to every good American, than the hard, scoffing spirit which treats the allegation of dishonesty in a public man as a cause for laughter. Such laughter is worse than the crackling of thorns under a pot, for it denotes not merely the vacant mind, but the heart in which high emotions have been choked before they could grow to fruition.

There is any amount of good in the world, and there never was a time when loftier and more disinterested work for the betterment of mankind was being done than now. The forces that tend for evil are great and terrible, but the forces of truth and love and courage and honesty and generosity and sympathy are also stronger than ever before. It is a foolish and timid, no less than a wicked, thing to blink the fact that the forces of evil are strong, but it is even worse to fail to take into account the strength of the forces that tell for good. Hysterical sensationalism is the very poorest weapon wherewith to fight for lasting righteousness. The men who, with stern sobriety and truth, assail the many evils of our time, whether in the public press, or in magazines, or in books, are the leaders and allies of all engaged in the work for social and political betterment. But if they give good reasons for distrust of what they say, if they chill the ardor of those who demand truth as a primary virtue, they thereby betray the good cause, and play into the hands of the very men against whom they are nominally at war.

In his "Ecclesiastical Polity" that fine old Elizabethan divine, Bishop Hooker, wrote:

> He that goeth about to persuade a multitude that they are not so well governed as they ought to be shall never want attentive and favorable hearers, because they know the manifold defects whereunto every kind of regimen is subject; but the secret lets and difficulties which in public proceeding are innumerable and inevitable, they have not ordinarily the judgment to consider."

This truth should be kept constantly in mind by every free people desiring to preserve the sanity and poise indispensable to the permanent success of self-government. Yet, on the other hand, it is vital not to permit this spirit of sanity and self-command to degenerate into mere mental stagnation. Bad though a state of hysterical excitement is, and evil though the results are which come from the violent oscillations such excitement invariably produces, yet a sodden acquiescence in evil is even worse. At this moment we are passing through a period of great unrest — social, political, and industrial unrest. It is of the utmost importance for our future that this should prove to be not the unrest of mere rebelliousness against life, of mere dissatisfaction with the inevitable inequality of conditions, but the unrest of a resolute and eager ambition to secure the betterment of the individual and the nation. So far as this movement of agitation throughout the country takes the form of a fierce discontent with evil, of a determination to punish the authors of evil, whether in industry or politics, the feeling is to be heartily welcomed as a sign of healthy life.

If, on the other hand, it turns into a mere crusade of appetite against appetite, a contest between the brutal greed of the "have-nots" and the brutal greed of the "haves," then it has no significance for good, but only for evil. If it seeks to establish a line of cleavage, not along the line which divides good men from bad, but along that other line, running at right angles thereto, which divides those who are well off from those who are less well off, then it will be fraught with immeasurable harm to the body politic.

We can no more and no less afford to condone evil in the man of capital than evil in the man of no capital. The wealthy man who exults because there is a failure of justice in the effort to bring some trust magnate to an account for his misdeeds is as bad as, and no worse than, the so-called labor leader who clamorously strives to excite a foul class feeling on behalf of some other labor leader who is implicated in murder. One attitude is as bad as the other and no worse; in each case the accused is entitled to exact justice; and in neither case is there need of action by others which can be construed into an expression of sympathy for crime. There is nothing more antisocial in a democratic republic like ours than such vicious class-consciousness. The multi-millionaires who band together to prevent the enactment of proper laws for the supervision of the use of wealth, or to assail those who resolutely enforce such laws, or to exercise a hidden influence upon the political destinies of parties or individuals in their own personal interest, are a menace to the whole community; and a menace at least as great is offered by those laboring men who band together to defy the law, and by their openly used influence to coerce law-upholding public officials. The apologists for either class of offenders are themselves enemies of good citizenship; and incidentally they are also, to a peculiar degree, the enemies of every honest-dealing corporation and every law-abiding labor-union.

It is a prime necessity that if the present unrest is to result in permanent good, the emotion shall be translated into action, and that the action shall be marked by honesty, sanity, and self-restraint. There is mighty little good in a mere spasm of reform. The reform that counts is that which comes through steady, continuous growth; violent emotionalism leads to exhaustion.

It is important to this people to grapple with the problems connected with the amassing of enormous fortunes and the use of those fortunes, both corporate and individual, in business. We should discriminate in the sharpest way between fortunes well won and fortunes ill won; between those gained as an incident to performing great services to the community as a whole, and those gained in evil fashion by keeping just within the limits of mere law-honesty. Of course no amount of charity in spending such fortunes in any way compensates for misconduct in making them. As a matter of personal conviction, and without pretending to discuss the details or formulate the system, I feel that we shall ultimately have to consider the adoption of some such scheme as that of a progressive tax on all fortunes, beyond a certain amount, either given in life or devised or bequeathed upon death to any individual — a tax so framed as to put it out of the power of the owner of one of these enormous fortunes to hand on more than a certain amount to any one individual; the tax, of course, to be imposed by the national and not the State government. Such taxation should, of course, be aimed merely at the inheritance or transmission in their entirety of those fortunes swollen beyond all healthy limits.

Again, the national government must in some form exercise supervision over corporations engaged in interstate business — and all large corporations are engaged in interstate business, — whether by license or otherwise, so as to permit us to deal with the far-reaching evils of over-capitalization. This year we are making a beginning in the direction of serious effort to settle some of these economic problems by the railway rate legislation. Such legislation, if so framed, as I am sure it will be, as to secure definite and tangible results, will amount to something of itself; and it will amount to a great deal more in so far as it is taken as a first step in the direction of a policy of superintendence and control over corporate wealth engaged in interstate commerce, this superintendence and control not to be exercised in a spirit of malevolence toward the men who have created the wealth, but with the firm purpose both to do justice to them and to see that they in their turn do justice to the public at large.

The first requisite in the public servants who are to deal in this shape with corporations, whether as legislators or as executives, is honesty. This honesty can be no respecter of persons. There can be no such thing as unilateral honesty. The danger is not really from corrupt corporations; it springs from the corruption itself, whether exercised for or against corporations.

The eighth commandment reads, "Thou shalt not steal." It does not read, "Thou shalt not steal from the rich man." It does not read, "Thou shalt not steal from the poor man." It reads simply and plainly, "Thou shalt not steal." No good whatever will come from that warped and mock morality which denounces the misdeeds of men of wealth and forgets the misdeeds practised at their expense; which denounces bribery, but blinds itself to blackmail;

which foams with rage if a corporation secures favors by improper methods, and merely leers with hideous mirth if the corporation is itself wronged. The only public servant who can be trusted honestly to protect the rights of the public against the misdeeds of a corporation is that public man who will just as surely protect the corporation itself from wrongful aggression. If a public man is willing to yield to popular clamor and do wrong to the men of wealth or to rich corporations, it may be set down as certain that if the opportunity comes he will secretly and furtively do wrong to the public in the interest of a corporation.

But, in addition to honesty, we need sanity. No honesty will make a public man useful if that man is timid or foolish, if he is a hot-headed zealot or an impracticable visionary. As we strive for reform, we find that it is not at all merely the case of a long up-hill pull. On the contrary, there is almost as much of breeching work as of collar work; to depend only on traces means that there will soon be a runaway and an upset. The men of wealth who to-day are trying to prevent the regulation and control of their business in the interest of the public by the proper government authorities will not succeed, in my judgment, in checking the progress of the movement. But if they did succeed, they would find that they had sown the wind and would surely reap the whirlwind, for they would ultimately provoke the violent excesses which accompany a reform coming by convulsion instead of by steady and natural growth.

On the other hand, the wild preachers of unrest and discontent, the wild agitators against the entire existing order, the men who act crookedly, whether because of sinister design or from mere puzzle-headedness, the men who preach destruction without proposing any substitute for what they intend to destroy, or who propose a substitute which would be far worse than the existing evils, — all these men are the most dangerous opponents of real reform. If they get their way, they will lead the people into a deeper pit than any into which they could fall under the present system. If they fail to get their way, they will still do incalculable harm by provoking the kind of reaction which, in its revolt against the senseless evil of their teaching, would enthrone more securely than ever the very evils which their misguided followers believe they are attacking.

More important than aught else is the development of the

broadest sympathy of man for man. The welfare of the wage-worker, the welfare of the tiller of the soil — upon this depends the welfare of the entire country; their good is not to be sought in pulling down others; but their good must be the prime object of all our statesmanship.

Materially we must strive to secure a broader economic opportunity for all men, so that each shall have a better chance to show the stuff of which he is made. Spiritually and ethically we must strive to bring about clean living and right thinking. We appreciate that the things of the body are important; but we appreciate also that the things of the soul are immeasurably more important. The foundation-stone of national life is, and ever must be, the high individual character of the average citizen.

World Wars I and II: Crises and Controversies

World Wars I and II:
Crises and Controversies

The outbreak of World War I in 1914 had a great impact on political thought in this country and exerted a corresponding effect on the nature of American public address.

The war began in a blaze of violence. With its superbly mechanized and well-trained armies Germany thrust suddenly through the Lowlands and into France. Vainly did France, England, and Russia try to stop the avalanche of power. Inevitably the United States had an important role to play in this struggle.

With the outbreak of the war, President Woodrow Wilson enunciated a policy of strict neutrality "in word, deed, and thought." He hoped that if the country followed such a policy this nation might become the best agency for the re-establishment of peace and the promotion of a permanent world organization to avoid future wars. In contradiction to the President's policy, there were a number of prominent Americans who spoke out vigorously against the idea of neutrality.

President Wilson found strict neutrality difficult to maintain as changing events brought crisis after crisis. American shipping was being sunk by German submarines, and other American ships were being taken into custody when they attempted to run the Allied blockade. Espionage and foreign intrigue threatened our industries. Worst of all, the American public was shocked by the horrible war atrocities committed by the Germans and worried over the imminent defeat of our historic allies — England and France. These influences caused the President to modify his neutrality doctrine. He wrote strong protests to Germany complaining against its cruel conduct of the war, and he gave notice that there was a limit to how much this country was willing to withstand.

The principle of neutrality with its resulting crises produced many outstanding examples of patriotic eloquence. Foremost were the many great speeches made by President Wilson himself in defense of his policies. Almost next in importance and undoubtedly equal in effectiveness were the speeches of Theodore Roosevelt denouncing our foreign policy and advocating complete preparedness. When Bryan resigned as Secretary of State in 1915, he made a speaking tour on behalf of world peace which took him to all parts of the country. On one appearance he spoke in New York's Madison Square Garden to 20,000 people although some 100,000 sought admittance.

The extent and quality of the eloquence of this period cannot be demonstrated adequately in a limited space. Specific reference, however, to a few leading speeches may prove illustrative of the speaking of the time. On May 10, 1915, President Wilson made his famous "Too Proud to Fight Speech" (included in this section) which set off a torrent of oratory. A few of the speeches that followed were "The Plattsburg Speech on Preparedness" by Theodore Roosevelt on August 25, 1915; "The Kansas City Speech on Preparedness" by President Wilson on February 2, 1916; "Bankrupt Diplomacy" by Elihu Root on February 15, 1916; "America and the Allies" by James M. Beck on July 5, 1916; "Essential Terms of Peace in Europe" by President Wilson on January 22, 1917; and "On the Wilson Peace Message" by Henry Cabot Lodge on February 1, 1917.

This period of controversy came to an unsurprising but dramatic end; neutrality proved untenable and the United States went to war. President Wilson appeared before the combined houses of Congress to deliver his war message on April 2, 1917. This brilliant address inspired a long chain of powerful speeches. Two days later, while the Declaration of War was still being debated, Senator Robert M. LaFollette made his highly persuasive, courageous, and almost violent speech "Against the War with Germany" before the Senate. The speech nearly cost him his seat in the Senate and his liberty as an American citizen. The editors, without taking sides about subject matter, consider it one of the great contemporary speeches of American eloquence. Both President Wilson's speech asking for the declaration of war and Senator LaFollette's speech against it are given in this section.

On April 7, 1917, Congress voted the declaration of war. Immediately, many vital questions arose for debate in Congress, and important speeches became part of the literature of oratory. The great bulk of the eloquence, however, was composed of brilliant, highly patriotic cheerleading oratory designed to build national morale and to win the war. These speeches were numerous and were made by such notable Americans as Theodore Roosevelt, Henry Cabot Lodge, Elihu Root, Charles Evans Hughes, Joseph H. Choate, James M. Beck, Robert Lansing, and many others.

The power and determination of the American people in partnership with the heroic people of the Allied nations finally won the war. At last, Germany and the nations who supported her were defeated, and an armistice was signed on November 11, 1918.

The historic Peace Conference met at Versailles to negotiate a peace that would prevent future wars. President Wilson fought hard for the principles upon which he believed a lasting peace could be established. His structure for world security lay on the cornerstone of a league of nations. The leaders of the Allies finally accepted President Wilson's views and the terms of a treaty were agreed upon. The President triumphantly returned to this country only to find that the people would not follow his leadership. His idealism was crushed when the Senate refused to confirm the treaty. The strain of controversy broke his health and power and led to the incapacity and death of one of the great men of modern history.

The debate on the League of Nations was one of the most significant issues that has ever been argued before the forum of American public opinion. President Wilson took his case to the people in defiance of the Senate and made a vigorous personal speaking crusade for the League. He was supported by such dedicated public figures as William Howard Taft and A. Lawrence Lowell. But he was opposed by such equally dedicated public figures as Henry Cabot Lodge, William E. Borah, and Hiram W. Johnson. The League could not survive its opposition, and the controversy came to an end. To illustrate the speaking on this issue William Howard Taft's address in support of the League, Henry Cabot Lodge's speech opposing the proposed plan for the League, and William E. Borah's speech opposing the League idea itself will be found in this section.

Freed from the hardships and bickerings of the war the United States entered upon a period of intense nationalism and strong isolationism. The country experienced a few years of unprecedented economic prosperity followed by a catastrophic financial crash. To meet this new crisis, Franklin D. Roosevelt inaugurated his New Deal and with it an era of new political thinking. Unfortunately, the oratory on this subject is far too extensive to be included in this collection.

The United States had hardly put its economic house in order before World War II broke out with a fury that made World War I appear a mere skirmish. The country was strongly isolationist because of its unhappy experiences of some twenty years before. The United States had come out of its recent war effort disillusioned and resentful. The contribution of this nation to victory had been almost uniformly belittled, and the millions of dollars of war debts owed this country were in the main repudiated or forgiven under duress. The United States, however, was inevitably drawn into the war for reasons almost identical to those which had forced its entry into the previous war. The American people would not countenance the atrocities of Hitler's legions, nor could it stand by and watch the destruction of its historic allies.

The problems of World War II presented a surprising parallelism with those of World War I. In 1939, Congress passed a

Neutrality Act similar to the one passed in 1915. In 1939, President Roosevelt urged the cause of neutrality as President Wilson had done in 1915. Neutrality, however, failed in World War II as it had failed in World War I. The country's safety and security drove President Roosevelt to appear before Congress on December 8, 1941, to ask for a declaration of war as President Wilson had done on April 2, 1917. Then on the evening of December 9 Roosevelt delivered a greatly expanded war message in the form of a fireside chat to the people in which he discussed fully the Japanese attack as a challenge "flung at the United States of America" and the acceptance of the challenge by the American people. Since radio had, between 1915 and 1939, developed into a great source of communication, President Roosevelt — a master of the radio speaking technique — was able to carry both his neutrality message of September 3, 1939, and his expanded war message of December 9, 1941, directly to the people. Both of these speeches are given in this section to show the similarity of the issues with those faced by President Wilson in 1915 and 1917.

The conduct of World War II, the peace which followed, the increasingly important role of the United States in world affairs, and the important domestic developments which have come in increasing numbers have produced important speeches, but sheer numbers compel the reader to await another collection. Then, too, many of these speeches are too recent to permit an accurate evaluation of their place in history.

So this collection must content itself with noting only a few issues, printing a few examples of eloquence, and giving the names of a few courageous men whose voices rang out in the public forums of our nation. It must, therefore, conclude with President Franklin D. Roosevelt's momentous Fireside Chat of December 9, 1941.

WOODROW WILSON

(1856-1924)

As a young man Thomas Woodrow Wilson, who later was to
become the twenty-eighth President of the United States, was convinced that vigorous healthy government was possible only through
strong personal leadership which, in turn, was possible only through
a mastery of the arts of persuasion, especially oratory. Wilson felt
that to be a successful leader of men, he must be able to communicate his thoughts clearly, accurately, strikingly; he must, in
other words, develop a style. To be sure, he recognized that ideas
were important, but not less important was the vehicle in which
they were carried.

Clearly decisive in Wilson's consciousness of the importance of
thoughtful, careful expression was the tutoring the elder Wilson
gave his son in the proper use of the English language.

> He never permitted the use of an incorrect word or sentence. If
> there was any doubt, the boy was sent flying for the dictionary, and
> there was often great discussion of the exact meaning of a word or
> a phrase. . . .
>
> "What do you mean by that?" the Doctor would ask the boy
> when he fumbled a sentence.
>
> Tommy would explain.
>
> "Then why don't you say so?"
>
> . . . The Doctor believed that there could be no clear thought
> without clear expression. And back of clear thought lay clear
> observation, the activity of an alert mind. An idea must not be left
> ragged at the edges, every word must do its definite work, every
> sentence must be clear.[1]

[1] Ray Stannard Baker, *Woodrow Wilson, Life and Letters,* I, Doubleday &
Company, Inc., New York, pp. 37-38.

For the rest of his life and in whatever capacity he found himself, Woodrow Wilson reaped the benefits of this early but exacting instruction. Both as a college student at Davidson, Princeton, University of Virginia, and Johns Hopkins, and as a teacher at Wesleyan and Princeton, Wilson consistently earned top honors as an active participant in each school's literary and debating society. The student body at Princeton annually voted him the most popular lecturer. Furthermore, his remarkable skill at energizing ideas certainly was a contributing factor in his rise to the high offices of President of Princeton, Governor of New Jersey, and President of the United States.

Truly, then, Woodrow Wilson's appeal as a leader to the masses of men may be traced in large measure to his ability as a speaker, to his talent for articulate, imaginative statement.

Woodrow Wilson's famous "Too Proud to Fight" speech was delivered in Convention Hall, Philadelphia, on May 11, 1915. The occasion was a special program in honor of 4,000 newly naturalized American citizens. The New York Times of that same day relates that "when the President's party arrived at Convention Hall, the streets outside were black with people and Mr. Wilson was repeatedly cheered. Inside, practically every seat had been taken." A crowd of some 15,000 persons marked the President's entrance into the Hall with cheering, waving of flags, and singing.

With reference to the speech itself, according to the Times, "the President was constantly interrupted by spontaneous outbursts of applause. He spoke clearly and . . . could be heard distinctly in all parts of the great hall."

Wilson's redefinition of what America stands for might well be reread periodically by all Americans.

> You have just taken an oath of allegiance to the United States. Of allegiance to whom? Of allegiance to no one, unless it be God — certainly not of allegiance to those who temporarily represent this great Government. You have taken an oath of allegiance to a great ideal, to a great body of principles, to a great hope of the human race. . . . [the] longing and utterance of the human heart. . . . for liberty and justice.

Furthermore, remarked the President, "you cannot become thorough Americans if you think of yourselves in groups, America does not consist of groups. A man who thinks of himself as belonging to a particular national group in America has not yet become an American. . . ."

In addition to redefining the American ideal, the President intimated the probable course of action the government would take concerning the recent loss of American lives on the ill-fated Lusitania.

> The example of America must be the example not merely of peace because it will not fight, but of peace because peace is the healing and elevating influence of the world and strife is not. There is such a thing as a man being too proud to fight. There is such a thing as a nation being so right that it does not need to convince others by force that it is right.

"These remarks," observes the Times, "precipitated a tumult of applause and patriotic enthusiasm, attended by a waving of thousands of small American flags. The President had made no direct reference to the Lusitania tragedy, but the audience did not hesitate to read the application of the statement."

The Times reports that "a tremendous ovation" greeted the President as he concluded his speech, a speech in which he had eloquently stressed the true meaning of America and the determination of the government to seek ways other than war to settle America's disputes with Germany.

Unfortunately, however, relations with Germany steadily worsened, and with the initiation in early 1917 of unrestricted submarine warfare by the Germans the die was cast; war was to be the final arbiter. On March 21 the President called for Congress to meet on April 2.

About twenty minutes past eight on the rainy evening of April 2, 1917, President Wilson left the White House for the Capitol where he was to execute a Constitutional duty, the painful and overwhelming implications of which had kept him awake the previous night. To his intimate friend and visitor that sleepless night, Frank Cobb, he had exclaimed, "If there is any alternative, for God's sake, let's take it." But alternatives had been exhausted. Only one course of action remained and, with great anguish, Wilson took it. Though in agony over what must be done, though besieged with terrible doubts, he would appear before Congress, specially convened for an Executive message, to ask that it recognize the existence of a state of war between the United States and the Imperial German Government.

As he walked in and ascended the Speaker's platform he got such a reception as Congress had never given him before in any of his visits to it. The Supreme Court Justices rose from their chairs, facing the place where he stood, and led the applause, while Representatives and Senators not only cheered, but yelled. It was two minutes before he could begin his address.[2]

The intense drama and almost unbearable tension of this moment in history is best conveyed in the words of Josephus Daniels, Secretary of the Navy under Wilson:

Any stranger would have chosen Wilson as the leader if he had looked down upon that gathering of the great. Erect, with stern sense of responsibility, his face marked with determination . . . there was a gravity and distinction in his bearing which made him the voice and inspiration of a great people about to embark on what he and his hearers alike regarded as a noble struggle. He looked inches taller in his immaculate dress. . . . He was pale, for he had come to that moment through great travail of mind and heart. . . . he turned to the manuscript he held in his hands and an air of calm and confidence settled upon him. . . . He spoke clearly and solemnly. . . . the great audience seemed hushed as the chosen leader, in sentences so vascular they would have bled if cut, recounted the tragic events which had culminated in the necessity for war. The spirit of the Covenanter flashed from his eyes as he proclaimed: "the world must be made safe for democracy." It was to be a war "without rancor and without selfish object" and without revenge. Why did he counsel war — why must we fight? He answered: "For democracy, for the right of those who submit to authority to have a voice in their own governments, for the rights and liberties of small nations, for a universal dominion of right by such concert of free peoples as shall bring peace and safety to all nations and make the world at last free."

The chamber breathed its approval and consecration. When he came to the climax: "there is one choice we cannot make, we are incapable of making. We will not choose the path of submission," all observed the tall and commanding and venerable Chief Justice rise to his feet — he looked ten feet high — and lead the cheering

---

[2] New York Times, April 3, 1917.

with which the chamber rang. As he applauded, his face moved
convulsively and great tears rolled down his cheeks. . . .

The memorable address ended with the inspiring prayer, borrowed from the immortal Luther, as Wilson spoke for America
"privileged to spend her blood and her might for the principles that
gave her birth and happiness and the peace which she has treasured." —

"God helping her, she can do no other."[3]

According to the New York Times,

The President ended at 9:11, having spoken thirty-six minutes.
Then the great scene which had been enacted at his entrance was
repeated. The diplomats, the Supreme Court, the galleries, the
House and Senate, Republicans and Democrats alike, stood in their
places and the Senators waved flags they had brought in with them.
Those who were wearing, not carrying flags, tore them from their
lapels or their sleeves and waved with the rest, and they all cheered
wildly.[4]

Quickly the President left the House chamber, but not before
Senator Lodge had congratulated him. "Mr. President, you have
expressed in the loftiest manner possible, the sentiments of the
American people." Daniels then remarks, "If I should live a thousand years, there would abide with me the reverberation of the
fateful, ominous sound of the hoofs of the cavalry horses as they
escorted Mr. and Mrs. Wilson back to the White House."[5]

Having returned to the White House, relates Joseph Tumulty,
his private secretary, Wilson "sat silent and pale in the Cabinet
Room. At last he said: 'Think what it was they were applauding
[speaking of the people lined along the streets on his way to the
Capitol]. My message to-day was a message of death for our young
men. How strange it seems to applaud that.'"[6] Later, writes
Tumulty, "the President drew his handkerchief from his pocket,
wiped away great tears that stood in his eyes, and then laying his
head on the Cabinet table, sobbed as if he had been a child."[7]

[3] Josephus Daniels. The Wilson Era — Years of War and After, 1917-1923,
The University of North Carolina Press, Chapel Hill, pp. 32-33.
[4] April 3, 1917.
[5] Op. cit., p. 34.
[6] Woodrow Wilson As I Know Him, p. 258.
[7] Ibid., p. 259.

The United States was at war, a war that proved too much for Wilson's rather frail constitution to bear. In 1919 the President suffered a disabling stroke from which he never really recovered. His life ended on February 3, 1924, but as long as man shall value unswerving devotion to moral principles his name will be remembered.

"TOO PROUD TO FIGHT" SPEECH

by

Woodrow Wilson

Delivered in Philadelphia in Convention Hall on May 11, 1915.

IT WARMS MY HEART that you should give me such a reception; but it is not of myself that I wish to think to-night; but of those who have just become citizens of the United States.

This is the only country in the world which experiences this constant and repeated rebirth. Other countries depend upon the multiplication of their own native people. This country is constantly drinking strength out of new sources by the voluntary association with it of great bodies of strong men and forward-looking women out of other lands. And so by the gift of the free will of independent people it is being constantly renewed from generation to generation by the same process by which it was originally created. It is as if humanity had determined to see to it that this great Nation, founded for the benefit of humanity, should not lack for the allegiance of the people of the world.

You have just taken an oath of allegiance to the United States. Of allegiance to whom? Of allegiance to no one, unless it be God —certainly not of allegiance to those who temporarily represent this great Government. You have taken an oath of allegiance to a great ideal, to a great body of principles, to a great hope of the human race. You have said, "We are going to America not only to earn a living, not only to seek the things which it was more difficult to obtain where we were born, but to help forward the great enterprises of the human spirit — to let men know that everywhere in the world there are men who will cross strange oceans and go where a speech is spoken which is alien to them if they can but satisfy their quest for what their spirits crave; knowing that whatever the speech there is but one longing and utterance of the human heart, and that is for liberty and justice." And while you bring all countries with you, you come with a purpose of leaving all other countries behind you — bringing what is best of their spirit, but not looking over your shoulders and seeking to perpetuate what you intended to leave behind in them. I certainly would not be one even to suggest that a man cease to love the home of his birth and the nation of his origin — these things are very sacred and ought not to be put out of our hearts — but it is one thing to love the place where you were born and it is another thing to dedicate yourself to the place to which you go. You cannot dedicate yourself to America unless you become in every respect and with every purpose of your will thorough Americans. You cannot become thorough Americans if you think of yourselves in groups. America does not consist of groups. A man who thinks of himself as belonging to a particular national group in America has not yet become an American, and the man who goes among you to trade upon your nationality is no worthy son to live under the Stars and Stripes.

My urgent advice to you would be, not only always to think first of America, but always, also, to think first of humanity. You do not love humanity if you seek to divide humanity into jealous camps. Humanity can be welded together only by love, by sympathy, by justice, not by jealousy and hatred. I am sorry for the man who seeks to make personal capital out of the passions of his fellowmen. He has lost the touch and ideal of America, for America was created to unite mankind by those passions which lift and not by the passions which separate and debase. We came to America, either ourselves or in the persons of our ancestors, to better the ideals of men, to make them see finer things than they had seen before, to get rid of the things that divide and to make sure of the things that unite. It was but an historical accident no doubt that this great country was called the "United States"; yet I am very thankful that it has that word "United" in its title, and the man who seeks to divide man from man, group from group, interest from interest in this great Union is striking at its very heart.

It is a very interesting circumstance to me, in thinking of those of you who have just sworn allegiance to this great Government, that you were drawn across the ocean by some beckoning finger of hope, by some belief, by some vision of a new kind of justice, by some expectation of a better kind of life. No doubt you have been disappointed in some of us. Some of us are very disappointing. No doubt you have found that justice in the United States goes only with a pure heart and a right purpose as it does everywhere else in the world. No doubt what you found here did not seem touched for you, after all, with the complete beauty of the ideal which you had conceived beforehand. But remember this: If we had grown at all poor in the ideal, you brought some of it with you. A man does not go out to seek the thing that is not in him. A man does not hope for the thing that he does not believe in, and if some of us have forgotten what America believed in, you, at any rate, imported in your own hearts a renewal of the belief. That is the reason that I, for one, make you welcome. If I have in any degree forgotten what America was intended for, I will thank God if you will remind me. I was born in America. You dreamed dreams of what America was to be, and I hope you brought the dreams with you. No man that does not see visions will ever realize any high hope or undertake any high enterprise. Just because you brought dreams with you, America is more likely to realize dreams such as you brought. You are enriching us if you came expecting us to be better than we are.

See, my friends, what that means. It means that Americans must have a consciousness different from the consciousness of every other nation in the world. I am not saying this with even the slightest thought of criticism of other nations. You know how it is with a family. A family gets centered on itself if it is not careful and is less interested in the neighbors than it is in its own members. So a nation that is not constantly renewed out of new sources is apt to have the narrowness and prejudice of a family; whereas, America must have this consciousness, that on all sides it touches elbows and touches hearts with all the nations of mankind. The example of America must be a special example. The example of America must be the example not merely of peace because it will not fight, but of peace because peace is the healing and elevating influence of the world and strife is not. There is such a thing as a man being too proud to fight. There is such a thing as a nation being so right that it does not need to convince others by force that it is right.

You have come into this great Nation voluntarily seeking something that we have to give, and all that we have to give is this: We cannot exempt you from work. No man is exempt from work anywhere in the world. We cannot exempt you from the strife and the heartbreaking burden of the struggle of the day — that is common to mankind everywhere; we cannot exempt you from the loads that you must carry. We can only make them light by the spirit in which they are carried. That is the spirit of hope, it is the spirit of liberty, it is the spirit of justice.

When I was asked, therefore, by the Mayor and the committee that accompanied him to come up from Washington to meet this great company of newly admitted citizens, I could not decline the invitation. I ought not to be away from Washington, and yet I feel that it has renewed my spirit as an American to be here. In Washington men tell you so many things every day that are not so, and I like to come and stand in the presence of a great body of my fellow-citizens, whether they have been my fellow-citizens a long time or a short time, and drink, as it were, out of the common fountains with them and go back feeling what you have so generously given me — the sense of your support and of the living vitality in your hearts of the great ideals which have made America the hope of the world.

WAR MESSAGE

by
Woodrow Wilson

Delivered before a joint session of Congress on April 2, 1917.

GENTLEMEN OF THE CONGRESS: I have called the Congress into extraordinary session because there are serious, very serious choices of policy to be made, and made immediately, which it was neither right nor constitutionally permissible that I should assume the responsibility of making.

On the third of February last I officially laid before you the extraordinary announcement of the Imperial German Government that on and after the first day of February it was its purpose to put aside all restraints of law or of humanity and use its submarines to sink every vessel that sought to approach either the ports of Great Britain and Ireland or the western coasts of Europe or any of the ports controlled by the enemies of Germany within the Mediterranean. That had seemed to be the object of the German submarine warfare earlier in the war, but since April of last year the Imperial Government had somewhat restrained the commanders of its undersea craft in conformity with its promise then given to us that passenger boats should not be sunk and that due warning would be given to all other vessels which its submarines might seek to destroy, when no resistance was offered or escape attempted, and care taken that their crews were given at least a fair chance to save their lives in their open boats. The precautions taken were meager and haphazard enough, as was proved in distressing instance after instance in the progress of the cruel and unmanly business, but a certain degree of restraint was observed. The new policy has swept every restriction aside. Vessels of every kind, whatever their flag, their character, their cargo, their destination, their errand, have been ruthlessly sent to the bottom without warning and without thought of help or mercy for those on board, the vessels of friendly neutrals along with those of belligerents. Even hospital ships and ships carrying relief to the sorely bereaved and stricken people of Belgium, though the latter were provided with safe conduct through the proscribed areas by the German Government itself and were distinguished by unmistakable marks of identity, have been sunk with the same reckless lack of compassion or of principle.

I was for a little while unable to believe that such things would in fact be done by any government that had hitherto subscribed to humane practices of civilized nations. International law had its origin in the attempt to set up some law which would be respected and observed upon the seas, where no nation had right of dominion and where lay the free highways of the world. By painful stage after stage has that law been built up, with meager enough results, indeed, after all was accomplished that could be accomplished, but always with a clear view, at least, of what the heart and conscience of mankind demanded. This minimum of right the German Government has swept aside, under the plea of retaliation and necessity and because it had no weapons which it could use at sea except these which it is impossible to employ as it is employing them without throwing to the wind all scruples of humanity or of respect for the understandings that were supposed to underlie the intercourse of the world. I am not now thinking of the loss of property involved, immense and serious as that is, but only of the wanton and wholesale destruction of the lives of non-combatants, men, women, and children, engaged in pursuits which have always, even in the darkest periods of modern histoy, been deemed innocent and legitimate. Property can be paid for; the lives of peaceful and innocent people cannot be. The present German submarine warfare against commerce is a warfare against mankind.

It is a war against all nations. American ships have been sunk, American lives taken, in ways which it has stirred us very deeply to learn of, but the ships and people of other neutral and friendly nations have been sunk and overwhelmed in the waters in the same way. There has been no discrimination. The challenge is to all mankind. Each nation must decide for itself how it will meet it. The choice we make for ourselves must be made with a moderation of counsel and a temperateness of judgment befitting our character and our motives as a nation. We must put excited feeling away. Our motive will not be revenge or the victorious assertion of the physical might of the nation, but only the vindication of right, of human right, of which we are only a single champion.

When I addressed the Congress on the twenty-sixth of February last I thought that it would suffice to assert our neutral rights with arms, our right to use the seas against unlawful interference, our right to keep our people safe against unlawful violence. But armed neutrality, it now appears, is impracticable. Because submarines are in effect outlaws when used as the German submarines have been used against merchant shipping, it is impossible to defend ships against their attacks as the law of nations has assumed that merchantmen would defend themselves against privateers or cruisers, visible craft giving chase upon the open sea. It is common prudence in such circumstances, grim necessity indeed, to endeavor to destroy them before they have shown their own intention. They must be dealt with upon sight, if dealt with at all. The German Government denies the right of neutrals to use arms at all within the areas of the sea which it has proscribed, even in the defense of rights which no modern publicist has ever before questioned their right to defend. The intimation is conveyed that the armed guards which we have placed on our merchant ships will be treated as beyond the pale of law and subject to be dealt with as pirates would be. Armed neutrality is ineffectual enough at best; in such circumstances and in the face of such pretensions it is worse than ineffectual; it is likely only to produce what it was meant to prevent; it is practically certain to draw us into the war without either the rights or the effectiveness of belligerents. There is one choice we cannot make, we are incapable of making; we will not choose the path of submission and suffer the most sacred rights of our nation and our people to be ignored or violated. The wrongs against which we now array ourselves are no common wrongs; they cut to the very roots of human life.

With a profound sense of the solemn and even tragical character of the step I am taking and of the grave responsibilities which it involves, but in unhesitating obedience to what I deem my constitutional duty, I advise that the Congress declare the recent course of the Imperial German Government to be in fact nothing less than war against the Government and people of the United States; that it formally accept the status of belligerent which has thus been thrust upon it; and that it take immediate steps not only to put the country in a more thorough state of defense, but also to exert all its power and employ all its resources to bring the Government of the German Empire to terms and end the war.

What this will involve is clear. It will involve the utmost practicable cooperation in counsel and action with the governments now at war with Germany, and, as incident to that, the extension to those governments of the most liberal financial credits, in order that our resources may so far as possible be added to theirs. It will involve the organization and mobilization of all the material resources of the country to supply the materials of war and serve the incidental needs of the nation in the most abundant and yet the most economical and efficient way possible. It will involve the immediate full equipment of the navy in all respects but particularly in supplying it with the best means of dealing with the enemy's submarines. It will involve the immediate addition to the armed forces of the United States already provided for by law in case of war of at least five hundred thousand men, who should, in my opinion, be chosen upon the principle of universal liability to service, and also the authorization of subsequent additional increments of equal force so soon as they may be needed and can be handled in training. It will involve also, of course, the granting of adequate credits to the Government, sustained, I hope, so far as they can equitably be sustained by the present generation, by well-conceived taxation.

I say sustained so far as may be equitable by taxation because it seems to me that it would be most unwise to base the credits which will now be necessary entirely on money borrowed. It is our duty, I most respectfully urge, to protect our people so far as we may against the very serious hardships and evils which would be likely to arise out of the inflation which would be produced by vast loans.

In carrying out the measures by which these things are to be accomplished we should keep constantly in mind the wisdom of interfering as little as possible in our own preparation and in the equipment of our own military forces with the duty — for it will be a very practical duty — of supplying the nations already at war with Germany with the materials which they can obtain only from us or by our assistance. They are in the field and we should help them in every way to be effective there.

I shall take the liberty of suggesting, through the several executive departments of the Government, for the consideration of your committees, measures for the accomplishment of the several objects I have mentioned. I hope that it will be your pleasure to deal with them as having been framed after very careful thought by the branch of the Government upon whom the responsibility of conducting the war and safeguarding the nation will most directly fall.

While we do these things, these deeply momentous things, let us be very clear, and make very clear to all the world, what our motives and our objects are. My own thought has not been driven from its habitual and normal course by the unhappy events of the last two months, and I do not believe that the thought of the nation has been altered or clouded by them. I have exactly the same things in mind now that I had in mind when I addressed the Senate on the twenty-second of January last; the same that I had in mind when I addressed the Congress on the third of February and on the twenty-sixth of February. Our object now, as then, is to vindicate the principles of peace and justice in the life of the world as against selfish and autocratic power, and to set up among the really free and self-governed peoples of the world such a concert of purpose and of action as will henceforth ensure the observance of those principles. Neutrality is no longer feasible or desirable where the peace of the world is involved and the freedom of its peoples, and the menace to that peace and freedom lies in the existence of autocratic governments, backed by organized force which is controlled wholly by their will, not by the will of their people. We have seen the last of neutrality in such circumstances. We are at the beginning of an age in which it will be insisted that the same standards of conduct and of responsibility for wrong done shall be observed among nations and their governments that are observed among the individual citizens of civilized States.

We have no quarrel with the German people. We have no feeling towards them but one of sympathy and friendship. It was not upon their impulse that their government acted in entering this war. It was not with their previous knowledge or approval. It was a war determined upon as wars used to be determined upon in the old, unhappy days when peoples were nowhere consulted by their rulers and wars were provoked and waged in the interest of dynasties or of little groups of ambitious men who were accustomed to use their fellow-men as pawns and tools. Self-governed nations do not fill their neighbor states with spies or set the course of intrigue to bring about some critical posture of affairs which will give them an opportunity to strike and make conquest. Such designs can be successfully worked out only under cover and where no one has the right to ask questions. Cunningly contrived plans of deception or aggression, carried, it may be, from generation to generation, can be worked out and kept from the light only within the privacy of courts or behind the carefully guarded confidences of a narrow and privileged class. They are happily impossible where public opinion commands and insists upon full information concerning all the nation's affairs.

A steadfast concert for peace can never be maintained except by a partnership of democratic nations. No autocratic government could be trusted to keep faith within it or observe its covenants. It must be a league of honor, a partnership of opinion. Intrigue would eat its vitals away; the plottings of inner circles who could plan what they would and render account to no one would be a corruption seated at its very heart. Only free peoples can hold their purpose and their honor steady to a common end and prefer the interests of mankind to any narrow interest of their own.

Does not every American feel that assurance has been added to our hope for the future peace of the world by the wonderful and heartening things that have been happening within the last few weeks in Russia? Russia was known by those who knew her best to have been always in fact democratic at heart in all the vital habits of her thought, in all the intimate relationships of her people that spoke their natural instinct, their habitual attitude towards life. The autocracy that crowned the summit of her political structure, long as it had stood and terrible as was the reality of its power, was not in fact Russian in origin, character, or purpose; and now it has been shaken off and the great, generous Russian people have been added, in all their naïve majesty and might, to the forces that are fighting for freedom in the world, for justice, and for peace. Here is a fit partner for a League of Honor.

One of the things that has served to convince us that the Prussian autocracy was not and could never be our friend is that from the very outset of the present war it has filled our unsuspecting communities, and even our offices of government, with spies and set criminal intrigues everywhere afoot against our national unity of counsel, our peace within and without, our industries and our commerce. Indeed, it is now evident that its spies were here even before the war began; and it is unhappily not a matter of conjecture but a fact proved in our courts of justice that the intrigues which have more than once come perilously near to disturbing the peace and dislocating the industries of the country have been carried on at the instigation, with the support, and even under the personal direction of official agents of the Imperial Government accredited to the Government of the United States. Even in checking these things and trying to extirpate them we have sought to put the most generous interpretation possible upon them because we knew that their source lay, not in any hostile feeling of the German people toward us (who were, no doubt, as ignorant of them as we ourselves were), but only in the selfish designs of a government that did what it pleased and told its people nothing. But they have played their part in serving to convince us at last that that government entertains no real friendship for us, and means to act against our peace and security at its convenience. That it means to stir up enemies against us at our very doors the intercepted note to the German Minister at Mexico City is eloquent evidence.

We are accepting this challenge of hostile purpose because we know that in such a government, following such methods, we can never have a friend; and that in the presence of its organized power, always lying in wait to accomplish we know not what purpose, there can be no assured security for the democratic governments of the world. We are now about to accept the gauge of battle with this natural foe to liberty and shall, if necessary, spend the whole force of the nation to check and nullify its pretensions and its power. We are glad, now that we see the facts with no veil of false pretense about them, to fight thus for the ultimate peace of the world and for the liberation of its peoples, the German peoples included; for the rights of nations, great and small, and the privilege of men everywhere to choose their way of life and of obedience. The world must be made safe for democracy. Its peace must be planted upon the tested foundations of political liberty. We have no selfish ends to serve. We desire no conquest, no dominion. We seek no indemnities for ourselves, no material compensation for the sacrifices we shall freely make. We are but one of the champions of the rights of mankind. We shall be satisfied when those rights have been made as secure as the faith and the freedom of nations can make them.

Just because we fight without rancor and without selfish object, seeking nothing for ourselves but what we shall wish to share with all free peoples, we shall, I feel confident, conduct our operations as belligerents without passion and ourselves observe with proud punctilio the principles of right and of fair play we profess to be fighting for.

I have said nothing of the government allied with the Imperial Government of Germany because they have not made war upon us or challenged us to defend our right and our honor. The Austro-Hungarian Government has, indeed, avowed its unqualified endorsement and acceptance of the reckless and lawless submarine warfare adopted now without disguise by the Imperial German Government, and it has therefore not been possible for this Government to receive Count Tarnowski, the Ambassador recently accredited to this Government by the Imperial and Royal Government of Austria-Hungary; but that Government has not actually engaged in warfare against citizens of the United States on the seas, and I take the liberty, for the present at least, of postponing a discussion of our relations with the authorities at Vienna. We enter this war only where we are clearly forced into it because there are no other means of defending our rights.

It will be all the easier for us to conduct ourselves as belligerents in a high spirit of right and fairness because we act without animus, not with enmity toward a people or with the desire to bring any injury or disadvantage upon them, but only in armed opposition to an irresponsible government which has thrown aside all considerations of humanity and of right and is running amuck. We are, let me say again, the sincere friends of the German people, and shall desire nothing so much as the early reëstablishment of intimate relations of mutual advantage between us, — however hard it may be for them, for the time being, to believe that this is spoken from our hearts. We have borne with their present government through all these bitter months because of that friendship, exercising a patience and forbearance which would otherwise have been impossible. We shall, happily, still have an opportunity to prove that friendship in our daily attitude and actions toward the millions of men and women of German birth and native sympathy who live among us and share our life, and we shall be proud to prove it towards all who are in fact loyal to their neighbors and to the Government in the hour of test. They are, most of them, as true and loyal Americans as if they had never known any other fealty or allegiance. They will be prompt to stand with us in rebuking and restraining the few who may be of a different mind and purpose. If there should be disloyalty, it will be dealt with with a firm hand of stern repression; but, if it lifts its head at all, it will lift it only here and there and without countenance except from a lawless and malignant few.

It is a distressing and oppressive duty, Gentlemen of the Congress, which I have performed in thus addressing you. There are, it may be, many months of fiery trial and sacrifice ahead of us. It is a fearful thing to lead this great peaceful people into war, into the most terrible and disastrous of all wars, civilization itself seeming to be in the balance. But the right is more precious than peace, and we shall fight for the things which we have always carried nearest our hearts — for democracy, for the right of those who submit to authority to have a voice in their own governments, for the rights and liberties of small nations, for a universal dominion of right by such a concert of free peoples as shall bring peace and safety to all nations and make the world itself at last free. To such a task we can dedicate our lives and our fortunes, everything that we are and everything that we have, with the pride of those who know that the day has come when America is privileged to spend her blood and her might for the principles that gave her birth and happiness and the peace which she has treasured. God helping her, she can do no other.

ROBERT M. LaFOLLETTE

(1855-1925)

Four years governor of Wisconsin, nineteen years a U. S. Senator, "Fighting Bob" LaFollette was one of the most colorful and dynamic political figures of the first half of the twentieth century. As Wisconsin's governor from 1901 to 1905, he fought valiantly and successfully for such reform or progressive legislation as the direct primary; the civil service law; the anti-lobbying law; and the adequate taxation and regulation of the railroads. As a member of the United States Senate from 1906 to 1925, LaFollette was the acknowledged spokesman for that minority group of insurgent Republicans known as the Progressives — those who struggled (1) to promote a more popular or representative type of government, and (2) to secure legislation in the national or public interest. This small band of Senators — often verbally crucified by both their colleagues and the press for their frequent unpopular stand on proposed legislation — were unswerving in their determination to oppose the never-ending stream of private interests which descended upon Congress seeking special privileges and advantages at the expense of the people as a whole.

LaFollette, Norris, Johnson, and others, were dedicated completely to the principle that the Republican party must represent not the entrenched vested interests but the people generally. According to LaFollette, the constant danger to a truly representative government was "the encroachment of the powerful few upon the rights of the many."

Certainly instrumental in LaFollette's frequent success in combating "the powerful few" was his ability as a public speaker and debater. The following quote taken by Edward Doan from an article in the Milwaukee Journal calls attention to one of the prin-

311

cipal strengths of LaFollette as a speaker; that is, the characteristic energy and determination that he regularly brought to bear on his speech efforts.

"Below the ordinary height, he is compactly built. . . . impresses one who sees him for the first time as possessed of a solidity and bulldog determination. . . . a trained and impressive public speaker. . . . intense and continued display of energy is one of the strong characteristics of the man, as expressed in his work as a public speaker, and it rarely fails to bring his hearers to him and to hold their attention. . . . LaFollette is infinite in facial expression and gesture. . . . And Mr. LaFollette is sometimes sarcastic. His words bite like coals of fire. . . . there is a certain fine frenzy in the man. . . . Disgust, hope, honor, avarice, despair, love, anger, all the passions of man, he paints in strong words and still stronger gestures. . . . He carries his subject and his hearers both, and compels the latter to listen, if he cannot compel them to endorse what he may say. . . . he impresses even the unbelievers among his hearers that he believes himself and believes in the truth and force of his statements." . . .[1]

Not only was there genuine, deep feeling giving rise to a vigorous style but also careful, thorough speech preparation. Perhaps benefitted by his legal training, LaFollette did not often make unfounded generalizations; he derived his conclusions from a substantial array of evidence, of facts. So completely was he the master of any subject on which he spoke that the New York Times commented that anyone who dared oppose him in debate without first having devoted " 'a couple of years to the subject' " would " 'retire from the contest much the worse for wear.' "[2]

On April 4, 1917, from the floor of the United States Senate, Robert M. LaFollette gave one of the finest speeches of his long and distinguished political career. An avowed champion of the rights and problems of the common man he vehemently protested our entry into World War I, because he was convinced that the average American citizen was unalterably opposed to our involvement. Despite the war fever that was sweeping Washington like a prairie fire and despite the wildly enthusiastic acceptance of Wilson's War Message of April 2 by both Congress and the press,

[1] Edward Doan, The LaFollettes and the Wisconsin Idea, Rinehart & Company, Inc., New York, pp. 31-33.
[2] Belle and Fola LaFollette, Robert M. LaFollette, I, 227.

LaFollette boldly attacked the very grounds on which the President had justified his request to Congress for a declaration of war against Germany. According to Belle and Fola LaFollette, he spoke nearly three hours that Wednesday afternoon, reading his speech as he stood beside his desk in the first row of the middle aisle — directly opposite the presiding officer. The crowded galleries and the eighty-eight Senators present listened attentively as LaFollette argued forcibly from a wealth of evidence against our fighting the Germans. But those who urged American participation in the European war were not to be denied; by a vote of eighty-two to six the Senate supported the President's appeal for a declaration of war.

Unmistakably, LaFollette once again had pleaded earnestly and persuasively for what he believed was right for his country. Knowing full well the savage denunciation of himself that would inevitably follow, the man, consistent with his character, had stood firm and spoken his mind. He had given voice to his convictions even when such action seriously threatened to jeopardize his political future. Why? The answer, appropriately, is revealed through his own words in a penciled note found after his death: "I would be remembered as one who in the world's darkest hour kept a clear conscience and stood to the end for the ideals of American democracy."

AGAINST WAR WITH GERMANY

by

Robert M. LaFollette

Delivered in the United States Senate on April 4, 1917*

MR. PRESIDENT. I HAD supposed until recently that it was the duty of Senators and Representatives in Congress to vote and act

*Editors' Note: Senator LaFollette's speech as it appears in the Congressional Record cannot be printed in its entirety because of its length. The version given here has been abridged in a manner designed to preserve the main arguments as well as the style.

according to their convictions on all public matters that came before them for consideration and decision.

Quite another doctrine has recently been promulgated by certain newspapers, which unfortunately seems to have found considerable support elsewhere, and that is the doctrine of "standing back of the President," without inquiring whether the President is right or wrong. For myself I have never subscribed to that doctrine and never shall. I shall support the President in the measures he proposes when I believe him to be right. I shall oppose measures proposed by the President when I believe them to be wrong. The fact that the matter which the President submits for consideration is of the greatest importance is only an additional reason why we should be sure that we are right and not to be swerved from that conviction or intimidated in its expression by any influence of power whatsoever. If it is important for us to speak and vote our convictions in matters of internal policy, though we may unfortunately be in disagreement with the President, it is infinitely more important for us to speak and vote our convictions when the question is one of peace or war, certain to involve the lives and fortunes of many of our people and, it may be, the destiny of all of them and of the civilized world as well. If, unhappily, on such momentous questions the most patient research and conscientious consideration we could give to them leave us in disagreement with the President, I know of no course to take except to oppose, regretfully but not the less firmly, the demands of the Executive.

On the 2d of this month the President addressed a communication to the Senate and House in which he advised that the Congress declare war against Germany and that this Government "assert all its powers and employ all its resources to bring the Government of the German Empire to terms and end the war."

On February 26, 1917, the President addressed the Senate and the House upon the conditions existing between this Government and the German Empire, and at that time said, "I am not now proposing or contemplating war or any steps that need lead to it. . . . I request that you will authorize me to supply our merchant ships with defensive arms, should that become necessary, and with the means of using them" against what he characterized as the unlawful attacks of German submarines.

A bill was introduced, and it was attempted to rush it through the closing hours of the last session of Congress, to give the President the powers requested, namely, to arm our merchant ships, and to place upon them guns and gunners from our Navy, to be used against German submarines, and to employ such other instrumentalities and methods as might in his judgment and discretion seem necessary and adequate to protect such vessels. That measure did not pass.

It is common knowledge that the President, acting without authority from Congress, did arm our merchant ships with guns and gunners from our Navy, and sent them into the prohibited "war zone." At the time the President addressed us on the 2d of April there was absolutely no change in the conditions between this Government and Germany. The effect of arming merchant ships had not been tested as a defensive measure. Late press reports indicate, however, that the *Aztec*, a United States armed merchantman, has been sunk in the prohibited zone, whether with mines or a torpedo, I believe, has not been established, so the responsibility for this sinking can not, so far as I know at this time, be placed.

When the request was made by the President on February 26 for authority to arm merchant ships, the granting of such authority was opposed by certain Members of the House and by certain Senators, of which I was one. I made at that time a careful investigation of the subject, and became convinced that arming our merchant ships was wholly futile and its only purpose and effect would be to lure our merchantmen to danger, and probably result in the destruction of the vessels and in the loss of the lives of those on board. The representatives of the President on this floor then having that bill in charge saw fit, by methods I do not care to characterize, to prevent my speaking upon the measure and giving to the Senate and to the country such information as I had upon the subject.

Under the circumstances, I did the only thing that seemed practical to me, and that was to give such publicity as I was able through the press to the fact that the proposition to arm merchant ships would be wholly futile, and could only result in loss of the lives and property of our own people, without accomplishing the results intended. I regret to say that the President, according to statements in the public press purporting to emanate from him, and which have never been denied, saw fit to characterize as "willful" the conduct of the Senators who, in obedience to their consciences and their oaths of office, opposed the armed-ship bill, and to charge that in so doing they were not representing the people by whose suffrages they are here. I know of no graver charge that could be made against the official conduct of any Member of this body than that his official action was the result of a "willful" — that is, an unreasoned and perverse — purpose. . . .

Mr. President, let me make another suggestion. It is this: That a minority in one Congress — mayhap a small minority in one Congress — protesting, exercising the rights which the Constitution confers upon a minority, may really be representing the majority opinion of the country, and if, exercising the right that the Constitution gives them, they succeed in defeating for the time being the will of the majority, they are but carrying out what was in the mind of the framers of the Constitution; that you may have from time to time in a legislative body a majority in numbers that really does not represent the principle of democracy; and that if the question could be deferred and carried to the people it would be found that a minority was the real representative of the public opinion. So, Mr. President, it was that they wrote into the Constitution that a President — that one man — may put his judgment against the will of a majority not only in one branch of the Congress but in both branches of the Congress; that he may defeat the measure that they have agreed upon and may set his one single judgment above the majority judgment of the Congress. That seems, when you look at it nakedly, to be in violation of the principle that the majority shall rule; and so it is. Why is that power given? It is one of those checks provided by the wisdom of the fathers to prevent the majority from abusing the power that they chance to have, when they do not reflect the real judgment, the opinion, the will of the majority of the people that constitute the sovereign power of the democracy.

We have had three immigration bills passed by Congress much in the same form, varying in some particulars, which have been vetoed by President Taft and twice vetoed by President Wilson. At recurring elections the people send back the Members who have passed that bill by an overwhelming majority; and still the President, exercising that power — that one-man power — vetoes the legislation ratified by the people at the polls through the election of Members of Congress — through the election and re-election of Members of Congress with that legislation one of the paramount issues. Mr. President, that might have been characterized as the exercise of a willful disposition, but it was not.

So, too, Mr. President, we find that the framers of that great instrument wrote into it that one-fifth of the Members of either one of the two bodies of Congress might hold in check the autocratic use of power by the majority on any question whatsoever. They armed a minority of one-fifth of the body with the power to filibuster; the power to demand a roll call — not a roll call, as some of the State constitutions provide, only upon matters which carry appropriations, but a roll call on every single question upon which it pleases one-fifth of the body to demand a roll call.

What was the purpose of it? Not to make a record, for parliamentary legislative history shows that they had that right prior to that time, and always had it and could exercise it. No, no; it was the foresight of the makers of the Constitution of this great Government of ours desiring to perpetuate not the semblance of democracy but real democracy, and they said, "There may be times when a majority, swept either by passion or misinformation, may do a wrongful thing to this Republic, and we will arm the minority in such emergencies against the undue exercise of majority power by placing in the hands of one-fifth the right to demand a roll call on every question." Exercised in the late hours of the session of a Congress it would easily be possible for them to demand roll calls in such a way as to make an extra session necessary. But, oh, Mr. President, we have always and ever in this Republic of ours back of Congresses and statutes and back of Presidents the supreme power, the sovereign power of the people, and they can correct our errors and mistakes and our wrongdoings. They can take us out of our places, and if we abuse any power which the Constitution puts in the hands of a minority, it lies with them to call us to account; and the more important, the more profoundly and intensely important the question upon which such a power is abused by a minority, the more swift and sweeping will be the punishment by the people for the wrongful exercise of it.

We need not disturb ourselves because of what a minority may do. There is always lodged, and always will be, thank the God above us, power in the people supreme. Sometimes it sleeps, sometimes it seems the sleep of death; but, sir, the sovereign power of the people never dies. It may be suppressed for a time, it may be misled, be fooled, silenced. I think, Mr. President, that it is being denied expression now. I think there will come a day when it will have expression.

The poor, sir, who are the ones called upon to rot in the trenches, have no organized power, have no press to voice their will upon this question of peace or war; but, oh, Mr. President, at some time they will be heard. I hope and I believe they will be heard in an orderly and a peaceful way. I think they may be heard from before long. I think, sir, if we take this step, when the people to-day who are staggering under the burden of supporting families at the present prices of the necessaries of life find those prices multiplied, when they are raised a hundred per cent, or 200 per cent, as they will be quickly, aye, sir, when beyond that those who pay taxes come to have their taxes doubled and again doubled to pay the interest on the nontaxable bonds held by Morgan and his combinations, which have been issued to meet this war, there will come an awakening; they will have their day and they will be heard. It will be as certain and as inevitable as the return of the tides, and as resistless, too.

I promise my colleagues that I will not be tempted again to turn aside from the thread of my discussion as I have outlined it here, and I will hasten with all possible speed.

Now that the President has in his message to us of April 2 admitted the very charge against the armed-ship bill which we made I trust that he is fully convinced that the conduct of the Senators on the occasion in question was not unreasoned and obstinate, but that it was inspired by quite as high purposes and motives as can inspire the action of any public official.

I would not, however, have made this personal reference did not the question it suggests go to the very heart of the matter now under consideration. If the President was wrong when he proposed arming the ships; if that policy was, as he now says, "certain to draw us into the war without either the rights or the effectiveness of belligerents,"is it so certain he is right now when he demands an unqualified declaration of war against Germany? If those Members of Congress who were supporting the President then were wrong, as it appears from the President's statement now they were, should not that fact prompt them to inquire carefully whether they are right in supporting the proposed declaration of war? If the armed-ship bill involved a course of action that was hasty and ill advised, may it not well be that this proposed declaration of war, which is being so hotly pressed, is also ill advised? With that thought in mind let us, with the earnestness and the singleness of purpose which the momentous nature of the question involves, be calm enough and brave enough to examine further the President's address of April 2.

In his address of April 2 the President says:

Since April of last year the Imperial Government had somewhat restrained the commands of its undersea craft in conformity with its promise then given to us that passenger boats should not be sunk, and that due warning would be given to all other vessels which its submarines might seek to destroy when no resistance was offered or escape attempted, and care taken that their crews were given at least a fair chance to save their lives in their open boats.

Beside that statement I wish to place exactly what the German Government did say:

The German Government, moreover, is prepared to do its utmost to confine the operations of war for the rest of its duration to the fighting forces of the belligerents, thereby also insuring the freedom of the seas, a principle upon which the German Government believes, now as before, to be in agreement with the Government of the United States. . . .

But neutrals can not expect that Germany, forced to fight for her existence, shall, for the sake of neutral interest, restrict the use of an effective weapon if her enemy is permitted to continue to apply at will methods of warfare violating the rules of international law. Such a demand would be incompatible with the character of neutrality, and the German Government is convinced that the Government of the United States does not think of making such a demand, knowing that the Government of the United States has repeatedly declared that it is determined to restore the principle of the freedom of the seas, from whatever quarter it is violated.

It must be perfectly apparent therefore that the promise, so called, of the German Government was conditioned upon England's being brought to obedience of international law in her naval warfare. Since no one contends that England was brought to conduct her naval operations in accordance with international law, and even the poor protests our Government has lodged against her show that she has not done so, was it quite fair to lay before the country a statement which implies that Germany had made an unconditional promise which she has dishonorably violated?

This is a time of all times when the public mind should be calm, not inflamed; when accuracy of statement is vitally essential to presenting the issues to the Congress and to the people of the country. . . .

In his message of April 2 the President said:

> We have no quarrel with the German people — it was not upon their impulse that their Government acted in entering this war; it was not with their previous knowledge or approval.

Again he says:

> We are, let me say again, sincere friends of the German people and shall desire nothing so much as the early reestablishment of intimate relations of mutual advantage between us.

At least, the German people, then, are not outlaws. What is the thing the President asks us to do to these German people of whom he speaks so highly and whose sincere friend he declares us to be?

Here is what he declares we shall do in this war. We shall undertake, he says —

> The utmost practicable cooperation in council and action with the Governments now at war with Germany, and as an incident to that, the extension to these Governments of the most liberal financial credits in order that our resources may, so far as possible, be added to theirs.

"Practicable cooperation!" Practicable cooperation with England and her allies in starving to death the old men and women, the children, the sick and the maimed of Germany. The thing we are asked to do is the thing I have stated. It is idle to talk of a war upon a government only. We are leagued in this war, or it is the President's proposition that we shall be so leagued, with the hereditary enemies of Germany. Any war with Germany, or any other country for that matter, would be bad enough, but there are not words strong enough to voice my protest against the proposed combination with the entente allies. When we cooperate with those Governments we indorse their methods, we indorse the violations of international law by Great Britain, we indorse the shameful methods of warfare against which we have again and again protested in this war; we indorse her purpose to wreak upon the German people the animosities which for years her people have been taught to cherish against Germany; finally when the end comes, whatever it may be, we find ourselves in cooperation with our ally, Great Britain, and if we can not resist now the pressure she is exerting to carry us into the war, how can we hope to resist, then, the thousandfold greater pressure she will exert to bend us to her purposes and compel compliance with her demands?

We do not know what they are. We do not know what is in the minds of those who have made the compact, but we are to subscribe to it. We are irrevocably, by our votes here, to marry ourselves to a nondivorceable proposition veiled from us now. Once enlisted, once in the copartnership, we will be carried through with the purposes, whatever they may be, of which we now know nothing.

Sir, if we are to enter upon this war in the manner the President demands, let us throw pretense to the winds, let us be honest, let us admit that this is a ruthless war against not only Germany's army and her navy but against her civilian population as well, and frankly state that the purpose of Germany's hereditary European enemies has become our purpose.

Again, the President says "we are about to accept the gage of battle with this natural foe of liberty and shall, if necessary, spend the whole force of the Nation to check and nullify its pretensions and its power." That much, at least, is clear; that program is definite. The whole force and power of this Nation, if necessary, is to be used to bring victory to the entente allies, and to us as their ally in this war. Remember, that not yet has the "whole force" of one of the warring nations been used. Countless millions are suffering from want and privation; countless other millions are dead and rotting on foreign battlefields; countless other millions are crippled and maimed, blinded, and dismembered; upon all and upon their children's children for generations to come has been laid a burden of debt which must be worked out in poverty and suffering, but the "whole force" of no one of the warring nations has yet been expended; but our "whole force" shall be expended, so says the President. We are pledged by the President, so far as he can pledge us, to make this fair, free and happy land of ours the same shambles and bottomless pit of horror that we see in Europe to-day.

Just a word of comment more upon one of the points in the President's address. He says that this is a war "for the things which we have always carried nearest to our hearts — for democracy, for the right of those who submit to authority to have a voice in their own government." In many places throughout the address is this exalted sentiment given expression.

It is a sentiment peculiarly calculated to appeal to American hearts and, when accompanied by acts consistent with it, is certain to receive our support; but in this same connection, and strangely enough, the President says that we have become convinced that the German Government as it now exists — "Prussian autocracy" he calls it — can never again maintain friendly relations with us. His expression is that "Prussian autocracy was not and could never be our friend," and repeatedly throughout the address the suggestion is made that if the German people would overturn their Government it would probably be the way to peace. So true is this that the dispatches from London all hailed the message of the President as sounding the death knell of Germany's Government.

But the President proposes alliance with Great Britain, which, however liberty-loving its people, is a hereditary monarchy, with a hereditary ruler, with a hereditary House of Lords, with a hereditary landed system, with a limited and restricted suffrage for one class and a multiplied suffrage power for another, and with grinding industrial conditions for all the wageworkers. The President has not suggested that we make our support of Great Britain conditional to her granting home rule to Ireland, or Egypt, or India. We rejoice in the establishment of a democracy in Russia, but it will hardly be contended that if Russia was still an autocratic Government, we would not be asked to enter this alliance with her just the same. Italy and the lesser powers of Europe, Japan in the Orient; in fact, all of the countries with whom we are to enter into alliance, except France and newly revolutionized Russia, are still of the old order — and it will be generally conceded that no one of them has done as much for its people in the solution of municipal problems and in securing social and industrial reforms as Germany.

Is it not a remarkable democracy which leagues itself with allies already far overmatching in strength the German nation and holds out to such beleaguered nation the hope of peace only at the price of giving up their Government? I am not talking now of the merits or demerits of any government, but I am speaking of a profession of democracy that is liked in action with the most brutal and domineering use of autocratic power. Are the people of this country being so well represented in this war movement that we need to go abroad to give other people control of their governments? Will the President and the supporters of this war bill submit it to a vote of the people before the declaration of war goes into effect? Until we are willing to do that, it illy becomes us to offer as an excuse for our entry into the war the unsupported claim that this war was forced upon the German people by their Government "without their previous knowledge or approval."

Who has registered the knowledge or approval of the American people of the course this Congress is called upon to take in declaring war upon Germany? Submit the question to the people, you who support it. You who support it dare not do it, for you know that by a vote of more than ten to one the American people as a body would register their declaration against it.

In the sense that this war is being forced upon our people without their knowing why and without their approval, and that wars are usually forced upon all peoples in the same way, there is some truth in the statement; but I venture to say that the response which the German people have made to the demands of this war shows that it has a degree of popular support which the war upon which we are entering has not and never will have among our people. The espionage bills, the conscription bills, and other forcible military measures which we understand are being ground out of the war machine in this country is the complete proof that those responsible for this war fear that it has no popular support and that armies sufficient to satisfy the demand of the entente allies can not be recruited by voluntary enlistments. . . .

This case of ours in going into this war will not be tried by history upon technicalities, but upon great fundamental, underlying principles, and the declaration of London was the expression — the codification of the well-settled and accepted principles of international law on the subjects covered relating to naval warfare by the most advanced governments of the world. And the Government of Germany that is arraigned here every hour as the most bloodthirsty Government on earth, responding to the inquiry of our Government, agreed that she would suspend or wipe out her right to use the submarine in conformity with our suggestions provided that the rules laid down in the London declaration were adhered to by all of those who had participated in it and who were then parties to the war. . . .

For reasons which become clearer as we advance it suited England's policy to disregard the rules of civilized naval warfare as the same were codified and clearly set forth in the declaration of London and revert to that indefinite and conflicting body of precedents called international law, in which can be found authority for doing anything you have the power to do.

The declaration of London, promulgated in 1909, as I have stated, was the work of the accredited representatives of the leading nations of the world, who met in London at England's request. Among the nations represented were Germany, the United States, Austria, Russia, France, Great Britain, Italy, Japan, Holland, and other leading nations. The way had been prepared for such a great conference by the various Hague conventions and the discussions therein. The sentiment of the civilized world demanded such a conference, and the nations of the world accepted the declaration of London as being the best and most humane statement of the rules of naval warfare which could be prepared. The very first paragraph of the declaration is:

> The signatory powers are agreed in declaring that the rules contained in the following chapters correspond in substance with the generally recognized principles of international law.

Article 65 provided, "the provisions of the present declaration form an indivisible whole."

When, therefore, Great Britain made waste paper of this declaration, as she did early in the war, it ought not to have been difficult to have foreseen the inevitable result. There are a few simple propositions of international law embodied in the declaration of London to which in this connection it is important to call attention. One is that "a blockade must be limited to the ports and coasts belonging to or occupied by the enemy." (See art. 1)

That has been international law ever since we have had a body of international rules called international law, and that was expressed in the London declaration, which was joined in by the representatives of Great Britain. If that had been adhered to, no declaration taking this country into the war would be before us this afternoon.

I repeat it. One of the declarations reads as follows:

A blockade must be limited to the ports and coasts belonging to or occupied by the enemy. (See art. 1)

Another is that a blockade in order to be binding upon anyone must be "maintained by a force sufficiently large to prevent access to the enemy coast." (See art. 2) Not by sowing the open sea with deadly contact mines, but by a force which shall maintain the blockade of the ports. (See art. 2)

Another is that a blockade must under no circumstances bar access to the ports or to the coasts of neutral countries. . . .

Another important service rendered by the declaration of London to a civilized world was the clear statement it furnished of articles which were contraband, conditional contraband, and those which under no circumstances could be declared contraband. (See arts. 22 to 27)

Talk about making war, about hurling this Government into the bottomless pit of the European conflict to sustain the principles of international law under which we have suffered the loss of some ships and some human lives, when England, by her course in rejecting the declaration of London and in the manner of conducting her naval warfare, has wiped out the established rules of international law which had grown up through the centuries and opened the pathway and set us upon the road we have followed straight to the proceedings which engage the attention of the Senate.

The distinction between articles that are contraband and those that are conditional contraband and free is well understood. I will not trespass upon the time of the Senate to discuss it. Articles which are contraband are always liable to capture by one belligerent if shown to be destined to territory belonging to or occupied by the enemy, or if it was destined to the armed forces of the enemy, no matter to what particular port the contraband might be billed. Of this class, according to the declaration of London, were all kinds of arms, ammunition, projectiles powder, clothing and equipment of purely a military character, and other articles used exclusively for war. Conditional contraband was not liable to capture if bound for a neutral port, and in any case the government asserting the right to capture it, even when it was moving direct to the enemy country, was obliged to prove that it was destined for the use of the enemy armed forces and not to the civilian population. Conditional contraband, according to the declaration of London, included food of all kinds, clothing, vehicles, tools, and a vast multitude of other things enumerated which, while they might be used by the armed forces, were also susceptible of use by the civilian population. Goods on the free list could move unhindered to the enemy country in either direct or indirect trade. Among the articles on the free list, according to the declaration of London, was raw cotton, wool, substantially all other raw materials, and a great variety of other articles necessary for a civilian population. Goods from the enemy could not be stopped, except by an effective blockade.

There is no escape from these propositions. They are to be found in every work upon international law, approved by every court that has ever passed upon the questions relating to contraband, as shown by an unbroken line of decisions.

As late as the Boer War, Lord Salisbury — now get this into your minds if your attention has not been directed to it before — when asked the position of the British Government regarding foodstuffs, which were and always had been conditional contraband, Lord Salisbury said:

> Foodstuffs with a hostile destination can be considered contraband of war only if they are supplied for the enemy's forces. It is not sufficient that they are capable of being so used; it must be shown that this was in fact their destination at the time of the seizure. (Hales' *American Rights at Sea*, p. 11)

In the very first days of the war with Germany, Great Britain set aside and reversed this well-established rule announced by Lord Salisbury as to foodstuffs. Had she obeyed that rule of law Germany would have received food for her civilian population through neutral merchantmen and our neutral commerce would not have been attacked by German submarines. Now, that is the way history is going to record it, Senators. That is the undisputed fact and there is nothing else to be said about it. It has pleased those who have been conducting this campaign through the press to make a jumble of the issues, until the public sees nothing, thinks of nothing but the wrongs committed by the German submarine, and hears nothing, knows nothing of wrongdoing of England that forced Germany to take the course she has taken or submit to the unlawful starving of her civilian population.

Now, I want to repeat: It was our absolute right as a neutral to ship food to the people of Germany. That is a position that we have fought for through all of our history. The correspondence of every Secretary of State in the history of our Government who has been called upon to deal with the rights of our neutral commerce as to foodstuffs is the position stated by Lord Salisbury, just quoted. He was in line with all of the precedents that we had originated and established for the maintenance of neutral rights upon this subject.

In the first days of the war with Germany, Great Britain set aside, so far as her own conduct was concerned, all these rules of civilized naval warfare.

According to the declaration of London, as well as the rules of international law, there could have been no interference in trade between the United States and Holland or Scandinavia and other countries, except in the case of ships which could be proven to carry absolute contraband, like arms and ammunition, with ultimate German destination. There could have been no interference with the importation into Germany of any goods on the free list, such as cotton, rubber, and hides. There could have properly been no interference with our export to Germany of anything on the conditional contraband list, like flour, grain, and provisions, unless it could be proven by England that such shipments were intended for the use of the German Army. There could be no lawful interference with foodstuffs intended for the civilian population of Germany, and if those foodstuffs were shipped to Germany, no question could be raised that they were not intended for the use of the civilian population.

It is well to recall at this point our rights as declared by that declaration of London and as declared without the declaration of

London by settled principles of international law, for we have during the present war become so used to having Great Britain utterly disregard our rights on the high seas that we have really forgotten that we have any, as far as Great Britain and her allies are concerned.

Great Britain, by what she called her modifications of the declaration of London, shifted goods from the free list to the conditional contraband and contraband lists, reversed the presumption of destination for civilian population, and abolished the principle that a blockade to exist at all must be effective. . . .

It is not my purpose to go into detail into the violations of our neutrality by any of the belligerents. While Germany has again and again yielded to our protests, I do not recall a single instance in which a protest we have made to Great Britain has won for us the slightest consideration, except for a short time in the case of cotton. I will not stop to dwell upon the multitude of minor violations of our neutral rights, such as seizing our mails, violations of the neutral flag, seizing and appropriating our goods without the least warrant or authority in law, and impressing, seizing, and taking possession of our vessels and putting them into her own service. I have constituents, American citizens, who organized a company and invested large sums of money in the purchase of ships to engage in foreign carrying. Several of their vessels plying between the United States and South America were captured almost in our own territorial waters, taken possession of by the British Government, practically confiscated, and put into her service or the service of her admiralty. They are there to-day, and that company is helpless. When they appealed to our Department of State they were advised that they might "file" their papers. And were given the further suggestion that they could hire an attorney and prosecute their case in the English prize court. The company did hire an attorney and sent him to England, and he is there now, and has been there for almost a year, trying to get some redress, some relief, some adjustment of those rights.

But those are individual cases. There are many others. All these violations have come from Great Britain and her allies, and are in perfect harmony with Britain's traditional policy as absolute master of the seas.

I come now, however, to one other event in the naval policy of Great Britain during this war, which to my mind is absolutely controlling upon the action we should take upon the question under consideration.

On the 2d of November, 1914, only three months after the beginning of the war, England issued a proclamation, the most ruthless and sweeping in its violation of neutral rights that up to that time had ever emanated from a civilized government, engaged in prosecuting a war, announcing that on three days' notice all of the North Sea, free under international law to the trade of the world, would be entered by our merchant ships at their peril. She based her action upon an assertion that the German Government had been scattering mines in waters open to the world's commerce. . . .

The North Sea, a great stretch of the Atlantic Ocean, extending from Scotland to Iceland, was barred to the commerce of the world, the neutral commerce, that had the same right there that you have to walk down Pennsylvania Avenue.

Before considering the piratical character of this document as a whole it will be noted that while it proposes to use every effort to warn neutral shipping it allows just three days for the warning.

Do you observe that the country with whom we are about to yoke ourselves issued this proclamation, unheard of before in the history of the world, mining a great area of the Atlantic Ocean with deadly contact mines, and gave to the neutral nations only three days' notice? It issued its declaration on the 2d of November, and it went into effect on the 5th of November.

Of the preliminary allegations in the note concerning the scattering of mines by Germany in the open sea around the British Isles, no proof of it has ever been furnished, so far as I am aware; and, even if it were true, it certainly would not have remedied the condition to mine a much larger portion of the sea upon which neutral ships must travel. I say this because of the high-sounding but obviously false and hypocritical assertion contained in the proclamation that Britain is taking this action in order to maintain trade between neutral countries within the limits of international law. She was, in fact, by her action absolutely destroying trade between neutral countries, and the penalties for disobeying her orders, and which operate automatically and inexorably, was the destruction by mines of all ships and passengers venturing into the prohibited portion of the sea.

Now we come to the most unfortunate part of our record. The

present administration agreed to this lawless act of Great Britain. I make this statement deliberately and fully appreciating its consequences. If we had entered into a contract with Great Britain, signed and sealed under the great seals of the respective countries, agreeing that she should commit the act of piracy involved in mining the North Sea, we would not more completely have been bound by such contract than we are bound by the conduct of the present administration. It will be recalled that when Secretary Bryan made his request of Great Britain to adhere to the declaration of London, and she refused, and he notified her that the request was withdrawn, he declared in substance that he would nevertheless hold her responsible for any violations of international law, so far as they affected our right as a neutral Nation. And from that time protest after protest was made by us; many against Germany and some against Great Britain and her allies, whenever we claimed that international law had been violated.

The fact remains, however, that from November 2, when England declared her settled purpose to mine large areas of the public sea contrary to every principle of international law, the Government through the present administration has never uttered a word of protest.

If you think you can escape the responsibility of that act and hold other belligerents to the strict requirements of international law by play upon a phrase you are mistaken. You may make this country declare war in your attempt to do it, but your war will not have the support of the people. Until the omission of this administration to uphold our rights against Great Britain is corrected we can never hope for popular support for a war waged to enforce the same right against the country at war with Great Britain. . . .

The only reason why we have not suffered the sacrifice of just as many lives from the violation of our rights by the war zone and the submarine mines of Great Britain, as we have through the unlawful acts of Germany in making her war zone in violation of our neutral rights, is simply because we have submitted to Great Britain's dictation. If our ships had been sent into her forbidden high-sea war zone, as they have into the proscribed area Germany marked out on the high seas as a war zone, we would have had the same loss of life and property in the one case as in the other; but because we avoided doing that in the case of England, and acquiesced in her violation of law, we have not only a legal but a moral responsibility for the position in which Germany has been placed by our collusion and cooperation with Great Britain. By suspending the rule with respect to neutral rights in Great Britain's case, we have been actively aiding her in starving the civil population of Germany. We have helped to drive Germany into a corner, her back to the wall, to fight with what weapons she can lay her hands on to prevent the starving of her women and children, her old men and babes. . . .

Days, weeks, and months went by, and still no protest came from the American Government against this unlawful act on the part of Great Britain.

She did this unlawful thing on the 5th day of November. Germany waited and waited, week after week, for this Government to assert its neutral commerce. She waited in vain for three long months for this Government to take some action, and not until the 4th day of February — that is my recollection of the date; I do not know that I have it here — did she in retaliation serve notice upon this Government of the establishment of her war zone.

Germany then did as a matter of retaliation and defense what Great Britain had done months previously purely as an offensive measure — established a war zone or war area. She included in it portions of the sea about the British islands, and gave notice that ships coming within it would be destroyed by mines or submarines, even as English mines in the North Sea destroyed the ships which entered there.

It is Germany's insistence upon her right to blindly destroy with mines and submarines in the area she has declared a war zone all ships that enter there, that causes the whole trouble existing between us and Germany to-day. It is for this, and this only, that we are urged to make war. Yet in asserting this warning, Germany is doing only that which England is doing in her proscribed area, with our consent. Here is the parting of the ways. When England, having previously violated all neutral rights on the high seas, mined the North Sea and asserted the right to blindly destroy, and mines can only destroy blindly, all ships that traversed it, one of two courses was open to us.

We chose to acquiesce, but a singular thing transpired. I suppose all Senators have secured the published copies of the diplomatic correspondence which has been issued by the State Department.

I find all the correspondence about the submarines of Germany; I find them arrayed; I find the note warning Germany that she would be held to a "strict accountability" for violation of our neutral rights; but you will search in vain these volumes for a copy of the British order in council mining the North Sea.

I am talking now about principles. You can not distinguish between the principles which allowed England to mine a large area of the Atlantic Ocean and the North Sea in order to shut in Germany, and the principle on which Germany by her submarines seeks to destroy all shipping which enters the war zone which she has laid out around the British Isles.

The English mines are intended to destroy without warning every ship that enters the war zone she has proscribed, killing or drowning every passenger that can not find some means of escape. It is neither more nor less than that which Germany tries to do with her submarines in her war zone. We acquiesced in England's action without protest. It is proposed that we now go to war with Germany for identically the same action upon her part.

At this point, sir, I say, with all deference but with the absolute certainty of conviction, that the present administration made a fatal mistake, and if war comes to this country with Germany for the present causes it will be due wholly to that mistake. The present administration has assumed and acted upon the policy that it could enforce to the very letter of the law the principles of international law against one belligerent and relax them as to the other. That thing no nation can do without losing its character as a neutral nation and without losing the rights that go with strict and absolute neutrality. . . .

I quote now from the President's address of February 3, 1917, before the two Houses of Congress:

> In order, however, to avoid any possible misunderstanding, the Government of the United States notifies the Imperial Government that it can not for a moment entertain, much less discuss, a suggestion that respect by German naval authorities for the rights of citizens of the United States upon the high seas should in any way or in the slightest degree be made contingent upon the conduct of any other Government affecting the rights of neutrals and noncombatants. Responsibility in such matters is single, not joint; absolute, not relative.

That phrase the President has used repeatedly in his addresses; he has used it at least three times, I think, and he has referred to it as being a complete and sufficient answer to this proposition. It misstates the law; it asserts a principle that can not be maintained for one moment with a decent regard for equal rights between nations with whom we are dealing upon a basis of neutrality.

The offenses of Great Britain and Germany against us can not be treated as they might be treated if those nations were not at war with each other. Undoubtedly, if those nations were not at war with each other we could suffer one to violate international law to our injury and make no protest and take no action against the nation so offending and hold the other to strict accountability and compel her to respect to the limit our rights under international law, and if she refused we would be justified in going to war about it. But when we are dealing with Germany and Great Britain, warring against each other, so evenly balanced in strength that a little help to one or a little hindrance to the other turns the scale and spells victory for one and defeat for the other, in that situation I say the principle of international law steps in which declares that any failure on our part to enforce our rights equally against both is a gross act of unneutrality.

That is precisely what we have done, as I have shown. In the early days of the conflict in this matter of the war zones of each belligerent, in submitting to Great Britain's dictation concerning what might be treated as contraband, resulting finally in a practical cessation of shipping to German ports, we have done Germany as much harm as though we had landed an army in France to fight beside the entente allies. How will history regard this conduct of ours? How will our own people regard it when they come to understand it? We can never justify it.

Jefferson asserted that we could not permit one warring nation to curtail our neutral rights if we were not ready to allow her enemy the same privileges, and that any other course entailed the sacrifice of our neutrality.

That is the sensible, that is the logical position. No neutrality could ever have commanded respect if it was not based on that equitable and just proposition; and we from early in the war threw our neutrality to the winds by permitting England to make a mockery of it to her advantage against her chief enemy. Then we expect to say to that enemy, "You have got to respect my rights as a neutral." What is the answer? I say Germany has been patient with us. Standing strictly on her rights, her answer would be, "Maintain your neutrality; treat these other Governments warring against me as you treat me if you want your neutral rights respected."

I say again that when two nations are at war any neutral nation, in order to preserve its character as a neutral nation, must exact the same conduct from both warring nations; both must equally obey the principles of international law. If a neutral nation fails in that, then its rights upon the high seas — to adopt the President's phrase — are relative and not absolute. There can be no greater violation of our neutrality than the requirement that one of two belligerents shall adhere to the settled principles of law and that the other shall adhere to the vantage of not doing so. The respect that German naval authorities were required to pay to the rights of our people upon the high seas would depend upon the question whether we had exacted the same rights from Germany's enemies. If we had not done so we lost our character as a neutral nation, and our people unfortunately had lost the protection that belongs to neutrals. Our responsibility was joint in the sense that we must exact the same conduct from both belligerents. No principle of international law is better settled than that which is stated by Oppenheim, the great English authority on international law, in volume 2, second edition, page 365. He says:

> Neutrality as an attitude of impartiality involves the duty of abstaining from assisting either belligerent either actively or passively. . . .

The best and clearest exposition of the exact question, however, was made long ago by one of the greatest of Democrats and statesmen of this country — Thomas Jefferson. Mr. Jefferson, then Secretary of State, in writing to Thomas Pinckney, United States minister to Great Britain regarding England's stoppage of our food shipments to France, with whom England was then at war, dealt with precisely the same situation that confronts President Wilson in the war between Germany and England, but Secretary Jefferson dealt with the situation in precisely the opposite manner from that adopted by President Wilson. In this letter, under date of September 7, 1793, Secretary Jefferson said:

The first article of it (the British order) permits all vessels laden wholly or in part with corn, flour, or meal, bound to any port in France to be stopped and sent into any British port, to be purchased by that Government or to be released only on the condition of security given by the master that he will proceed to dispose of his cargo in the ports of some country in amity with his majesty.

This article is so manifestly contrary to the law of nations that nothing more would seem necessary than to observe that it is so. . . .

And with a firmness which it would have been well had the present administration emulated, it is said:

It is with concern, however, I am obliged to observe that so marked has been the inattention of the British court to every application which has been made to them on any subject by this Government (not a single answer, I believe, having ever been given to one of them, except in the act of exchanging a minister) that it may become unavoidable in certain cases, where an answer of some sort is necessary, to consider their silence as an answer.

Had the plain principle of international law announced by Jefferson been followed by us, we would not be called on to-day to declare war upon any of the belligerents. The failure to treat the belligerent nations of Europe alike, the failure to reject the unlawful "war zones" of both Germany and Great Britain, is wholly accountable for our present dilemma. We should not seek to hide our blunder behind the smoke of battle, to inflame the mind of our people by half truths into the frenzy of war, in order that they may never appreciate the real cause of it until it is too late. I do not believe that our national honor is served by such a course. The right way is the honorable way.

One alternative is to admit our initial blunder to enforce our rights against Great Britain as we have enforced our rights against Germany; demand that both those nations shall respect our neutral rights upon the high seas to the letter; and give notice that we will enforce those rights from that time forth against both belligerents and then live up to that notice.

The other alternative is to withdraw our commerce from both. The mere suggestion that food supplies would be withheld from both sides impartially would compel belligerents to observe the principle of freedom of the seas for neutral commerce.

WILLIAM H. TAFT

(1857-1930)

Few men have ever had the background for the Presidency to equal that of William Howard Taft. His family heritage of legal accomplishment, his own early training in the law, his reputation for honesty and fairness, and his friendly manner, all were natural stepping stones to the office of Chief Executive. As Governor General of the Philippines and then as Secretary of War, Taft so pleased President Roosevelt that he received Roosevelt's full endorsement as the Republican Presidential candidate in the 1908 election. The election itself produced a landslide victory for Taft and prefaced a four-year term fraught with problems and controversies.

Taft was not a great public speaker — the campaigning for the 1908 election illustrated this point very well — but he had two qualities which helped him immensely. He was a very large man with a large smile, and when he beamed at an audience before starting a speech, the impression of overwhelming cordiality melted practically all resistance. Concerning his speaking, Albert Bushnell Hart says:

> Taft was no silver-tongued orator, though a very agreeable public speaker — his periods sometimes punctuated by that delightful chuckle which was a national possession. He spoke easily, he spoke well. . . .[1]

And a man who traveled with him through the course of several speeches adds:

[1] "William Howard Taft: His Place in American History," *Current History* 32:291 (May '30).

"There was no gesturing — almost none — for most of the time his hands were on his hips or in his pockets or reposing against his midriff. Sometimes he leaned a little forward to be emphatic. There was no spread-eagle oratory at all. No attempt at elocution. All was simple, straightforward, genial, kindly."[2]

Defeated in the 1912 Presidential contest, Taft elected to take a position with the Yale Law School. In that way he felt he could retire from the public eye most gracefully. But storm clouds hung over Europe, and in 1914 World War I broke out. Peaceful by nature, Taft was shocked by the ensuing brutality and loss of life, and decided to act. In June of 1915, he became President of the newly-formed League to Enforce Peace. His subsequent efforts to promote some sort of association of nations were unceasing; he traveled all over the nation speaking for his cause. Finally, he gave what many might call "that full measure of devotion" when he agreed to appear with the leader of "the other party" — President Woodrow Wilson — in a joint appearance on behalf of the League of Nations.

The program was held in the Metropolitan Opera House on March 4, 1919, the day before Wilson was to sail for Europe with what he hoped would be an endorsement of his League plan. It was a truly gala occasion; Caruso sang, the house was packed (4,000), and thousands more who had to be turned away were milling around in front of the building. Ex-President and President joined forces to defend the idea of a peaceful community of nations, and were warmly received. Wilson sailed for Europe the next day with high hopes of success.

These hopes, however, were never realized. The United States of America never joined the organization its leader so strongly advocated, and Wilson and Taft were both greatly disappointed. But Taft's long service to the nation in this and other endeavors were not forgotten by the next President, Warren Harding. For in 1921, William Howard Taft had his one great ambition in life fulfilled — he became Chief Justice of the United States Supreme Court. The position came to him in the twilight of his life, but he filled it with rare dignity, integrity, and wisdom.

Unfortunately, his health had been seriously impaired during his term as Governor General of the Philippines, and his life began

[2] Ibid., p. 292.

to ebb slowly away. Ironically, the League of Nations for which he had struggled so valiantly was likewise growing weaker with each succeeding year. Perhaps it is a small blessing that Taft never saw the inglorious collapse of the League, for certainly he would have been terribly saddened by it. This devoted American, called by many historians the father of the League idea, passed away in 1930, mourned by the nation he had so honestly served.

FOR THE LEAGUE OF NATIONS

by

William H. Taft

Delivered in New York in the Metropolitan Opera House on March 4, 1919.

WE ARE HERE TO-NIGHT in the sight of a League of Peace, of what I have ever regarded as the "Promised Land." Such a war as the last is a hideous blot on our Christian civilization. The inconsistency is as foul as was slavery under the Declaration of Independence. If Christian nations cannot now be brought into a united effort to suppress a recurrence of such a contest it will be a shame to modern society.

During my administration I attempted to secure treaties of universal arbitration between this country and France and England, by which all issues depending for their settlement upon legal principles were to be submitted to an international court for final decision. These treaties were emasculated by the Senate, yielding to the spirit which proceeds, unconsciously doubtless, but truly, from the conviction that the only thing that will secure to a nation the justice it wishes to secure is force; that agreements between nations to settle controversies justly and peaceably should never be given any weight in national policy; that in dealings between civilized nations we must assume that each nation is conspiring to deprive us of our independence and our prosperity; that there is no impartial tribunal to which we can entrust the decision of any question vitally affecting our interests or our honor, and that we can afford to make no agreement from which we may not immediately withdraw, and whose temporary operation to our detriment may not be expressly a ground for ending it. This is the doctrine of despair. It leads necessarily to the conclusion that our only recourse to avoid war is competitive armament, with its dreadful burdens and its constant temptation to the war it seeks to avoid.

The first important covenant with reference to peace and war in the Constitution of the League is that looking to a reduction of armament by all nations. The Executive Council, consisting of representatives of the United States, the British Empire, France, Italy, Japan, and of four other nations to be selected by the body of delegates, is to consider how much the armaments of the nations should be reduced, having regard to the safety of each of the nations and their obligations under the League. Having reached a conclusion as to the proportionate limits of each nation's armament, it submits its conclusion to each nation, which may or may not agree to the limit thus recommended; but when an agreement is reached it covenants to keep within that limit until, by application to the Executive Council, the limit may be raised. In other words, each nation agrees to its own limitation. Having so agreed it must keep within it.

The importance of providing for a reduction of armament every one recognizes. It is affirmed in the newly proposed Senate resolution. Can we not trust our Congress to fix a limitation safe for the country and to stick to it? If we can't, no country can. Yet all the rest are anxious to do this and they are far more exposed than we.

The character of this obligation is affected by the time during which the covenants of the League remain binding. There is no stipulation as to how long this is. In my judgment there should be a period of ten years or a permission for any member of the League to withdraw from the covenant by giving a reasonable notice of one or two years of its intention to do so.

The members of the League and the non-members are required, the former by their covenant, the latter by an enforced obligation, to submit all differences between them not capable of being settled by negotiation to arbitration before a tribunal composed as the parties may agree. They are required to covenant to abide the award. Should either party deem the question one not proper for arbitration then it is to be taken up by the Executive Council of the League. The Executive Council mediates between the parties and secures a voluntary settlement of the question if possible; if it fails, it makes a report. If the report is unanimous, the Executive Council is to recommend what shall be done to carry into effect its recommendation. If there is a dissenting vote, then the majority report is published, and the minority report, if desired, and no further action is taken. If either party of the Executive Council itself desires, the mediating function is to be discharged by the body of delegates in which every member of the league has one vote. There is no direction as to what shall be done with reference to the recommendation of proper measures to be taken, and the whole matter is then left for such further action as the members of the League agree upon. There is no covenant by the defeated party that it will comply with the unanimous report of the Executive Council or the Body of the League.

And right here I wish to take up the objection made to the League that under this machinery we might be compelled to receive immigrants contrary to our national desire from Japan or China. We could and would refuse to submit the issue to arbitration. It would then go to mediation. In my judgment the Council as a mediating body should not take jurisdiction to consider such a difference. Immigration by international law is a domestic question completely within the control of the government into which immigration is sought, unless the question of immigration is the subject of treaty stipulation between two countries. If, however, it be said that there is no limitation in the covenant of the differences to be mediated, clearly we would run no risk of receiving from the large body of delegates of all the members of the League a unanimous report recommending a settlement by which Japanese immigrants shall be admitted to our shores or Japanese applicants be admitted to our citizenship, contrary to our protest. But were it made, we are under no covenant to obey such recommendation. If it could be imagined that all of the other nations of the world would thus unite their military forces to compel us to receive Japanese immigrants under the covenant, why would they not do so without the covenant?

These articles compelling submission of differences either to arbitration or mediation are not complete machinery for settlement by peaceable means of all issues arising between nations. But they are a substantial step forward. They are an unambitious plan to settle as many questions as possible by arbitration or mediation. They illustrate the spirit of those who drafted this covenant and their sensible desire not to attempt more till after actual experience.

The next covenant is that the nations shall not begin war until three months after the arbitration award or the recommendation of compromise, and not then if the defendant nation against whom the award or recommendation has been made shall comply with it. This is the great restraint of war imposed by the covenant upon members of the League and non-members. It is said that this would prevent our resistance to a border raid of Mexico or self-defense against any invasion. This is most extreme construction. If a nation refuses submission at all, as it does when it begins an attack, the nation attacked is released instanter from its obligation to submit and is restored to the complete power of self-defense. Had this objection not been raised in the Senate one would not have deemed it necessary to answer so unwarranted a suggestion.

If the defendant nation does not comply with the award or unanimous report, then the plaintiff nation can begin war and carry out such complete remedy as the circumstances enable it to do. But if the defendant nation does comply with the award or unanimous report, then the plaintiff nation must be content with such compliance. It runs the risk of not getting all it thought it ought to have or might have by war, but as it is asking affirmative relief it must be seeking some less vital interest than its political independence or territorial integrity, and the limitation is not one which can be dangerous to its sovereignty.

The third covenant, the penalizing covenant, is that if a nation begins war, in violation of its covenant, then *ipso facto* that it is an act of war against every member of the League, and the members of the League are required definitely and distinctly to levy a boycott on the covenant-breaking nation and to cut off from it all commercial, trade, financial, personal, and official relations between them and their citizens and it and its citizens. Indeed, the boycott is compound or secondary, in that it is directed against any non-members of the League continuing to deal with the outlaw nation. This is an obligation operative at once on each member of the League. With us the Executive Council would report the violation of the covenant to the President and that would be reported to Congress, and Congress would then, by reason of the covenant of the League, be under an honorable legal and moral obligation to levy an embargo and prevent all intercourse of every kind between this nation and the covenant-breaking nation.

The extent of this penalty and its heavy withering effect when the hostile action includes all members of the League, as well as non-members, may be easily appreciated. The prospect of such an isolation would be likely to frighten any member of the League from a reckless violation of its covenant to begin war. It is inconceivable that any small nation, dependent as it must be on larger nations for its trade and sustenance, indeed for its food and raw material, would for a moment court such a destructive ostracism as this would be.

Other covenants of the penalizing article impose on the members of the League the duty of sharing the expense of a boycott with any nation upon which it has fallen with uneven weight and of supporting such a nation in its resistance to any special measures directed against it by the outlaw nation. But there is no specific requirement as to the character of the support beyond the obligation of the boycott, the contribution of expenses and the obligation of each member of the League to permit the passage through its territory of forces of other members of the League coöperating with military forces against the outlaw nation.

If, however, the boycott does not prove sufficient, then the Executive Council is to recommend the number of the military and naval forces to be contributed by the members of the League to protect the covenants of the League in such a case. There is no specific covenant by which they agree to furnish any amount of force, or, indeed, any force at all, to a League army. The use of the word "recommended" in describing the functions of the Executive Council shows that the question whether such forces shall be contributed and what shall be their amount must ultimately address itself to the members of the League for their discussion and action. There is this radical and important difference, therefore, between the obligation to lay a boycott and the obligation to furnish military force, and doubtless this distinction was insisted upon and reached by a compromise. The term "recommendation" cannot be interpreted to impose any imperative obligation on those to whom the recommendation is directed.

By Article X, the high contracting parties undertake to respect and preserve against external aggression the political independence and territorial integrity of every member of the League, and when these are attacked or threatened the Executive Council is to advise as to the proper means to fulfill this obligation. The same acts or series of acts which made Article X applicable will be a breach of the covenant which creates an outlaw nation under Article XVI, so that all nations must begin a boycott against any nation thus breaking the territorial integrity or overthrowing the independence of a member of the League. Indeed, Article X will usually not be applicable until a war shall be fought to the point showing its specific purpose. Protection against it will usually be necessary in preventing a treaty of peace, the appropriation of territory or the interference with the sovereignty of the attacked and defeated nation. We have seen this in the construction of the Monroe Doctrine put upon it by Secretary Seward and President Roosevelt. The former, when Spain attacked Chili and Chili appealed to the United States to protect it, advised Spain that under the policy of the United States it would not interfere to prevent the punishment by war of an American nation by a non-American nation, provided it did not extend to a permanent deprivation of its territory or an overthrow of its sovereignty. President Roosevelt, in the Venezuelan matter, also announced that the Monroe Doctrine did not prevent nations from proceeding by force to collect their debts provided oppressive measures were not used which would deprive the nation of its independence or territorial integrity. This furnishes an analogy for the proper construction of Article X.

The fact that the Executive Council is to advise what means shall be taken to fulfill the obligation shows that they are to be such as each nation shall deem proper and fair under the circumstances, considering its remoteness from the country and the fact that the nearer presence of other nations should induce them to furnish the requisite military force. It thus seems to me clear that the question, both under Article XVIII, and under Article X, as to whether the United States shall declare war and what forces it shall furnish, are remitted to the voluntary action of the Congress of the United States under the constitution, having regard for a fair division between all the nations of the burden to be borne under the League and the proper means to be adopted, whether by the enjoined and inevitable boycott alone, or by the advance of loans of money, or by the declaration of war, and the use of military force. This is as it should be. It fixes the obligation of action in such a way that American nations will attend to America and European nations will attend to Europe and Asiatic nations to Asia, unless all deem the situation so threatening to the world and to their own interests that they should take a more active part. It seems to me that appropriate words might be added to the pact which should show distinctly this distribution of obligation. This will relieve those anxious in respect to the Monroe Doctrine to exclude from forcible intervention European or Asiatic nations in issues between American nations until requested by the United States or an executive council of the American nations framed for the purpose.

Objection is made that Great Britain might have more delegates in the Executive Council than other countries. This is an error. The British Empire, which, of course, includes its dominions, is limited to one delegate in the Executive Council. Provision is made by which upon a vote of two-thirds of the body of delegates new members may be admitted who are independent states or self-governing dominions or colonies. Under this Canada and Australia and South Africa might be admitted as delegates. I presume, too, the Philippines might be admitted. But the function of the body of delegates is not one which makes its membership of great importance. When it acts as a mediating and compromising body its reports must be unanimous to have any effect. The addition of members, therefore, is not likely to create greater probability of unanimity. More than this, the large number of countries who will become members will minimize any important British influence from the addition of such dominions and colonies since they are really admitted because they have different interests from their mother country. The suggestion that Great Britain will have any greater power than any other member nations in shaping the policy of the League in really critical matters, when analyzed, will be seen to have no foundation whatever.

A proposed resolution in the Senate recites that the Constitution of the League of Nations in the form now proposed should not be accepted by the United States, although the sense of the Senate is that the nations of the world should unite to promote peace and general disarmament. The resolution further recites that the negotiations on the part of the United States should immediately be directed to the utmost expedition of the urgent business of negotiating peace terms with Germany satisfactory to the United States and the nations with whom the United States is associated in the war against the German government, and that the proposal for a League of Nations to insure the permanent peace of the world should then be taken up for careful and serious consideration. It is said that this resolution will be supported by thirty-seven members of the new Senate, and thus defeat the confirmation of any treaty which includes the present proposed covenant of Paris.

The President of the United States is the authority under the Federal Constitution which initiates the form of treaties and which at the outset determines what subject matter they shall include. Therefore, if it shall seem to the President of the United States and to those acting with him and with similar authority for other nations that a treaty of peace cannot be concluded except with a covenant providing for a League of Nations in substance like that now proposed as a condition precedent to the proper operation and effectiveness of the treaty itself, it will be the duty of the President and his fellow delegates to the conference to insert such a covenant in the treaty. If, accordingly, such a covenant shall be incorporated in a treaty of peace, signed by the representatives of the Powers and shall be brought back by the President and submitted by him to the Senate, the question which will address itself to the proponents of this Senate resolution will be not whether they would prefer to consider a League of Nations after the treaty of peace but whether they will feel justified in defeating or postponing a treaty because it contains a constitution of a League of Nations deemed by the President necessary to the kind of peace which all seek.

The covenant of Paris, which is now a covenant only between the nations at war with Germany, including the seven nations who actually won the war, is essential to an effective treaty of peace to accomplish the purposes of the war; for the purposes of the war were to defeat militarism, to make the world safe for democracy, and to secure permanent peace.

Under the informal agreement between the nations who won this war, outlined in the President's message of January 8, 1918, as qualified by the Entente Allies before the armistice, we are to create and recognize as independent states four nations forming a bulwark between Germany and Russia to prevent future intrigues by Germany to secure control of Russia. In the process we are to carve these new nations out of the great autocracies, Russia, Germany, and Austria. We are to give German and Austrian Poland to the republic of Poland, to set up the Czecho-Slovak state of ten million inhabitants between Germany and Austria-Hungary, as well as the Jugo-Slav state carved out of Austria, and Hungary in the South. We are to fix new boundaries in the Balkans, with Rumania enlarged by Transylvania and Bessarabia, and to make an internationalized government at Constantinople, keeping ward over the passage between the Black Sea, and the Aegean, and to establish autonomous dominions in Palestine, Syria, Armenia, and Mesopotamia. This plan for the peace and the reasons for it were set out with great force and vision by Senator Lodge in a speech last January. The chief purpose of the plan is to take away the possibility that Germany shall ever again conceive and carry toward accomplishment her dream of the control of Russia and of a Middle European and Asiatic Empire, reaching from Hamburg to the Persian Gulf.

The plan thus requires not only the establishment but the continued maintenance of seven new republics in Europe and several autonomies in Asia Minor. We are to create twenty nations instead of four; and we are to carve the new ones out of the old ones. The peoples of the new republics will not have had experience in self-government. They are the children of the League of Nations, as Cuba has been our child. The League must continue to be a guardian of their internal stability, if they are to serve their purpose. Their natural resentment for past oppression against the neighboring countries out of which they have been carved and the corresponding hatred of them by the defeated peoples of those countries will at once produce controversies innumerable over the interpretation of the treaty and its application. Even the new countries as between themselves, with their natural lack of self-restraint and their indefinite ideas of their powers, have already come into forced conflict.

Unless there be some means for authoritatively interpreting the treaty and applying it, and unless the power of the League be behind it to give effect to such interpretation and application, the treaty instead of producing peace will produce a state of continued war.

More than this, in the dark background is the threatening specter of Bolshevism, hard, cruel, murderous, uncompromising, destructive of Christian civilization, militant in pressing its hideous doctrines upon other peoples and insidious in its propaganda among the lowest element in every country. Against the chaos and the explosive dangers of Bolshevism, throughout all the countries of Europe, a League of Nations must be established to settle controversies peaceably and to enforce the settlement.

If it be said that the European nations should unite in a league to maintain these independent states and settle the difficulties arising between them and the older states in the sphere of war, as well as to resist Bolshevism, it is sufficient to say that the withdrawal of the United States from the League of Nations will weaken it immeasurably. The disinterestedness of the United States, its position as the greatest Power in the world in view of its people and their intelligence and adaptability, its enormous natural resources, and its potential military power, demonstrated on the fields of France and Belgium, make its membership in the League indispensable. The confidence of the world in its disinterestedness and in its pure democracy will enormously enhance the prestige and power of the League's earnest desire for peace with justice.

For the United States to withdraw would make a league of other nations nothing but a return to the system of alliances and the balance of power with a certain speedy recurrence of war, in which the United States would be as certainly involved as it was in this war. The new inventions for the destruction of men and peoples would finally result in world suicide, while in the interval there would be a story of progressive competition in armaments, with all their heavy burdens upon the peoples of the nations, already oppressed almost to the point of exhaustion. With such a prospect and to avoid such results the United States should not hesitate to take its place with the other responsible nations of the world and make the light concessions and assume the light burdens involved in membership in the League.

No critic of the League has offered a single constructive suggestion to meet the crisis that I have thus summarily touched upon. The resolution of the Senate does not suggest or refer in any way to machinery by which the function of the League of Nations in steadying Europe and the maintaining of the peace agreed upon in the Peace Treaty shall be secured. Well may the President, therefore, decline to comply with the suggestions of the proposed resolution. Well may he say when he returns with the treaty, of which the covenant shall be a most important and indispensable part, "If you would postpone peace, if you would defeat it, you can refuse to ratify the Treaty. Amend it by striking out the covenant and you will have confusion worse confounded, with the objects of the war unattained and sacrificed and Europe and the world in dangerous chaos."

Objection is made that the covenant of the League is a departure from the traditional policy of the United States following the advice of Washington in avoiding entangling alliances with European nations. The European war into which we were drawn demonstrates that the policy is no longer possible for the United States. It has ceased to be a struggling nation. It has been made a close neighbor of Great Britain and France and Italy and of all nations of Europe, and is in such intimate trade relations that in a general European war it never can be a neutral again. It tried to be in this war and failed. Whatever nation secures the control of the seas will make the United States its ally, no matter how formal and careful its neutrality, because it will be the sole customer of the United States in food, raw material, and war necessities. Modern war is carried on in the mines and the workshops and on the farm, as well as in the trenches. The former are indispensable to the work in the latter. Hence the United States will certainly be drawn in, and hence its interests are inevitably involved in the preservation of European peace. These conditions and circumstances are so different from those in Washington's day, and are so unlike anything which we could have anticipated, that no words of his having relation to selfish offensive and defensive alliances such as he described in favor of one nation and against another should be given any application to the present international status.

Objection is made that the covenant destroys the Monroe Doctrine. The Monroe Doctrine was announced and adopted to keep European monarchies from overthrowing the independence of and fastening their system upon governments in this hemisphere. It has been asserted in various forms, some of them extreme, and others less so. I presume that no one now would attempt to sustain the declarations of Secretary Olney in his correspondence with Lord Salisbury. But all will probably agree that the sum and substance of the Monroe Doctrine is that we do not propose in our own interests to allow European nations or Asiatic nations to acquire, beyond what they now have, through war or purchase or intrigue, territory, political power, or strategical opportunity from the countries of this hemisphere. Article X of the constitution of the League is intended to secure this to all signatory nations, except that it does not forbid purchase of territory or power.

In some speeches in the Senate intimations have been made which enlarge the Monroe Doctrine beyond what can be justified. Those who would seek to enforce a doctrine which would make the western hemisphere our own preserve, in which we may impose our sovereign will on other countries in what we suppose to be their own interest, because, indeed, we have done that in the past, should not be sustained. Our conquests of western territory, of course, have worked greatly for the civilization of the world and for the usefulness and happiness of those who now occupy that territory; but we have reached a state in the world's history when its progress should be now determined and secured under just and peaceful conditions, and progress through conquest by powerful nations should be prevented.

To suppose that the conditions in America and in Europe can be maintained absolutely separate, with the great trade relations between North America and Europe, is to look backward, not forward. It does not face existing conditions.

The European nations desire our entrance into this League, not that they may control America but to secure our aid in controlling Europe, and I venture to think that they would be relieved if the primary duty of keeping peace and policing this western hemisphere were relegated to us and our western colleagues. I object, however, to such a reservation as was contained in the Hague Conference against entangling alliances, because the recommendation was framed before this war and contained provisions as to the so-called policy against entangling alliances that are inconsistent with the present needs of this nation and of the rest of the world if a peaceful future is to be secured to both. I would favor, however, a recognition of the Monroe Doctrine as I have stated it above by specific words in the covenant, and with further provision that the settlement of purely American questions should be remitted primarily to the American nations, with machinery like that of the present League, and that European nations should not intervene unless requested to do so by the American nations.

Objection is made to this League on constitutional grounds. This League is to be made by the treaty-making power of the United States. What does the treaty-making power cover? The Supreme Court of the United States, through Mr. Justice Field, in the Riggs case, has held that it covers the right to deal by contract with all subject-matters which are usually dealt with by contract in treaties between nations, except it cannot be used to change our form of government or to part with territory of a State without its consent. The Supreme Court has, over and over again, through Mr. Chief Justice Marshall, indicated that the United States was a nation and a sovereign capable of dealing with other nations as such, and with all the powers inferable from such sovereignty. It is said, however, that the League will change the form of our government. But no function or discretion is taken from any branch of the government which it now performs or exercises. It is asserted that the covenant delegates to an outside tribunal, viz., the Executive Council, the power vested by the Constitution in the Congress or the Senate. But the Executive Council has no power but to recommend to the nations of the League courses which those nations may accept or reject, save in the matter of increasing the limit of armament, to which the United States by its Congress, after full consideration, shall have consented. Neither the Executive Council nor the body of delegates in the machinery for the peaceful settling of differences does other than to recommend a compromise which the United States does not under the League covenant [have] to obey. In all other respects these bodies are mere instruments for conference by representatives for devising plans which are submitted to various governments of the League for their voluntary acceptance and adoption. No obligation of the United States under the League is fixed by action of either the Executive Council or the body of delegates.

Then it is said we have no right to agree to levy an embargo and a boycott. It is true that Congress determines what our commercial relations shall be with other countries of the world. It is true that if a boycott is to be levied Congress must levy it in the form of an embargo, as that which was levied by Congress in Jefferson's administration, and the validity of which was sustained by the Supreme Court, with John Marshall at its head. It is true that Congress might repudiate the obligation entered into by the treaty-making power and refuse to levy such an embargo. But none of these facts would invalidate or render unconstitutional a treaty by which the obligation of the United States was assumed.

In other words, the essence of sovereign power is that while the sovereign may make a contract, it retains the power to repudiate it, if it chooses to dishonor its promise. That does not render null the original obligation or discredit its binding moral force. The nations of Europe are willing to accept, as we must be willing to accept from them, mutual promises, the one in consideration of the other, in confidence that neither will refuse to comply with such promises honorably entered into.

Finally, it is objected that we have no right to agree to arbitrate issues. It is said that we might by arbitration lose our territorial integrity or our political independence. This is a stretch of imagination by the distinguished Senator who made it, at which we marvel. In the face of Article X, which is an understanding to respect the territorial integrity and political independence of every member of the League, how could a board of arbitration possibly reach such a result? More than that, we do not have to arbitrate. If we do not care to arbitrate, we can throw the matter into mediation and conciliation, and we do not covenant to obey the recommendation of compromise by the conciliating body. We have been arbitrating questions for one hundred years.

We have stipulated in treaties to arbitrate classes of questions long before the questions arise. How would we arbitrate under this treaty? The form of the issue to be arbitrated would have to be formulated by our treaty-making power — the President and the Senate of the United States. The award would have to be performed by that branch of the government which executes awards, generally the Congress of the United States. If it involved payment of money, Congress would have to appropriate it. If it involved limitation of armament, Congress would have to limit it. If it involved any duty within the legislative power of Congress under the Constitution, Congress would have to perform it. If Congress sees fit to comply with the report of the compromise by the conciliating body, Congress will have to make such compliance.

The covenant takes away the sovereignty of the United States only as any contract curtails the freedom of action of an individual which he has voluntarily surrendered for the purpose of the contract and to obtain the benefit of it. The covenant creates no super-sovereignty. It merely creates contract obligations. It binds nations to stand together to secure compliance with those obligations. That is all. This is no different from a contract that we make with one nation. If we enter into an important contract with another nation to pay money or to do other things of vital interest to that nation and we break it, then we expose ourselves to the just effort of that nation by force of arms to attempt to compel us to comply with our obligations. This covenant of all the nations is only a limited and loose union of the compelling powers of many nations to do the same thing. The assertion that we are giving up our sovereignty carries us logically and necessarily to the absurd result that we cannot make a contract to do anything with another nation because it limits our freedom of action as a sovereign.

Sovereignty is freedom of action and nations. It is exactly analogous to the liberty of the individual regulated by law. The sovereignty that we should insist upon, and the only sovereignty we have a right to insist upon, is a sovereignty regulated by international law, international morality, and international justice, a sovereignty enjoining the sacred rights which sovereignties of other nations may enjoy, a sovereignty consistent with the enjoyment of the same sovereignty of other nations. It is a sovereignty limited by the law of nations and limited by the obligation of contracts fully and freely entered into in respect to matters which are usually the subjects of contracts between nations.

The President is now returning to Europe. As the representative of this nation in the conference he has joined in recommending in this proposed covenant a League of Nations for consideration and adoption by the conference. He has, meantime, returned home to discharge other executive duties, and it has given him an opportunity to note a discussion of the League in the Senate of the United States and elsewhere. Some speeches, notably that of Senator Lodge, have been useful in taking up the League, article by article, criticizing its language, and expressing doubt either as to its meaning or as to its wisdom.

He will differ, as many others will differ, from Senator Lodge in respect to many of the criticisms, but he will find many useful suggestions in the constructive part of the speech which he will be able to present to his colleagues in the conference. They will be especially valuable in revising the form of the covenant and making reservations to which his colleagues in the conference may readily consent, where Senator Lodge or the other critics have misunderstood the purpose and meaning of the words used.

This covenant should be in the treaty of peace. It is indispensable in ending the war, if the war is to accomplish the declared purpose of this nation and the world in that war, and if it is to work the promised benefit to mankind. We know the President believes this and will insist upon it. Our profound sympathy in his purpose and our prayers for his success should go with him in his great mission.

HENRY CABOT LODGE

(1850-1924)

If being a controversial figure thirty years after your death makes one a classic politician, then Henry Cabot Lodge is as entitled to the honor as are his contemporaries, Wilson and Taft. This man, who virtually symbolized the Republican Party during the years of the Wilson administration, is still discussed and debated by politicians, students, and members of the generation that knew his work first-hand. Versatile figures are generally controversial, and Lodge was an exceedingly versatile man.

An historian would know Lodge's writings on famous American patriots, and would know that he once considered teaching history in college as a profession. A politician would know his rise to power through Massachusetts politics — a rise which carried him to the United States Senate. And an opponent would know his biting manner of speaking and overwhelming logic.

In Senate debates, Lodge more often than not found it hard to refrain from little taunts, fleers, and jibes — mannerisms further accented by his piping, irritating voice. Although he learned to control these unpleasant aspects of his speech delivery, he never mastered them completely; nor would he have been Henry Cabot Lodge if he had done so. A sarcastic phrase drove the point home; the voice twisted it.

"He was the only man in public life at that time who in his speech had style." He rose to speak as informally as in his library: his concise language and crisp voice held attention, while the clarity of his thought carried the Senators along with him. He did not hesitate to hold the Senate as long as he wished, for he never wished to speak after he was through with his subject. His mastery of the greater subjects, even to the least detail, was such that his hearers could not fail to follow his argument. Opposition to him kindled the forces of his brain and heated his blood. Hence he was most powerful before a bold antagonist: at times he was roused to anger when his hatred of injustice or apparent disloyalty touched him. And there were occasions when, in response to a taunt or vicious thrust, he, with his reserve of experience, knowledge, and brilliant mind, would . . . strike his opponent dumb with one slash.[1]

Although Lodge had many enemies, there were few among them who did not regard him as a formidable opponent. President Wilson, although he disliked Lodge intensely, was fully aware of Lodge's ability as an adversary. On no other issue did the viewpoints of Lodge and Wilson meet with such force as that of American membership in the League of Nations. Much has been made of this conflict; much that pictures Henry Cabot Lodge as anti-League and pro-isolation. This is not the whole truth. The March 2, 1919, edition of the New York Times accurately analyzes his stand:

Senator Lodge's position is different. He opposes the League's Constitution as drafted, but his criticism is constructive; he suggests amendments, changes which might make the plan acceptable. Even though he sets himself in opposition to the plans of the President, to the plans that fourteen nations represented in Paris have unanimously approved, we still consider him as a friend of the League, as one wishing to help the foundation idea to approval in a better form.

So Lodge was not anti-League in principle; he was anti-League as it was then constituted, and this League he fought with all of his might.

President Wilson needed the support of the Senate for his League of Nations proposal. He was to leave for France in early March of 1919, and wanted the United States — government and people — squarely behind him. The Senate discussed these proposals during the month before the President's departure, and it was inevitable that Henry Cabot Lodge would be a leading power in the fight against "Wilson's League." When it became known

[1] William Lawrence, Henry Cabot Lodge, pp. 128-129.

that the Senator would speak against the League on February 28, 1919, crowds flocked to the Senate Chambers. The speech itself was given to packed galleries, and, according to the New York Tribune (March 1, 1919), "so frequent were the bursts of applause that only the appeals of several senators, including Mr. Lodge himself and Mr. Reed, of Missouri, dissuaded the Vice-President from enforcing an order which he had given to the sergeant-at-arms to clear the galleries."

Even Lodge's opponents and critics considered the speech to be one of the Senator's finest, as witness these remarks by one of his biographers, John Garraty:

> . . . the tone of this speech was reasonable and the main point he raised was certainly one that merited thoughtful consideration from every citizen. If he betrayed his animosity through an occasional touch of sarcasm, he none the less refrained from personal criticism of Wilson, and his oration was nonpartisan in form at least, if not in intent. As Professor Fleming, a harsh critic of Lodge's position, has said, the speech was "moderate in tone" and "wholly reasonable," a "classic in any debate."[2]

Classic or not, the speech served its purpose. Wilson went to Europe with considerably less than full support for his League of Nations plan, and his own nation never did join the League. In what remained of Wilson's term, Lodge continued to be a political (and personal) vexation to the President.

His biggest battle fought and won, Lodge continued his position of leadership in the Senate with enhanced prestige. He fought other battles in his remaining years of service, but time was running out on him. This great Republican died in 1924, leaving behind him a brilliant record of service to Party and Nation. Quite unwittingly, he had delivered a speech in Boston some fourteen years earlier which stands as a virtual epitaph to his life and work:

> To her service I have given my all: no man can give more. Others may easily serve her better than I in those days yet to be; but of this I am sure: that no one can serve her with a greater love or deeper loyalty.

[2] Henry Cabot Lodge, p. 353.

AGAINST THE CONSTITUTION OF THE LEAGUE OF NATIONS

by

Henry Cabot Lodge

Delivered in the United States Senate on February 28, 1919.

MR. PRESIDENT, ALL people, men and women alike, who are capable of connected thought abhor war and desire nothing so much as to make secure the future peace of the world. Everybody hates war. Everyone longs to make it impossible. We ought to lay aside once and for all the unfounded and really evil suggestion that because men may differ as to the best method of assuring the world's peace in the future, anyone is against permanent peace, if it can be obtained, among all the nations of mankind. Because one man goes to the Capitol in Washington by one street and another man by a different street it does not follow that they are not both going to the Capitol. We all earnestly desire to advance toward the preservation of the world's peace, and difference in method makes no distinction in purpose. It is almost needless to say that the question now before us is so momentous that it transcends all party lines. Party considerations and party interests disappear in dealing with such a question as this. I will follow any man and vote for any measure which in my honest opinion will make for the maintenance of the world's peace. I will follow no man and vote for no measures which, however well intended, seem in my best judgment to lead to dissensions rather than to harmony among the nations or to injury, peril, or injustice to my country. No question has ever confronted the United States Senate which equals in importance that which is involved in the league of nations intended to secure the future peace of the world. There should be no undue haste in considering it. My one desire is that not only the Senate, which is charged with responsibility, but that the press and the people of the country should investigate every proposal with the utmost thoroughness and weigh them all carefully before they make up their minds. If there is any proposition or any plan which will not bear, which will not court the most thorough and most public discussion, that fact makes it an object of suspicion at the very outset. Beware of it; be on your guard against it. Demand that those who oppose the plan now offered present arguments and reasons, based on facts and history, and that those who favor it meet objections with something more relative than rhetoric, personal denunciation, and shrill shrieks that virtue is to be preferred to vice and that peace is better than war. Glittering and enticing generalities will not serve. We must have facts, details, and sharp, clear-cut definitions. The American people can not give too much thought to this subject, and that they shall look into it with considerate eyes is all that I desire.

In the first place, the terms of the league — the agreements which we make — must be so plain and so explicit that no man can misunderstand them. We must, so far as it can be done by human ingenuity, have every agreement which we make so stated that it will not give rise to different interpretations and to consequent argument. Misunderstandings as to terms are not a good foundation for a treaty to promote peace. We now have before us the draft of a constitution for a league of nations, prepared by a commission or committee, which is to be submitted to the representatives of the nations. The nations, through their delegates, have not agreed to it. It has not passed beyond the stage of a committee report. It is open to amendment and change in the peace conference. The Senate can take no action upon it, but it lies open before us for criticism and discussion. What is said in the Senate ought to be placed before the peace conference and published in Paris, so that the foreign Governments may be informed as to the various views expressed here.

In this draft prepared for a constitution of a league of nations, which is now before the world, there is hardly a clause about the interpretation of which men do not already differ. As it stands there is serious danger that the very nations which sign the constitution of the league will quarrel about the meaning of the various articles before a twelvemonth has passed. It seems to have been very hastily drafted, and the result is crudeness and looseness of expression, unintentional, I hope. There are certainly many doubtful passages and open questions obvious in the articles which can not be settled by individual inference, but which must be made so clear and so distinct that we may all understand the exact meaning of the instrument to which we are to be asked to set our hands. The language of these articles does not appear to me to have the precision and unmistakable character which a constitution, a treaty, or a law ought to present. The language only too frequently is not the language of laws or statutes. The article concerning mandatories, for example, contains an argument and a statement of existing conditions. Arguments and historical facts have no place in a statute or a treaty. Statutory and legal language must assert and command, not argue and describe. I press this point because there is nothing so vital to the peace of the world as the sanctity of treaties. The suggestion that we can safely sign because we can always violate or abrogate is fatal not only to any league but to peace itself. You can not found world peace upon the cynical "scrap of paper" doctrine so dear to Germany. To whatever instrument the United States sets its hand it must carry out the provisions of that instrument to the last jot and tittle, and observe it absolutely both in letter and in spirit. If this is not done the instrument will become a source of controversy instead of agreement, of dissension instead of harmony. This is all the more essential because it is evident, although not expressly stated, that this league is intended to be indissoluble, for there is no provision for its termination or for the withdrawal of any signatory. We are left to infer that any nation withdrawing from the league exposes itself to penalties and probably to war. Therefore, before we ratify, the terms and the language in which the terms are stated must be as exact and as precise, as free from any possibility of conflicting interpretations, as it is possible to make them. [*Interruption by* Mr. Gore . . .]

The explanation or interpretation of any of these doubtful passages is not sufficient if made by one man, whether that man be the President of the United States, or a Senator, or anyone else. These questions and doubts must be answered and removed by the instrument itself.

It is to be remembered that if there is any dispute about the terms of this constitution there is no court provided that I can find to pass upon differences of opinion as to the terms of the constitution itself. There is no court to fill the function which our Supreme Court fills. There is provision for tribunals to decide questions submitted for arbitration, but there is no authority to decide differing interpretations as to the terms of the instrument itself.

What I have just said indicates the vast importance of the form and the manner in which the agreements which we are to sign shall be stated. I now come to questions of substance, which seem to me to demand the most careful thought of the entire American people, and particularly those charged with the responsibility of ratification. We abandon entirely by the proposed constitution the policy laid down by Washington in his Farewell Address and the Monroe Doctrine. It is worse than idle, it is not honest, to evade or deny this fact, and every fair-minded supporter of this draft plan for a league admits it. I know that some of the ardent advocates of the plan submitted to us regard any suggestion of the importance of the Washington policy as foolish and irrelevant. Perhaps it is. Perhaps the time has come when the policies of Washington should be abandoned; but if we are to cast them aside I think that at least it should be done respectfully and with a sense of gratitude to the great man who formulated them. For nearly a century and a quarter the policies laid down in the Farewell Address have been followed and adhered to by the Government of the United States and by the American people. I doubt if any purely political declaration has ever been absorbed by any people for so long a time. The principles of the Farewell Address in regard to our foreign relations have been sustained and acted upon by the American people down to the present moment. Washington declared against permanent alliances. He did not close the door on temporary alliances for particular purposes. Our entry into the great war just closed was entirely in accord with and violated in no respect the policy laid down by Washington. When we went to war with Germany we made no treaties with the nations engaged in the war against the German Government. The President was so careful in this direction that he did not permit himself ever to refer to the nations by whose side we fought as "allies," but always as "nations associated with us in the war." The attitude recommended by Washington was scrupulously maintained even under the pressure of the great conflict. Now, in the twinkling of an eye, while passion and emotion reign, the

Washington policy is to be entirely laid aside and we are to enter upon a permanent and indissoluble alliance. That which we refuse to do in war we are to do in peace deliberately, coolly, and with no war exigency. Let us not overlook the profound gravity of this step.

Washington was not only a very great man but he was also a very wise man. He looked far into the future and he never omitted human nature from his calculations. He knew well that human nature had not changed fundamentally since mankind had a history. Moreover, he was destitute of any personal ambitions to a degree never equaled by any other very great man known to us. In all the vital questions with which he dealt, it was not merely that he thought of his country first and of himself second. He thought of his country first and never thought of himself at all. He was so great a man that the fact that this country had produced him was enough of itself to justify the Revolution and our existence as a Nation. Do not think that I overstate this in the fondness of patriotism and with the partiality of one of his countrymen. The opinion I have expressed is the opinion of the world. Fifteen years after Washington's death Byron wrote the famous and familiar lines:

> Where may the wearied eye repose
>   When gazing on the Great,
> Where neither guilty glory glows,
>   Nor despicable state?
> Yes, One — the first — the last — the best —
> The Cincinnatus of the West,
>   Whom Envy dared not hate —
> Bequeathed the name of Washington,
> To make man blush there was but one!

That was the opinion of mankind then, and it is the opinion of mankind to-day, when his statue has been erected in Paris and is about to be erected in London. If we throw aside the political testament of such a man, which has been of living force down to the present instant, because altered circumstances demand it, it is a subject for deep regret and not for rejoicing. When Washington prepared the Farewell Address he consulted Hamilton, perhaps the greatest constructive mind among modern statesmen, who prepared a large part of the draft; Madison, one of the chief framers of the Constitution and President of the United States; John Jay, Chief Justice and one of the great lawyers in our history. Following them came Thomas Jefferson, James Monroe, and John Quincy Adams, bringing the Monroe doctrine to complete and round out the principles of Washington to which they were all alike devoted. If we are to be driven by modern exigencies to dismiss Washington and his counselors and the men who declared the Monroe doctrine from our consideration, we ought, at least, as these stately figures pass off the stage of guiding influence, to pay our homage to them and not relegate them to the shades of the past with jeers and laughter directed against their teachings.

But if we put aside forever the Washington policy in regard to our foreign relations, we must always remember that it carries with it the corollary known as the Monroe doctrine. Under the terms of this league draft reported by the committee to the peace conference the Monroe doctrine disappears. It has been our cherished guide and guard for nearly a century. The Monroe doctrine is based on the principle of self-preservation. To say that it is a question of protecting the boundaries, the political integrity, of the American States is not to state the Monroe doctrine. Boundaries have been changed among American States since the Monroe doctrine was enunciated. That is not the kernel of the doctrine. The real essence of that doctrine is that American questions shall be settled by Americans alone; that the Americas shall be separated from Europe and from the interference of Europe in purely American questions. That is the vital principle of the doctrine.

I have seen it said that the Monroe doctrine is preserved under article 10; that we do not abandon the Monroe doctrine, we merely extend it to all the world. How anyone can say this passes my comprehension. The Monroe doctrine exists solely for the protection of the American Hemisphere, and to that hemisphere it was limited. If you extend it to all the world, it ceases to exist, because it rests on nothing but the differentiation of the American Hemisphere from the rest of the world. Under this draft of the constitution of the league of nations American questions and European questions and Asian and African questions are all alike put within the control and jurisdiction of the league. Europe will have the right to take part in the settlement of all American questions, and we, of course, shall have the right to share in the settlement of all questions in Europe and Asia and Africa. Europe and Asia are to take part in policing the American Continent and the Panama Canal, and in return we are to have, by way of compensation, the right to police the Balkans and Asia Minor when we are asked to do so. Perhaps the time has come when it is necessary to do this, but it is a very grave step, and I wish now merely to point out that the American people ought never to abandon the Washington policy and the Monroe doctrine without being perfectly certain that they earnestly wish to do so. Standing always firmly by these great policies, we have thriven and prospered and have done more to preserve the world's peace than any nation, league, or alliance which ever existed. For this reason I ask the press and the public and, of course, the Senate to consider well the gravity of this proposition before it takes the heavy responsibility of finally casting aside these policies which we have adhered to for a century and more and under which we have greatly served the cause of peace both at home and abroad.

Very complete proof must be offered of the superiority of any new system before we reject the policies of Washington and Monroe, which have been in our foreign relations the Palladium of the Republic. Within the memory of those to whom I now speak the Monroe doctrine stopped the incursions of England upon the territory of Venezuela and settled the boundary question finally by arbitration. Under the Monroe doctrine we arrested the attempt of Germany to take Venezuelan territory on another occasion. In these two instances the doctrine was enforced by a Democratic President and by a Republican President, and they were supported in so doing by all the people of the United States without regard to party. I mention these cases merely to show that we are not cutting away dead limbs from the body politic, but that we are abandoning two cardinal principles of American government, which, until the presentation of this draft for the constitution of the league of nations, were as vital as on the day when Washington addressed the people of the United States for the last time or when President Monroe announced his policy to the world. What has happened since November 11, 1918, to make them so suddenly valueless, to cause them to be regarded as injurious obstacles to be cast out upon the dust heaps of history? It seems to me that that is a question which at least deserves our consideration before we take action upon it.

Two other general propositions, and I shall proceed to examine these league articles in detail. In article 10 we, in common, of course, with the other signatories and members of the projected league, guarantee the territorial integrity and the political independence of every member of the league. That means that we ultimately guarantee the independence and the boundaries, as now settled or as they may be settled by the treaty with Germany, of every nation on earth. If the United States agrees to guaranties of that sort we must maintain them. The word of the United States, her promise to guarantee the independence and the boundaries of any country, whether she does it alone or in company with other nations, whether she guarantees one country or all the countries of the world, is just as sacred as her honor — far more important than the maintenance of every financial pledge, which the people of this country would never consent to break.

I do not now say the time has not come when, in the interest of future peace, the American people may not decide that we ought to guarantee the territorial integrity of the far-flung British Empire, including her self-governing dominions and colonies, of the Balkan States, of China or Japan, or of the French, Italian, and Portuguese colonies in Africa; but I do suggest that it is a very grave, a very perilous promise to make, because there is but one way by which such guaranties, if ever invoked, can be maintained, and that way is the way of force — whether military or economic force, it matters not. If we guarantee any country on the earth, no matter how small or how large, in its independence or its boundaries, that guarantee we must maintain at any cost when our word is once given, and we must be in constant possession of fleets and armies capable of enforcing these guaranties at a moment's notice. There is no need of arguing whether there is to be compulsive force behind this league. It is there in article 10 absolutely and entirely by the mere fact of these guaranties. The ranks of the armies and the fleets of the navy made necessary by such pledges are to be filled and manned by the sons, husbands, and brothers of the people of America. I wish them carefully to consider, therefore, whether they are willing to have the youth of America ordered to war by other nations without regard to what they or their representatives desire. I would have them determine after much reflection whether they are willing to have the United States forced into war by other nations against her own will. They must bear in mind constantly that we have only one vote in the executive council, only one vote in the body of delegates, and a majority of the votes rules and is decisive.

I am not here to discuss the constitutional question of the sole right of Congress to declare war. That is a detail, as it relates only to the Constitution, which we may decide later. In my own opinion, we shall be obliged to modify the Constitution. I do not think, and I never can admit, that we can change or modify the Constitution by a treaty negotiated by the President and ratified by the Senate. I think that must be done, and can only be done, in the way prescribed by the Constitution itself, and to promise to amend our Constitution is a serious task and a doubtful undertaking.

I hope the American people will take time to consider this promise before they make it — because when it is once made it can not be broken — and ask themselves whether this is the best way of assuring perfect peace throughout the future years, which is what we are aiming at, for we all are aiming at the same object. A world's peace which requires at the outset preparations for war — for war either economic or military — in order to maintain that peace presents questions and awakens thoughts which certainly ought to be soberly and discreetly considered.

The second general proposition to which I would call attention is this: We now in this draft bind ourselves to submit every possible international dispute or difference either to the league court or to the control of the executive council of the league. That includes immigration, a very live question, to take a single example. Are we ready to give to other nations the power to say who shall come into the United States and become citizens of the Republic? If we are ready to do this, we are prepared to part with the most precious of sovereign rights, that which guards our existence and our character as a Nation. Are we ready to leave it to other nations to determine whether we shall admit to the United States a flood of Japanese, Chinese, and Hindu labor? If we accept this plan for a league, this is precisely what we promise to do. I know that by following out all the windings of the provision for referring to the council or allowing the council to take charge of what has been called hitherto a nonjusticiable question, we shall probably reach a point where it would not be possible to secure unanimous action by the league upon the question of immigration. But, Mr. President, I start with the proposition that there should be no jurisdiction in the league at all over that question; that it should be separated absolutely and entirely from any jurisdiction of the league. Are we prepared to have a league of nations — in which the United States has only one vote, which she could not cast on a dispute to which she was a party — open our doors, if they see fit, to any and all immigration from all parts of the world?

Mr. Taft has announced, in an article which appeared in the *National Geographic Magazine*, that the question of immigration will go before the international tribunal, and he says now that all organized labor is for the league. If American labor favors putting the restriction of immigration in the control of other nations they must have radically changed their minds and abandoned their most cherished policy. Certainly the gravity of such promises as are involved in the points I have suggested is sufficient to forbid haste. If such promises are to be given they must be given in cold blood with a full realization of what they mean and after the American people and those who represent them here have considered all that is involved with a serious care such as we have never been called upon to exercise before. We are asked to abandon the policies which we have adhered to during all our life as a Nation. We are asked to guarantee the political independence and the territorial integrity of every nation which chooses to join the league — and that means all nations, as the President stated in his speech at Manchester. We are asked to leave to the decision of other nations, or to the jurisdiction of other nations, the question of what immigrants shall come to the United States. We are asked also to give up in part our sovereignty and our independence and to subject our own will to the will of other nations, if there is a majority against our desires. We are asked, therefore, in a large and important degree to substitute internationalism for nationalism and an international state for pure Americanism. Certainly such things as these deserve reflection, discussion, and earnest thought.

I am not contending now that these things must not be done. I have no intention of opposing a blank negative to propositions which concern the peace of the world, which I am as anxious to see promoted as any living man can be; but I do say, in the strongest terms, that these things I have pointed out are of vast importance not only to us but to the entire world, and a mistake now in making the league of nations might result in more war and trouble than the old system in its worst days. What I ask, and all I ask, is consideration, time, and thought.

The first and most practical question for us to consider and decide is whether the terms of this committee draft of a constitution for the league of nations really make for harmony among the nations or will tend to produce dissension and controversy. We all desire peace, but in our zeal for peace we must be careful not to create new obligations and new and untried conditions, which may lead to fostering war rather than peace. For this reason I am going now to examine the articles in the draft of the constitution for the league of nations one by one.

Upon the preamble we need not pause. It states purposes and objects with which everybody, of course, is in sympathy.

Article 1 deals with the officers and the delegates, and they are sufficiently and clearly provided for, and also that there shall be an international secretariat. I think nothing is omitted so far as the creation of offices goes.

Nothing is said about how the delegates shall be chosen. That, of course, is a matter which is left to each nation to determine, but I venture, with all respect, to suggest that delegates representing the United States in what is to be a world state, to which we are to give a portion of our sovereignty and independence, ought to represent the United States; they ought to be selected by the people of the United States or appointed as ambassadors and consuls are appointed. I think these delegates, who are certainly as important as ambassadors or consuls, should be appointed by the usual method of the President and the Senate, and not ever be allowed to be irresponsible personal agents. That, however, is something we can attend to here, I think, when the league of nations is submitted to us in treaty form.

Article 2 refers to the meetings of the body of delegates, and also provides that "each of the high contracting parties shall have one vote but may not have more than three representatives." Therefore the voting in the body of delegates proceeds on the well-settled principle of international law that each national sovereignty is equal to every other national sovereignty, and the United States will have one vote and so will Siam.

In article 3 we come to the executive council, which is of the greatest possible importance, for it is in the provision stated here

— and also, I am sure, as practice will show — the controlling force of the entire league:

> The executive council shall consist of representatives of the United States of America, the British Empire, France, Italy, and Japan, together with representatives of four other States members of the league.

What other States shall be selected has not yet been disclosed to us, but there must be four other States. The executive council now has five members — three from Europe, one from Asia, and one from America. Ultimately it will have nine members. I assume, and I think I have the right to assume, on the best authority, that there is no intention of making Germany one of the four nations to be added to the existing five which will compose the nine members of the executive council. I think it is probable that Germany will have a period of probation before she is even admitted to the league, and that seems to me to be eminently wise.

Then the article provides for the meeting of the council, and then says in the last paragraph:

> Invitations shall be sent to any power to attend a meeting of the council at which matters directly affecting its interests are to be discussed, and no decision taken at any meeting will be binding on such powers unless so invited.

This, of course, looks to having the executive council consider the affairs of every country in the world, whether they are members of the league or not, and all the council has to do in order to make its action binding on such powers is to invite them to be present. It is a paragraph not without importance.

> ART. 4. All matter of procedure at meetings of the body of delegates or the executive council, including the appointment of the committees to investigate particular matters, shall be regulated by the body of delegates or the executive council, and may be decided by a majority of the States represented at the meeting.

It is to be decided by the executive council, where we shall have one vote in five, or, when the council is enlarged, one vote in nine, and in the body of delegates, of course, only one vote.

Then comes article 5, which provides for the secretariat and concerns only offices and provisions for expenses. The words creating offices and providing for salaries leave no room for doubts or questionings.

Article 6 is a matter of course. It simply gives the delegates diplomatic immunities and privileges.

Article 7 covers the admission to the league of States and, when a State is invited to adhere, "requires the assent of not less than two-thirds of the States represented in the body of delegates, and shall be limited to fully self-governing countries, including dominions and colonies."

The inclusion of dominions and colonies, of course, covers the four great self-governing dominions of Great Britain. I have no fault to find with the arrangement. Canada, New Zealand, South Africa, and Australia are far more worthy and more valuable members of a league of nations than some of the nations which I think will find their way into the body. But the fact remains that in the body of delegates England has five votes to one vote of any other country.

The next paragraph says:

> No State shall be admitted to the league unless it is able to give effective guaranties of its sincere intention to observe its international obligations.

I do not wish to seem hypercritical, but I think that in a document of this kind we should know a little better what an "effective guaranty of a sincere intention" is.

How can we have an effective guaranty of a sincere intention?

I merely throw this out as one of the points which it seems to me ought to be made clear. Let us know what it means. How are we to test the sincerity of the intention? How are we to get a guaranty for the sincerity of the intention in advance? I think it would be well to have that more precisely defined.

We now come to article 8, which refers to disarmament, a most important question, one of the most important in the constitution of the league, with the purpose of which everybody must be in the keenest sympathy. The reduction of armaments, if it can be brought about successfully, will be of the greatest value to the world and relieve the people of all countries from a burden of taxation which has become intolerable. But its very importance makes it necessary, in my opinion, to express what is to be done with the utmost clearness. The article says:

> The high contracting parties recognize the principle that the maintenance of peace will require the reduction of national armaments to the lowest point consistent with national safety and the enforcement by common action of international obligations —

That is, the reduction must be consistent with the "enforcement by common action of international obligations," words to be considered and which the instrument itself must explain.

Here we are dealing solely with military force which we are seeking to reduce, and it is recognized that in disarmament one of the elements to be considered is the "enforcement by common action of international obligations," which, I assume — we have to assume more or less as we pass along through these articles — refers to the obligations of the league. We certainly owe no international obligation to anybody else to-day as to what fleets and armies we shall have. Yet this article contemplates as one of the tests of disarmament the amount of force which will be needed to carry out the purposes of the league. The article continues:

> having special regard to the geographical situation and circumstances of each State, and the executive council shall formulate plans for effecting such reduction.

I do not know how far the formulation has a binding effect, but the article goes on to say:

> The executive council shall also determine for the consideration and action of the several Governments what military equipment and armament is fair and reasonable in proportion to the scale of forces laid down in the program of disarmament —

"Laid down." Again I have to interpret. Laid down, I assume, by the executive council itself, because it is they who make the program —

> and these limits, when adopted, shall not be exceeded without the permission of the executive council.

There comes in an absolutely binding provision. It says "when adopted." Adopted by whom? The natural inference is, adopted by the several governments, if you trace it back through the wording of the previous paragraphs. Ought not an instrument of this vital character to be drafted with the ordinary care which a clerk gives in drafting a clause in an appropriation bill for a Senate committee? Ought it not to be stated clearly, "thus adopted by the several governments," and then there can be no question that each government will decide on the program itself and its own share before it is put in a position where it can never exceed that program without the permission of the executive council — I assume the majority of the executive council. That is another thing which apparently it has not been thought worth while to state, but I do not think you can be too clear when you are exacting from nations these great promises and laying upon them these heavy burdens.

The high contracting parties agree that the manufacture by private enterprise of munitions and implements of war lends itself to grave objections, and direct the executive council to advise how the evil effects attendant upon such manufacture can be prevented.

That, I take it, is mere advice to be laid before the body of delegates, but it is not explained how far the advice goes.

The high contracting parties —

The last paragraph says —

undertake in no way to conceal from each other the condition of such of their industries as are capable of being adapted to warlike purposes or the scale of their armaments, and agree that there shall be full and frank interchange of information as to their military and naval program.

An admirable proposition! Certainly it can not but add to the prospect of the peace of the world if every nation shall explain to every other nation just what military and naval program it has; but there seems to be no method expressed here by which they can be compelled to give that information, except by saying that if they do not do it they fail in a moral obligation and will be guilty of what some people might define as "moral obliquity."

Article 9 says:

> A permanent commission shall be constituted to advise the league on the execution of the provisions of article 8 and on military and naval questions generally.

A very useful body, but constituted by whom? There is not one syllable in the article to show by whom it shall be constituted. It may be unnecessary to do it; we may be able to infer it; but when you get into the misty region of inferences by individuals you must have some tribunal established like our Supreme Court, who can declare whether the inference is correct or not.

Article 10 is probably the most important article in the whole constitution — I have already referred to it — because to me it is graver than anything else with perhaps one exception in this entire treaty. It is also perfectly clear:

> The high contracting parties undertake to respect and preserve as against external aggression the territorial integrity and existing political independence of all States members of the league. In case of any such aggression, or in case of any threat or danger of such aggression, the executive council shall advise upon the means by which the obligation shall be fulfilled.

The executive council is to have the power of advice, which I do not suppose is binding at all, but the guaranty remains, and, as I have already said — it can not be too often repeated — that when one nation guarantees the political independence and the territorial integrity of another, that guaranty must be maintained, and guaranties can only be maintained by the exercise in the last resort of the force of the nation. If we were to guarantee the political independence and territorial integrity of Mexico or Guatemala, or any of those States, we should have to stand behind them with our armies and our fleets when the guaranty was invoked, and there is no escape from that obligation. Those plain words demand it. I am not now arguing whether we should give the guaranty or whether we should not give the guaranty, but I beg my fellow countrymen to consider well before they give this promise to invoke the mighty power of the United States in order to enforce a guaranty which extends to the boundaries of every State on the face of the earth. It is a tremendous promise, and if we give it this country must carry it out. The United States must never be guilty of in any way impairing the sanctity of treaties. But let us think well before we do it. Let us consider it. In the presence of such promises as that is it unreasonable to ask that the American people should have time to consider, to realize, just what it means before they give the promise? If they decide coolly and deliberately, there is nothing more to be said; we bow to it, and Congress will fulfill it; but that is too weighty a promise to make by simply saying, "I am in favor of a league of nations and of the eternal peace of the world." We are all in favor of the peace of the world. A mere title does not carry with it any explanation of the responsibility which is undertaken.

Article 11. Any war or threat of war, whether immediately affecting any of the high contracting parties or not, is hereby declared a matter of concern to the league, and the high contracting parties reserve the right to take any action that may be deemed wise and effectual to safeguard the peace of nations —

"Any action" covers war —

It is hereby also declared and agreed to be the friendly right of each of the high contracting parties to draw the attention of the body of delegates —

Which I suppose means the five who are now assigned and the four who are to join with them, making nine in all —

to draw the attention of the body of delegates or of the executive council to any circumstances affecting international intercourse which threaten to disturb international peace or the good understanding between nations upon which peace depends.

Everyone must agree to that, except for the slight uncertainties of statement, but it embodies in practice one of the paragraphs of The Hague convention.

Now we come to the disputes. Those articles relating to the settlement of disputes would require a long time by themselves, if we touched nothing else, to discuss, and also to understand. I merely wish to call attention to a few points which occur on a casual reading. It says in article 12 "disputes." It says in article

13 "any disputes." That means any dispute that may arise among nations, of any kind, whether involving domestic or internal matters or foreign relations. The words "any disputes" covers everything. On that point I wish to reiterate what I have already said. I am not going further into it.

It is no reply to the point that is made about immigration to say that, if you follow it through all the windings of the provisions here for justiciable and nonjusticiable questions you will find it reaches a point where the league could do nothing about immigration into the United States unless it was unanimous, and that it is very unlikely they would ever be unanimous. Grant it; it is unlikely that the league will ever be unanimous about anything, but the possibility is there. I deny the jurisdiction. I do not think we should leave to the league any question as to immigration, because immigration lies at the very root of national character and national economy; it ought to be made plain that the league has no jurisdiction whatever over such questions in any way. We do not want a narrow alley of escape from the jurisdiction of the league. We want to prevent any jurisdiction whatever. As we stand to-day no nation or nations can say who shall come into the United States. There is only one rule as to that, and that is the rule of the United States. It should so remain. What I say for the United States I mean for every other nation. No nation should be compelled to admit anyone within its borders whom it does not choose to admit.

Some of these points I think it might be well for those who prepared this draft to consider. Perhaps I do not regard the drafting committee with the veneration which the Senator from Nebraska [Mr. Hitchcock] feels toward them; I know some of them, and, without reflecting upon them in any way, I do not think their intellect or position in the world are so overpowering that we can not suggest amendments to this league. I can not say I know them all; I do not believe anybody here could get up and say who the 14 members of that commission are.

But there is a practical question to which I was about to call attention. This constitution here says until three months there shall be "no resort to war without previously submitting the question and matters involved either to arbitration or to inquiry by the executive council and until three months after award by the arbitrators or a recommendation by the executive council."

That binds the members of the league; but there have been outlaws among the nations before now. As a matter of history, the sudden manner in which Frederick the Great threw aside all his most solemn promises and poured his armies over Silesia, which Prussia has held ever since he tore it from Austria. How was this present war begun? By the sudden precipitation of an enormous war machine on the unprepared lands of Belgium and the nearly unprepared territory of France.

Suppose we had a Mexican raid across our border. It has happened. Perhaps Mexican nature has changed and it will never happen again, but it may happen. We are members of the league, we will suppose, and mean to carry out, as we must, every provision in absolute good faith. Mexico does not happen, we will say, to be a member of the league, or she is a member and breaks her covenants; she has not yet given "effective guaranties of sincere intention"; she breaks across our border, and under this article we have got to wait three months before we do anything. That, I think, would be a little hard on the people who live on the border. [Interruption by MR. REED. . . .]

Article 13 reads:

> The high contracting parties agree that whenever any dispute or difficulty shall arise between them which they recognize to be suitable for submission to arbitration —

That is, disputes which a majority of the high contracting parties recognize to be suitable for submission to arbitration —

> and which can not be satisfactorily settled by diplomacy, they will submit the whole matter to arbitration.

Of course, the only people who can submit a matter to arbitration are the people who are parties to the dispute. Those who have no dispute can not submit anything to arbitration, because they have nothing to submit.

The reason I bring this apparently trivial point up at this time is that it will be well to differentiate these "theys" and show that in one case the reference is to the high contracting parties who agree that any dispute that arises among them suitable for submission shall be submitted, and, in the other that those between whom the dispute arises will submit it. This is clearly the meaning, I think, but it might be expressed a little more luminously.

The executive council "proposes," I suppose, by a majority, although it does not say so; and how binding the proposal is does not appear. I think it ought to be explicitly stated that a majority of the executive council shall have the power to propose and declare whether the proposal is binding or not. The word "propose" does not imply a binding character, I am well aware; but I should like to get rid of one of the implications of which this document is full.

Article 14 provides that "the executive council shall formulate plans for the establishment of a permanent court of international justice."

Then comes article 15, which is very important, and which provides for those disputes "likely to lead to rupture," which are not submitted to arbitration, but which the high contracting parties agree they will refer to the executive council through the secretary general. They are to make their statements of the case there and such recommendations are to be made as the executive council thinks just and proper for the settlement of the dispute, and "if the report is unanimously agreed to by the members of the council other than the parties to the dispute the high contracting parties agree that they will not go to war with any party which complies with the recommendations."

Unless the council is unanimous, I take it, they are at liberty to go to war. And "if any party shall refuse so to comply the council shall propose measures necessary to give effect to the recommendation." There is no explanation of what measures. I presume we must take it to mean all measures. I will not follow the referred dispute through all its tortuous pathway, but it comes eventually to the body of delegates, and in that connection the proposed constitution says:

All the provisions of this article and of article 12 relating to the action of the executive council shall apply to the action and powers of the body of delegates.

This means that the body of delegates, as I take it, must unanimously agree, and if they do not unanimously agree it appears to me to leave the whole matter open. This may be a protection in certain cases, but in other cases, it seems to me, it does not offer a very strong resistance or create a very serious obstacle to war.

Now we come to article 16, which says that —

Should any of the high contracting parties break or disregard its covenants under article 12 it shall thereby ipso facto be deemed to have committed an act of war against all the other members of the league, which hereby undertake immediately to subject it to the severance of all trade or financial relations, the prohibition of all intercourse between their nationals and the nationals of the covenant-breaking State, and the prevention of all financial, commercial, or personal intercourse between the nationals of the covenant-breaking State and the nationals of any other State, whether a member of the league or not.

There can be no doubt, under the conditions given, that we shall be called upon to enter on an economic war with any State on earth, whether a member of the league or not, if that State breaks or disregards any of the covenants relating to arbitration. I merely call attention to it because I venture to think that cutting off our intercourse with another nation and opening our territory to the passage of troops is a very serious promise to make; and I think it ought to be honored with more consideration than perhaps it has yet received.

Article 16 contemplates also the duties of the executive council in such cases "to recommend what effective military or naval forces the members of the league shall severally contribute to the armed forces to be used to protect the covenants of the league."

Here it is apparent that there can be no question that the armed forces of the United States are to be called upon for work of this kind; and if we are to act in good faith, it seems to me we are morally bound by this clause to contribute what the executive council recommends to the armed forces called forth to protect the covenants of this league. We may say their recommendation does not bind, but it certainly binds us morally if we agree to it; and I do not think that we can afford to enter a league of nations for the preservation of the peace of the world with any misunderstanding on a point of this kind. It seems to me that, in any event, this is a direct interference with the power of Congress to raise armies and maintain navies, and we shall be compelled to have a constitutional amendment in order that this provision may be carried out. However, I am not going at this time to enter upon constitutional questions, which are regarded by most advocates of the league as either humorous or academic.

Article 17 refers to the case of disputes between members of the league and other States not members, and makes various provisions raising many of the questions which are raised by the preceding article.

Article 19 is one of the great articles of the proposed constitution. It provides for the States of the league being mandatories and taking charge of other States classified under various descriptions in the article, which I will not read. Oddly enough, it does not say who is to select the mandatories; at least, I can find nothing in the article stating who is to choose the mandatories, whether the body of the delegates or the executive council; nor does it appear whether a mandatory is bound if once selected. I presume not; but it is not stated. I do not think it is hypercriticism to suggest that when a mandatory is to be selected to take charge of the fortunes of another people, or of another State, there should be some provision for the selection of the mandatory, and it should be made clear, at least, whether the nation so selected is bound.

I am not going into the general question of taking up the work of the mandatories and holding States in tutelage. That was so thoroughly covered by the Senator from Iowa [MR. CUMMINS] that it is not necessary for me to take the time of the Senate to discuss it further; but I suggest this thought — and I shall keep on suggesting it — that before the United States binds itself in any way it should be made clear to what extent it is bound, for I have no sympathy with the proposition that we can refuse this and refuse that; in other words, that we can violate the principles of the treaty whenever we feel like it. I think that idea ought to be finally dismissed. What we are bound to in honor we are bound to do, and I think whether we should be prepared to take charge of other countries and of other peoples is an important question for the American people to decide. I am not speaking now of States which we are to establish as a result of the war. We must help in the establishment of such States. But that belongs to the German peace. The peace with Germany will settle the boundaries of Poland and the Jugo-Slav and the Czecho-Slovak States and the rest. That is part of the German peace which we are bound to see through; but this article 19 is a promise to enter upon the

work of trusteeship for all time, and I venture ~~~~ it is very
serious and deserves much thoughtful considerati~~

Of course article 20, for securing or maintaining ~~~~
mane conditions of labor for men, women, and child~~ hu-
article in which everyone must sympathize. ~~~~ an

Now, article 21:

> The high contracting parties agree that provision shall be made
> through the instrumentality of the league to secure and maintain
> freedom of transit and equitable treatment for the commerce of all
> States members of the league —

"Freedom of transit." Does that mean transit by land alone, or
does it mean transit by land and water? If it means transit by land
and water we shall have to repeal our coastwise laws.

"Equitable treatment for the commerce of all States members of
the league." Under that phrase, every tariff duty which any other
nation thought was inequitable the league of nations could take
hold of, and "recommend" or "advise," or "decide," whatever the
word may be. If we leave this loose language there the tariff and
all import duties of every nation will come before the league. If
we think that there is an unjust discrimination against some American goods by any country we have a right to take it before the
league and see if we can not get equitable treatment. I think this
opens up a wide field of dispute. It does not seem to me, moreover, that to throw all questions of tariff or import duties into the
jurisdiction of the league can do anything to promote peace. I
think, on the contrary, it will be a breeder of dissension. I do not
see how it can be anything else.

That is the first very vital objection to it in my mind; but I also
have a feeling — and, of course, I am aware it is an old-fashioned
one — that the Constitution gives to the House of Representatives
the right to originate all bills to raise revenue; and this meddling
of the league with tariff rates, of course, would affect revenue very
seriously.

Next come the international bureaus, in article 22, to which
no one would object.

Then comes article 23, which provides that no such treaty or
international engagement, when once made, shall be binding until
it has been registered by the secretary general. Our Constitution

380

...all become binding after it has been ratified by the ...says ... ratifications have been exchanged; and this seems to ...Senew condition to the constitutional conditions. I am told ...ad...nds of this treaty that we can hold back ratification until the ...stry has taken place, but while this ingenious scheme undoubt-...dly slips by the Constitution, it seems to me that it would be just as well to make it plain and avoid a constitutional objection which would get into our courts if nowhere else.

Article 24 is not very clear, but it says:

> It shall be the right of the body of delegates from time to time to advise the reconsideration by State members of the league of treaties which shall become inapplicable and of international conditions of which the continuance may endanger the peace of the world.

I confess I do not clearly understand what is meant by this. I have no doubt that there are Senators, who like the league just as it is printed, who perhaps can explain that thoroughly; but "international conditions of which the continuance may endanger the peace of the world" and "the league of treaties" — I think it must be misprinted; but, at all events, it needs some examination.

Article 25 provides that we solemnly engage not to enter hereafter into any engagements inconsistent with the terms of the league of nations. Now, that is a distinct limitation upon the treaty-making power of the Constitution. That is a new provision which must be added, in my judgment, by constitutional amendment if this article remains unchanged. The Constitution gives us very well-defined powers as to treaty making, and here we promise that we will not enter upon any engagement inconsistent with the terms of the league of nations. The object is excellent, of course, but it nevertheless raises a very obvious constitutional difficulty.

The provision for amendments to the constitution of the league makes amendment very difficult, if not practically impossible. That is another reason why I am anxious, perhaps unduly anxious, as to the importance of getting this article clear and precise now, before we are asked to approve it. When our Constitution was formed we had in the convention some 50 of the ablest men in the country, and some of the ablest men, I believe, in the world. They took some three months, as I recall, in their work. They had a committee on style, headed by Gouverneur Morris, and that is the reason the language of the Constitution of the United States is so extremely clear, precise, and excellent; and yet, precise and clear as those articles are, under them, and especially under the grant in regard to commerce between the States, have arisen questions the decisions of which by the Supreme Court would fill volumes, showing the extreme difficulty and also the need of extreme care in phraseology. I think a committee on style in this league, to redraft the proposed constitution and put it in legal language, would not have been amiss.

Finally, as I come to the end, the Senate will observe that there is no provision for withdrawal. That is very important. We are making an indissoluble treaty. The old fashion of treaties, always beginning by swearing eternal friendship, common certainly as late as the seventeenth century, has been abandoned in modern times entirely. Almost all treaties now contain provisions for terminating the treaty on due notice. Others limit the life of the treaty. An indissoluble treaty, without the right of withdrawal, is very unusual.

It has been pointed out to me — not once but many times — that we can abrogate, that we can violate, that we can overrule any treaty by the action of Congress. I know that. We can denounce it. I know that. I think, however, that to form a league of this kind and leave it in such a form that no nation can get out of it except by abrogation, by violation, or by denunciation — action which usually in the intercourse of nations means war — is very serious. If the right of withdrawal were preserved, a nation could withdraw — on due notice, of course — without shattering the league or impairing in any way the sanctity of treaties. It seems to me there ought to be some such provision. If you leave a country — I am not speaking merely of the United States — tied hard and fast, so that they can not get out of this league without tearing everything to pieces by denouncing it or by abrogating it or violating it, you create a situation which in my mind does not promote the peace of nations, but the very reverse.

I have seen here not so many years ago an occasion when, in a burst of passion, the House of Representatives swept away a treaty with a friendly nation, which contained provisions for notice and withdrawal, without any regard for the terms of the treaty. The resolution was modified here so as to avoid insult and offense; but that was the way it passed the House in a moment of anger and excitement. Passion and emotion are not going to perish or die out of men because we sign an agreement for a league of nations. They will remain. The case to which I have referred, which was with Russia, involved the good relations of the United States with one nation; but such treatment of the provisions of the league would involve a similar feeling on the part of all nations of the earth, practically all members of the league. I think this is a very serious danger, a danger to the peace of the world which we are all seeking to promote. It must be avoided by a simple amendment.

Thus, very imperfectly, I have reviewed these articles. I have stated some of the doubts and questionings which have arisen in my own mind, and I could print in the Record letters which I have received showing other points and questions which have occurred to other minds. This demonstrates the uncertainties which cloud this instrument from beginning to end. When the United States enters into an indissoluble permanent alliance there ought to be, as I have said, no uncertainties in the terms of the agreement. I earnestly desire to do everything that can be done to secure the peace of the world, but these articles as they stand in this proposed constitution seem to give a rich promise of being fertile in producing controversies and misunderstandings. They also make some demands which I do not believe any nation would submit to in a time of stress. Therefore this machinery would not promote the peace of the world, but would have a directly opposite effect. It would tend to increase the subjects of misunderstanding and dispute among the nations. Is it not possible to draft a better, more explicit, less dangerous scheme than the one here and now presented? Surely we are not to be shut up to this as the last and only word to take or leave.

To those who object that the criticism of this tentative draft plan of the committee of the peace conference must be not only destructive but constructive it might be said that the burden of proof lies upon those who propose, in order to establish the future peace of the world, that the United States must curtail its independence, part with a portion of its sovereignty, and abandon all the international policies which have been so successful for more than a hundred years. Those who support the present draft of the constitution for the league must demonstrate that it is an improvement before they can expect its general acceptance. But the Senate can not at this time undertake to make plans for a league, because we are in the process of negotiation, and the Senate does not begin to act until the stage of ratification is reached. At the same time there are certain constructive propositions which it would be well, I think, for the peace conference to consider. If it is said that you can preserve the Monroe doctrine by extending it, which appears to me clearly to mean its destruction and to be a contradiction in terms, then let us put three lines into the draft for the league which will preserve the Monroe doctrine beyond any possibility of doubt or question. It is easily done. Let us also have, if we enter the league, a complete exclusion from the league's jurisdiction of such questions as are involved in immigration and the right of each country to say who shall come within its borders and become citizens. This and certain other questions vital to national existence ought to be exempted from any control or jurisdiction by the league or its officials by a very few words, such as can be found in the arbitration treaties of 1907. There should be some definite provision for peaceful withdrawal from the league if any nation desires to withdraw. Lastly, let us have a definite statement in the constitution of the league as to whether the league is to have an international force of its own or is to have the power to summon the armed forces of the different members of the league. Let it be stated in plain language whether the "measures," the "recommendations," or the suggestions of the executive council are to be binding upon the members of the league and are to compel them, technically or morally, to do what the league delegates and the executive council determine to be necessary. On the question of the use of force we should not proceed in the dark. If those who support the league decline to make such simple statements as these — I mean statements in the body of the instrument, not individual statements — it is impossible to avoid the conclusion that they are seeking to do by indirection and the use of nebulous phrases what they are not willing to do directly, and nothing could be more fatal to the preservation of the world's peace than this, for every exercise of power by the executive council which the signatories to the league might fairly consider to be doubtful would lead to very perilous controversies and to menacing quarrels.

Unless some better constitution for a league than this can be

drawn, it seems to me, after such examination as I have been able
to give, that the world's peace would be much better, much more
surely promoted, by allowing the United States to go on under the
Monroe doctrine, responsible for the peace of this hemisphere,
without any danger of collision with Europe as to questions among
the various American States, and if a league is desired it might be
made up by the European nations whose interests are chiefly concerned, and with which the United States could cooperate fully
and at any time, whenever cooperation was needed. I suppose I
shall make myself the subject of derision for quoting from the
Farewell Address, but it states a momentous truth so admirably
that I can not refrain from giving it, for I think it ought to be
borne in mind. Washington says:

> Europe has a set of primary interests which to us have none or a
> very remote relation. Hence she must be engaged in frequent con-
> troversies the causes of which are essentially foreign to our concerns.
> Hence, therefore, it must be unwise in us to implicate ourselves by
> artificial ties in the ordinary vicissitudes of her politics or the ordi-
> nary combinations and collisions of her friendships or enmities.

It must also be remembered that if the United States enters any
league of nations it does so for the benefit of the world at large,
and not for its own benefit. The people of the United States are
a peace-loving people. We have no boundaries to rectify, no
schemes, and no desires for the acquisition or conquest of territory.
We have in the main kept the peace in the American hemisphere.
The States of South America have grown constantly more stable,
and revolutions have well-nigh disappeared in the States south of
those bordering on the Caribbean. No one questions that the
United States is able to prevent any conflicts in the American
hemisphere which would involve the world in any way or be more
than passing difficulties, which in most cases could be settled by
arbitration. If we join a league, therefore, it must be with a view
to maintaining peace in Europe, where all the greatest wars have
originated, and where there is always danger of war, and in Asia,
where serious conflicts may arise at any moment. If we join a
league, of course, we have in mind the danger of European conflicts springing up in such a way as to involve us in the defense
of civilization, as has just happened in the war with Germany. But

such wars as that are, fortunately, rare; so rare that one has never before occurred, and when the time came we took our part; but in the main our share in any league must be almost wholly for the benefit of others. We have the right, therefore, to demand that there shall be nothing in any agreement for the maintenance of the world's peace which is likely to produce new causes of difference and dissension, or which is calculated to injure the United States, or compel from us undue sacrifice, or put us in a position where we may be forced to serve the ambitions of others. There is no gain for peace in the Americas to be found by annexing the Americas to the European system. Whatever we do there we do from almost purely altruistic motives, and therefore we are entitled to consider every proposition with the utmost care in order to make sure that it does not do us injustice or render future conditions worse instead of better than they are at present.

To me the whole subject is one of enormous difficulties. We are all striving for a like result; but to make any real advances toward the future preservation of the world's peace will take time, care, and long consideration. We can not reach our objects by a world constitution hastily constructed in a few weeks in Paris in the midst of the excitement of a war not yet ended. The one thing to do, as I said in the Senate some time ago, and that which I now wish above all others, is to make the peace with Germany — to make a peace which by its terms will prevent her from breaking out again upon the world; to exclude Turkey from Europe, strengthen Greece, and give freedom and independence to the Armenians and to the Jewish and Christian populations of Asia Minor; to erect the barrier States for the Poles, Czecho-Slovaks, and Jugo-Slavs; to take possession of the Kiel Canal; to establish the Baltic States and free them from Russia and restore Danish Schleswig to Denmark. Provision must be made for indemnities or reparation, or by whatever name we choose to call the damages to be exacted from Germany. We ought, in my judgment, to receive indemnities which would enable us to provide for the *Lusitania* claims and for the destruction of our ships by submarines — to go no further. But the enormous losses of England and Italy in shipping should be made good, either in money or in kind. Belgium must be restored and fully compensated for her terrible injuries.

Finally there is France, and the indemnities to France ought to be ample and complete. The machinery taken from her factories should be restored. The cattle driven from her fields should be brought back. The debt of the free and civilized world to France is inestimable. Our own debt to her is very large. France has been our outpost and our bulwark. She has bared her breast to the storm and stood between us and the advancing hordes of Germany in the darkest days. It was France, aided by the small but gallant army of England, which checked the onrush of the Germans at the first battle of the Marne. It is her land which has been desolated and her villages and cities which have been destroyed. She should have compensation to the utmost limit in every way. Eternal justice demands it. But it is also to our immediate and selfish interest as a Nation that France should be made as strong as possible. Alsace and Lorraine she must have without question and without reduction, and other barriers if necessary to make her impregnable to German assault, for on the strength of France more than anything else, because she is the neighbor of Germany, rests the future peace of the world. We ought then to make this peace with Germany and make it at once. Much time has been wasted. The delays have bred restlessness and confusion everywhere. Germany is lifting her head again. The whining after defeat is changing to threats. She is seeking to annex nine millions of Germans in German Austria. She is reaching out in Russia and reviving her financial and commercial penetration everywhere. Her fields have not been desolated nor her factories destroyed. Germany is again threatening, and the only source of a great war is to be found in the future as in the past in Germany. She could be chained and fettered now and this menace to the world's peace should be removed at once. Whatever else we fought for certainly our first and paramount purpose was to defeat Germany. The victory over Germany is not yet complete. Let it be made so without delay.

That which I desire above everything else, that which is nearest to my heart, is to bring our soldiers home. The making of a league of nations will not do that. We can only bring our soldiers home, entirely and completely, when the peace with Germany is made and proclaimed. Let that peace be made and I can assure the world that when the treaty of peace with Germany comes to this Chamber there will be no delay in the Senate of the United States. We must bring our men back from France — the men who fought the war, the men who made the personal sacrifice. Let us get them back at once, and to that end let us have the peace made with Germany, made now, and not delay it until the complicated questions of the league of nations can be settled with the care and consideration which they demand. What is it that delays the peace with Germany? Discussions over the league of nations; nothing else. Let us have peace now, in this year of grace 1919. That is the first step to the future peace of the world. The next step will be to make sure if we can that the world shall have peace in the year 1950 or 2000. Let us have the peace with Germany and bring our boys home.

This is the immediate thing to do toward the establishment of the world's peace, but there is an issue involved in the league constitution presented to us which far overshadows all others. We are asked to depart now for the first time from the foreign policies of Washington. We are invited to move away from George Washington toward the other end of the line at which stands the sinister figure of Trotzky, the champion of internationalism.

We have in this country a Government of the people, for the people, and by the people, the freest and best Government in the world, and we are the great rampart to-day against the anarchy and disorder which have taken possession of Russia and are trying to invade every peaceful country in the world. For Lincoln's Government of the people, for the people, and by the people we are asked to substitute in the United States on many vital points government of, for, and by other people. Pause and consider well before you take this fateful step. I do not say that agreements may not be made among the nations which stand for ordered freedom and civilization, which will do much to secure and preserve the peace of the world; but no such agreement has yet been presented to us. We must beware of the dangers which beset our path. We must not lose by an improvident attempt to reach eternal peace all that we have won by war and sacrifice. We must build no bridges across the chasm which now separates American freedom and order from Russian anarchy and destruction. We must see to it that the democracy of the United States, which has prospered so mightily in the past, is not drawn by any hasty error or by any glittering delusions, through specious devices of supernational government, within the toils of international socialism and anarchy. I wish nothing but good to all the races of men. I hope and pray that peace, unbroken peace, may reign everywhere on earth. But

America and the American people are first in my heart now and always. I can never assent to any scheme no matter how fair its outward seeming which is not for the welfare and for the highest and best interest of my own beloved people of whom I am one — the American people — the people of the United States.

WILLIAM E. BORAH

(1865-1940)

From 1907 to his death in 1940, William E. Borah served continuously and conspicuously as a member of the United States Senate — the only public office that he ever held. Independent as a lawyer back in Boise, Idaho, before coming to Washington, Borah continued to maintain his independence in the Senate. Although nominally a Republican, he voted as he thought best despite the stand of his party. Virtually immune to party pressures, he subscribed wholly to Edmund Burke's observation that "your representative gives you not his industry only but his judgement. And he betrays you instead of serving you if he sacrifices it to your opinion." Independent judgment was the very essence of Borah, the Lion of Idaho.

Borah's principal and self-appointed role in the Senate was to act as a kind of Senatorial gadfly — questioning, critically weighing proposed legislation, and vigorously opposing it if he thought opposition necessary. Contrary to the feelings of many observers, Borah believed he performed a constructive function in subjecting legislative proposals to a searching examination. Looking back at his past record, he once wrote in the New York Times (Feb. 13, 1927): ". . . the votes which I am proudest of were 'no' votes. If as a Senator I have rendered any service that is of merit, the best of that service has been in opposition. My highest claim for credit is for what I may have helped to prevent."

A powerful intelligence plus the gift of eloquent expression combined to produce one of the most exciting and effective debaters ever heard in the Senate chamber. The fact that he was to speak was sufficient to pack not only the galleries but the Senate floor as well.

Borah of Idaho is thought by many connoisseurs of such things to be the premier debater of the whole world. In any case he is certainly the pampered and adulated champion debating matador of the American senatorial arena.

When Borah rises to speak, his fellow-Senators come flocking in from the cloakrooms exhibiting on their faces those expressions of amused and pleased expectancy which always adorn the human countenance when there is in prospect some spectacle which will be attended by skill in the performer and by a casualty in the life of the performer's adversary.

Seldom are Borah's colleagues balked of their happy anticipations.[1]

As a debater, Borah was fair to his opponents, objective and logical in his argument; he stuck to issues, not personalities. He spoke extemporaneously because he felt that a manuscript was too restricting. "If you don't have a new thought while speaking," he was fond of saying, "you'd better sit down."

On November 19, 1919, from the floor of the Senate, Borah made one of the most stirring appeals of his life. Because he was convinced that the Senate would vote that day to accept the League of Nations, with the reservations that had been proposed, he took the opportunity to declare forcibly his fundamental objections to such a commitment. If we join this League, he argued, we will "have forfeited and surrendered, once and for all, the great policy of 'no entangling alliances' upon which the strength of this Republic has been founded for one hundred and fifty years." Furthermore, charged Borah, the League "imperils what I conceive to be the underlying, the very first principles of this Republic. It is in conflict with the right of our people to govern themselves free from all restraint, legal or moral, of foreign powers." He went on to warn his colleagues that,

. . . when you shall have committed this Republic to a scheme of world control based upon force, upon the combined military force of the four great nations of this world, you will have soon destroyed the atmosphere of freedom, of confidence in the self-governing capacity of the masses, in which alone a democracy may thrive. We may become one of the four dictators of the world, but we shall no longer be master of our own spirit.

[1] William Hard, "Borah the Individual," *Review of Reviews* 71: 149(F '25).

The effect on the audience of Borah's impassioned plea for national sovereignty may best be suggested by a remark made by Senator Henry Cabot Lodge: "When I find myself with tears in my eyes I know I am hearing a great speech."

Borah, of course, lived to witness the triumph of his cause, the final rejection of the League proposal. But victory per se had never been and would never be the man's chief concern. The philosophy which guided this truly dedicated public servant has been recorded for us in his own words: "I would sooner lose in a right cause than win in a wrong cause. As long as I can distinguish between right and wrong, I shall do what I believe to be right — whatever the consequences."[2]

AGAINST THE LEAGUE OF NATIONS

by

William E. Borah

Delivered in the United States Senate on November 19, 1919.

MR. PRESIDENT, AFTER Mr. Lincoln had been elected President before he assumed the duties of the office and at a time when all indications were to the effect that we would soon be in the midst of civil strife, a friend from the city of Washington wrote him for instructions. Mr. Lincoln wrote back in a single line, "Entertain no compromise; have none of it." That states the position I occupy at this time and which I have, in an humble way, occupied from the first contention in regard to this proposal.

My objections to the league have not been met by the reservations. I desire to state wherein my objections have not been met.

[2] William Hutchinson, *News Articles on the Life and Works of Honorable William E. Borah*, p. 55.

Let us see what our attitude will be toward Europe and what our position will be with reference to the other nations of the world after we shall have entered the league with the present reservations written therein. With all due respect to those who think that they have accomplished a different thing and challenging no man's intellectual integrity or patriotism, I do not believe the reservations have met the fundamental propositions which are involved in this contest.

When the league shall have been formed, we shall be a member of what is known as the council of the league. Our accredited representative will sit in judgment with the accredited representatives of the other members of the league to pass upon the concerns not only of our country but of all Europe and all Asia and the entire world. Our accredited representatives will be members of the assembly. They will sit there to represent the judgment of these 110,000,000 of people, just as we are accredited here to represent our constituencies. We can not send our representatives to sit in council with the representatives of the other great nations of the world with mental reservations as to what we shall do in case their judgment shall not be satisfactory with us. If we go to the council or to the assembly with any other purpose than that of complying in good faith and in absolute integrity with all upon which the council or the assembly may pass, we shall soon return to our country with our self-respect forfeited and the public opinion of the world condemnatory.

Why need you gentlemen across the aisle worry about a reservation here or there, when we are sitting in the council and in the assembly and bound by every obligation in morals, which the President said was supreme above that of law, to comply with the judgment which our representative and the other representatives finally form? Shall we go there, to sit in judgment, and in case that judgment works for peace join with our allies, but in case it works for war withdraw our cooperation? How long would we stand as we now stand, a great Republic commanding the respect and holding the leadership of the world, if we should adopt any such course?

So, sir, we not only sit in the council and in the assembly with our accredited representatives, but bear in mind that article 11 is untouched by any reservation which has been offered here; and with article 11 untouched, and its integrity complete, article 10 is perfectly superfluous. If any war or threat of war shall be a matter of consideration for the league, and the league shall take such action as it deems wise to deal with it, what is the necessity of article 10? Will not external aggression be regarded as a war or threat of war? If the political independence of some nation in Europe is assailed will it be regarded as a war or threat of war? Is there anything in article 10 that is not completely covered by article 11?

It remains complete, and with our representatives sitting in the council and the assembly, and with article 11 complete, and with the assembly and the council having jurisdiction of all matters touching the peace of the world, what more do you need to bind the United States if you assume that the United States is a Nation of honor?

We have said that we would not send our troops abroad without the consent of Congress. Pass by now for a moment the legal proposition. If we create executive functions, the Executive will perform those functions without the authority of Congress. Pass that question by and go to the other question. Our members of the council are there. Our members of the assembly are there. Article 11 is complete, and it authorizes the league, a member of which is our representative, to deal with matters of peace and war, and the league through its council and its assembly deals with the matter, and our accredited representative joins with the others in deciding upon a certain course, which involves a question of sending troops. What will the Congress of the United States do? What right will it have left, except the bare technical right to refuse, which as a moral proposition it will not dare to exercise? Have we not been told day by day for the last nine months that the Senate of the United States, a coordinate part of the treaty-making power, should accept this league as it was written because the wise men sitting at Versailles had so written it, and has not every possible influence and every source of power in public opinion been organized and directed against the Senate to compel it to do that thing? How much stronger will be the moral compulsion upon the Congress of the United States when we ourselves have indorsed the proposition of sending our accredited representatives there to vote for us?

Ah, but you say that there must be unanimous consent, and that there is vast protection in unanimous consent.

I do not wish to speak disparagingly; but has not every division and dismemberment of every nation which has suffered dismemberment taken place by unanimous consent for the last three hundred years? Did not Prussia and Austria and Russia by unanimous consent divide Poland? Did not the United States and Great Britain and Japan and Italy and France divide China, and give Shantung to Japan? Was that not a unanimous decision? Close the doors upon the diplomats of Europe, let them sit in secret, give them the material to trade on, and there always will be unanimous consent.

How did Japan get unanimous consent? I want to say here, in my parting words upon this proposition, that I have no doubt the outrage upon China was quite as distasteful to the President of the United States as it is to me. But Japan said: "I will not sign your treaty unless you turn over to me Shantung, to be turned back at my discretion," and you know how Japan's discretion operates with reference to such things. And so, when we are in the league, and our accredited representatives are sitting at Geneva, and a question of great moment arises, Japan, or Russia, or Germany, or Great Britain will say, "Unless this matter is adjusted in this way I will depart from your league." It is the same thing, operating in the same way, only under a different date and under a little different circumstances.

If you have enough territory, if you have enough material, if you have enough subject peoples to trade upon and divide, there will be no difficulty about unanimous consent.

Do our Democratic friends ever expect any man to sit as a member of the council or as a member of the assembly equal in intellectual power and in standing before the world with that of our representative at Versailles? Do you expect a man to sit in the council who will have made more pledges, and I shall assume made them in sincerity, for self-determination and for the rights of small peoples, than had been made by our accredited representative? And yet, what became of it? The unanimous consent was obtained nevertheless.

But take another view of it. We are sending to the council one man. That one man represents 110,000,000 people.

Here, sitting in the Senate, we have two from every State in the Union, and over in the other House we have Representatives in accordance with population, and the responsibility is spread out in accordance with our obligations to our constituency. But now we are transferring to one man the stupendous power of representing the sentiment and convictions of 110,000,000 people in tremendous questions which may involve the peace or may involve the war of the world.

However you view the question of unanimous consent, it does not protect us.

What is the result of all this? We are in the midst of all of the affairs of Europe. We have entangled ourselves with all European concerns. We have joined in alliance with all the European nations which have thus far joined the league, and all nations which may be admitted to the league. We are sitting there dabbling in their affairs and intermeddling in their concerns. In other words — and this comes to the question which is fundamental with me — we have forfeited and surrendered, once and for all, the great policy of "no entangling alliances" upon which the strength of this Republic has been founded for one hundred and fifty years.

My friends of reservations, tell me where is the reservation in these articles which protects us against entangling alliances with Europe?

Those who are differing over reservations, tell me what one of them protects the doctrine laid down by the Father of our Country. That fundamental proposition is surrendered, and we are a part of the European turmoils and conflicts from the time we enter this league.

Let us not underestimate that. There has never been an hour since the Venezuelan difficulty that there has not been operating in this country, fed by domestic and foreign sources, a powerful propaganda for the destruction of the doctrine of no entangling alliances.

Lloyd-George is reported to have said just a few days before the conference met at Versailles that Great Britain could give up much, and would be willing to sacrifice much, to have America withdraw from that policy. That was one of the great objects of the entire conference at Versailles, so far as the foreign representatives were concerned. Clemenceau and Lloyd-George and others like them were willing to make any reasonable sacrifice which would draw America away from her isolation and into the internal affairs and concerns of Europe. This league of nations, with or without reservations, whatever else it does or does not do, does surrender and sacrifice that policy; and once having surrendered and become a part of the European concerns, where, my friends, are you going to stop?

You have put in here a reservation upon the Monroe doctrine. I think that, in so far as language could protect the Monroe doctrine, it has been protected. But as a practical proposition, as a working proposition, tell me candidly, as men familiar with the history of your country and of other countries, do you think that you can intermeddle in European affairs and keep Europe from intermeddling in your affairs?

When Mr. Monroe wrote to Jefferson, he asked him his view upon the Monroe doctrine, and Mr. Jefferson said, in substance, our first and primary obligation should be never to interfere in European affairs; and, secondly, never permit Europe to interfere in our affairs.

He understood, as every wise and practical man understands, that if we intermeddle in her affairs, if we help to adjust her conditions, inevitably and remorselessly Europe then will be carried into our affairs, in spite of anything you can write upon paper.

We can not protect the Monroe doctrine unless we protect the basic principle upon which it rests, and that is the Washington policy. I do not care how earnestly you may endeavor to do so, as a practical working proposition, your league will come to the United States. Will you permit me to digress long enough to read a paragraph from a great French editor upon this particular phase of the matter, Mr. Stephen Lausanne, editor of Le Matin, of Paris:

> When the executive council of the league of nations fixes "the reasonable limits of the armament of Peru"; when it shall demand information concerning the naval program of Brazil; when it shall tell Argentina what shall be the measure of the "contribution to the armed forces to protect the signatures of the social covenant"; when it shall demand the immediate registration of the treaty between the United States and Canada at the seat of the league, it will control, whether it will or no, the destinies of America. And when the American States shall be obliged to take a hand in every war or menace of war in Europe (art. 11), they will necessarily fall afoul of the fundamental principle laid down by Monroe, which was that Americans should never take part in a European war.
>
> If the league takes in the world, then Europe must mix in the affairs of America; if only Europe is included, then America will

violate of necessity her own doctrine by intermixing in the affairs of Europe.

If the league includes the affairs of the world, does it not include the affairs of all the world? Is there any limitation of the jurisdiction of the council or of the assembly upon the question of peace or war? Does it not have now, under the reservations, the same as it had before, the power to deal with all matters of peace or war throughout the entire world? How shall you keep from meddling in the affairs of Europe or keep Europe from meddling in the affairs of America?

There is another and even a more commanding reason why I shall record my vote against this treaty. It imperils what I conceive to be the underlying, the very first principles of this Republic. It is in conflict with the right of our people to govern themselves free from all restraint, legal or moral, of foreign powers. It challenges every tenet of my political faith. If this faith were one of my own contriving, if I stood here to assert principles of government of my own evolving, I might well be charged with intolerable presumption, for we all recognize the ability of those who urge a different course. But I offer in justification of my course nothing of my own — save the deep and abiding reverence I have for those whose policies I humbly but most ardently support. I claim no merit save fidelity to American principles and devotion to American ideals as they were wrought out from time to time by those who built the Republic and as they have been extended and maintained throughout these years. In opposing the treaty I do nothing more than decline to renounce and tear out of my life the sacred traditions which through fifty years have been translated into my whole intellectual and moral being. I will not, I can not, give up my belief that America must, not alone for the happiness of her own people, but for the moral guidance and greater contentment of the world, be permitted to live her own life. Next to the tie which binds a man to his God is the tie which binds a man to his country, and all schemes, all plans, however ambitious and fascinating they seem in their proposal, but which would embarrass or entangle and impede or shackle her sovereign will, which would compromise her freedom of action I unhesitatingly put behind me.

Sir, since the debate opened months ago those of us who have stood against this proposition have been taunted many times with being little Americans. Leave us the word American, keep that in your presumptuous impeachment, and no taunt can disturb us, no gibe discompose our purposes. Call us little Americans if you will, but leave us the consolation and the pride which the term American, however modified, still imparts. Take away that term and though you should coin in telling phrase your highest eulogy we would hurl it back as common slander. We have been ridiculed because, forsooth, of our limited vision. Possibly that charge may be true. Who is there here that can read the future? Time, and time alone, unerring and remorseless, will give us each our proper place in the affections of our countrymen and in the esteem and commendation of those who are to come after us. We neither fear nor court her favor. But if our vision has been circumscribed it has at all times within its compass been clear and steady. We have sought nothing save the tranquility of our own people and the honor and independence of our own Republic. No foreign flattery, no possible world glory and power have disturbed our poise or come between us and our devotion to the traditions which have made us a people, or the policies which have made us a Nation, unselfish and commanding. If we have erred we have erred out of too much love for those things which from childhood you and we together have been taught to revere — yes, to defend even at the cost of limb and life. If we have erred it is because we have placed too high an estimate upon the wisdom of Washington and Jefferson, too exalted an opinion upon the patriotism of the sainted Lincoln. And blame us not therefore if we have, in our limited vision, seemed sometimes bitter and at all times uncompromising, for the things for which we have spoken, feebly spoken, the things which we have endeavored to defend have been the things for which your fathers and our fathers were willing to die.

Senators, even in an hour so big with expectancy we should not close our eyes to the fact that democracy is something more, vastly more, than a mere form of government by which society is restrained into free and orderly life. It is a moral entity, a spiritual force as well. And these are things which live only and alone in the atmosphere of liberty. The foundation upon which democracy rests is faith in the moral instincts of the people. Its ballot boxes, the franchise, its laws, and constitutions are but the outward manifestations of the deeper and more essential thing — a continuing trust in the moral purposes of the average man and woman. When this is lost or forfeited your outward forms, however democratic in terms, are a mockery. Force may find expression through institutions democratic in structure equally with the simple and more direct processes of a single supreme ruler. These distinguishing virtues of a real republic you can not commingle with the discordant and destructive forces of the Old World and still preserve them. You can not yoke a government whose fundamental maxim is that of liberty to a government whose first law is that of force and hope to preserve the former. These things are in eternal war, and one must ultimately destroy the other. You may still keep for a time the outward form, you may still delude yourself, as others have done in the past, with appearances and symbols, but when you shall have committed this Republic to a scheme of world control based upon force, upon the combined military force of the four great nations of the world, you will have soon destroyed the atmosphere of freedom, of confidence in the self-governing capacity of the masses, in which alone a democracy may thrive. We may become one of the four dictators of the world, but we shall no longer be master of our own spirit. And what shall it profit us as a Nation if we shall go forth to the dominion of the earth and share with others the glory of world control and lose that fine sense of confidence in the people, the soul of democracy.

Look upon the scene as it is now presented. Behold the task we are to assume, and then contemplate the method by which we are to deal with this task. Is the method such as to address itself to a Government "conceived in liberty and dedicated to the proposition that all men are created equal"? When this league, this combination, is formed four great powers representing the dominant people will rule one-half of the inhabitants of the globe as subject peoples — rule by force, and we shall be a party to the rule of force. There is no other way by which you can keep people in subjection. You must either give them independence, recognize their rights as nations to live their own life and to set up their own form of government, or you must deny them these things by force. That is the scheme, the method proposed by the league. It proposes no other. We will in our time become inured to its inhuman precepts and its soulless methods, strange as this doctrine now seems to a free people. If we stay with our contract, we will come in time to declare with our associates that force — force, the creed of the Prussian military oligarchy — is after all the true foundation upon which must rest all stable governments. Korea, despoiled and bleeding at every pore; India, sweltering in ignorance and burdened with inhuman taxes after more than a hundred years of dominant rule; Egypt, trapped and robbed of her birthright; Ireland, with 700 years of sacrifice for independence — this is the task, this is the atmosphere, and this is the creed in and under which we are to keep alive our belief in the moral purposes and self-governing capacity of the people, a belief without which the Republic must disintegrate and die. The maxim of liberty will soon give way to the rule of blood and iron. We have been pleading here for our Constitution. Conform this league, it has been said, to the technical terms of our charter and all will be well. But I declare to you that we must go further and conform to those sentiments and passions for justice and freedom which are essential to the existence of democracy. You must respect not territorial boundaries, not territorial integrity, but you must respect and preserve the sentiments and passions for justice and for freedom which God in his infinite wisdom has planted so deep in the human heart that no form of tyranny however brutal, no persecution however prolonged can wholly uproot and kill. Respect nationality, respect justice, respect freedom, and you may have some hope of peace, but not so if you make your standard the standard of tyrants and despots, the protection of real estate regardless of how it is obtained.

Sir, we are told that this treaty means peace. Even so, I would not pay the price. Would you purchase peace at the cost of any part of our independence? We could have had peace in 1776 — the price was high, but we could have had it. James Otis, Sam Adams, Hancock, and Warren were surrounded by those who urged peace and British rule. All through that long and trying struggle, particularly when the clouds of adversity lowered upon the cause there was a cry of peace — let us have peace. We could have had peace in 1860; Lincoln was counseled by men of great influence and accredited wisdom to let our brothers — and, thank heaven, they are brothers — depart in peace. But the tender, loving Lincoln, bending under the fearful weight of impending civil war, an apostle of peace, refused to pay the price, and a reunited country will praise his name forevermore — bless it because he refused peace at the price of national honor and national integrity. Peace upon any other basis than national independence, peace purchased at the cost of any part of our national integrity, is fit only for slaves, and even when purchased at such a price it is a delusion, for it can not last.

But your treaty does not mean peace — far, very far, from it. If we are to judge the future by the past it means war. Is there any guaranty of peace other than the guaranty which comes of the control of the war-making power by the people? Yet what great rule of democracy does the treaty leave unassailed? The people in whose keeping alone you can safely lodge the power of peace or war nowhere, at no time and in no place, have any voice in this scheme for world peace. Autocracy which has bathed the world in blood for centuries reigns supreme. Democracy is everywhere excluded. This, you say, means peace.

Can you hope for peace when love of country is disregarded in your scheme, when the spirit of nationality is rejected, even scoffed at? Yet what law of that moving and mysterious force does your treaty not deny? With a ruthlessness unparalleled your treaty in a dozen instances runs counter to the divine law of nationality. Peoples who speak the same language, kneel at the same ancestral tombs, moved by the same traditions, animated by a common hope, are torn asunder, broken in pieces, divided, and parceled out to antagonistic nations. And this you call justice. This, you cry, means peace. Peoples who have dreamed of independence, struggled and been patient, sacrificed and been hopeful, peoples who were told that through this peace conference they should realize the aspirations of centuries, have again had their hopes dashed to earth. One of the most striking and commanding figures in this war, soldier and statesman, turned away from the peace table at Versailles declaring to the world, "The promise of the new life, the victory of the great humane ideals for which the peoples have shed their blood and their treasure without stint, the fulfillment of their aspirations toward a new international order and a fairer and better world are not written into the treaty." No; your treaty means injustice. It means slavery. It means war. And to all this you ask this Republic to become a party. You ask it to abandon the creed under which it has grown to power and accept the creed of autocracy, the creed of repression and force.

I turn from this scheme based upon force to another scheme, planned one hundred and forty-three years ago in old Independence Hall, in the city of Philadelphia, based upon liberty. I like it better. I have become so accustomed to believe in it that it is difficult for me to reject it out of hand. I have difficulty in subscribing to the new creed of oppression, the creed of dominant and subject peoples. I feel a reluctance to give up the belief that all men are created equal — the eternal principle in government that all governments derive their just powers from the consent of the governed. I can not get my consent to exchange the doctrine of George Washington for the doctrine of Frederick the Great translated into mendacious phrases of peace. I go back to that serene and masterful soul who pointed the way to power and glory for the new and then weak Republic, and whose teachings and admonitions even in our majesty and dominance we dare not disregard.

I know well the answer to my contention. It has been piped about of late from a thousand sources — venal sources, disloyal sources, sinister sources — that Washington's wisdom was of his day only and that his teachings are out of fashion — things long since sent to the scrap heap of history —that while he was great in character and noble in soul he was untrained in the arts of statecraft and unlearned in the science of government. The puny demagogue, the barren editor, the sterile professor now vie with each other in apologizing for the temporary and commonplace expedients which the Father of our County felt constrained to adopt in building a republic!

What is the test of statesmanship? Is it the formation of theories, the utterance of abstract and incontrovertible truths, or is it the capacity and the power to give to a people that concrete thing called liberty, that vital and indispensable thing in human happiness called free institutions and to establish over all and above all the blessed and eternal reign of order and law? If this be the test, where shall we find another whose name is entitled to be written beside the name of Washington? His judgment and poise in the hour of turmoil and peril, his courage and vision in times of adversity, his firm grasp of fundamental principles, his almost inspired power to penetrate the future and read there the result, the effect of policies, have never been excelled, if equalled, by any of the world's commonwealth builders. Peter the Great, William the

Silent, and Cromwell the Protector, these and these alone perhaps are to be associated with his name as the builders of States and the founders of governments. But in exaltation of moral purpose, in the unselfish character of his work, in the durability of his policies, in the permanency of the institutions which he more than anyone else called into effect, his service to mankind stands out separate and apart in a class by itself. The works of these other great builders, where are they now? But the work of Washington is still the most potent influence for the advancement of civilization and the freedom of the race.

Reflect for a moment over his achievements. He led the Revolutionary Army to victory. He was the very first to suggest a union instead of a confederacy. He presided over and counseled with great wisdom the convention which framed the Constitution. He guided the Government through its first perilous years. He gave dignity and stability and honor to that which was looked upon by the world as a passing experiment, and finally, my friends, as his own peculiar and particular contribution to the happiness of his countrymen and to the cause of the Republic, he gave us his great foreign policy under which we have lived and prospered and strengthened for nearly a century and a half. This policy is the most sublime confirmation of his genius as a statesman. It was then, and it now is an indispensable part of our whole scheme of government. It is to-day a vital, indispensable element in our entire plan, purpose, and mission as a nation. To abandon it is nothing less than a betrayal of the American people. I say betrayal deliberately, in view of the suffering and the sacrifice which will follow in the wake of such a course.

But under the stress and strain of these extraordinary days, when strong men are being swept down by the onrushing forces of disorder and change, when the most sacred things of life, the most cherished hopes of a Christian world seem to yield to the mad forces of discontent — just such days as Washington passed through when the mobs of Paris, wild with new liberty and drunk with power, challenged the established institutions of all the world, but his steadfast soul was unshaken — under these conditions come again we are about to abandon this policy so essential to our happiness and tranquility as a people and our stability as a Government. No leader with his commanding influence and his unquailing courage stands forth to stem the current. But what no leader can or will do experience, bitter experience, and the people of this country in whose keeping, after all, thank God, is the Republic, will ultimately do. If we abandon his leadership and teachings, we will go back. We will return to this policy. Americanism shall not, can not die. We may go back in sackcloth and ashes, but we will return to the faith of the fathers. America will live her own life. The independence of this Republic will have its defenders. Thousands have suffered and died for it, and their sons and daughters are not of the breed who will be betrayed into the hands of foreigners. The noble face of the Father of his Country, so familiar to every boy and girl, looking out from the walls of the Capitol in stern reproach, will call those who come here for public service to a reckoning. The people of our beloved country will finally speak, and we will return to the policy which we now abandon. American disenthralled and free in spite of all these things will continue her mission in the cause of peace, of freedom, and of civilization.

FRANKLIN D. ROOSEVELT

(1882-1945)

A few short years after his death, Franklin Delano Roosevelt had already become a legend. In fact, it is quite possible to claim that this remarkable man actually had become a legend during his own lifetime. Born of wealthy parents, he became known as a "defender of the poor"; raised and schooled in the conservative tradition, he soon developed into a "reformer"; crippled by polio when he was thirty-nine, he overcame his handicap and became our thirty-second President. This is material enough for most legends, yet there is more. He was elected to the nation's highest office not once, but four times. And his fame as a humanitarian had spread so throughout the world that his death was mourned everywhere. Certainly Roosevelt has made his mark in history, through his own abilities as statesman and politician to be sure, but with a helping hand from modern-day developments in communication and transportation.

For Franklin D. Roosevelt's fame resulted in large measure from his ability to make himself known to the people. The fact that radio was a fully developed medium when he first took office as President in 1933, plus the fact that modern methods of transportation enabled him to reach almost any part of the country with reasonable ease, meant that more people could see and hear him than had ever before been able to see or hear a President.

There was more than the mere existence of technical facilities behind Roosevelt's tremendous popularity, however; he knew just how to use these facilities. Too, he himself was blessed with an excellent radio voice: John Carlile, production director of the Co-

lumbia Broadcasting System, called it "one of the finest on the radio," while Brandenburg and Braden state that:

Roosevelt was admirably equipped to make use of the new medium. His style of speaking, direct and conversational; his clear pronunciation; his excellent voice; his ability to read orally; and his extrovertive personality were readily adaptable to the microphone. Each listener received the impression that Roosevelt was talking directly to him. Millions of Americans sat at their radios and agreed that "they could practically feel him physically in the room." His voice communicated his expansive personality; it registered what was in him and what he wanted other people to grasp — conviction, sympathy, humility, gravity, humor — in harmony with situations as he saw them.[1]

The President was to see a great variety of "situations" during his years of office, ranging from the depression to the greatest war in man's history. As the leader of a great nation, he was required to speak on a bewildering variety of topics. By itself, his knowledge was insufficient, so he expanded a device which he had first used when Governor of New York State (1928-1932), namely, a "brain trust" — a group of experts on matters ranging from military science to commerce. The main job of this group was to give the President advice on matters of state, and to assist him in the preparation of his numerous speeches. The playwright Robert E. Sherwood, a member of this group, has given us a colorful picture of the sort of work the brain trust and Roosevelt did together.

When he wanted to give a speech for some important purpose, whether it was connected with a special occasion or not, he would discuss it first at length with Hopkins, Rosenman, and me, telling us what particular points he wanted to make, what sort of audience he wished primarily to reach and what the maximum word limit was to be. He would dictate pages and pages, approaching his main topic, sometimes hitting it squarely on the nose with terrific impact, sometimes rambling so far away from it that he couldn't get back, in which case he would say, "Well — something along those lines — you boys can fix it up."[2]

---

[1] Marie K. Hochmuth (ed.), *A History and Criticism of American Public Address,* III, 527.

[2] *Roosevelt and Hopkins,* pp. 371-372.

Some people claim that Roosevelt left most of his speeches to be "fixed up" by his "boys." This claim is correct if one means by "most of" the innumerable minor speeches that Roosevelt had to make. But Hopkins, Sherwood, and even the President's "ally-turned-opponent," Raymond Moley, all state that Roosevelt's major addresses were primarily his own. This fact becomes quite evident in the case of the President's "fireside chats" — another device from his period as Governor, incidentally — in which the language is pure Roosevelt, i.e., simple, direct, friendly, even colloquial at times. On such occasions Roosevelt was interested in just "chatting" with the people. John Gunther puts his finger squarely on the essence of Roosevelt's popularity here when he says,

He gave the impression, on the radio, of speaking to every listener personally, like a sympathetic, authoritative, and omniscient friend; as almost every American knows, you could practically feel him physically in the room. Europeans who never heard him on the radio may be puzzled by this phenomenon. But nobody will ever really understand FDR who did not hear him talk and catch something of his magnificent delivery.[3]

It took all of the magnificent delivery at Roosevelt's command to put across the message of his September 3, 1939, Fireside Chat on the outbreak of war in Europe. Bluntly he informed the American people of a very distasteful fact.

You must master at the outset a simple but unalterable fact in modern foreign relations between nations. When peace has been broken anywhere, the peace of all countries everywhere is in danger.

It is easy for you and me to shrug our shoulders and to say that conflicts taking place thousands of miles from the continental United States, and, indeed, thousands of miles from the whole American Hemisphere, do not seriously affect the Americas — and that all the United States has to do is to ignore them and go about its own business. Passionately though we may desire detachment, we are forced to realize that every word that comes through the air, every ship that sails the sea, every battle that is fought, does affect the American future.

[3] *Roosevelt in Retrospect*, p. 38.

At the same time, however, Roosevelt attempted to reassure his listeners with these words: "Let no man or woman thoughtlessly or falsely talk of America sending its armies to European fields. At this moment there is being prepared a proclamation of American neutrality. . . . And I trust that in the days to come our neutrality can be made a true neutrality." In his memorable peroration the President again emphasized his determination to keep the United States out of war.

> This Nation will remain a neutral Nation, but I cannot ask that every American remain neutral in thought as well. Even a neutral has a right to take account of facts. Even a neutral cannot be asked to close his mind or his conscience.
>
> I have said not once, but many times, that I have seen war and that I hate war. I say that again and again.
>
> I hope the United States will keep out of this war. I believe that it will. And I give you assurance and reassurance that every effort of your Government will be directed toward that end.
>
> As long as it remains within my power to prevent, there will be no black-out of peace in the United States.

Unknown at the time, however, the days of peace were numbered; they ended abruptly on Sunday morning, December 7, 1941, with the Japanese attack on Pearl Harbor. Again, the President spoke directly to the people when he told them, "We are going to win the war and we are going to win the peace that follows." This Fireside Chat, delivered December 9, 1941, repeated much of what Roosevelt had stated the day before in his Declaration of War message against Japan. Through it all appeared the same courage and determination to win which had pulled him through the dark days of his illness, which had helped to lift the nation he served through the depression, and which would now see his country to the ultimate victory which he himself was not privileged to see.

Although Franklin Delano Roosevelt may well be a legend, the legend is not a universally accepted one. Some of his political moves were born of sheer brilliance; others were very nearly disastrous. He had his supporters and he had his critics.

When all was said and done, however, these critics could not drown out the sound of the golden voice with its warmth and confidence; they could not erase the vision of that infectious smile as shown in the newsreels and in the candid shots; they could not obliterate the magnificent presence of the man who appeared serenely before millions although he could not walk; no, nor could they erase from the hearts and minds of people all over the world the visions of hope which his words aroused. Roosevelt had something which none of his detractors could take away from him.[4]

A PLEA FOR NEUTRALITY

by

Franklin D. Roosevelt

Radio Fireside Chat from Washington, D. C., on September 3, 1939.

TONIGHT MY SINGLE DUTY is to speak to the whole of America. Until four-thirty this morning I had hoped against hope that some miracle would prevent a devastating war in Europe and bring to an end the invasion of Poland by Germany.

For four long years a succession of actual wars and constant crises have shaken the entire world and have threatened in each case to bring on the gigantic conflict which is today unhappily a fact.

It is right that I should recall to your minds the consistent and at times successful efforts of your Government in these crises to throw the full weight of the United States into the cause of peace. In spite of spreading wars I think that we have every right and every reason to maintain as a national policy the fundamental moralities, the teachings of religion and the continuation of efforts to restore peace — for some day, though the time may be distant, we can be of even greater help to a crippled humanity.

[4] Harold F. Gosnell, *Champion Campaigner — Franklin D. Roosevelt*, pp. 2-4.

It is right, too, to point out that the unfortunate events of these recent years have, without question, been based on the use of force and the threat of force. And it seems to me clear, even at the outbreak of this great war, that the influence of America should be consistent in seeking for humanity a final peace which will eliminate, as far as it is possible to do so, the continued use of force between nations.

It is, of course, impossible to predict the future. I have my constant stream of information from American representatives and other sources throughout the world. You, the people of this country, are receiving news through your radios and your newspapers at every hour of the day.

You are, I believe, the most enlightened and the best informed people in all the world at this moment. You are subjected to no censorship of news, and I want to add that your Government has no information which it withholds or which it has any thought of withholding from you.

At the same time, as I told my press conference on Friday, it is of the highest importance that the press and the radio use the utmost caution to discriminate between actual verified fact on the one hand, and mere rumor on the other.

I can add to that by saying that I hope the people of this country will also discriminate most carefully between news and rumor. Do not believe of necessity everything you hear or read. Check up on it first.

You must master at the outset a simple but unalterable fact in modern foreign relations between nations. When peace has been broken anywhere, the peace of all countries everywhere is in danger.

It is easy for you and for me to shrug our shoulders and to say that conflicts taking place thousands of miles from the continental United States, and, indeed, thousands of miles from the whole American Hemisphere, do not seriously affect the Americas — and that all the United States has to do is to ignore them and go about its own business. Passionately though we may desire detachment, we are forced to realize that every word that comes through the air, every ship that sails the sea, every battle that is fought, does affect the American future.

Let no man or woman thoughtlessly or falsely talk of America sending its armies to European fields. At this moment there is being prepared a proclamation of American neutrality. This would have been done even if there had been no neutrality statute on the books, for this proclamation is in accordance with international law and in accordance with American policy.

This will be followed by a Proclamation required by the existing Neutrality Act. And I trust that in the days to come our neutrality can be made a true neutrality.

It is of the utmost importance that the people of this country, with the best information in the world, think things through. The most dangerous enemies of American peace are those who, without well-rounded information on the whole broad subject of the past, the present and the future, undertake to speak with assumed authority, to talk in terms of glittering generalities, to give to the nation assurances or prophesies which are of little present or future value.

I myself cannot and do not prophesy the course of events abroad — and the reason is that, because I have of necessity such a complete picture of what is going on in every part of the world, I do not dare to do so. And the other reason is that I think it is honest for me to be honest with the people of the United States.

I cannot prophesy the immediate economic effect of this new war on our nation, but I do say that no American has the moral right to profiteer at the expense either of his fellow citizens or of the men, the women and the children who are living and dying in the midst of war in Europe.

Some things we do know. Most of us in the United States believe in spiritual values. Most of us, regardless of what church we belong to, believe in the spirit of the New Testament — a great teaching which opposes itself to the use of force, of armed force, of marching armies and falling bombs. The overwhelming masses of our people seek peace — peace at home, and the kind of peace in other lands which will not jeopardize our peace at home.

We have certain ideas and certain ideals of national safety, and we must act to preserve that safety today, and to preserve the safety of our children in future years.

That safety is and will be bound up with the safety of the Western Hemisphere and of the seas adjacent thereto. We seek to keep war from our own firesides by keeping war from coming to the Americas. For that we have historic precedent that goes back to the days of the Administration of President George Washington.

It is serious enough and tragic enough to every American family in every State in the Union to live in a world that is torn by wars on other continents. Those wars today affect every American home. It is our national duty to use every effort to keep them out of the Americas.

And at this time let me make the simple plea that partisanship and selfishness be adjourned; and that national unity be the thought that underlies all others.

This Nation will remain a neutral Nation, but I cannot ask that every American remain neutral in thought as well. Even a neutral has a right to take account of facts. Even a neutral cannot be asked to close his mind or his conscience.

I have said not once, but many times, that I have seen war and that I hate war. I say that again and again.

I hope the United States will keep out of this war. I believe that it will. And I give you assurance and reassurance that every effort of your Government will be directed toward that end.

As long as it remains within my power to prevent, there will be no black-out of peace in the United States.

AMERICA'S ANSWER TO
JAPAN'S CHALLENGE

by

Franklin D. Roosevelt

Radio Fireside Chat from Washington, D. C., on December 9, 1941.

THE SUDDEN CRIMINAL ATTACKS perpetrated by the Japanese in the Pacific provide the climax of a decade of international immorality.

Powerful and resourceful gangsters have banded together to make war upon the whole human race. Their challenge has now been flung at the United States of America. The Japanese have treacherously violated the long-standing peace between us. Many American soldiers and sailors have been killed by enemy action. American ships have been sunk; American airplanes have been destroyed.

The Congress and the people of the United States have accepted that challenge.

Together with other free peoples, we are now fighting to maintain our right to live among our world neighbors in freedom and in common decency, without fear of assault.

I have prepared the full record of our past relations with Japan, and it will be submitted to the Congress. It begins with the visit of Commodore Perry to Japan eighty-eight years ago. It ends with the visit of two Japanese emissaries to the Secretary of State last Sunday, an hour after Japanese forces had loosed their bombs and machine guns against our flag, our forces and our citizens.

I can say with utmost confidence that no Americans today or a thousand years hence need feel anything but pride in our patience and in our efforts through all the years toward achieving a peace in the Pacific which would be fair and honorable to every nation, large or small. And no honest person, today or a thousand years hence, will be able to suppress a sense of indignation and horror at the treachery committed by the military dictators of Japan under the very shadow of the flag of peace borne by their special envoys in our midst.

The course that Japan has followed for the past ten years in Asia has paralleled the course of Hitler and Mussolini in Europe and in Africa. Today, it has become far more than a parallel. It is collaboration, actual collaboration so well calculated that all the continents of the world, and all the oceans, are now considered by the Axis strategists as one gigantic battlefield.

In 1931, ten years ago, Japan invaded Manchukuo — without warning.

In 1935, Italy invaded Ethiopia — without warning.

In 1938, Hitler occupied Austria — without warning.

In 1939, Hitler invaded Czecho-Slovakia — without warning.

Later in 1939, Hitler invaded Poland — without warning.

In 1940, Hitler invaded Norway, Denmark, the Netherlands, Belgium and Luxembourg — without warning.

In 1940, Italy attacked France and later Greece — without warning.

And in this year, 1941, the Axis Powers attacked Yugoslavia and Greece and they dominated the Balkans — without warning.

In 1941 also, Hitler invaded Russia — without warning.

And now Japan has attacked Malaya and Thailand — and the United States — without warning.

It is all of one pattern.

We are now in this war. We are all in it — all the way. Every single man, woman and child is a partner in the most tremendous undertaking of our American history. We must share together the bad news and the good news, the defeats and the victories — the changing fortunes of war.

So far, the news has been all bad. We have suffered a serious set-back in Hawaii. Our forces in the Philippines, which include the brave people of that commonwealth, are taking punishment, but are defending themselves vigorously. The reports from Guam and Wake and Midway Islands are still confused, but we must be prepared for the announcement that all these three outposts have been seized.

The casualty lists of these first few days will undoubtedly be large. I deeply feel the anxiety of all families of the men in our armed forces and the relatives of people in cities which have been bombed. I can only give them my solemn promise that they will get news just as quickly as possible.

This government will put its trust in the stamina of the American people and will give the facts to the public as soon as two conditions have been fulfilled; first, that the information has been definitely and officially confirmed; and, second, that the release of the information at the time it is received will not prove valuable to the enemy directly or indirectly.

Most earnestly I urge my countrymen to reject all rumors. These ugly little hints of complete disaster fly thick and fast in wartime. They have to be examined and appraised.

As an example, I can tell you frankly that until further surveys are made, I have not sufficient information to state the exact damage which has been done to our naval vessels at Pearl Harbor. Admittedly the damage is serious. But no one can say how serious until we know how much of this damage can be repaired and how quickly the necessary repairs can be made.

I cite as another example a statement made on Sunday night that a Japanese carrier had been located and sunk off the Canal Zone. And when you hear statements that are attributed to what they call "an authoritative source," you can be reasonably sure that under these war circumstances the "authoritative source" was not any person in authority.

Many rumors and reports which we now hear originate with enemy sources. For instance, today the Japanese are claiming that as a result of their one action against Hawaii they have gained naval supremacy in the Pacific. This is an old trick of propaganda which has been used inuumerable times by the Nazis. The purposes of such fantastic claims are, of course, to spread fear and confusion among us, and to goad us into revealing military information which our enemies are desperately anxious to obtain.

Our government will not be caught in this obvious trap — and neither will our people.

It must be remembered by each and every one of us that our free and rapid communication must be greatly restricted in wartime. It is not possible to receive full, speedy, accurate reports from distant areas of combat. This is particularly true where naval operations are concerned. For in these days of the marvels of radio it is often impossible for the commanders of various units to report their activities by radio, for the very simple reason that this information would become available to the enemy, and would disclose their position and their plan of defense or attack.

Of necessity there will be delays in officially confirming or denying reports of operations, but we will not hide facts from the country if we know the facts and if the enemy will not be aided by their disclosure.

To all newspapers and radio stations — all those who reach the eyes and ears of the American people — I say this: You have a most grave responsibility to the nation now and for the duration of this war.

If you feel that our government is not disclosing enough of the truth, you have every right to say so. But — in the absence of all the facts, as revealed by official sources — you have no right to deal out unconfirmed reports in such a way as to make people believe they are gospel truth.

Every citizen, in every walk of life, shares this same responsibility. The lives of our soldiers and sailors — the whole future of this nation — depend upon the manner in which each and every one of us fulfills his obligation to our country.

Now a word about the recent past — and the future. A year and a half has elapsed since the fall of France, when the whole world first realized the mechanized might which the Axis nations had been building for so many years. America has used that year and a half to great advantage. Knowing that the attack might reach us in all too short a time, we immediately began greatly to increase our industrial strength and our capacity to meet the demands of modern warfare.

Precious months were gained by sending vast quantities of our war matériel to the nations of the world still able to resist Axis aggression. Our policy rested on the fundamental truth that the defense of any country resisting Hitler or Japan was in the long run the defense of our own country. That policy has been justified. It has given us time, invaluable time, to build our American assembly lines of production.

Assembly lines are now in operation. Others are being rushed to completion. A steady stream of tanks and planes, of guns and ships, of shells and equipment — that is what these eighteen months have given us.

But it is all only a beginning of what has to be done. We must be set to face a long war against crafty and powerful bandits. The attack at Pearl Harbor can be repeated at any one of many points in both oceans and along both our coast lines and against all the rest of the hemisphere.

It will not only be a long war, it will be a hard war. That is the basis on which we now lay all our plans. That is the yardstick by which we measure what we shall need and demand; money, materials, doubled and quadrupled production — ever increasing. The production must be not only for our own Army and Navy and air forces. It must reinforce the other armies and navies and air forces fighting the Nazis and the war lords of Japan throughout the Americas and the world.

I have been working today on the subject of production. Your government has decided on two broad policies.

The first is to speed up all existing production by working on a seven-day-week basis in every war industry, including the production of essential raw materials.

The second policy, now being put into form, is to rush additions to the capacity of production by building more new plants, by adding to old plants, and by using the many smaller plants for war needs.

Over the hard road of the past months we have at times met obstacles and difficulties, divisions and disputes, indifference and callousness. That is now all past — and, I am sure, forgotten.

The fact is that the country now has an organization in Washington built around men and women who are recognized experts in their own fields. I think the country knows that the people who are actually responsible in each and every one of these many fields are pulling together with a teamwork that has never before been excelled.

On the road ahead there lies hard work — gruelling work — day and night, every hour and every minute.

I was about to add that ahead there lies sacrifice for all of us.

But it is not correct to use that word. The United States does not consider it a sacrifice to do all one can, to give one's best to our nation, when the nation is fighting for its existence and its future life.

It is not a sacrifice for any man, old or young, to be in the Army or the Navy of the United States. Rather is it a privilege.

It is not a sacrifice for the industrialist or the wage-earner, the farmer or the shopkeeper, the trainman or the doctor, to pay more taxes, to buy more bonds, to forego extra profits, to work longer or harder at the task for which he is best fitted. Rather, it is a privilege.

It is not a sacrifice to do without many things to which we are accustomed if the national defense calls for doing without.

A review this morning leads me to the conclusion that at present we shall not have to curtail the normal articles of food. There is enough food for all of us and enough left over to send to those who are fighting on the same side with us.

There will be a clear and definite shortage of metals of many kinds for civilian use for the very good reason that in our increased program we shall need for war purposes more than half of that portion of the principal metals which during the past year have gone into articles for civilian use. We shall have to give up many things entirely.

I am sure that the people in every part of the nation are prepared in their individual living to win this war. I am sure they will cheerfully help to pay a large part of its financial cost while it goes on. I am sure they will cheerfully give up those material things they are asked to give up.

I am sure that they will retain all those great spiritual things without which we cannot win through.

I repeat that the United States can accept no result save victory, final and complete. Not only must the shame of Japanese treachery be wiped out, but the sources of international brutality, wherever they exist, must be absolutely and finally broken.

In my message to the Congress yesterday I said that we "will make very certain that this form of treachery shall never endanger us again." In order to achieve that certainty, we must begin the great task that is before us by abandoning once and for all the illusion that we can ever again isolate ourselves from the rest of humanity.

In these past few years — and, most violently, in the past few days — we have learned a terrible lesson.

It is our obligation to our dead — it is our sacred obligation to their children and our children — that we must never forget what we have learned.

And what we all have learned is this:

There is no such thing as security for any nation — or any individual — in a world ruled by the principles of gangsterism.

There is no such thing as impregnable defense against powerful aggressors who sneak up in the dark and strike without warning.

We have learned that our ocean-girt hemisphere is not immune from severe attack — that we cannot measure our safety in terms of miles on any map.

We may acknowledge that our enemies have performed a brilliant feat of deception, perfectly timed and executed with great skill. It was a thoroughly dishonorable deed, but we must face the fact that modern warfare as conducted in the Nazi manner is a dirty business. We don't like it — we didn't want to get in it — but we are in it and we're going to fight it with everything we've got.

I do not think any American has any doubt of our ability to administer proper punishment to the perpetrators of these crimes.

Your government knows that for weeks Germany has been telling Japan that if Japan did not attack the United States, Japan would not share in dividing the spoils with Germany when peace came. She was promised by Germany that if she came in she would receive the complete and perpetual control of the whole of the Pacific area — and that means not only the Far East, not only all of the islands in the Pacific, but also a stranglehold on the west coast of North, Central and South America.

We also know that Germany and Japan are conducting their military and naval operations in accordance with a joint plan. That plan considers all peoples and nations which are not helping the Axis powers as common enemies of each and every one of the Axis powers.

That is their simple and obvious grand strategy. That is why the American people must realize that it can be matched only with similar grand strategy.

We must realize, for example, that Japanese successes against the United States in the Pacific are helpful to German operations in Libya; that any German success against the Caucasus is inevitably an assistance to Japan in her operations against the Dutch East Indies; that a German attack against Algiers or Morocco opens the way to a German attack against South America.

On the other side of the picture, we must learn to know that guerrilla warfare against the Germans in Serbia helps us; that a successful Russian offensive against the Germans helps us; and that British successes on land or sea in any part of the world strengthen our hands.

Remember always that Germany and Italy, regardless of any formal declaration of war, consider themselves at war with the United States at this moment just as much as they consider themselves at war with Britain and Russia. And Germany puts all the other republics of the Americas into the category of enemies. The people of the hemisphere can be honored by that.

The true goal we seek is far above and beyond the ugly field of battle. When we resort to force, as now we must, we are determined that this force shall be directed toward ultimate good as well as against immediate evil. We Americans are not destroyers — we are builders.

We are now in the midst of a war, not for conquest, not for vengeance, but for a world in which this nation, and all that this nation represents, will be safe for our children. We expect to eliminate the danger from Japan, but it would serve us ill if we accomplished that and found that the rest of the world was dominated by Hitler and Mussolini.

We are going to win the war and we are going to win the peace that follows.

And in the dark hours of this day — and through dark days that may be yet to come — we will know that the vast majority of the members of the human race are on our side. Many of them are fighting with us. All of them are praying for us. For, in representing our cause, we represent theirs as well — our hope and their hope for liberty under God.

SELECTED BIBLIOGRAPHY

Articles

"Borah the Individual," *Review of Reviews* 71:149 ff. (F '25). Contains some colorful comments on Borah's skill as a debater.

"Borah and World Politics," *Current History* 37:513 ff. (F '33).

"Bryan," *McClure's Magazine* 15:232 ff. (Jl 1900). Noted journalist evaluates "The Cross of Gold Speech" and decides it was effective but unwise.

"Bryan, the Democratic Leader in 1900," *Review of Reviews* 22:41 ff. (Jl 1900). Deals with Bryan's qualities as a man.

"Daniel Webster's Social Hours," *Harper's* 13:216 ff.; 354 ff.; 495 ff.; 634 ff. (Je-N 1856). Interesting sidelights on the man.

"The Dividing Line Between Federal and Local Authority" (authored by Stephen A. Douglas), *Harper's* 19:519 ff. (S 1859). Reprinted in Sheahan's biography of Douglas.

"Henry Clay; as an Orator," *The New Englander* 2:105 ff. (1944). Good critical account.

"Henry Clay as an Orator," *Putnam's Monthly Magazine* 3:493 ff. (1854). Authored by one who heard Clay speak.

"Henry Clay — Personal Anecdotes, Incidents, etc.," *Harper's* 5:392 ff. (Je-N 1852).

"Henry Clay: Reminiscences by His Executor," *Century Magazine* 33:170 ff. (D 1886).

"In Plain Black and White," *Century Magazine* (Ap 1885). Grady defines the attitude of the South toward the Negro question. Written in reply to George W. Cable's opposing point of view — see *Century* (Ja 1885).

"John C. Calhoun and the Secession Movement of 1850," *American Antiquarian Society* (new series) 28:19 ff. (Ap '18).

"The Lone Lion of Idaho," *Colliers* 75:6 ff. (S 12 '25). Interesting sketch of Borah's career.

"Old Wine in a New Bottle," *Virginia Quarterly Review* 11:239 ff. (1935). Points up a Southern attitude that Grady had to take into consideration.

"The Speeches of Henry Clay," *Magazine of American History* 16:58 ff. (Jl-D 1886). Critical appraisal.

"Taft's Labors for International Peace," *Current History* 32:295 ff. (My 30 '30). Stresses prominent role of Taft in support of a League of Nations.

"William Howard Taft: His Place in American History," *Current History* 32:290 ff. (My 30 '30). Keen assessment.

"William Jennings Bryan — a Character Sketch," *Review of Reviews* 14:161 ff. (Au 1896). Contains an interesting discussion of Bryan's speech methods.

Books

Anderson, John M. (ed.). *Calhoun: Basic Documents*, 1952. See fine introduction on Calhoun's political philosophy.

Bailey, Thomas A. *Woodrow Wilson and the Great Betrayal*, 1945. Clear, readable, critical analysis of the U. S. decision not to accept the Versailles treaty or to join the League of Nations.

Bailey, Thomas A. *Woodrow Wilson and the Lost Peace*, 1944. Good critical analysis.

Baker, Ray S. and Dodd, William E. *The Public Papers of Woodrow Wilson*, 6 vols., 1925-27. Nearly all of Wilson's important public addresses are included here.

Baker, Ray S. *Woodrow Wilson: Life and Letters*, 8 vols., 1927-40. The authorized biography of the man.

Beveridge, Albert J. *Abraham Lincoln*, 1809-1858, 2 vols., 1928. Fascinating, detailed.

Beveridge, Albert J. *The Art of Public Speaking*, 1924. A brief statement of the basic principles of public speaking by one of America's greatest speakers.

Birley, Robert. *Speeches and Documents in American History*, Vol. 3, 1942-44. Contains a brief but effective evaluation of Bryan's "The Cross of Gold Speech."

Bowers, Claude G. *Beveridge and the Progressive Era*, 1932. Sensitive biography of Beveridge which as the author says "is the story of an era."

Buck, Paul H. *The Road to Reunion*, 1937. Splendid background of the Reconstruction Era.

Capers, Gerald M. *Stephen A. Douglas, Defender of the Union*, 1959. A recent and favorable re-examination of Douglas' role in pre-Civil War politics.

Channing, Edward. *A History of the United States*, 6 vols., 1905-25. Commendable in all respects.

Coit, Margaret. *John C. Calhoun*, 1950. Comprehensive, critical treatment.

Collected Works of Abraham Lincoln, Vol. 3, 1953-55. Contains copy of Cooper Institute Address that is extensively annotated.

Cramer, C. H. *Royal Bob*, 1952. A recent and interesting biography of Ingersoll.

Curtis, George T. *Life of Daniel Webster*, 2 vols., 1870. Excellent.

Eaton, Clement. *Henry Clay and the Art of American Politics*, 1957. Relates Clay to issues of the times.

Friedel, Frank. *Franklin D. Roosevelt: The Apprenticeship*, 1952. Extremely thorough on Roosevelt's early years — up to end of World War I.

Fuess, Claude. *Carl Schurz*, 1932. Excellent, comprehensive biography.

Fuess, Claude. *Daniel Webster*, 2 vols., 1930. Excellent biography.

Garraty, John A. *Henry Cabot Lodge*, 1953. A well-written and objective critical biography.

Gosnell, Harold Foote. *Champion Campaigner — Franklin D. Roosevelt*, 1952. A fine book about the specific campaigns of FDR, plus a good running account of some of his speech techniques.

Groves, Charles. *Henry Cabot Lodge, the Statesman*, 1925. A wholly favorable account of Lodge's political career.

Gunther, John. *Roosevelt in Retrospect — A Profile in History*, 1950. Excellent all around portrait of FDR.

Hagedorn, Herman (ed.). *The Theodore Roosevelt Treasury: A Self-Portrait from His Writings*, 1957.

Harris, Joel C. *Henry W. Grady: His Life, Writings, and Speeches*, 1890. Contains, too, many tributes paid Grady upon his death which frequently attest to his speaking effectiveness.

Hendrick, Burton J. *The Life and Letters of Walter H. Page*, 3 vols., 1922-25. Walter Hines Page was our Ambassador to England during the administration of President Wilson. The critical issues leading to our entrance into World War I are presented in this colorful and dramatic biography.

Herndon, William H. and Weik, Jesse W. *Abraham Lincoln*, 1892. Chapter 11 of the second volume offers an interesting, detailed account of Lincoln's personality, character, and intellectual qualities.

Hibben, Paxton. *The Peerless Leader: William Jennings Bryan*, 1929. Useful biography.

Hofstadter, Richard. *The American Political Tradition*, 1948. Contains detailed portraits of Calhoun, Lincoln, Bryan, T. Roosevelt, Wilson, and F. Roosevelt.

Houston, David F. *Eight Years with Wilson's Cabinet*, 1926. Wilson's Secretary of Agriculture provides us with his personal estimate of the President.

Johnson, Allen. *Stephen A. Douglas*, 1908. Rather objective biography.

Johnson, Claudius O. *Borah of Idaho*, 1926. An early but useful biography even though it does not include the last five years of Borah's life.

Johnson, Gerald W. *America's Silver Age*, 1939. Chapter 16 discusses circumstances surrounding Compromise of 1850.

Kerney, James. *The Political Education of Woodrow Wilson*, 1926. Early but critical appraisal.

Kittredge, Herman E. *Ingersoll: A Biographical Appreciation*, 1911. A not very critical biography by one who knew Ingersoll personally.

LaFollette, Belle and Fola. *Robert M. LaFollette*, 2 vols., 1953. Superbly written, rich in detail.

LaFollette, Robert M. *Autobiography: A Personal Narrative of Political Experiences*, 1913.

Lawrence, William. *Henry Cabot Lodge*, 1925. A friendly biographical sketch.

Lewis, William D. *The Life of Theodore Roosevelt*, 1919. Nicely written, thorough account of the man and his career.

Link, Arthur S. *Wilson, the Road to the White House*, 1947. Excellent history, biography.

Lodge, Henry C. *Daniel Webster*, 1883. Good single-volume biography.

Lodge, Henry Cabot. *Early Memories*, 1913.

Milton, George F. *The Eve of Conflict*, 1934. In the words of the author, a "glimpse into the gestation of the Civil War, and the effort of Stephen Arnold Douglas to prevent it. . . ." Completely pro-Douglas.

Morison, Samuel E. and Commager, Henry. *The Growth of the American Republic*, 2 vols., 1950. Indispensable as a general survey.

Nixon, Raymond B. *Henry Grady, Spokesman of the New South*, 1943. Very good biography.

Parrington, Vernon L. *Main Currents in American Thought*, Vol. 2., 1927. Essential to an understanding of pre-Civil War America.

Peck, Harry T. *Twenty Years of the Republic*, 1920. Contains a colorful eulogistic narrative of "The Cross of Gold Speech."

Pringle, Henry F. *The Life and Times of William Howard Taft*, 1939. Informative, complete.

Pringle, Henry F. *Theodore Roosevelt*, 1931. Informative, discerning single-volume biography.

Pritchett, John P. *Calhoun: His Defense of the South*, 1937. Brief but good.

Putnam, Carleton. *Theodore Roosevelt: The Formative Years, 1858-1886*, Vol. 1., 1958. The first of a proposed four-volume exhaustive study.

Putnam, G. H. *The Political Debates Between Abraham Lincoln and Stephen A. Douglas*, 1912. Contains the complete texts of the seven meetings plus a brief but helpful general introduction to the debates as a whole.

Reminiscences of Carl Schurz, Vol. 3., 1907-1908. See pp. 315-455 for a sketch of Schurz's political career.

Rhodes, James F. *History of the United States from the Compromise of 1850*, 8 vols., 1893-1919. Unmatched for details.

Rothe, B. M. *Daniel Webster Reader*, 1956. A general view of the man.

Schurz, Carl. *Life of Henry Clay*, 2 vols., 1887. A definitive work.

Seymour, Charles (ed.). *The Intimate Papers of Colonel House*, 4 vols., 1926-28. An invaluable look at President Wilson and his administration from the vantage point of his closest advisor.

Sheahan, James W. *The Life of Stephen A. Douglas*, 1860. A kindly first biography with extracts from some of Douglas' important speeches.

Sherwood, Robert E. *Roosevelt and Hopkins*, 1948. Lively account of the President behind the scenes, told by a member of his "brain trust."

Shurter, E. D. *Masterpieces of Modern Oratory*, 1906. Introductory note on Schurz presents selected biographical data plus a brief comment on the man's ability as a speaker.

Spain, August. *Political Theory of John Calhoun*, 1951. Excellent.

Styron, Arthur. *The Cast-Iron Man*, 1935. Calhoun as a political philosopher.

Sullivan, Mark. *Our Times*, Vol. 1., 1926-35. A lively and interesting report by a distinguished journalist of the accomplishments of Bryan.

Thayer, William Roscoe. *The Life and Letters of John Hay*, 2 vols., 1915. John Hay entered government service under President Lincoln and was Secretary of State in the Cabinet of President Theodore Roosevelt. The biography presents a vivid picture of events at the beginning of the twentieth century.

Van Deusen, Glyndon G. *The Life of Henry Clay*, 1937. Excellent biographical study.

Vinson, John C. *William E. Borah and the Outlawry of War*, 1957. Careful study of Senator Borah's career from 1917 to 1931 in relation to the debate on the League of Nations.

Willis, H. P. *Stephen A. Douglas*, 1910. Emphasizes Douglas as a participant in national politics — not too complimentary.

Wiltse, Charles M. *John C. Calhoun*, 3 vols., 1944-51. An excellent study.

Works of John C. Calhoun, Vol. 1., 1851-56. Contains Calhoun's Disquisition on Government and A Discourse on the Constitution of the United States.